Epistemic Luck

Epistemic Luck

Duncan Pritchard

CLARENDON PRESS · OXFORD

This book has been printed digitally and produced in a standard specification in order to ensure its continuing availability

OXFORD
UNIVERSITY PRESS

Great Clarendon Street, Oxford OX2 6DP

Oxford University Press is a department of the University of Oxford.
It furthers the University's objective of excellence in research, scholarship,
and education by publishing worldwide in

Oxford New York

Auckland Cape Town Dar es Salaam Hong Kong Karachi
Kuala Lumpur Madrid Melbourne Mexico City Nairobi
New Delhi Shanghai Taipei Toronto
With offices in
Argentina Austria Brazil Chile Czech Republic France Greece
Guatemala Hungary Italy Japan South Korea Poland Portugal
Singapore Switzerland Thailand Turkey Ukraine Vietnam

Oxford is a registered trade mark of Oxford University Press
in the UK and in certain other countries

Published in the United States
by Oxford University Press Inc., New York

ISBN 978-0-19-928038-4

For my wife, Mandi, the most sceptical person I know

It is always by favour of Nature that one knows something

Wittgenstein, *On Certainty*

None of us can think or act without the acceptance of truths, not intuitive, not demonstrated, yet sovereign.

John Henry Newman, *An Essay in Aid of a Grammar of Assent*

Acknowledgements

Most of this book was written while on a two-year Leverhulme Trust Special Research Fellowship, and I am immensely grateful to the Leverhulme Trust for this award, and also to the Department of Philosophy at Stirling for sponsoring me for the award in the first place. I enjoyed my two years working on this project a great deal. Throughout this time I benefited from the support of my wife, Mandi ('the sceptic'), who is blessed with the gift of being unable to hear any philosophical statement that I might presume to utter without responding with some humorous wisecrack or other. I cannot recommend such irreverence enough. (Our giant fur-ball of a cat, Mitzy, managed to maintain a similar level of condescension throughout.) I'd also like to take this opportunity to thank my parents for their constant support over the years, financial and otherwise. This support is all the more remarkable given that (understandably, and like most people) they still have very little idea of what it is that philosophers actually *do*. Hopefully, this book will constitute something tangible that can help to rectify this situation.

An earlier version of this book was the topic of the Stirling Department of Philosophy reading group, and I am extremely grateful to the members of this group—Michael Brady, Rowan Cruft, Antony Duff, Phyllis McKay, and Alan Millar—for going to such lengths to provide me with comments on the manuscript. Michael Brady deserves a special mention in this respect, since he has had the misfortune to have read through and commented on no fewer than *three* earlier versions of this book.

Much of the material in this book has also been tried out on a number of occasions outside of the Stirling Philosophy Department. These occasions include: the University of Glasgow; the *Society for Skeptical Studies* session at the 2002 Pacific meeting of the American Philosophical Association in Seattle; the 2002 *Joint Session of the Mind and Aristotelian Society* in Glasgow; the University of Edinburgh; the University of Aberdeen; the 2002 *Scots Philosophical Club* annual meeting hosted by the University of Stirling; the University of Bristol; the University of Leeds; two talks at the 2003 Pacific meeting of the American Philosophical Association in San Francisco (one of which was to the *Society for Skeptical Studies* session); a conference on *Skepticism* at the Free University,

Acknowledgements

Amsterdam (along with a separate talk to the Faculty of Philosophy); the Department of Psychology at the University of Stirling; a NAMICONA workshop on *Theories of Knowledge* in Kolding, Demark; two talks at the NAMICONA pre-conference to *Modalism and Mentalism in Contemporary Epistemology* at the University of Copenhagen; a workshop on *McDowell on Perceptual Experience* at the University of Warwick; the University of Edinburgh Philosophy Society; a workshop on *Contemporary Epistemology* at the University of Stirling; a conference on *Epistemological Contextualism* at the University of Stirling; the Inland Northwest Annual Philosophy Conference on *Knowledge and Skepticism*, Moscow, USA; a conference on *Contextualism* in Bled, Slovenia; a conference on *Contextualism* at the Free University, Amsterdam; a conference on *Virtue Epistemology* at the University of Stirling; and the University of York. I am grateful to all the audiences on these occasions.

Many people have been of assistance to me in writing this book, whether in small ways by discussing specific points or by passing on relevant unpublished work, or in more substantial ways by reading and commenting on draft chapters. In this regard my thanks go to: Guy Axtell, Kent Bach, Will Barrett, Peter Bauman, Kelly Becker, Martijn Blaauw, Tim Black, Tom Blackson, Bill Brenner, Jessica Brown, Tony Brueckner, E. J. Coffman, Stew Cohen, Keith DeRose, Mylan Engal, Bryan Frances, Brian Garrett, Mikkel Gerken, Sandy Goldberg, Maurice Goldsmith, Richard Greene, Patrick Greenough, Lars-Bo Gundersen, Vincent Hendricks, Chris Hookway, Jesper Kallestrup, Klemens Kappel, Antti Karjalainen, Jonathan Kvanvig, Bob Lockie, Andrew McGonigal, Cornelis van Putten, Daniele Moyal-Sharrock, Brian Ribeiro, Bruce Russell, Nico Silins, Matthew Smith, Declan Smithies, Walter Sinnott-Armstrong, David Sosa, Ernie Sosa, Finn Spicer, Karl Halvor Teigen, Charles Travis, Jonathan Vogel, René van Woudenberg, Michael Williams, Tim Williamson, Crispin Wright, and Linda Zagzebski. Whist this list is meant to be exhaustive and thereby as uninvidious as possible, it is almost *bound* to be the case that I have missed someone out. If so, my sincerest apologies. Special thanks go to the following people who read an early version of the book in its entirety and provided me with invaluable and subtle comments: Berit Brogaard, Neil Gascoigne, John Greco, and Ram Neta. As ever, and despite all this help, my errors are my own.

I also benefited from the comments of two anonymous referees engaged by Oxford University Press to read the manuscript, and from the continual help and encouragement of my editor, Peter Momtchiloff. Thanks also to my copy editor, Conan Nicholas, and to Jacqueline Baker and Rupert Cousens at OUP.

Whilst several of the key ideas in this book have been aired in previous articles of mine, the process of weaving and integrating these ideas together has tended to result in much of this earlier work being substantially revised and rewritten. Nevertheless, some of it does survive in the final manuscript.

The main body of Chapter 4 is based on 'The Structure of Sceptical Arguments', *Philosophical Quarterly* 55 (2005), 37–52.

The early sections of Chapter 5 on how to define luck draw on work published in 'The Psychology and Philosophy of Luck' (co-written with Matthew Smith), *New Ideas in Psychology* 22 (2004), 1–28.

The later sections of Chapter 5 that discuss different types of benign epistemic luck, and the early and later sections of Chapter 6 which contrast two non-benign varieties of epistemic luck, are based on work published in 'Epistemic Luck', *Journal of Philosophical Research* 29 (2004), 193–22.

Chapter 7 draws on work published as 'Virtue Epistemology and Epistemic Luck', *Metaphilosophy* 34 (2003), 106–30. This paper is reprinted in *Moral and Epistemic Virtues*, (eds.) M. S. Brady and D. H. Pritchard (Oxford: Blackwell, 2003).

Much of the material on Pyrrhonian scepticism in Chapter 8 is derived from 'Doubt Undogmatized: Pyrrhonian Scepticism, Epistemological Externalism, and the "Metaepistemological" Challenge', *Principia—Revista Internacional de Epistemologia* 4 (2000), 187–218.

The discussion of Wittgenstein and McDowell on reasons that appears in Chapter 9 makes use of material from 'McDowell on Reasons, Externalism and Scepticism', *European Journal of Philosophy* 11 (2003), 273–94.

Finally, the general thread of argument found in Chapters 6, 8, and 9— concerning the relationship between the two main varieties of epistemic luck that I identify and the problem of scepticism—can be found in a shortened form in 'Scepticism, Epistemic Luck and Epistemic *Angst*', *Australasian Journal of Philosophy* 83 (2005).

I thank the editors concerned for their permission to make use of this material.

Contents

Contents

Introduction

It is quite rare in philosophy that one finds consensus, and when one does this tends to provoke a sense of unease. After all, one of the morals that can be gleaned from the study of the history of philosophy is that the emergence of a consensus is often the result of a shared mistake rather than a common understanding. The philosophical consensus that is the focus of this book, and which I argue is most definitely a cause for disquiet, concerns the seemingly universal intuition that *knowledge excludes luck,* or, to put it another way, that the *epistemic luck* that sometimes enables one to have true beliefs (and sometimes even fully justified true beliefs) is incompatible with knowledge. One can see the attraction of the intuition. Knowledge does appear to be a cognitive achievement of some sort, and luck seems to militate against genuine achievements. Accordingly, to say that an agent has knowledge is to imply that she didn't gain that knowledge *simply* via good fortune. Henceforth, we will call this claim that knowledge excludes luck the '*epistemic luck platitude*'.

The problem, however, is that it is difficult to take this thesis entirely at face-value, despite its initial plausibility. After all, there certainly are instances where luck plays a substantial role in the acquisition of apparently bona fide knowledge. Think, for example, of the history of scientific endeavour and those key discoveries that were gained via luck (such as the well-known, though possible apocryphal, story of Alexander Fleming's supposedly accidental discovery of penicillin), or of familiar tales of plucky detectives who just happen on the vital piece of incriminating evidence at the eleventh hour. Clearly we have here cases—possibly even paradigm cases—in which the agent's true belief constitutes a cognitive achievement even despite the possibly malign influence of luck. Are we to say that the epistemic luck platitude prevents one from ascribing knowledge in these instances?

Nevertheless, whilst there is this tension over just how we are to understand the intuition that knowledge excludes luck, it is clear that there is *something* right about it. Setting aside the issue of whether a guess could ever be an instance of belief for a moment, it is certainly true that your lucky guess that the horse 'Looby-Loo' would win the 4.20 p.m. meeting at Kempton racecourse is hardly knowledge, and at least part of the explanation of why this is so is that it is just plain luck that you were right. Indeed, lucky guesses are an extremal case in this regard, since the point is perfectly general and applies to examples even where no guesswork is involved. The beliefs of the gullible or the epistemically unconscientious, even when true, are often not knowledge, and a good explanation of why this is the case is that the beliefs formed by these agents tend to be only luckily true, and where they are true in such cases it does not represent a cognitive achievement on the part of the agent. We thus need to be careful that in granting knowledge to the Alexander Flemings of this world we do not thereby become so permissive in our knowledge ascriptions as to likewise grant knowledge to those agents whose gullibility or lack of epistemic conscientiousness did not, as it happens, impede them in gaining true beliefs. (And this is not to mention the folly of ascribing knowledge to those epistemically reckless agents who form their true beliefs via lucky guesses.)

Here, then, in essence, is the prima facie worry about the claim that knowledge excludes luck. On the one hand, if we construe it too inclusively then we may end up rejecting bona fide cases of knowledge. On the other hand, if we read it too restrictively then we may end up being unable to capture the very sense in which knowledge is a cognitive achievement at all. The issue of how we are to understand the relationship between knowledge and luck is thus central to our understanding of what knowledge is and therefore goes right to the heart of the epistemological project.

The parallel to the more widely discussed debate regarding moral luck is instructive in this regard. Very roughly, the analogy between the two cases goes something like this: just as one cannot take epistemic credit for forming a true belief in a lucky fashion, so one cannot take moral credit for a good consequence of one's action that arose out of luck rather than design (or, for that matter, be morally *blamed* for a bad consequence of one's action that arose out of luck). In short, we are, seemingly, only morally responsible for the consequences of our actions that are in some sense in our control.

Suppose, for example, that by flipping the light switch in my hotel room one evening I inadvertently electrocute the guest in the room next door, with fatal consequences—the result, let us say, of faulty wiring in the hotel that is nothing to do with me, and of which I am (blamelessly) unaware. Clearly, it is just bad luck, in one sense at least, that this happened, and certainly no responsibility of mine. Accordingly, so the intuition runs, I cannot be held morally responsible for this consequence of my actions and thus I am in this respect immune to moral censure. Similarly, the same goes for inadvertent and unforeseeable *good* consequences of my actions, such as if the flipping of this light switch had electrocuted my next-door neighbour *thereby saving his life* (he had, let us suppose, just collapsed from a heart attack, and the burst of current prompted his cold heart back into action). This may be a good consequence that we might loosely describe as being the result of an action of mine, but the luck involved in this good consequence coming about prevents me from taking any moral credit for it.

As with the case of epistemic luck, however, the fact that luck pervades our lives means that there are inevitably going to be cases where understanding moral responsibility in such a way that it *completely* excludes the influence of luck will jar with intuition. For example, consider the case of the otherwise conscientious motorist who just happens to hit a pedestrian at the one moment when his attention is not on the road. It is, we might say in a sympathetic tone, merely a matter of bad luck that this happened and, as in the examples just described, there is certainly a strong case that could be made for thinking that this consequence is both inadvertent and, we can stipulate, unforeseeable (there are usually no pedestrians around this area and, furthermore, the driver had no good reason for thinking that a pedestrian would be around this time). Does this mean, however, that we would be willing to say that this agent is *not* morally responsible for this consequence of his actions (and if we do, would we expect the courts to think likewise)? Clearly our intuitions here are not so straightforward. Thus, as with the phenomenon of epistemic luck, the concern is that we need some way of understanding the claim that moral responsibility excludes luck in such a way that it is neither unduly restrictive nor unduly permissive. And this behoves us to examine in more detail the underlying motivations for this thesis, and the various nuanced ways in which it can be understood.

Although I will be saying something about the problem posed by moral luck, my primary goal in this book is to deal with the far less explored difficulty presented by epistemic luck. Indeed, given the importance of epistemic luck to our understanding of knowledge, it is surprising that there has not yet been a sustained critical discussion of the specific problem posed by epistemic luck. As we will see, a closer examination of this problem highlights some important epistemological truths that have far-reaching ramifications for contemporary epistemology. Furthermore, as I will argue at the end of the book, this discussion of epistemic luck has important implications for the debate about moral luck as well.

In noting that hardly anyone has seriously examined the problem of epistemic luck, I am not claiming that the core thesis in this regard—that knowledge excludes luck—is never *mentioned* (explicitly or otherwise) in the recent epistemological literature, only that it is never really *discussed*. Indeed, as befitting its status as a *universal* intuition—what these days we philosophers tendentiously call a 'platitude'—one finds this thesis both everywhere and nowhere at the same time. That is, whilst this line of thinking is clearly being presupposed in much of contemporary epistemological thought, the thesis itself is rarely drawn up to the surface of discussion, and even then it is left to stand as it is: a pure platitudinous intuition that is in need of no further explication. For example, Matthias Steup (2001: 2), in a recent survey article on the analysis of knowledge, writes that 'it is uncontroversial that knowledge is incompatible with epistemic luck', and simply leaves the matter at that.

My contention here is not that such a claim *is* controversial as it stands, much less that it is straightforwardly false, but rather that we have yet to be given any clear sense of what this claim involves. Given that one core way of understanding the epistemological project is such that it is concerned, in some substantive respect, with providing an account of our key epistemic concepts which explains their incompatibility with epistemic luck, then it is essential that we interpret this supposed platitude correctly. Indeed, it is central to the thesis that I defend in this book that there are various ways of understanding the claim that knowledge excludes luck, not all of them plausible, and that they each pose a different challenge to epistemology.

Consider, for example, some of the areas of epistemological discussion in which the issue of epistemic luck is implicated. One such topic that springs immediately to mind in this regard is the debate concerning the counter-examples to the classical tripartite account of knowledge that were famously presented by Edmund Gettier. These examples work by highlighting the possibility that one might have a true belief that is gained on the basis of excellent grounds (and which therefore meets the rubric set down by the classical tripartite account of knowledge), but which is, nonetheless, and through some strange twist of fate, not knowledge. In effect, what Gettier presented were scenarios in which agents met the conditions specified by the classical tripartite account, but did so in a way that was infected with serendipity.

That just about everyone has been quick to conclude that such examples are successful in their stated aim—in that it is universally acknowledged that the cases described are clearly not instances of knowledge—speaks directly in favour of the claim that knowledge excludes luck. And, indeed, that these examples work because of the incompatibility of luck and knowledge is often explicitly noted. In a relatively recent textbook on contemporary epistemology, for example, we find Jonathan Dancy making the following remark:

justification and knowledge must somehow not depend on coincidence or luck. *This was just the point* of the Gettier counter-examples; nothing in the tripartite definition excluded knowledge by luck. (Dancy 1985: 134, *my italics*)

This is a fairly standard way of understanding the challenge posed by the Gettier counter-examples. Knowledge excludes luck, and thus examples which indicate that one has met the conditions set down by a theory of knowledge, but in such a way that is consistent with a substantive degree of luck being involved, are thereby conclusive counter-examples to that theory of knowledge. Accordingly, it should come as no surprise to learn that it is hard to find anyone these days who would seriously defend the classical tripartite theory of knowledge.

This neat picture of the relationship between knowledge and luck is complicated, however, once one considers how the issue of epistemic luck figures in other epistemological debates. A good contrast in this regard is the debate regarding radical scepticism. Again, we often get the intuition expressed that part of the sceptical challenge is to offer an analysis of knowledge that does not allow that our putative 'knowledge' is susceptible, in a wholesale manner, to luck. Just such an intuition seems to be behind, for example, infallibility-based approaches to scepticism where the leading idea seems to be that our knowledge must be infallible because otherwise it would be subject to the vagaries of luck.

Nevertheless, it is also interesting to note that in the debate regarding scepticism a certain degree of *acceptance* of some form of epistemic luck is often countenanced as well. One finds, for example, Michael Williams arguing as follows:

Knowledge and justification always involve an element of *epistemic luck*. A belief whose truth is *wholly* accidental cannot count as knowledge. But getting things right is never wholly nonaccidental either. (Williams 1999: 59, *italics in original*)

Similarly, Linda Zagzebski (1999: 109) has recently written that 'epistemic luck permeates the human condition, whether for good or ill'. Without any specification of what is involved in epistemic luck, however, it is far from clear what these concessions, if that's what they are, amount to. Moreover, neither is it clear just how allowing some degree of epistemic luck in this case is meant to be compatible with apparently not allowing *any* degree of epistemic luck in the Gettier cases.

The principal goal of this book is to capture what is involved in epistemic luck, and thus to identify the sense in which luck is incompatible with knowledge and the sense (if any) in which it isn't. Since one finds the most explicit discussions of epistemic luck in the debate regarding radical scepticism, the first part of the book focuses on this debate. (Indeed, as we will see in Part II, the fundamental problem posed by epistemic luck is a sceptical problem.)

In Chapter 1 I examine the way in which scepticism is often motivated via an appeal to some kind of infallibility thesis—as expressed, for example, in the work of Peter Unger—and highlight how this construal of the sceptical problem presupposes a certain view about epistemic luck. Furthermore, I explore the manner in which an infallibilism-based scepticism gives rise to the kind of template sceptical argument that is the focus for much of the contemporary discussion of scepticism and which turns on the principle that knowledge is 'closed' under known entailments (the so-called 'closure' principle).

In Chapter 2 I critically examine two of the main responses to the closure-based sceptical argument. In particular, I look at the case that has been made for the rejection of closure by, for example, Fred Dretske and Robert Nozick, and examine the so-called 'sensitivity' condition on knowledge that they advocate in this respect. I then evaluate this approach in the light of the attributer contextualist response to scepticism, as developed by such figures as Stewart Cohen, Keith DeRose, and David Lewis. In both cases I argue that these antisceptical approaches suffer by being motivated by diverse and incompatible intuitions, principally as regards their ambivalent endorsement of epistemological externalism. An exploration of the relationship between the sceptical problem and the epistemic externalism–internalism distinction is thus presented.

In Chapter 3 I contend that in so far as the contemporary debate about scepticism has formulated the sceptical problem correctly, and in so far as one is entitled to adopt epistemological externalism as part of one's antisceptical strategy, then one should reject both the arguments for non-closure and for attributer contextualism, and advance instead the kind of neo-Moorean position—as defended in the recent literature by, amongst others, Ernest Sosa and myself—which turns on the so-called 'safety' condition on knowledge. This chapter is thus devoted to exploring the implications of this approach for the sceptical problem, including the manner in which it needs to be distinguished from the more familiar 'Moorean' approach to scepticism that is associated with G. E. Moore's famous proof of an external world. A key component of this chapter in this respect is an account of the conversational rules that govern our ascriptions of knowledge (including self-ascriptions) which can do justice to the intuitions that motivate attributer contextualism whilst also explaining why the kind of antisceptical assertions made by Moore are so problematic. As regards the latter, I enlist elements of Wittgenstein's critique of Moore's response to the sceptic from *On Certainty*. I conclude that what these considerations highlight is a deep and important (and also surprising) truth about the structure of reasons.

Crucially, however, I do not pretend (as others do) that the neo-Moorean approach is able, by itself at any rate, to resolve the sceptical problem. As I explain in Chapter 4, the reason for this is that the contemporary discussion has misunderstood what the focus of scepticism is, and thus even the most plausible of the three main antisceptical theories in the literature misses its intended target. In order to illustrate this, I contrast the closure-based template sceptical argument with its analogue argument expressed in terms of the 'underdetermination' principle that can be found in ancient Pyrrhonian sceptical writings and which merely demands that one's evidence should favour one's beliefs over incompatible alternatives. I show how the latter argument brings to the fore just what is wrong with the contemporary debate regarding scepticism, which is its failure to respond to the specifically internalist and evidentialist character of the sceptical doubt.

At this point the reader might begin to wonder—entirely legitimately I think—just what all this has to do with epistemic luck. For whilst, as noted above, there is a clear sense in which the sceptical problem seems to trade on intuitions we have about the relationship between luck and knowledge, it is not immediately obvious why a deeper analysis of epistemic luck should cast any light on the sceptical debate. As I show in Part II, however, the confused understanding of the sceptical problem in the contemporary epistemological debate is indicative of a deeper confusion regarding the status of the claim that knowledge excludes luck. The reader is thus asked for patience while I set out the main responses to scepticism in the literature, since the extensive groundwork of Part I is necessary if the detailed discussions of epistemic luck in Part II are to be possible.

Indeed, there is a second sense in which the groundwork on scepticism undertaken in Part I is necessary for the specific discussion on epistemic luck that takes place in Part II, and this concerns how it is in response to the problem of scepticism that most of the main currents of contemporary epistemology have been motivated. In particular, sensitivity-based, safety-based, and attributer contextualist theories of knowledge all started out as antisceptical theories but are now theories of knowledge motivated on grounds that are independent of the problem of radical scepticism. Identifying a problem regarding epistemic luck that lies at the heart of the debate about radical scepticism is thus tantamount to discovering that contemporary epistemology as a whole is in trouble. The extended critique of Part I thus introduces all the main positions and thereby sets the scene for the second part of the book where critique starts to give way in favour of reconstruction.

I begin Part II with an overview of the various claims that have been made concerning epistemic luck and present an elucidation of the concept of luck in the light of this discussion that, I argue, captures the essence of the notion. With this elucidation in mind, I then identify—with the help of Unger— several varieties of luck that might be referred to as epistemic and which are entirely compatible with knowledge possession.

With these benign types of epistemic luck set to one side, I then turn, in Chapter 6, to the two species that remain and explain how they feature in the main epistemological debates. The first species of epistemic luck—what I call 'veritic' luck—can be handled with a modest 'relevant alternatives' account of knowledge that is specifically defined so that it counters this type of epistemic luck. As I explain, such a theory is essentially a version of the safety-based neo-Moorean thesis that we looked at in Chapter 3. I develop this view by considering some of the main examples that are discussed in epistemology— such as Gettier counter-examples, the 'lottery' puzzle, and 'barn façade' examples—and show how the neo-Moorean account can in each case generate the right result. Along the way the formulation of this anti-veritic-luck thesis is refined in response to potential challenges that might be presented to the view.

Significantly, however, the chapter closes by arguing that there is a second species of epistemic luck—what I call 'reflective luck'—that is epistemically problematic and which is not dealt with by the neo-Moorean account. The bulk of the rest of the book is devoted to getting to grips with this type of epistemic luck. In particular, in Chapter 7, I argue that such a notion raises important questions about the centrality to epistemology of a conception of justification which demands that one is able to take cognitive responsibility for one's beliefs. I also look (critically, as it turns out) at some of the recent 'virtue epistemo- logies' that have been put forward in the recent literature which (in essence) define knowledge in terms of the epistemic virtues (and also, in some cases, the cognitive faculties).

More specifically, I contrast broadly externalist construals of the virtue- theoretic thesis—such as the 'agent reliabilism' advanced, for example, by Sosa and John Greco—with virtue epistemologies that roughly fall into the internalist camp—in particular, 'neo-Aristotelian' theories, such as the view defended by Zagzebski. I claim that in each case a key part of the motivation for offering such a view lies in a desire to eliminate a species of epistemic luck that

8

is thought to be left uneliminated by rival theories of knowledge. In the case of agent reliabilism, the rival view is the similarly externalist 'process reliabilist' theory of knowledge advanced by, for example, Alvin Goldman. For the neo-Aristotelians, in contrast, the rival views are externalist theories of knowledge more generally, including agent reliabilism itself. Crucially, however, I maintain that whilst the kind of epistemic luck that Greco and company are focusing upon is specifically veritic, those offering a Zagzebski-style virtue theory are, it turns out, concerned also with the exclusion of reflective luck. In general, I claim that externalists and internalists in epistemology often speak past one another precisely because they are concerned with these different types of epistemic luck, and that disambiguating the species of epistemic luck at issue in this debate can help us to find a way of reconciling both internalist and externalist intuitions about knowledge.

More dramatically still, I conclude this chapter by arguing that once the ambiguous role of epistemic luck in the development of these virtue epistemological theories is made explicit, then the motivation to offer a specifically *virtue*-theoretic theory of knowledge subsides. In particular, I show how, pending further detail about the virtue-theoretic account at least, one can achieve everything that virtue epistemologists claim to achieve with their theories without adopting the core virtue-theoretic claim that knowledge must be defined in terms of the epistemic virtues (and cognitive faculties). Accordingly, there is no need to endorse the more radical theory of knowledge proposed by virtue theorists. A close analysis of epistemic luck thus not only helps us to see a way through the apparently intractable debate between epistemic externalists and internalists, but also appears to undercut the motivation for one of the most influential epistemological proposals of recent years.

In Chapter 8 I return to the sceptical challenge in the light of this distinction between veritic and reflective epistemic luck and argue that the inadequacy of the antisceptical proposals considered in Part I is a result of how they only (at best) eliminate veritic luck, and thus do not engage with the problem of reflective luck at all. Crucially, however, I claim that it is the specific challenge posed by reflective luck that is central to the sceptical problem, and yet that there is a fundamental sense in which this type of epistemic luck is ineliminable. In order to add some content to this claim, I argue that it is this sceptical problem that informs the Pyrrhonian sceptical challenge of antiquity. Moreover, I further maintain that the so-called 'metaepistemological' sceptical challenge that features prominently in contemporary epistemological debate—as advanced, for example, by Barry Stroud and Richard Fumerton—is best understood in terms of the specific sceptical problem regarding the ineliminability of reflective luck.

Introduction

Chapter 9 presents a more in-depth discussion of the difficulty posed by the ineliminability of reflective luck and offers one way of responding to the difficulty. I begin by reconsidering Wittgenstein's remarks on knowledge from *On Certainty* that we looked at in Chapter 3, and consider in particular the specific claims he makes about the so-called 'hinge' propositions that contextually determine the nature of epistemic evaluation. I claim that what underlies Wittgenstein's remarks in this respect is a certain view about the ultimately groundless nature of our reason-giving practices. This way of thinking about the structure of reasons is, I argue, correlative to the thesis described here regarding the ineliminability of reflective luck. Moreover, I contend that it is our implicit philosophical recognition of this problem that gives rise to a certain kind of general anxiety about our epistemic position that I refer to as epistemic *angst*. This contention is further illustrated by critically evaluating John McDowell's content externalist response to the sceptic which incorporates a strongly antisceptical account of reasons in the light of the opposing Wittgensteinian scepticism-friendly account.

This final chapter of the main body of the book is not completely pessimistic, however, in that it closes by arguing that whilst there is no epistemic response available to the problem posed by reflective luck, there is a plausible *pragmatic* resolution to this difficulty. Indeed, I claim that an antisceptical thesis of this sort can be discerned from Wittgenstein's own fragmentary remarks on scepticism, and I develop such a view in the light of Hans Reichenbach's pragmatic response to the problem of inductive scepticism, which I maintain is cast along similar lines.

The book closes with a postscript which outlines how this analysis of epistemic luck has ramifications for the supposedly parallel debate regarding moral luck. As noted above, both discussions seem to rest upon the assumption that the moral and epistemic states in question are (in some sense) achievements and so cannot be subject to luck. Nevertheless, and as we also noted above, whilst tacit acceptance of this brute intuition is common in contemporary epistemology, contemporary moral theory has been conspicuous in its sustained scrutiny of this claim. Focusing on the two classic papers in this area by Thomas Nagel and Bernard Williams that sparked the modern debate on this subject, I examine the arguments and examples put forward in this regard and highlight how the primarily epistemological analysis offered here can be put into service to cast light on the corresponding moral debate. In particular, I show that these authors fail to distinguish a specifically moral problem, and that what difficulties they do highlight are parasitic on the problem of reflective epistemic luck that is identified here. I therefore conclude that there is a strong prima facie case for thinking that there is no such thing as moral luck, and that the only reason why many think that there is is because they are confusing the non-existent problem of moral luck with the entirely genuine problem of reflective epistemic luck. Our discussion of epistemic luck thus has repercussions which extend beyond the purely epistemological realm.

Part One
Scepticism

1

Scepticism in Contemporary Debate

1.0. Introduction

Interest in the debate regarding radical scepticism has seen a dramatic resurgence in recent years, with a number of novel (and, in some cases, sympathetic) approaches to the problem being offered.[1] The enduring appeal of this debate owes a great deal to our underlying commitment to some version of the 'epistemic luck' platitude—the intuitive thought that knowledge is incompatible with luck. For what the sceptic claims to be highlighting to us is how our putative 'knowledge' is in fact acquired in an extremely lucky fashion. This is particularly apparent when the scepticism is motivated via an appeal to sceptical hypotheses, which is probably the most common way in which sceptical arguments have been understood in the contemporary literature. For example, one might think that one is currently seated by the fire, but one could just as well be merely dreaming that one is. Or one might think that one is living a life full of varied causal engagement with the world, but one could just as well be merely a stationary brain-in-a-vat (BIV) who is being 'fed' her experiences by futuristic neuroscientists. And so on. In each case the point is that it is merely a matter of luck, in some sense to be specified, that circumstances are as we take them to be, and thus that we cannot have knowledge of what we believe about the world, even if these beliefs are in fact true.

The peculiarity of the sceptical challenge regarding epistemic luck, however, is that it does not just raise the possibility that luck has illicitly intervened to defeat our putative knowledge, but also invokes the further thought that there is no way in which we might improve our epistemic situation so as to definitively establish that, after all, there is no luck at issue in these cases. For whilst one could respond to an ordinary 'epistemic luck' challenge of this general sort by looking closer at the facts to ensure that there was no luck in play (or by identifying what one would need to do to improve one's epistemic position so as to ensure that the luck in question is eliminated in future), this is, the sceptic claims, *impossible* when it comes to the sceptic's epistemic luck challenge.

For example, suppose someone were to say that you didn't really know that your brother was in town yesterday, despite seeing him drive past you in the High Street, because his doppelgänger was also in town (and drives a similar car) and it was just luck that you happened to form your (true) belief in response to seeing your brother rather than the doppelgänger. In response to this, one could attempt to eliminate this 'local' epistemic luck challenge by checking to see whether one would have been able to tell the doppelgänger and one's brother apart after all (or at least their cars). If one is able to show that one would have (perhaps because the doppelgänger has longer hair, and one would have noticed this difference on the day given the view one had of the driver), then this would, ordinarily at least, suffice to neutralize this challenge to one's knowledge.

Moreover, even if one were to agree that one did not really have the knowledge in question in this case because of the luck involved, one could at the very least identify an incremental improvement in one's epistemic position that would have ensured that the knowledge was not lucky in the way described. In this case, for example, this might involve getting a better view of the driver, or having the chance to speak to him. The sceptical case is very different. The point of the sceptic's epistemic luck challenge is that there is no possible incremental improvement in one's epistemic position that could settle the issue in your favour. There is, the sceptic claims, no possible test that could determine that you were not, say, a BIV in the scenario described above. It is not just an incidental epistemic lack on our part that the sceptic claims to be drawing our attention to, then, but an epistemic lack that is constitutive of our epistemic position. Such is the drama of the radical sceptical argument.

Sceptical arguments are also meant to be (at least in one sense) *paradoxes*, in that they highlight a cluster of claims which, when taken individually, we all regard as intuitively true but which, collectively, entail an intellectually devastating and unacceptable conclusion—that it is impossible for us to possess any knowledge, or at least any knowledge of substance. This puts an extra dialectical burden on the antisceptic, since she has to not only explain where this apparent paradox goes wrong, but also diagnose why we were ever taken in by it in the first place. A simple rejection of one of the premises of the paradox would do little to assuage our sense of philosophical unease since it would leave open the possibility of a second-order scepticism which claimed that we have no good reason *not* to be sceptics, and this second-order scepticism seems little better than its first-order analogue. In particular, what we want from the antisceptic is not just the identification of which premiss (or premisses) should be rejected, but also a diagnosis of how we were ever taken in by this puzzle in the first place.[2]

Given the intellectually devastating conclusions of sceptical arguments, the desire to meet the challenge is obvious. Nevertheless, the fact that sceptical arguments have been the mainstay of epistemological reflection for most of its history should indicate to us that we should regard recent 'resolutions' of this age-old problem with great caution. Indeed, it is a key component of the main argument of this first part of the book that none of these contemporary responses to scepticism gets to the bottom of the problem, and part of the reason for this is a failure to be clear about what these intuitions about epistemic luck that sceptical arguments trade upon involve.

This chapter begins by noting some of the ways in which scepticism has been motivated in the contemporary discussion, and primarily considers how 'infallibilist' intuitions, even if unpersuasive when considered in isolation, appear to be behind the recent move to cast the sceptical argument in terms of a certain template argument which essentially employs the so-called 'closure' principle for knowledge. The aim of this chapter is to prepare the ground so that the main antisceptical arguments proposed in the recent literature can be surveyed and shown to be ultimately inadequate to the task. This first part of the book is thus primarily negative, but that is to be expected. As so often in philosophy, before the constructive work can begin, some deconstruction must take place.

1.1. Infallibilism and Absolute Certainty

Perhaps the most obvious way in which sceptical arguments trade upon epistemic luck is when those arguments are understood in terms of a demand for *infallibility*. Very roughly (we will consider various alternative formulations in a moment), the demand for infallibility here involves something like the requirement that there be no possibility of error. Accordingly, in order to know a proposition, one must be able to rule out all possibilities of error associated with that proposition. And since, intuitively at least, this is an impossible demand to make as regards nearly all (if not all) of our beliefs, the sceptical conclusion that it is impossible to possess knowledge to any substantive degree immediately follows. So understood, infallibilism-based scepticism appears to arise out of a very literal reading of the epistemic luck platitude. If knowledge is incompatible with luck, then it must also be incompatible with the possibility of error since to leave a possibility of error unelimitated is to leave one's belief open to being undermined by the bad epistemic luck that this possibility of error obtains. We might express this thought in ordinary language, for example, by saying that unless one eliminates every possibility of error, then one's putative knowledge is 'left open to chance'. That, at any rate, seems to be the general form of the intuition in play here—that knowledge is not the kind of thing that can be left open to chance, nor which can therefore admit of even the smallest degree of epistemic luck.

The problem for infallibilism-based scepticism, however, is that whilst we all have the intuition that knowledge is in some sense incompatible with luck, we *also* have the fairly strong intuition that one can possess knowledge whilst nevertheless having a belief about the proposition at issue which is fallible. That is, infallibility does not appear to be an obvious part of the epistemic demands that we make when it comes to the possession of knowledge (most of it, at any rate). The sceptic thus has some work to do to convince us that we should understand the epistemic luck platitude in this austere manner.

One influential way that infallibilism has been motivated in the recent literature is via the claim that in order to possess knowledge it must be epistemically legitimate for the agent in question to be absolutely certain about the target proposition, where absolute certainty here is most naturally understood as demanding that the agent has eliminated all possibilities of error associated with that proposition. One thus gets infallibilism from the demand for absolute certainty. Of course, it might seem just as problematic to suppose that knowledge demands absolute certainty as that it demands infallibility, and if this is so then the appeal to absolute certainty will not help the sceptic's case in this respect. Nevertheless, as Peter Unger (1971, 1974, 1975) has famously argued, there *are* grounds available in support of the demand for absolute certainty.

Essentially, Unger's claim is that once we factor out the weakened senses of 'know' that we use in quotidian discourse, we discover a strict sense of 'know' that demands absolute certainty and which can thus be put into service in a sceptical argument. And since the sceptical use of the term is held to be the paradigm usage (with our quotidian usage as somehow derivative), the sceptic is able to marshal everyday (i.e. non-philosophical) intuitions about our epistemic terms in order to defend her scepticism, thereby ensuring the paradoxical nature of her doubt. Unger's strategy can thus concede the fallibilist nature of our everyday usage of the term 'know' without thereby conceding that our epistemic intuitions are with fallibilism.

Unger makes his case for the claim that knowledge demands absolute certainty by adducing examples of statements which he claims are inconsistent, such as the following, 'He really *knew* that it was raining, but he *wasn't* absolutely *certain* that it was' (Unger 1974: 2, *italics in the original*). And since, he argues, we all share the intuition that claiming knowledge whilst simultaneously admitting a lack of absolute certainty is inconsistent, hence we must all implicitly agree that knowledge demands absolute certainty, and thus that we do not really know anything (or anything of substance at any rate).

Of course, in saying this Unger does not deny that sometimes we are happy to ascribe knowledge to agents where the agent is not absolutely certain about the target proposition, but his claim is that these cases simply reflect a 'loose' usage of the term. For example, he describes the case of someone who unhesitatingly went to the right spot to find his cufflinks even whilst doubting that they were there, arguing that 'our readiness to say that he knew might only indicate loose usage of those words by us, while we are more strict in our use when the word "certain" enters the picture' (Unger 1974: 2). Unger's point is that once we make explicit the connection between knowledge and absolute certainty— as we do when we make assertions like 'He really *knew* that it was raining, but he *wasn't* absolutely *certain* that it was'—we recognize that our everyday ascriptions of knowledge are unduly permissive and hence, strictly speaking, false.

Unger argues that this contrast between our permissive 'loose' usage of the term 'knowledge' and a stricter scepticism-friendly usage reflects the fact that 'knowledge', like 'flat' or 'empty', is an 'absolute term'. Just as we realize on reflection that nothing is ever *really* flat (since even a 'flat' road has some imperfections), and that nothing is ever *really* empty (since there is no such thing as a vacuum), so reflection also reveals to us that no (hardly any) proposition is ever *really* known because in order to possess knowledge one must be (rightly) absolutely certain and we have no just cause to be absolutely certain about anything (or, at least, hardly anything). Our everyday ascriptions of knowledge in the absence of absolute certainty are thus akin to our claims that pool tables are 'flat' even though we grant that no pool table has a surface which is a frictionless plane. In both cases, we are using the terms involved in a loose fashion even though we recognize, when called upon to do so, that what we say in such cases is, strictly speaking, false.

There are a number of points to make about this general line of argument. For one thing, it is somewhat controversial to straightforwardly conclude on the basis that a certain assertion is conversationally inappropriate that the assertion is thereby (literally) expressing a proposition that is false. After all, the apparent falsity of an assertion could be due to the fact that this assertion, whilst (literally) true, generates a false conversational implicature. We will return to this point at a later juncture. For now, the more pressing issue is that it is not entirely obvious that the claims that Unger focuses upon really are incoherent. Would we really find it odd to hear it said that someone knows a proposition despite not being absolutely certain of it? I'm inclined to think not. Indeed, if anything, it seems more intuitive to suppose that we would *not* take it as given upon hearing that knowledge is being ascribed to an agent that the agent in question is absolutely certain about the target proposition.

Of course, Unger can accede this much to us, since he can respond by noting that this reluctance to find such assertions incoherent merely reflects loose everyday epistemic standards. But this move is problematic. Recall that Unger's claim was the plausible contention that whilst we *unthinkingly* allow weak epistemic standards in everyday contexts which do not demand absolute certainty, on reflection we discover that knowledge really does require absolute certainty. The difficulty, however, is that the kind of assertions that Unger is focusing upon are precisely cases where this supposed feature of our epistemic standards has been brought to our attention (this is why Unger is making use of these examples in the first place). So whilst we might ascribe knowledge in the absence of absolute certainty in everyday contexts, by the lights of Unger's account we ought not to be willing to ascribe knowledge and *explicitly grant that the agent is not absolutely certain*, even in otherwise 'everyday' contexts. That these assertions are not obviously incoherent is thus a major difficulty for Unger's view.

This point is strengthened once one looks more closely at the everyday cases in which we are happy to ascribe knowledge even in the absence of absolute certainty. Consider again the 'cufflink' example noted above. Unger weakens the force of this example by considering a case in which the agent unerringly manages to find his cufflinks even whilst *professing that he doubts* that they are where he thinks they are. The difficulty with this example is that the problem from Unger's point of view is precisely not with cases such as this where a temptation to ascribe knowledge coexists with the presence of a doubt, but rather lies in otherwise similar cases where the agent has *no doubts* and may in fact be certain of what he believes, but is just not *absolutely* certain.[3] After all, one of the problems facing any example that deals with a case of doubt is that doubt has a tendency to undermine one's *belief* (thereby potentially preventing one from meeting one of the necessary conditions for knowledge). It is little wonder then that we find ourselves sympathetic with Unger's claim that in these cases the temptation to ascribe knowledge should probably be resisted. But what about those cases where there is no doubt and in fact justifiable cause for the agent to express a (non-absolute) degree of certainty? Why should we resist the temptation to ascribe knowledge in *these* cases? The problem, however, is that if one reruns the above example but stipulates that there was no doubt in play—nor, indeed, any specific need for doubt—then the 'intuition' that the agent does indeed know that the cufflinks were where he thought they were is considerably strengthened. Given that this is the case, merely contending that our intuitions here are *simply* a mistaken response to the 'loose' standards in play in everyday contexts is not going to be particularly persuasive.

Nevertheless, there is clearly *something* right about Unger's defence of infalli-bilism. This is that whilst it does not seem particularly troubling to ascribe knowledge whilst explicitly allowing that the agent is not absolutely certain about the proposition in question, it *does* seem problematic to ascribe knowledge whilst allowing that there is a *specific* possibility that the agent is unable to rule out. That is, an assertion of the following form does seem to be incoherent: 'X knows that P, but X is unable to rule out an error possibility associated with P.' For example, consider an assertion of the following sentence: 'John knows that his car is parked on the driveway, but for all he knows it could've been stolen in the last few minutes.' This assertion has a 'Moorean' air about it.

One philosopher who seems aware of this point is David Lewis. He charac-terizes the intuition behind infallibilism as follows:

The sceptical argument is nothing new or fancy. It's just this: it seems as if knowledge must be by definition infallible. If you claim that S knows that P, and yet you grant that S cannot eliminate a certain possibility in which not-P, it certainly seems as if you have granted that S does not after all know that P. To speak of fallible knowledge, of knowledge despite uneliminated possibilities of error, just *sounds* contradictory. (Lewis 1996: 549)

Note that Lewis is not endorsing here (at least not directly) the general claim that knowledge demands absolute certainty or (where this is thought to be different) the elimination of all possibility of error, but only the more specific claim that knowledge demands the elimination of every error-possibility associated with the target proposition *where those error-possibilities are currently being entertained* (either by the agent herself, or by the one who is ascribing the knowledge to the agent)[4]. However, given that the context in which one engages with the problem of scepticism is one in which all manner of error-possibilities are under consideration—including sceptical hypotheses which, the sceptic claims, no one could ever know to be false—this specific concession to the sceptic can very quickly be converted into a general concession that agents need to rule out all possibilities of error, and thus (rightly) be absolutely certain, before they can have knowledge.

That the Lewisian version of infallibilism only focuses on entertained error-possibilities explains why we are so permissive in our ascriptions of knowledge in everyday contexts, since in these contexts it is only mundane and generally eliminable possibilities of error that are at issue. We will credit an agent with knowing that his car is parked outside just so long as he can eliminate the possibility that, for example, it is not his wife's car on the driveway, or that it was not stolen last night. He does not need to be able to rule out possibilities of error that aren't at issue in that context, such as whether it has just this minute been stolen, or whether it has been removed and replaced with a hologram image. And this seems perfectly sensible, in that 'knowledge' here is serving the function of indicating that agents can eliminate the possibilities of error that *we are interested in* in that context. The trouble is, of course, if there is no bar in principle to the raising of possibilities of error, then in more demanding contexts we will expect our usage of the term 'knowledge' to tighten up to reflect this. On this view, the sceptical context in which almost every possibility of error is relevant to the possession of knowledge—even uneliminable ones, such as sceptical error-possibilities (that one is a BIV, and so forth)—lies at one end of a continuum of epistemic rigour.[5]

Indeed, if 'knowledge' really is an absolute term, as Unger suggests, then this is just what we should expect. The epistemic standards governing our everyday ascriptions of 'knowledge' will be as demanding as they need to be relative to the kinds of error-possibilities that are at issue in that context. Given that in everyday contexts it is only quite mundane error-possibilities that are at issue (and certainly not sceptical error-possibilities), these standards won't be very demanding at all and thus a great deal of 'knowledge' will be ascribed. In sceptical contexts in which the most onerous error-possibilities are in play, however, the epistemic standards will be maximally austere, and here we realize that, strictly speaking, hardly anyone has any genuine knowledge. On this view, the truth of scepticism is something that we discover when we enter the sceptical context and which we realize was hitherto hidden by the arbitrarily limited epistemic standards in operation in ordinary non-sceptical contexts.

Moreover, if Unger is right that 'knowledge' is an absolute term, then the usage of this term in sceptical contexts where all possibilities of error are relevant will have a theoretical ascendancy over the usage of the term in everyday contexts. According to Unger, just as we speak loosely and, strictly speaking, falsely in asserting that a pool table, despite the imperfections on its surface, is flat, so we speak loosely and, strictly speaking, falsely in asserting that an agent, despite being unable to eliminate all possibilities of error and thus not (legitimately) being absolutely certain, has knowledge.

Accordingly, the apparently weaker way of expressing the infallibilist point in terms of entertained error-possibilities proposed by Lewis collapses into an infallibilist thesis that is just as demanding as that put forward by Unger. There is one interesting difference between the two presentations of infallibilism, however, despite the fact that they are ultimately epistemically demanding to the same degree. This is that whilst Unger motivates his infallibilism via an appeal to the need for absolute certainty, on the Lewisian model the demand for absolute certainty plays no essential role at all, the focus instead being simply on the need to eliminate all entertained possibilities of error.

We must tread carefully here, however, since this infallibilist conclusion is not the only one licensed by this observation. To begin with, as noted above, the incoherence of these assertions could merely reflect the fact that these assertions are conversationally inappropriate, perhaps because an ascription of knowledge in a sceptical conversational context generates the false implicature that there is no uneliminated possibility of error. Furthermore, even if we cannot escape the infallibilist conclusion via this particular manoeuvre, it still does not follow that we must endorse infallibilism. Lewis himself, for example, argues that the appropriate moral to be drawn is not infallibilism but rather *contextualism*, where the epistemic standards that are relevant to the correct usage of the term 'know' are context-sensitive such that in *some* contexts one can have knowledge even despite being unable to eliminate all possibilities of error (and thus without being absolutely certain).[6]

We will return to consider these two alternative possibilities below. For now the point is that there is at least a prima facie case for this particular rendering of infallibilism, and thus for the related thesis that knowledge demands absolute certainty (though recall that we also noted that the plausibility of the latter thesis seems to be dependent upon the plausibility of infallibilist intuitions, rather than vice versa as Unger suggests). Accordingly, there are grounds for reading the epistemic luck platitude in a robust manner that lends support to scepticism.

1.2. From Infallibilism to the Closure-based Template Sceptical Argument

There is thus one prima facie plausible version of infallibilism-based scepticism which demands that, strictly speaking, in order to have knowledge one must be able to rule out all the error-possibilities associated with the target proposition, and therefore concludes that we do not have any knowledge (or, at any rate, any knowledge of substance). As it stands, however, this infallibilism-based sceptical line of thought is incomplete in that it still remains to be made explicit just why we are unable to rule out the error-possibilities in question (we have heard some suggestive remarks in this regard, of course, such as the straight-forward assertion of the intuition that we cannot rule out all relevant error-possibilities, but this is not yet an *argument*). Since it is clearly the case that we are able to rule out some error-possibilities, in order to meet this challenge the sceptic therefore needs to further argue that there are error-possibilities within the class of relevant error-possibilities that are *ineliminable*—that is, error-possibilities which agents are unable to rule out. To this end, the sceptic typically adduces a special kind of error-possibility—*viz. sceptical hypotheses*. Crucially, this type of error-possibility has the special feature that, intuitively, no agent could ever rule it out.

For simplicity, we will stick to the BIV sceptical hypothesis, since this is clearly the most popular sceptical hypothesis in the recent literature. We will take this to be the scenario that at some point in one's adult life one's brain was removed and placed in a vat of nutrients. Once there, it was 'fed' 'experiences' by neuro-scientists (we will not trouble ourselves how), where the 'experiences' in question have the same general phenomenal character as the experiences one would expect to have if one were not a BIV and had instead been living the kind of normal life that one had been living prior to having one's brain 'harvested' in this way.[7]

The problem that a sceptical hypothesis such as the BIV hypothesis poses is that it is subjectively indistinguishable to the agent whether her experiences indicate that the world is as she takes it to be as opposed to being completely unlike how she takes it to be, which it would be if she were the victim of the sceptical hypothesis. And given this subjective indistinguishability, it seems that there will be nothing cognitively available to the agent which will suffice to indicate to her that she is in the non-sceptical scenario as opposed to the scep-tical scenario. So whereas the standard error-possibilities merely raise *incidental* difficulties for the epistemic status of one's beliefs—in that there are possible incremental improvements in one's epistemic position that one could envisage that would enable one to meet the challenge posed by these error-possibilities— sceptical error-possibilities pose an *in principle* difficulty for the epistemic status of one's beliefs. Just so long as sceptical error-possibilities are relevant to knowledge in the way that infallibilism demands so that they must be eliminated before one can have knowledge, then scepticism appears to quickly follow. It is little wonder then that we have the intuition that it is never epistemically legitimate for us to adopt an attitude of absolute certainty regarding a proposi-tion, since there will always be a (sceptical) error-possibility associated with that proposition that cannot be ruled out, even in principle.

One natural way of understanding what is involved in 'ruling out' an error-possibility is that of the agent knowing that error-possibility to be false. Indeed, we often treat these two notions as equivalent, in that if we heard an agent assert that she could rule out a certain error-possibility (e.g. that her car has just been stolen) we would naturally infer that she knows this error-possibility to be false. Conversely, if we heard an agent assert that she knew a certain error-possibility to be false, then we would naturally infer that she is able to rule out this possibility. Moreover, just as an assertion of the form, 'X knows that P, but X is unable to rule out an error possibility associated with P', sounds incoherent, so too does an assertion of the form, 'X knows that P, but X does not know that an error possibility associated with P is false'. For example, the assertion, 'John knows that his car is parked on the driveway, but he does not know that it hasn't been stolen in the last few minutes', sounds problematic.

At any rate, the standard reading of the phrase 'rule out' in the contemporary literature is 'know to be false', and we will follow suit for now (though we will return later on to examine this supposed equivalence in more detail). On this construal, infallibilism licenses the following 'infallibility principle':

The infallibility principle
For all agents, φ, if an agent knows a proposition φ, then that agent knows that all error-possibilities associated with φ are false.

In itself, this still leaves it open that the sceptical problem may just be concerned with an incidental epistemic lack on the agent's part. When this principle is combined with the further claim that agents are unable to know the falsity of all sceptical error-possibilities that are associated with a proposition, however, then one can derive the radical sceptical conclusion that it is impossible to have knowledge of most (if not all) of what we ordinarily take ourselves to know (call these propositions that we ordinarily take ourselves to know 'everyday' propositions). The basic form of the argument is therefore as follows, where the infallibility principle is the motivation for the major premiss, (I1), and the argument is understood as reflecting features of our epistemic concepts that we discover in the context of philosophical reflection:

The template infallibilism-based radical sceptical argument

(I1) If one is to have knowledge of a wide range of everyday propositions, then one must know the denials of all error-possibilities that are associated with these propositions, including radical sceptical hypotheses.

(I2) One cannot know the denials of radical sceptical hypotheses.

(IC) One cannot have knowledge of a wide range of everyday propositions.

Indeed, so understood, one can weaken the argument further without loss, since the sceptic only needs *one* suitably general sceptical hypothesis to be at issue in order to generate the radical sceptical conclusion, and so one could simply demand that the agent should rule this particular hypothesis out in (I1). For our purposes, for example, we could just focus on the BIV sceptical hypothesis:

The infallibilism-based BIV radical sceptical argument

(IB1) If one is to have knowledge of a wide range of everyday propositions, then one must know the denial of the BIV sceptical hypothesis.

(IB2) One cannot know the denial of the BIV sceptical hypothesis.

(IBC) One cannot have knowledge of a wide range of everyday propositions.

So the state of play is that we have seen that there is a prima facie plausibility in the idea that one cannot coherently simultaneously ascribe knowledge to an agent whilst granting that there is a specific error-possibility associated with the target proposition that the agent does not know to be false. And since the sceptic introduces a context in which a wide range of error-possibilities— including, crucially, *sceptical* error-possibilities—are at issue, so we get the demand that the possession of knowledge is contingent upon the putatively knowing agent being able to do the impossible and rule out even sceptical error-possibilities. Unger tried to motivate this sceptical line of argument via an appeal to absolute certainty, but it seems that the demand for absolute certainty falls out of considerations to do with infallibilism rather than the other way around. In any case, with this infallibilist claim in play combined with the further thesis that one is unable to know the denials of sceptical error-possibilities, it follows that one lacks knowledge of much (if not all) of what one believes, *no matter what incremental improvements one might make to one's epistemic position*. Hence, if the underlying plausibility of infallibilism lies in a robust reading of the epistemic luck platitude, then scepticism is a consequence of the apparently impossible demand that one's knowledge should not be subject to luck.

We will return to the issue of whether it is possible to know the denials of radical sceptical hypotheses below. What is more interesting for our present purposes is the relationship between the infallibilism-based argument that we have just set out, and the formulation of the sceptical argument that is most prominent in the contemporary literature which turns on the principle that knowledge is 'closed' under known entailment, or the 'closure' principle for short. Roughly, we can express this principle as follows:

The closure principle for knowledge
For all agents, φ, ψ, if an agent knows that φ, and knows that φ entails ψ, then that agent knows that ψ.[8]

This principle is extremely plausible, in that it seems difficult to imagine how one could know one proposition, such as that the murder was committed in the lobby, know that this entails a second proposition, such as that the murder was not committed in the kitchen, and yet fail to know the second proposition. This principle is also logically weaker than the infallibilist principle that motivates (I1) and (IB1), since whilst that principle demands that the agent knows the denials of *all* error-possibilities associated with the target proposition, the closure principle only requires that the agent knows the denials of those error-possibilities which she knows to be inconsistent with the target proposition. Closure therefore allows a possibility that is ruled out by the infallibility principle, *viz.* that there may be error-possibilities associated with a proposition that are not known by the agent to be entailed by that proposition, and which can therefore be legitimately ignored by the agent.[9]

Crucially, however, although closure is logically weaker it will do the sceptic's bidding just as well. After all, since it is (typically at least) a trivial conceptual truth that our everyday beliefs are inconsistent with the truth of sceptical hypotheses, we can legitimately suppose that most agents know that this entailment holds. Moreover, in so far as this entailment does hold, then closure demands that knowledge of the 'everyday' propositions which we ordinarily take ourselves to know will demand knowledge of the denials of sceptical hypotheses, and since (as (I2) states) we cannot know that such hypotheses are false, the radical sceptical conclusion immediately follows.

We thus have the following closure-based template radical sceptical argument which is based on the logically weaker principle of closure but which generates the same intellectually devastating conclusion as that which is at issue in the infallibilism-based sceptical argument:[10]

The template closure-based radical sceptical argument

(C1) If one is to have knowledge of a wide range of everyday propositions, then one must know the denials of all radical sceptical hypotheses that one knows to be incompatible with the relevant everyday propositions.

(C2) One cannot know the denials of radical sceptical hypotheses.

(CC) One cannot have knowledge of a wide range of everyday propositions.[11]

And since, as with the infallibilism-based template radical sceptical argument formulated above, the sceptic only needs one suitably general radical sceptical hypothesis in order to motivate her sceptical conclusion, we can reformulate this example using the BIV sceptical hypothesis without loss:

The closure-based BIV radical sceptical argument

(CB1) If one is to have knowledge of a wide range of everyday propositions, then one must know the denial of the BIV sceptical hypothesis.

(CB2) One cannot know the denial of the BIV sceptical hypothesis.

(CBC) One cannot have knowledge of a wide range of everyday propositions.

Given that both sceptical arguments generate the same intellectually devastating sceptical conclusion, there are obvious advantages to opting for the closure-based formulation of the argument that is motivated by a logically weaker epistemic principle. Clearly, the considerations that motivate the infallibilism principle have just as much motivating force when it comes to the closure principle. If it is incoherent to ascribe knowledge to an agent whilst granting that she is unable to know that an error-possibility associated with the target proposition is false, then it is going to be just as incoherent (if not more incoherent) to ascribe knowledge to that agent whilst granting that there is an error-possibility that she knows to be inconsistent with the target proposition and which she does not know to be false. Furthermore, since the assumption that most agents know the relevant sceptical entailment—i.e. that the everyday propositions entail the denials of sceptical hypotheses—is uncontentious, we need not concern ourselves unduly with the issue of what to make of agents who have never considered sceptical error-possibilities, and so are employing the term 'knowledge' in a loose way that is insensitive to the supposed need to rule out these possibilities. If agents can ordinarily be supposed to know that the falsity of these error-possibilities is a consequence of what they take themselves to know, then at least in this sense these error-possibilities are already relevant to the instances of everyday knowledge in question, whether the problem of radical scepticism has been explicitly raised or not.

A further advantage of employing the closure-based argument is that it dispels the temptation to *simply* respond to an infallibilism-based scepticism by adopting a fallibilist view of knowledge. The motivation for this manoeuvre might naturally arise from the thought that whilst we can satisfy our loose everyday concept of 'knowledge' without meeting infallibilist epistemic standards, the standards that one does meet will at least *approximate* to infallibilist standards. Accordingly, whilst we must renounce any claim to have knowledge in the sense demanded by the infallibilist and the sceptic (and by reflection as well, if the infallibilist and the sceptic are right), we can still claim that our beliefs have met an important 'knowledge-approximating' epistemic rubric.

The problem, however, is that the contrast between the infallibilist conception of knowledge and our everyday conception is not merely to do with the *range* of error-possibilities that need to be eliminated, but is also concerned with the *type* of error-possibilities at issue. If it were just the range that was important then we could respond to infallibilism by simply identifying a weaker sense of 'knowledge' that simply involved eliminating a smaller range of error-possibilities. The sceptical error-possibility is not just one more error-possibility to be eliminated however, but an in principle *ineliminable* error-possibility. It is not then as if someone who met the loose everyday epistemic standards would be *closer* to meeting the stricter infallible epistemic standards than one who had met no epistemic standards at all (as the 'approximation' model would suggest). Instead, they are both just as worse off when it comes to the elimination of sceptical error-possibilities.

The difference between everyday error-possibilities and sceptical error-possibilities is thus not, in this sense at least, one of degree but of kind. Accordingly, what makes infallibilism sceptic-friendly is not just that it makes a wide *range* of error-possibilities relevant to knowledge, but more specifically that it makes error-possibilities of a certain *sort* relevant to knowledge. Closure brings this point to the fore, given that we grant knowledge of the relevant entailment from putative everyday knowledge to antisceptical knowledge. If closure holds, then sceptical error-possibilities are relevant to knowledge, and their relevance ensures (it seems) that we lack knowledge of everyday propositions even though we might understand 'knowledge' in fallibilist terms as not demanding the elimination of all possibilities of error.

So just as long as our concept of knowledge is infallibilist enough to license closure—relatedly, just so long as our interpretation of the epistemic luck platitude is robust enough to license closure—then we need not concern ourselves with whether it conforms completely to the more demanding infallibilist picture. Conversely, if we could show that there was something amiss with the closure principle, then this would suffice to meet both the closure-based sceptical argument and its infallibilist counterpart that is based on the logically stronger infallibility principle. The problem, however, is that the logical weakness of the closure principle relative to the infallibility principle means that the sceptical argument is now even more compelling, and therefore even more difficult to respond to. Biting the bullet and denying infallibilism is one thing; biting the bullet and denying closure quite another. For how could it be that I have knowledge of one proposition (that, say, I am sitting here now), and know that this entails a second proposition (that, say, I am not a disembodied BIV), without also having knowledge of the second entailed (and, it seems, *unknowable*) proposition? It is little wonder, then, that the contemporary discussion has tended to identify the infallibilist sceptical challenge with the closure-based sceptical challenge.

1.3. Concluding Remarks

We have thus seen the workings of a certain kind of infallibilist sceptical worry that could be regarded as motivated in terms of a particularly robust reading of the epistemic luck platitude. Crucially, however, we have also seen that one does not need to adduce a principle quite so strong as the infallibility principle in order to generate the sceptical conclusion because there is a related principle—the principle of closure for knowledge—which is able to produce the same result without being quite so epistemically austere. This has important ramifications for how we understand the relationship between scepticism and the issue of epistemic luck since it prevents us from identifying the sceptical challenge as simply arising out of an unduly demanding—indeed, an *unqualified*—reading of the claim that knowledge excludes luck. Our ordinary concept of knowledge may well allow a certain degree of luck to coexist with knowledge possession—such that one's knowledge is at least marginally open to the possibility of error—and yet this could be consistent with our putative knowledge being subject to the sceptical challenge nonetheless because of the correctness of the closure principle.

However one is to answer the sceptical problem, then, what is clear is that merely endorsing a slightly qualified version of the epistemic luck platitude which licenses fallibilism of some limited description will not suffice to do the trick. Instead, we need to, at the very least, engage with the closure-based template sceptical argument (indeed, as we will see later on in Chapter 4, dealing with the problem posed by the sceptic will require us to respond to sceptical arguments that are based on epistemic principles that are even weaker than closure).

Notes

1. Typically, this renewed interest in scepticism has tended to focus on those sceptical arguments that are directed at our empirical knowledge of contingent propositions. In what follows, I will do likewise.
2. A similar constraint on our dealings with the sceptic is offered by Wright (1991: 89). I discuss the relationship between a second-order scepticism of this sort and normal first-order radical scepticism in more detail in Pritchard (2001*b*). See also Ribeiro (2004).
3. Since Unger thinks that 'certainty' is an absolute term, he won't accept this distinction between certainty and absolute certainty. Thus, on his view, to not be absolutely certain is to not to be certain. I don't accept this conception of certainty, however, and indeed think that our use of this concept in ordinary language doesn't support it either (there are, I would argue, lots of cases where one can legitimately say 'I'm certain of P, but not absolutely certain'). We do not need to detain ourselves with this issue here, however, since the point would go through even if the agent in this example were not certain about where his cufflinks were. After all, that one has no doubts about P does not surely mean that one is absolutely certain about P, and thus it ought to be possible to be neither in doubt about a proposition that one believes nor absolutely certain of it. Accordingly, we would, I think, still ascribe knowledge to such a non-doubting subject who unerringly found his cufflinks in this way (pending further details about the example at least), and thus Unger's use of this example in his argument for infallibilism is contentious on *either* reading.
4. Actually, Lewis only mentions the error-possibilities considered by the one who is ascribing the knowledge in the quotation just cited. Nevertheless, it is clear from the context in which this quotation is taken that the error-possibilities that the agent is considering are also relevant to whether or not she has knowledge. We will examine in more detail the kind of attributer contextualist theory that Lewis goes on to develop in §2.4.
5. In a similar way, Craig (1990*b*: sect. X), whilst rejecting Unger's infallibilism, nevertheless grants that there is something right about infallibilism which is the way in which our concept of knowledge enjoins us to consider increasingly demanding 'objectifications' of our knowledge, where this means that we seek to eliminate increasingly far-fetched error-possibilities. Since there is in principle no bar to the kinds of error-possibilities that are permissible here, this process will eventually lead, if left unchecked, to the consideration of sceptical error-possibilities and thus, since such error-possibilities are by hypothesis ineliminable, to the kind of scepticism envisaged by infallibilists. For discussion of Craig's thesis in this respect, see Pritchard (2000*d*).
6. Unger himself, in later works, has moved towards a more contextual reading of infalli- bilism, albeit one that is somewhat different from Lewis's antisceptical model (see

Scepticism

Unger 1984, 1986). Here the idea that there is nothing to tell between an 'invariantist' reading of our epistemic terms that licenses infallibilism and thus scepticism (in every context), and an epistemologically contextualist reading that licenses scepticism only in 'sceptical' contexts in which the demand for absolute certainty is in play rather than also in quotidian contexts where the epistemic standards are much lower. And since there is nothing to tell between the two readings of our epistemic concepts, so we lack good reason to be antisceptics rather than sceptics. For discussion of Unger's position, both in its early and later forms, see Craig (1990*b*: sect. X and appendix).

7. This way of expressing the BIV scenario makes it immune to antisceptical arguments that are advanced on content-externalist grounds. The *locus classicus* in this respect is Putnam (1981: ch. 1), though see also Dretske (1983) and Davidson (1986). I set aside here the issue of whether the experiences one has when one is in the vat are the same as the experiences one has whilst out of it, or whether they are simply indistinguishable. Either interpretation will suffice for my purposes. The relationship between content externalism and scepticism is further explored in §9.2.

8. One might supplement this principle in a number of ways in order to deal with potential counter-examples of a trivial nature. One might, for example, stipulate that the agent has all the required beliefs, so that one does not have to worry about what might be the logical possibility that the agent lacks knowledge in the consequent proposition simply because she lacks the relevant belief. (Similar considerations will apply to the formulations given below of other closure-type principles.) Nevertheless, this basic formulation should suffice for our purposes here, at least provided that it is taken in the right spirit. Henceforth, when I refer to the 'closure' principle I will, unless otherwise indicated, be referring to the closure principle for knowledge (we will be considering analogue closure principles for epistemic terms other than knowledge below).

9. There is also a second sense in which the infallibility principle is logically stronger than the closure principle, in that there may be members of the class of error-possibilities that are associated with a proposition which are not inconsistent with the target proposition but only with the agent's *knowledge* of that proposition. Accordingly, a failure to eliminate these possibilities will be inconsistent with an agent's knowledge of the target proposition in light of the infallibility principle, but not by the lights of the closure principle. The dreaming hypothesis is an obvious example in this regard since whilst one cannot have knowledge of what one believes about the external world if that belief is formed whilst dreaming, the belief could nevertheless be true. Moore's story about the Duke of Devonshire who once dreamt that he was speaking in the House of Lords and awoke to find that he *was* speaking in the House of Lords is a classic example in this respect. See Moore (1959). For further discussion of this example, and of the nature of the dreaming hypothesis in general, see, in particular, Stroud (1984: ch. 1; cf. Williams 1978: app. 3; Rosenberg 2003: ch. 1).

10. This formulation of the sceptical argument has been advanced in a number of papers in the recent literature. See, for example, DeRose (1995); Sosa (1999); Vogel (1999); and Pritchard (2002*d*). See also, Pritchard (2002*c*: §§1–2).

11. It is important to note that not every radical sceptical argument that makes use of sceptical hypotheses will directly conform to this closure-based template. As noted above in note 9, the reason for this is that some sceptical hypotheses—such as, in particular, the hypothesis that one might be dreaming—do not entail the denials of everyday propositions. It could be, for example, that one is dreaming *and* that one has two hands. Such

arguments demand a modification to the template sceptical argument advanced above which captures the fact that although the denial of this hypothesis is not entailed by the *truth* of everyday propositions, it is entailed by the agent's *knowledge* of these everyday propositions. For discussion of dreaming scepticism in this regard, see Wright (1991; cf. Pritchard 2001*d*). As we will see below, this is not the only reason for not framing the sceptical challenge in terms of this closure-based template.

2

Closure and Context

2.0. Introduction

We saw in the last chapter how a certain formulation of the sceptical puzzle has come to the fore in recent debate which turns on the closure principle for knowledge. Significantly, this principle is logically weaker than the closely related infallibility principle which could be regarded as encapsulating the epistemic demands made by an unqualified reading of the epistemic luck platitude. Accordingly, the move to a closure-based template sceptical argument undermines one natural thought that one might have about the sceptical problem, *viz.* that it *simply* arises out of a robust reading of the claim that knowledge excludes luck. Whatever the moral of scepticism is, then, it is not simply that knowledge is compatible with a marginal degree of luck. We therefore need to delve more deeply into the nature of both the sceptical problem and the epistemic luck platitude if we are to resolve this issue. For now, we will focus our attention on the closure-based sceptical argument.

In this chapter we will examine two of the key antisceptical arguments that have been motivated with the closure-based formulation of the sceptical argument in mind. In particular, we will be looking at fallibilist arguments against the closure principle and arguments for epistemological contextualism. As we will see, both of these responses to scepticism are problematic in that they are *externalist* epistemological theories that are, at certain key junctures, implicitly motivated by *internalist* epistemological intuitions.

2.1. Fallibilism and the Denial of Closure

Fallibilists reject the infallibilist principle that we formulated above in §1.2, and thus maintain, at the very least, that agents can have knowledge even whilst being unable to rule out (i.e. know the denials of) all the error-possibilities associated with the target proposition. As we saw in the last chapter, however, merely arguing for a *minimal* fallibilism of this sort will not suffice to meet the sceptical challenge for the simple reason that minimal fallibilism could be true—in that agents need not eliminate every error-possibility associated with the proposition in question—without this having any effect on the *closure*-based sceptical argument which does not demand infallibility. As long as just one of the error-possibilities that agents have to eliminate is a sceptical error-possibility (which is what closure appears to demand), then, given the plausibility of the claim that we are unable to eliminate sceptical error-possibilities, this will suffice to motivate the sceptical conclusion, regardless of whether or not this demand is tied to infallibilism. The crux of the matter as far as a fallibilist antisceptical strategy is concerned is thus not the denial of the infallibility principle, but rather the denial of the logically weaker closure principle. More precisely, the issue is whether we should be fallibilists in the robust (i.e. non-minimal) sense which allows that agents can have knowledge of everyday propositions even whilst being unable to know the denials of sceptical hypotheses. As we will see, whilst motivating a minimal fallibilist thesis is fairly straightforward, offering a principled defence of a robust fallibilist thesis which is inconsistent with the closure principle is much more difficult.

The natural motivation for fallibilism (of either sort) is the intuition that in order to know one only needs to be able to rule out the error-possibilities that are (in some sense to be specified) *relevant*. In particular, one does not need to be able to rule out far-fetched error-possibilities, such as sceptical error-possibilities, since these are irrelevant to our everyday knowledge. In terms of the epistemic luck platitude, this thesis roughly translates as the claim that knowledge had better not be *completely* gained via luck, but that this does not mean that it must be infallible or even *quasi*-infallible. Fallibilism thus goes hand-in-hand with a certain *qualified* endorsement of the epistemic luck platitude.

This, at any rate, is the core *relevant alternatives* intuition behind fallibilism. There is certainly something plausible about this line of thought, in that our usual practice is only to demand that agents be able to rule out an error-possibility where a specific reason has been presented for taking that error-possibility into account. John Austin is one philosopher who has given expression to a relevant alternative thesis that attempts to be true to this feature of our everyday epistemic practice. Regarding an agent's putative knowledge that there is a goldfinch in her garden, Austin notes that there are clear constraints on the extent and the type of challenges that can be made against this 'knowledge':

If you say 'That's not enough', then you must have in mind some more or less definite lack. ... If there is no definite lack, ... then it's silly (outrageous) just to go on saying 'That's not enough'.

Enough is enough: it doesn't mean everything. Enough means enough to show that (within reason, and for present intents and purposes) it 'can't' be anything else, there is no room for an alternative, competing description of it. It does *not* mean, for example, enough to show that it isn't a *stuffed* goldfinch. (Austin 1961: 52)

If there is no specific reason that can be offered for thinking that this goldfinch might be stuffed (e.g. that there are stuffed goldfinch in the area, for whatever reason), then knowing that it's a goldfinch will not involve being able to rule out the possibility that it's a stuffed goldfinch. A fortiori, knowing that it's a goldfinch will not involve being able to rule out the possibility that one is a BIV having the relevant 'goldfinch' experiences. And this certainly seems true to our ordinary practice in these matters. So despite the infallibilist intuitions that we saw Unger noting above, there are also strong fallibilist intuitions that seem to count against treating sceptical error-possibilities as relevant to everyday knowledge.

Of course, the infallibilist will respond to this line of argument by arguing that this merely reveals the loose character of our everyday concept of 'knowledge', adding that there is, in any case, a context in which sceptical error-possibilities *are* relevant, and that is the *sceptical* context. Note, however, that Austin is quite clear that in order for an error-possibility to be relevant a *specific* lack on the part of the agent's epistemic position must be identified. This point is important because we do not ordinarily regard sceptical error-possibilities as being introduced because there is a *specific* lack in the agent's epistemic position, but rather because of a supposed *general* inadequacy of the agent's position. That is, sceptics do not offer specific grounds for think-ing that we might be BIVs in the way that one might offer specific (empirical) grounds for thinking that there could be stuffed goldfinches in the vicinity, but rather use the BIV sceptical error-possibility as a means of illustrating general a priori claims about the inadequacies of our epistemic position. If this is right, then there is no context in which the raising of a sceptical error-possibility will be legitimate. Austin's account thus offers the beginnings of a robust fallibilist thesis which can explain how our knowledge of everyday propositions can coexist with our lack of knowledge of the denials of sceptical hypotheses.

We therefore have a stand-off between our fallibilist intuition that Austin draws our attention to—that only error-possibilities that there is some specific reason to consider are relevant to knowledge—and the infallibilist intuition that we noted in §1.1 that it seems incoherent to ascribe knowledge to an agent whilst explicitly granting that there is an error-possibility associated with the target proposition that the agent is unable to discount. In the presence of such an *impasse*, we might be naturally inclined to opt for the fallibilist and sceptic-hostile intuitions over their infallibilist and sceptic-friendly rivals, perhaps seeking some further support for this move from contextualist considerations, whether they be pragmatic or (as we noted above with regard to Lewis's interpretation of infallibilism) semantic. This line of thought is further reinforced by the reflection that our assent to the general infallibilist principle that one should not ascribe knowledge to an agent whilst explicitly granting that there are error-possibilities associated with the target proposition that the agent cannot discount can be accounted for via the fallibilism that Austin recommends. After all, if Austin is right, then usually this principle *will* hold since our practice of making error-possibilities explicit is closely tied to there being specific reasons available for thinking that these error-possibilities are relevant. Where the sceptic goes wrong is in generalizing away from these concrete cases where specific grounds for doubt are at issue to formulate a universal infallibility principle that makes no mention of the particular considerations that motivate us when we contemplate an error-possibility.

The Austinian way of dealing with the sceptical problem does not reckon, however, with the extra hurdle posed by closure. For now the task for the fallibilist is not only to motivate this position *contra* the infallibility principle, but also to explain what is wrong with the highly intuitive closure principle. What is needed is thus a relevant alternative thesis that does more than merely respond to the infallibilist claim that everyday knowledge requires the elimination of sceptical error-possibilities, but which also combines this thesis with an account of how fallibilism can explain what is wrong with the closure principle.

Indeed, the Austinian point about the unspecific nature of the sceptical doubt also works in the sceptic's favour once we explicitly consider the implications of closure in this debate. For although we might agree that there is something illegitimate in actively *questioning* an agent's belief that what he sees is a goldfinch on the arbitrary grounds that it could be a make-believe stuffed goldfinch, we *would* normally suppose that what supports the agent's knowledge that the creature before him is a goldfinch *also* supports his knowledge that it is not a stuffed goldfinch (and much more besides). Part of the motivation for this is closure in that the knowledge is in this case transferring across a known entailment. Think of the questions that one might ask of this agent in order to determine if knowledge should be ascribed in this case. Are you a reliable detector of goldfinches? Can you see clearly that it is a goldfinch? Have you any special reason for thinking that the bird you see is not something that merely looks like a goldfinch? In so far as we are inclined to credit agents with knowledge in the goldfinch case, then we would expect a 'yes' answer to questions of this sort (and maybe many more beside), but a 'yes' answer to these questions also speaks in favour of crediting the agent with knowledge of the known entailment that the creature the agent sees is not a stuffed goldfinch.

Crucially, however, although this is the case when it comes to stuffed goldfinches, the same does not apply when we substitute the denial of a radical sceptical hypothesis for the known entailment. What supports my putative knowledge that I am sitting here now cannot be what supports my putative knowledge that I am not a BIV because, seemingly at least, *nothing* could act as epistemic support in this case. This is the crux of the problem that sceptical hypotheses raise—that it seems impossible to ever know that they are false— and it highlights the double-edged aspect of the 'unspecific' nature of sceptical questioning. Whilst we might treat the fact that the sceptic can offer no specific reasons in favour of her doubt as counting against the legitimacy of her doubt, once one reflects that it is equally true that nothing specific counts in favour of our *rejection* of sceptical hypotheses, then the boot is on the other foot. The specific empirical grounds one might have for thinking that one is looking at a goldfinch will also be specific empirical grounds for thinking that one is not looking at a stuffed make-believe goldfinch, but the specific empirical grounds one has for thinking that one is currently seated *cannot*, it seems, be specific empirical grounds for thinking that one is not a BIV because *there are no such grounds*.

This highlights the point made above that the sceptical problem posed by infallibilism and closure is not that they make a wide range of error-possibilities relevant to our knowledge of everyday propositions, but that they make specifically *sceptical* error-possibilities relevant to our knowledge of everyday propositions. We are attracted by fallibilism (and thus by the denial of closure) not because it allows us to have knowledge of goldfinches whilst being unable to know that the 'goldfinch' is not stuffed, but because it holds out the promise of allowing us to have knowledge of everyday propositions whilst being unable to know the denials of sceptical hypotheses. Indeed, once one separates out these two issues, then the motivation for denying closure in the first sense evaporates since in so far as we do have grounds that can support knowledge of everyday propositions, then we will thereby have grounds in support of our knowledge of the denials of lots of non-sceptical error-possibilities. The problem isn't that our knowledge is 'lucky' in the general sense that we cannot rule out non-sceptical possibilities of error associated with the proposition known, but that it is 'lucky' in the more specific sense that we are unable to rule out *sceptical* possibilities of error.

This confusion between these two issues regarding closure infects one of the key arguments against closure in the recent literature, due to Fred Dretske (1970, 1971).[1] What Dretske adds to previous contributions to this issue is to highlight that there are a great many sentential operators that do not, to use his phrase, always 'penetrate' across entailments (known or otherwise). Dretske (1970) gives the example of the sentential operators 'It is extraordinary that ...' and 'It is a mistake that ...' to illustrate his point. That I should bump into my next-door neighbour on the summit of mount Vesuvius is certainly extraordinary, but it is not extraordinary at all (given the extent of tourism in the area) that I should bump into *someone* on this summit, and the latter claim is clearly entailed by the former. Similarly, it could be a mistake that a production car is priced at such-and-such an amount even though it is not a mistake that the car is priced at less than a higher amount (because the car was meant to be priced much cheaper than it is), and the second proposition is clearly entailed by the first.

Dretske's idea is that epistemic sentential operators, such as 'It is known that ...' fail to penetrate across entailments (even known ones) in much the same way. More specifically, Dretske claims that epistemic operators fail to penetrate across entailments in a specific range of cases (he calls such operators 'semi-penetrating'). He writes:

> The general point may be put this way: there are certain presuppositions associated with a statement. These presuppositions, although their truth is entailed by the truth of the statement, are not part of what is *operated on* when we operate on the statement with one of our epistemic operators. The epistemic operators do not *penetrate to* these presuppositions. (Dretske 1970: 1014)

The best way to see what this thesis amounts to is to consider one of the key examples that Dretske offers in support of his view. Consider the following two propositions:

(P) The animals in the pen are zebras.
(Q) The animals in the pen are not cleverly disguised mules.

Put abstractly, Dretske's idea is that, at least in certain cases, one can know (P) whilst lacking knowledge of the (known) entailment (Q), because in these cases

39

the truth of (Q) is already presupposed in the agent's knowledge of (P). Accordingly, when we apply the knowledge operator to (P) in this case it does not penetrate to the (known) entailment (Q) because (Q), being a presupposition of the agent's knowledge of (P), is not part of what is operated on when we apply the knowledge operator to (P).

Rather less abstractly, we can express Dretske's intuition here by saying that most knowledge quite legitimately presupposes the truth of certain propositions that one does not know. Accordingly, it cannot be that the knowledge operator completely penetrates across (known) entailments since this would imply that one could gain new knowledge, and empirical knowledge at that, of what is presupposed in one's knowledge via a priori reflection on what the logical consequences are of what one knows. In effect, the failure of closure simply reflects the 'anti-bootstrapping' intuition that one cannot come to know the empirical truths that are presupposed in one's empirical knowledge simply by reflecting upon that knowledge.

Dretske's point here is confused, however, since it is far from clear that the grounds that support the agent's knowledge of (P) don't also support his knowledge of (Q). If the agent really does have grounds for thinking that the creature before him is a zebra (it looks like a zebra, it is in the clearly labelled zebra enclosure, there are no special reasons for thinking that any deception is taking place, and so on), then those grounds seem to equally support the agent's belief that the creature before him is not a cleverly disguised mule. Indeed, there is a sleight of hand in the way that Dretske motivates his point here. Consider the following passage:

If you are tempted to say [that the agent does know (Q) ...], think for a moment about the reasons that you have, what evidence you can produce in favour of this claim. The evidence you *had* for thinking them zebras has been effectively neutralized, since it does not count toward their *not* being mules cleverly disguised. Have you checked with the zoo authorities? Did you examine the animals closely enough to detect such a fraud? (Dretske 1970: 1016)

The problem is, of course, that if these issues really are relevant to the agent's knowledge of (Q), then they ought to be just as relevant to his knowledge of (P). In general, Dretske seems to want to separate the question of whether the agent knows (Q) from the question of whether the agent knows (Q) *given that he knows (P)*, and it is this latter question that is the pertinent one when it comes to closure. Since we are already meant to be granting that the agent does have sufficient grounds to support his knowledge of (P), the issue can't be settled by querying the grounds that the agent has for (Q) in isolation of the grounds he has for (P), since the grounds for (P) are also grounds for (Q) and *these* grounds are not meant to be in question. Moreover, notice that Dretske focuses on what it is appropriate for the agent to *say* about his epistemic position regarding (Q). Again, this should make us wary since, as we noted above (and will discuss further below), there may be all sorts of reasons why a claim to know could be inappropriate even though what is being claimed is true.

In any case, it is far from clear that Dretske's point about how our knowledge presupposes the truth of certain propositions is meant to work with the example that he adduces. Do I really need to *assume* or otherwise presuppose that there are no cleverly disguised mules around before I can know that what I see is a zebra? Intuitively, the answer to this question is 'no', since I have good empirical *grounds* for thinking that this error-possibility is false. Of course, if (Q) were the denial of a radical sceptical hypothesis then the point about presuppositions would have far more plausibility since I do not appear to have empirical grounds that suffice to support my belief that *this* error-possibility is false. The trouble is, if closure only fails in the sceptical case then it is far from clear how Dretske's remarks are to be persuasive at all. It is, after all, the *sceptic's* point that when it comes to our putative 'knowledge' of everyday propositions we must presuppose the falsity of sceptical error-possibilities, a presupposition which we can never have knowledge of, and all Dretske seems to be doing is reiterating this point as a supposedly *anti*-sceptical thesis.

As it stands, then, Dretske's argument against closure is not very persuasive as an antisceptical thesis, and this is because he confuses the general anti-closure thought that our knowledge can coexist with known to be entailed propositions which we do not know with the more specific claim that our knowledge of everyday propositions can coexist with known to be entailed *denials of sceptical hypotheses* which we *cannot* know. Whilst the former thesis, if defensible, would have enabled us to make some headway against the crucial latter thesis, and therefore against scepticism, simply proposing the latter thesis on its own gets us no further towards finding a plausible response to the sceptic.

Crucially, however, Dretske doesn't rest his case with these observations but goes on to develop a theory of knowledge which can add further support for endorsing this second thesis. We will return to consider this additional aspect of his antisceptical position in a moment. First, however, we will pause to consider in more detail what is at issue in the sceptic's use of closure.

2.2. Epistemological Internalism and Closure

The sceptical problem posed by closure is first and foremost a problem for epistemologically internalist theories of knowledge. In common with the contemporary literature, we will take epistemological internalism about justification to consist in the following thesis:

Epistemological internalism about justification
For all agents, φ, an agent's belief that φ is justified if, and only if, the agent is able to know the facts which determine that justification by reflection alone.

And by 'reflection' here, I mean a priori reasoning, introspective awareness of one's own mental states, and one's memory of knowledge that has been gained in either of these ways.[2]

This type of justification is most often associated with the work of Roderick Chisholm. He has argued, for example, that the 'concept of epistemic justification... is *internal* in that one can find out directly, by *reflection*, what one is justified in believing at any time' (1989: 7).[3]

One can see the attraction of the view in that, prima facie at least, facts which are outwith one's reflective ambit seem entirely irrelevant to the epistemic status of one's beliefs. If one has no good reflectively accessible reason available for believing what one does then, intuitively, one's belief is unjustified, regardless of whatever 'external' non-reflectively accessible facts can be cited (by others) in favour of that belief.

An epistemologically externalist theory of justification, in contrast, will precisely reject this intuition and hold instead that an agent's justification could be determined by facts which the agent is not in a position to know by reflection alone, such as facts concerning the reliability of the method by which the belief was formed.[4] On this view, just so long as one's belief is, as a matter of fact, formed in the right kind of way, then it is in the market for justification regardless of whatever reflectively accessible grounds one is able to cite in its favour. Externalists and internalists thus have very different, and competing, conceptions of what is involved in the concept of justification.[5]

Of course, the epistemic concept that we are focusing upon in our discussion of scepticism is knowledge, not justification. This adds an extra complication (one that is often overlooked in the epistemological literature) in that epistemological externalism about knowledge need not be inconsistent with epistemological internalism about justification. This is the reason why the focus for externalist epistemological theories is typically on knowledge rather than on justification, since it is only when it comes to the theory of knowledge that the

42

position is demarcated from internalism. A proponent of an externalist theory of knowledge could consistently allow an internalist conception of justification to play a role in her history. It could be, for example, that internalist justification is a sufficient condition for all knowledge, and it may even be that it is also necessary for certain types of knowledge. What is crucial to an externalist theory of knowledge is thus not the denial of the existence, or even the importance, of an internalist notion of justification, but rather the role that it accords to this notion within the theory of knowledge as a whole. In particular, externalists about knowledge will tend to hold that it is at least possible to have knowledge without meeting the justification condition, where this condition is understood along internalist lines in the fashion described above, just so long as the agent meets an appropriate 'external' epistemic condition, such as a reliability condition. The extent of the dispute between externalists and internalists in this respect therefore depends on the range of cases where they diverge. A modest externalist view might hold that internalist justification is necessary for most, but not all, knowledge, whereas a more radical externalist thesis might maintain that internalist justification is hardly ever a necessary component of knowledge.[6]

In order to give this discussion a focus, it is worthwhile pausing for a moment to look at one of the standard cases over which internalists and externalists disagree. Consider, for example, the notorious 'chicken-sexer' case that so divides externalists and internalists. In this example we are asked to imagine an agent who has a natural and highly reliable ability to distinguish male and female chicks, but who has no idea how she is doing this nor is even aware that she is reliable in this respect. (Some even supplement the example by saying that she is mistaken about how she is doing it, in that she believes that she is seeing or touching something distinctive when in fact she is guided by her unusually sensitive sense of smell.) Externalists are inclined to allow that the agent in this example can indeed have knowledge that, say, a sample pair of chicks are of a different gender, whilst internalists tend to demur. Internalists contend that this can't be knowledge because the agent lacks adequate reflectively accessible grounds in support of her belief in this regard. Externalists respond by arguing that the fact that the agent fails to meet an internalist justification condition doesn't preclude her from having knowledge, especially since, as in this case, she is exhibiting a highly reliable ability.[7]

Whatever one thinks of an example like this (and one's opinion will no doubt ultimately rest upon how the details of the example are spelt out), one thing that is clear is that internalists will be disinclined to ascribe knowledge in these cases whilst externalists are committed to ascribing knowledge, if not in this particular case, then at least in some cases of this general sort. Note, however, that this does not mean that externalists must hold that all knowledge is on a par with the type of knowledge possessed by the chicken-sexer since, after all, one would expect that the way in which agents typically acquire reliable beliefs is by gaining reflectively accessible grounds in support of those beliefs, and thus by meeting an internal epistemic condition.

In general, then, we can characterize epistemological internalism about knowledge as the following thesis, with epistemological externalism about knowledge consisting in the denial of this thesis:

Epistemological internalism about knowledge
For all agents, φ, if an agent knows that φ, then that agent's belief that φ is inter-nalistically justified.[8]

We will explore the motivations that have been offered for epistemological externalism and internalism about knowledge further below. Henceforth, unless otherwise specified, when I make reference to externalism or internalism I will specifically have in mind externalist and internalist *theories of knowledge*.

So far we have put the issue about closure by noting that it seems impossible to know the denials of sceptical hypotheses. Primarily, however, the problem is that it is impossible to be *internalistically justified* in believing the denials of sceptical hypotheses. If there is, *ex hypothesi*, no phenomenological difference available to the subject which could indicate to her that she is not a victim of this scenario, then it follows that there is not going to be anything reflectively available to the subject that could suffice to indicate to her that her belief in this antisceptical proposition is true. In this sense, then, she cannot be internalist-ically justified in believing this proposition, even if her belief is true. On the internalist account, however, internalist justification is necessary for know-ledge and this means that a lack of internalist justification for one's belief in the denial of a sceptical hypothesis entails a lack of knowledge in this proposition. With closure for knowledge in play, this lack of knowledge in an antisceptical proposition further entails a lack of knowledge in a wide class of everyday propositions that the agent knows entail the antisceptical proposition. Epistemological internalism when combined with closure for knowledge thus straightforwardly leads to radical scepticism.[9]

Not everyone has accepted this line of reasoning regarding the inconsistency of epistemological internalism and closure, and it is worthwhile briefly considering one of the key arguments that has been offered in this respect. One commentator who has explicitly defended the compatibility of epistemo-logical internalism and closure is Peter Klein (1981, 1995). Klein argues that whilst it might be true that the evidence which an agent has in support of her internalistically justified belief in one proposition might not suffice to internalistically justify her belief in a second proposition which she knows is entailed by the first, this conclusion alone will not suffice to demonstrate that epistemological internalism is inconsistent with closure. In particular, since the agent's belief in the antecedent proposition is, *ex hypothesi*, internalistically justified, it follows that the evidence that supports belief in the antecedent proposition is not the same as the evidence that supports belief in the consequent proposition since the latter includes as evidence the antecedent proposition (not to mention the entailment). On this view, the internalist case against closure is based on a mistaken conflation between the closure principle and a more demanding sister principle which demands that the *same* set of evidence is at issue as regards the agent's justification for the antecedent proposition and the consequent proposition. And if internalist justification can transfer across known entailments, then the internalist motivation for denying closure evaporates.

Klein's remarks were specifically directed at the kind of 'zebra' cases that Dretske discusses, and when it comes to these examples I think it is clear that the internalist moral to be drawn as regards closure is indeed moot. As we saw in the last section, this is because in so far as an agent has evidence which suffices to internalistically justify her belief that she is looking at a zebra then, intuitively, she also has evidence which suffices to internalistically justify her belief that she is not looking at a cleverly disguised mule. This is especially so if the agent in question has made the relevant inferential link and can therefore (as Klein points out) count the antecedent proposition (and the entailment) as being part of the evidence set that supports her belief in the consequent proposition.

As we noted above, however, the example that the sceptic has in mind is very different from this sort of scenario in that in the non-sceptical case there is no in principle difficulty in internalistically justifying one's belief that one is not looking at a cleverly disguised mule in the way that there *is* an in principle difficulty in internalistically justifying one's belief in the denial of a sceptical hypothesis. Given this feature of sceptical hypotheses, Klein's strategy for retaining epistemological internalism and closure will not be applicable here because there is *no* plausible sense in which there is a sufficient evidence base which could support an agent's belief in the relevant consequent proposition (the denial of the radical sceptical hypothesis), regardless of whether the agent is able to adduce the antecedent proposition as additional evidence in favour of this belief. More precisely, there is no such evidence base provided that we understand one's evidence in the usual internalistic way (as presumably Klein is understanding it), such that one's evidence is necessarily reflectively accessible to one. The challenge to closure on the internalist view thus does not arise from the zebra-style examples, as Dretske and Klein suppose, but rather from their specifically sceptical relatives. Provided that one keeps to the sceptical examples, then the case for the inconsistency of epistemological internalism and closure is compelling.[10,11]

Accordingly, a consistent epistemologically internalist response to scepticism would simply involve a rejection of the closure-based intuitions that we saw motivating the major premiss of the closure-based sceptical argument formulated above. As we noted earlier, however, such a strategy is highly implausible because it leaves the antisceptic in a kind of theoretical *impasse* with the sceptic, a stand-off that the sceptic can exploit at second-order. That is, the sceptic argues that we lack knowledge because reflection on closure reveals that there are unknowable antisceptical presuppositions in play regarding our everyday knowledge, whilst the core non-closure response to this argument is simply to say that we should allow such everyday knowledge *even despite* its reliance on unknowable antisceptical presuppositions. The stand-off is thus between our intuition that closure must be correct, but which leads to scepticism, and our intuition that scepticism must be false, but which leads to the denial of closure. Either way, this is not an intellectually desirable situation to be in since at the very least it seems to support the second-order sceptical contention that we have no good reason to *not* endorse scepticism and, as we noted in §1.0, this second-order scepticism seems little better than its first-order cousin.

The same is not true, however, of epistemological externalism, at least not directly. Since externalist theories do not regard internalist justification as being a necessary ingredient of knowledge, it follows that our in principle lack of internalist justification for our beliefs in the denials of sceptical hypotheses will not immediately translate into a lack of knowledge of these propositions. Accordingly, on the externalist view, there is not the straightforward tension between our apparent knowledge of everyday propositions and our apparent lack of knowledge of the (known to be entailed) denials of sceptical hypotheses that one gets on the internalist picture, and thus there is not the direct clash with the closure principle for knowledge. On the face of it, then, externalist theories of knowledge can resist the closure-based sceptical challenge.

The closure-based stand-off with the sceptic thus gets its initial support from epistemologically internalist intuitions about the unknowability of the denials of sceptical hypotheses. Prima facie, then, if one could motivate an *externalist* theory of knowledge then one could avoid this stand-off and thereby evade the sceptical problem altogether. This debate about the incompatibility of (an antisceptical version of) epistemological internalism and the closure principle for knowledge therefore raises the general issue of what motivates the sceptical premiss that we lack knowledge of the denials of sceptical hypotheses given that one endorses epistemological externalism. Clearly, we have intuitions here that speak in favour of this premiss, but if those intuitions can be put down to being the result of subscribing to a faulty epistemological theory then it is far from clear that we should concede anything to the sceptic on the basis of them. In particular, it is far from clear that we should deny so intuitive a principle as closure on the basis of internalist intuitions if we are already convinced of the correctness of epistemological externalism.

We will return to consider the status of the sceptical premiss that we are unable to know the denials of sceptical hypotheses below. For now, we will accept that there is a prima facie case for thinking that epistemological externalists might be able to reject this premiss (at least in an unqualified way), and explore the possibility that there may be a construal of the relevant alternatives thesis that can provide the necessary motivation for a move of this sort. Before we do this, however, it is necessary to first consider the way in which Dretske and others have developed the argument against closure along externalist lines via an appeal to a *sensitivity* condition on knowledge. If the diagnostic line just sketched is right, then we will find that an antisceptical externalist theory of knowledge which concedes that we are unable to know the denials of sceptical hypotheses, and which therefore rejects closure, will be illicitly based on incompatible intuitions that draw on *both* sides of the externalism–internalism distinction.

2.3. Knowledge as Sensitivity

Dretske's argument against closure does not just rest on the considerations considered above, since in subsequent work—especially Dretske (1971)—he also advocated a *sensitivity*-based theory of knowledge that can account for the anti-closure intuitions that he had previously motivated. Famously, of course, a similar sensitivity-based view was also later developed in an influential fashion by Robert Nozick (1981). The reason why the sensitivity-based view is so dialectically important is because this theory is not only independently plausible (i.e. plausible independently of considerations regarding scepticism), but is also a version of epistemological *externalism*.

The view in question essentially understands knowledge in terms of a sensitivity principle which, for our purposes, we can formulate as follows, where possible worlds are to be understood, in the standard way, as ordered in terms of their similarity to the actual world (i.e. so that 'distant' possible worlds are very unlike the actual world, whilst 'nearby' possible worlds are very alike the actual world):

The sensitivity principle
For all agents, φ, if an agent knows a contingent proposition φ, then the agent does not believe that φ in the nearest possible world or worlds in which $\neg \varphi$.[12]

The motivation for such a principle is the thought that knowledge requires the agent's belief to 'track' the truth of the proposition believed in such a way that, had the proposition been false, the agent would not have believed it. Dretske's idea is that there is nothing substantive that needs to be added to a theory of knowledge over and above sensitivity,[13] and certainly no need for an additional internalist justification condition.[14] Meeting the internalist justification condition might be a good way of ensuring that one's beliefs meet the sensitivity principle, but what is important is that one's beliefs are sensitive, not that they are internalistically justified. This principle thus forms part of an externalist theory of knowledge.

There is certainly a great deal of plausibility to the thesis that knowledge is essentially sensitivity to the truth. Take paradigm cases of knowledge. What explains the fact that I know that it is a computer that I see before me? Well, had it been false that there was a computer before me (if there were a typewriter there, for example, or a pile of books), then I wouldn't have believed that there was a computer before me. Similarly, what explains my knowledge that I am currently seated? Well, if I were not seated (if I were standing up, for example), then I wouldn't have believed that I was seated (I would have believed that I was standing up instead). And so on.

Sensitivity will also account for paradigm cases where agents lack knowledge. Take the case of 'Gullible Joe', the village idiot who believes whatever people tell him and who believes on this basis that the moon is made of cheese, something that he was told as a practical joke. Suppose further that, to everyone's surprise, it transpires that the moon really is made of a particularly hard form of cosmic cheese. Why doesn't Joe have knowledge of what he believes? Well, because in the nearest possible world in which Joe's belief is false—where the moon is *not* made of cheese—Joe will continue to believe, in his gullible way, that it is. It is thus the insensitivity of his belief that prevents him from having knowledge. And note how the very same belief held by the pioneering scientists who discover that the moon is made of cheese *will* be sensitive to the truth, and thus will be an instance of knowledge. After all, the nearest possible world in which their belief is false will be a world in which, for example, they conduct their experiments on moon rock and discover that it isn't made of cheese and so don't form the belief that it is. Again, it is sensitivity that is explaining why agents have, or lack, knowledge.

As we will see in Part II, sensitivity-based approaches are also able to deal with a wide range of difficult epistemological examples, such as the Gettier counter-examples and the so-called 'lottery' puzzle. Our present concern, however, is the problem of radical scepticism. We have already seen that sensitivity presents no bar to our conception of ourselves as knowing a great deal of the everyday propositions which we take ourselves to know (such as regards whether we see computers before us, or whether we are presently seated). And note that it does this without making any reference to whether or not we know the denials of sceptical hypotheses. This is all to the good, since on this view we lack knowledge of the denials of sceptical hypotheses because our belief in them is insensitive.

Suppose, for example, that I now believe that I am not a BIV and that this belief is true. The problem with this kind of belief, however, is that if it were false—if I were a BIV—then I would, by hypothesis, continue to believe that it was true. In other words, I cannot 'track' the truth of a proposition such as this. Hence, on this view, I can know everyday propositions such as that I am currently seated, know that this entails the denials of various sceptical hypotheses (such as the BIV hypothesis), whilst failing to know the denials of the relevant sceptical hypotheses. Making sensitivity an essential requirement on knowledge thus leads directly to the rejection of the closure principle for knowledge (and with it the infallibility principle).

Sensitivity also accommodates our relevant alternatives intuitions, as described above, in that the error-possibilities that need to be taken into account when evaluating a putative instance of knowledge are only those error-possibilities related to the satisfaction of the sensitivity condition, not also those error-possibilities the denials of which one knows to be entailed by what one knows (and certainly not *every* error-possibility). Accordingly, if we wanted to determine whether or not I knew I was currently seated, what would be relevant would be whether or not I would in fact be deceived about this matter in the nearest possible world or worlds in which this belief is false. Is the nearest world in which I am no longer seated a world where I still think that I am because, say, it is a world in which I have unknowingly ingested a mind-bending hallucinogen? If so, then this error-possibility is relevant to the issue of whether or not I know this proposition and can therefore defeat that knowledge. If not, then it isn't. In this sense, then, the issue of whether or not a certain error-possibility is relevant to my knowledge is settled by the proximity of the possible world in which this error-possibility obtains relative to the actual world. This is in contrast to infallibilism—which makes all error-possibilities relevant to knowledge, regardless of their modal proximity—and also (as we will see in a moment) attributer contextualism, which allows what is at issue in a conversational context to determine the range of relevant error-possibilities. In particular, sensitivity-based theories hold that if sceptical error-possibilities are modally 'far off', then we can disregard them with impunity. Knowledge is thus possible, *contra* the radical sceptic, provided that the antisceptical 'presuppositions' of our knowledge that Dretske talks of are true, whether we know them to be true or not. Just so long as our common-sense picture of the world which treats sceptical hypotheses as both false and far-fetched is correct, then we are in a position to have much of the knowledge that we take ourselves to have.

The dialectical situation regarding Dretske's denial of closure on sensitivity-based grounds is clearly very different from the stand-off we witnessed above where internalist and closure-based sceptical 'intuitions' vied with antisceptical and anti-closure 'intuitions'. This is because now we have an independently motivated theory of knowledge on offer that results in the rejection of closure, rather than just a set of alternative 'intuitions' about knowledge that are not so friendly to the sceptic. Moreover, since this is an externalist theory of knowledge that does not regard internalist justification as necessary for knowledge, the internalist intuitions discussed earlier are not directly relevant here.

The plausibility of this approach is further enhanced once one reflects that the natural objection that is often made to any antisceptical strategy of this sort lacks substance on closer consideration. It might be thought, for example, that this kind of antisceptical strategy is either impotent or irrelevant. Either we are already entitled to the presupposition that sceptical possible worlds are far off, in which case we do not need an antisceptical strategy in the first place; or else we aren't entitled to this presupposition, in which case finding out that we have knowledge provided this presupposition is true is of no help to us.[15] This objection misses the point, however, in that the sceptical conclusion is that knowledge is *impossible*, and the sensitivity-based antisceptical response is clearly the denial of this claim—that knowledge is *possible*. That the knowledge in question is only actually possessed given that certain further conditions obtain is thus neither here nor there since if the sceptical argument were correct then even this *conditional* knowledge would not be possible.

Moreover, the demand that we *show* that we are entitled to the presuppositions in question is clearly an implicit request for an internalist justification for believing those presuppositions. With this in mind, it is worth reminding ourselves that Dretske's claim that there are conditions that need to obtain if one is to have knowledge but which one is unable to have an internalist justification for believing have obtained is an explicit and *motivated* feature of his overall position (indeed, it is a key part of what makes his position an externalist theory of knowledge). Accordingly, it is somewhat empty to object to the position purely on the basis that it has this consequence (i.e. independently, for example, of offering a general critique of externalism).[16]

This is not to deny that there may be further worries that underlie this objection, only that it is not sound as it stands. We will return to consider whether there is any underlying substance to this charge below. For now, I want to focus on two interrelated features of the position that I think *are* immediately suspect.

The first is the asymmetry that is present on this view between how the relevant alternatives intuition that we noted earlier is understood when it comes to our knowledge of everyday propositions as opposed to how it is understood when it comes to our knowledge of the denials of sceptical hypotheses. We saw above that the core relevant alternatives intuition was that some error-possibilities, especially sceptical error-possibilities, were so far-fetched that they were not relevant to knowledge. The sensitivity-based view captures this intuition as it applies to knowledge of everyday propositions, since on this account one can possess such everyday knowledge whilst lacking knowledge of the denials of modally far-off sceptical error-possibilities. Curiously, however, a further consequence of the view is that we are unable to know the denials of sceptical error-possibilities because when it comes to knowledge of these propositions far-off sceptical possible worlds *are* relevant to knowledge.

Recall that the reason why we are unable to know the denial of a sceptical hypothesis—such as that one is not a BIV—is because in the nearest possible worlds in which the sceptical hypothesis is true—e.g. the world in which one is a BIV—one continues to believe, falsely, that one is not the victim of this sceptical hypothesis. Note, however, that the possible world in which the sceptical hypothesis obtains is, *ex hypothesi*, a *far-off* possible world, so that when it comes to our knowledge of the denials of sceptical hypotheses far-off sceptical possible worlds *are* relevant to knowledge. Accordingly, it appears that there is a kind of double-standard in play here. Everyday knowledge is only evaluated relative to error-possibilities that obtain in nearby possible worlds, whilst antisceptical knowledge is evaluated relative to error-possibilities that obtain in far-off (sceptical) possible worlds.

This asymmetry highlights an important ambiguity in our relevant alternatives intuition that far-off error-possibilities are irrelevant to knowledge. Indeed, there is a *three-way* ambiguity here. The first construal, which leads to the sensitivity-based approach and thus to the rejection of closure, reads this intuition as only applying to our knowledge of *everyday* propositions, and not also to our knowledge of the denials of sceptical hypotheses. A second interpretation takes this intuition more literally as applying to knowledge *simpliciter*, regardless of the kind of proposition in question. On this view, sceptical error-possibilities, in so far as they really are far-off, are irrelevant not only to our knowledge of everyday propositions but also to our knowledge of the denials of sceptical hypotheses. For reasons that will become apparent, we will call this view the 'neo-Moorean' interpretation of the relevant alternatives thesis. A third and final possible interpretation occupies a mid-ground between these two alternatives by maintaining that far-off error-possibilities are irrelevant to our knowledge of all propositions, but only in everyday conversational contexts where sceptical error-possibilities are not explicitly under consideration. In non-everyday *sceptical* conversational contexts where sceptical error possibilities are explicitly at issue, then such error-possibilities *are* relevant to the determination of knowledge (*all* knowledge).[17] This is the 'contextualist' rendering of the relevant alternatives intuition.

Given that there is this ambiguity in how we should understand the core relevant alternatives thesis, it follows that we should be wary of any view which proclaims itself to be the true heir to the relevant alternatives tradition. Furthermore, it is worth noting that each of these interpretations has ramifications for the construal that one adopts of the epistemic luck platitude. We have already seen that the sensitivity-based view seems to lead to a fallibilist rendering of that platitude in that it allows that a certain degree of luck is compatible with knowledge. More specifically, by licensing the rejection of closure, sensitivity-based views allow that an agent can have knowledge of a proposition even though this knowledge depends upon certain (known to be entailed) propositions being true which the agent is unable to know to be true. As we will see, whilst both the contextualist and the neo-Moorean views lead to a fallibilist reading of sorts of the epistemic luck platitude, since neither of them entail the denial of closure the fallibilism that is at issue here is very different from that which is in play when it comes to the sensitivity-based view. Getting clearer about how best to construe the relevant alternatives intuition thus has important consequences for how we should best formulate the epistemic luck platitude.

The second problem facing the Dretskean proposal also concerns how it is motivated, but this time the issue is the position's commitment to epistemological externalism rather than its use of the relevant alternatives intuition. We've already noted that Dretske endorses an externalist theory of knowledge that does not regard internalist justification as necessary for knowledge. What is curious about the view given this feature of it is that when it comes to motivating the claim that agents are unable to know the denials of sceptical hypotheses—a claim that a sensitivity-based approach to knowledge is meant to explain—Dretske does so by adducing *internalist* intuitions. Consider again this passage that we quoted above:

If you are tempted to say [that the agent does know (Q) . . .], think for a moment about the reasons that you have, what evidence you can produce in favour of this claim. The evidence you *had* for thinking them zebras has been effectively neutralised, since it does not count toward their *not* being mules cleverly disguised. Have you checked with the zoo authorities? Did you examine the animals closely enough to detect such a fraud? (Dretske 1970: 1016)

We noted above that there were a number of problems with this passage, in that it involves a problematic appeal to what it is appropriate to say and that it tends to disengage the question of whether the agent knows (Q) from the issue of whether the agent knows (Q) *given that he knows (P) and the entailment from (P) to (Q)*. Moreover, we also criticized the use of (Q) in that what seems to be needed here is a *radical* sceptical hypothesis, rather than a local one. Suppose that one rereads this passage with a radical sceptical hypothesis—such as the BIV hypothesis—in mind, and sets these other concerns aside. What is interesting is that Dretske would then appear to be arguing that what prevents an agent from knowing the denial of a sceptical hypothesis is that she is unable to adduce good empirical evidence in favour of thinking that this proposition is true. Since there is, intuitively at least, a close connection between the evidence that one is able to explicitly adduce and the evidence that is reflectively available to one, it follows that a natural way of reading this passage is as saying that agents are unable to know the denials of sceptical hypotheses because they lack internalist justification for their beliefs in these propositions. But if Dretske is an externalist who denies the necessity of internalist justification to knowledge, then it is far from clear why he should be motivating the denial of closure via a claim of this sort.[18,19]

Of course, what *does* follow from Dretske's remarks, properly understood, is that epistemological internalism, in so far as it does not directly lead to scepticism at any rate, is inconsistent with closure, but as we noted in the last section, there is no immediate reason why an epistemological externalist like Dretske should be concerned about *that*. The reason for this is that since epistemological internalists—unlike epistemological externalists, like Dretske—have no way of accounting for an agent's putative knowledge of the denials of antisceptical hypotheses, they likewise cannot maintain the antisceptical thesis that agents are able to know everyday propositions whilst closure is still in play. It is thus incumbent upon them to reject closure if they are to evade scepticism.

The sceptical issue thus ultimately turns on whether we are able to reject the minor premiss of the sceptical argument which claims that we lack knowledge of the denials of sceptical hypotheses. This point ties in with the issue just raised about the correct construal of the relevant alternatives thesis. If there is a way of understanding this thesis—whether along either neo-Moorean or contextualist lines—that enables us to makes sense of the sceptical problem without accepting this premiss (at least in an unqualified form), and thus without denying closure, then we should accord it serious consideration. We will begin by looking at the contextualist rendering of the relevant alternatives thesis.

2.4. Attributer Contextualist Antisceptical Theories

Essentially, epistemological contextualism involves allowing that the sceptical conclusion that we know very little is true, but limits the damage of this concession by arguing that this conclusion only holds in certain non-everyday contexts. Accordingly, the contextualist can maintain that we *do* know a great deal in everyday contexts, and is thereby able to prevent the sceptic from advancing her doubt in the universal fashion that is necessary if it is to generate the advertised intellectually devastating conclusion. We can live with the truth of scepticism, the contextualist argues, if that truth only obtains in certain restricted contexts far removed from everyday life. Moreover, this is also meant to be one way of construing the relevant alternatives intuition, in that it captures the idea that, at least in everyday contexts, we can legitimately ascribe knowledge to agents without concerning ourselves with the issue of whether the agents in question are able to rule out sceptical error-possibilities.

The dominant form of epistemological contextualism in the recent literature is *attributer* contextualism, as advanced by Keith DeRose (1995), Lewis (1996), and Stewart Cohen (e.g. 2000). This view focuses upon the *conversational* context of the one who is ascribing knowledge, and argues that 'knowledge' is a context-sensitive term in the sense that sentences of the form 'X knows that p' (henceforth, 'ascription sentences') express different propositions depending upon the attributer's conversational context.[20] Here, for example, is how Cohen describes the view:

I...defend the view that ascriptions of knowledge are context sensitive. According to this view, the truth value of sentences containing the words 'know', and its cognates will depend on contextually determined standards. Because of this, such a sentence can have different truth-values in different contexts. Now when I say 'contexts', I mean 'contexts of ascription'. . . . This view has the consequence that, given a fixed set of circumstances, a subject S, and a proposition p, two speakers may say 'S knows that p', and only of them thereby say something true. For the same reason, one speaker may say 'S knows p', and another say 'S does not know p' (relative to the same circumstances), and both speakers thereby say something true. (Cohen 2000: 94)

Note this last sentence. It is an immediate consequence of attributer contextualism as it is usually understood that the very same ascription sentence can simultaneously express a truth and a falsehood relative to two different contexts of utterance. This point is important because it allows the attributer contextualist to accommodate two apparently conflicting intuitions that help drive the sceptical argument. We can describe these intuitions as follows:

The infallibilist intuition
In sceptical conversational contexts we discover that we lack knowledge, and so may not legitimately ascribe it to agents.

The antisceptical intuition
In everyday (i.e. non-sceptical) conversational contexts we know a great deal, and so may legitimately ascribe knowledge to agents.

These two intuitions are apparently in conflict because all that may differ between the everyday conversational context where knowledge is widely ascribed and the sceptical conversational context where sceptical doubts are taken into account and knowledge is no longer widely ascribed are mere conversational factors and, intuitively, conversational factors alone (unlike changes in one's informational state, for example) cannot influence whether or not one knows. Accordingly, either the infallibilist is right and we lack knowledge *in every conversational context*, or else the fallibilist (such as the Dretskean) is right and we possess knowledge (at least of everyday propositions) *in every conversational context*. The contextualist attempts to dissolve this dichotomy by arguing that these two apparently conflicting intuitions can be reconciled if we are willing to allow that 'knowledge' is a context-sensitive term so that assertions of ascription sentences in everyday conversational contexts can be true even though the assertion of those same sentences in sceptical contexts would express falsehoods. The idea is that in entering the sceptical conversational context the epistemic standards are raised so that ascription sentences that once expressed truths now express falsehoods. As a result, it can both be true that our widespread ascriptions of knowledge to agents in everyday conversational contexts are correct *and* that our non-ascription of knowledge to those same agents in sceptical conversational contexts are also correct.

The antisceptical advantage gained by such a manoeuvre is obvious, since it allows the contextualist to accommodate both sceptical and antisceptical intuitions. The latter, because it ensures that our assertions of ascription sentences in everyday conversational contexts are true, just as we thought. The former, because it also acknowledges the force of sceptical arguments and their apparent power to destroy our sense that we know what we think we know. That the sceptic can wreak epistemic havoc in sceptical conversational contexts, however, does not affect the truth of our assertions of ascription sentences in everyday conversational contexts.

Moreover, the contextualist can argue that there are precedents for this sort of approach. We saw earlier that Unger motivated his infallibilism by comparing 'knowledge' to other absolute terms like 'flat' and 'empty'. The appropriate conclusion to draw from this parallel is moot, however, once one further reflects that our everyday (non-absolute) usage of terms like 'flat' and 'empty' seems perfectly in order. An alternative conclusion to draw from the comparison is thus not the infallibilism advanced by Unger, but rather a contextualist moral about the context-sensitivity of 'absolute' terms. In this way, just as the absolutism of terms such as 'flat' and 'empty' does not seem to mitigate against the correctness of our ascriptions of flatness and emptiness in normal conversational contexts (as regards 'flat' pool tables and 'empty' fridges, for example), so the same can be said of our use of 'knowledge' in non-sceptical conversational contexts.

For most of the recent versions of attributer contextualism, the motivation for this move comes from an earlier paper by Lewis (1979) on how one is to keep 'score' in a language game. The idea is that certain terms like 'knowledge', 'flat', 'empty', and so forth, are context-sensitive in that statements made using these terms can vary in their truth-value depending upon the standards employed in that particular conversational context. For example, relative to the standards employed in everyday conversational contexts, one asserts a truth by saying that the flat-to-the-naked-eye table before one is 'flat'. In contrast, in a scientific context where highly specialized instruments are being used which demand a far more refined degree of flatness, that same statement about the very same table will be false. The basic conversational contextualist line is that this kind of approach is equally applicable in the case of epistemic terms like 'knowledge', and that it is this feature of our use of epistemic terms which explains the enduring attraction of scepticism. There is thus, according to the attributer contextualist, independent linguistic support for treating 'knowledge' as a context-sensitive term.

A further advantage that attributer contextualism holds is that it is able to retain the closure principle and so can avoid the counter-intuitive consequences of rejecting this principle.[21] On this view, the apparent failure of closure is due to a shift between conversational contexts. Accordingly, provided one stays within the same conversational context, apparent counter-examples to closure disappear. For example, in everyday conversational contexts which employ low epistemic standards, assertions of ascription sentences involving everyday propositions will tend to express truths. Crucially, though, relative to the same everyday conversational context (and thus to the same epistemic standards), what would be expressed by an assertion of an ascription sentence where the proposition in question is the denial of a sceptical hypothesis would also be true.[22] As a result, one will not get a situation in which it can be simultaneously truly asserted, relative to the same conversational context, that an agent both knows an everyday proposition whilst lacking knowledge of a (known to be entailed) antisceptical proposition. Conversely, once one enters a sceptical conversational context which employs very demanding epistemic standards then assertions of ascription sentences involving everyday propositions will now tend to express falsehoods. Similarly, however, relative to this conversational context (and thus to these epistemic standards) assertions of ascription sentences where the proposition in question is the denial of a sceptical hypothesis will likewise express falsehoods. Again, then, one will not get a situation in which it can be simultaneously truly asserted, relative to the same conversational context, that an agent both knows an everyday proposition whilst lacking knowledge of a (known to be entailed) antisceptical proposition.

In general, the apparent failure of closure is diagnosed on the attributer contextualist account in terms of an illicit shift between conversational contexts. That is, it seems as if closure fails because whilst we ordinarily evaluate the conclusion of the sceptical argument that we lack knowledge of a wide class of everyday propositions relative to the *low* epistemic standards at issue in everyday conversational contexts (and therefore tend to find such a conclusion to be false), we evaluate the second premiss of the sceptical argument regarding whether we know the denials of sceptical hypotheses relative to the *high* epistemic standards at issue in sceptical conversational contexts (and therefore tend to grant to the sceptic that we do indeed lack such knowledge). Provided that we keep the contexts fixed throughout the closure-based inference (either from the second premiss of the sceptical argument to the conclusion, or from the negation of the sceptical conclusion back to the negation of the second premiss), then we get no tension over closure.

There are many differences between the contextualist theories expounded by the main protagonists, but we need not concern ourselves with these differences here.[23] What is important is that attributer contextualism incorporates a powerful diagnostic story since it can explain the attraction of scepticism in terms of the mistaken application of a non-contextualist theory about how epistemic terms such as 'knowledge' function. On this view, the temptation towards scepticism and infallibilism is simply the result of failing to recognize that the epistemic standards that we discover in operation in sceptical conversational contexts are not the same epistemic standards that are applicable in everyday conversational contexts. Similarly, the temptation towards a revisionistic fallibilist thesis like that advocated by Dretske which denies closure is the result of failing to see that the conversational context, and thus the applicable epistemic standard, has shifted midway through the relevant inference.

Furthermore, attributer contextualism also seems to accommodate some of our confusion about the correct construal of the epistemic luck platitude, since the moral to be drawn from the contextualist response to scepticism appears to be that the extent to which an agent's knowledge should not be gained through luck is dependent upon the epistemic standards in play in the relevant conversational context. On this view, our ambivalence towards the apparent need to eliminate luck from our knowledge (at least when faced with the problem of radical scepticism) is explained in terms of how different conversational contexts incorporate different degrees of epistemic rigour and thus demand different thresholds of luck exclusion.

The most obvious difficulty with attributer contextualism is its commitment to the counter-intuitive thesis that 'knowledge' is a context-sensitive term in the manner described, with the epistemic standards relevant to whether or not knowledge can be truly ascribed to an agent being determined by conversational factors. This problem is especially pertinent given that the natural conclusion to draw from the apparent context-sensitivity of our usage of the term 'knows' is that in different conversational contexts assertions of ascription sentences generate different conversational implicatures, so that what was assertible in one conversational context may not be assertible in another. On this view, the contextualist has been far too quick in converting claims about the pragmatics of our linguistic practice regarding epistemic terms (i.e. about what is properly assertible in this regard in the relevant conversational contexts) into semantic claims about the shifting content of what is expressed by these assertions in different conversational contexts. We will return to the issue of what the propriety conditions for assertions of ascription sentences (and knowledge claims in general) are below.

Even setting this issue aside, however, there are several core problems that remain, the most central of which for our purposes is the inconsistent motivation that is offered for the view. Recall that the Dretskean approach got into trouble by, on the one hand, employing epistemologically internalist intuitions in order to motivate the rejection of closure and then, on the other hand, developing an externalist theory of knowledge in order to accommodate those intuitions. As a result, the view appeared to lose all motivation, especially since it seemed to only be because of this 'mixed' set of intuitions that it incorporated an interpretation of the core relevant alternatives intuition which allowed far-off possible worlds to be relevant to the determination of knowledge, albeit only knowledge of the denials of sceptical hypotheses.

This problem about diverse motivation also crops up with the attributer contextualist approach because, primarily, attributer contextualism is an *externalist* theory of knowledge. There are a number of reasons why this should be so, but the main consideration that is relevant in this regard is that attributer contextualists are going to need to endorse epistemological externalism if they are to explain how we can have knowledge of the denials of sceptical hypotheses in *any* conversational context, even contexts which employ low epistemic standards. For recall that contextualism retains closure and thus allows such antisceptical knowledge, albeit at low epistemic standards. But as we have seen, whatever else is problematic about this type of knowledge, it is certainly true that no epistemologically internalist account of it is available. (And note that the problem here does not simply relate to the fact that one has insufficient reflectively accessible epistemic support for belief in this proposition, but rather concerns how one lacks *any* reflectively accessible epistemic support for belief in this proposition. Accordingly, the problem cannot be resolved merely by appealing to a reduced epistemic standard.) Any version of contextualism that retains closure—and this includes attributer contextualism—must thus reject epistemological internalism.

Most attributer contextualists are quite explicit about their endorsement of epistemological externalism, but it is perhaps worth pausing for a moment to consider Cohen's version of the attributer contextualist thesis since this is meant to be part of an *internalist* theory of knowledge. As a result, Cohen's account is faced with the onerous burden of explaining how agents can have (internalist) knowledge of the denials of sceptical hypothesis relative to *any* epistemic standard. His ingenious suggestion is that belief in these types of proposition is in some sense a priori rational, though not to a degree that licenses knowledge of these propositions in all conversational contexts. The problem, however, is that since such propositions are contingent, this makes him committed to the idea that there are contingent a priori propositions. Cohen is not altogether happy with this result, especially since the *apriocity* of the contingent propositions in question cannot be explained in terms of the standard Kripkean model of the contingent a priori (see Cohen 1999: 69). Nevertheless, he remarks that the only alternative would be to allow that in some sense agents are able to employ the reflectively accessible evidence that supports their belief in everyday propositions in order to support their belief in the denials of sceptical hypotheses, even though that evidence would not normally be allowed to perform this supporting role as regards belief in anti-sceptical propositions (recall that we criticized Klein for endorsing a thesis along these lines above). The choice is thus between a rock and a hard place. Here is Cohen:

What should we conclude? Our options seem to be accepting contingent a priori knowledge or endorsing what looks to be objectionable reasoning. However we go then, there is a distasteful consequence. But then again skepticism is a distasteful consequence—and I would maintain more so than any consequence of a contextualist account.

He continues, and here Cohen must surely be applauded for his intellectual honesty:

Which contextualist alternative is the best? I prefer the one that endorses a priori rationality, but that may be mostly a statement about which bullet I am most prepared to bite. (2000: 106)

There is no comfortable way to reconcile epistemological internalism and attributer contextualism, even by the lights of a proponent of such a reconciliation.[24,25]

As with the Dretskean proposal, however, once one recognizes that attributer contextualism must be allied to epistemological externalism, then the motivation for the view begins to subside. For if one is willing to allow that agents can know the denials of sceptical hypotheses—and, moreover, know these propositions relative to the externalist epistemic rubric—then the issue that arises is why the sophisticated theoretical machinery adduced by the contextualist is necessary at all. Why not just simply argue that agents know everyday propositions and thus, given closure, that agents can know the denials of sceptical hypotheses also? And note, we didn't make any mention of conversational contexts here at all, since the point was meant to apply in *all* conversational contexts. We thus evade the obvious worries regarding attributer contextualism which concern how it could possibly be the case that mere changes in the conversational context could influence whether or not an agent possesses knowledge.

Of course, a great deal needs to be said to explain how one could know the denials of sceptical hypotheses even on an externalist theory of knowledge. Moreover, rejecting attributer contextualism also means rejecting the most appealing element of it—its neat diagnostic account of what is wrong with sceptical arguments which also explains why they are so beguiling. Nevertheless, as we will see, an antisceptical account of our knowledge of the denials of sceptical hypotheses is available and, moreover, we can tie such an account to a general pragmatic thesis that incorporates the diagnostic element of the attributer contextualist position without thereby leading to the troubling conclusion that the truth-conditions of assertions of ascription sentences can be variable in response to conversational factors alone. There is therefore an antisceptical theory available which has all the key advantages of attributer contextualism, but without any of the problems associated with it.

2.5. Concluding Remarks

In this chapter we have seen that two of the dominant antisceptical arguments that have been put forward in the recent literature—the arguments for non-closure and for attributer contextualism—are, on closer inspection, question-able, in that they are motivated by diverse and incompatible intuitions which reflect *both* sides of the epistemological externalist–internalist distinction. We have also seen, however, that the very features of these antisceptical theses that are problematic point to a third antisceptical thesis which is consistently epistemologically externalist and which can incorporate the attractions of the other two views. This view is the 'neo-Moorean' response to scepticism, and it will be the topic of the next chapter.

Notes

1. Dretske (1970) is, perhaps, the first explicit exponent of a relevant alternatives response to scepticism, though see also Goldman (1976) and Stine (1976). Aside from Austin, one can find traces of a *proto*-relevant alternatives thesis in Wittgenstein (1969). I discuss Wittgenstein's remarks on knowledge in Chapters 3 and 9.
2. Sosa (in BonJour and Sosa 2003: 144) understands reflection as involving either '(a) intro-spection, (b) rational intuitions, (c) memory, (d) deduction, or (e) induction or ampliative reason which builds only on materials provided by (a)–(d).' The characterization of both epistemological internalism about justification and reflective access that I offer here conforms to the account given by Pryor (2001) in his extremely useful survey of recent trends in epistemology, though Sosa's definition would do equally well. For more on the epistemological externalism–internalism distinction, see the papers collected in the excellent anthology edited by Kornblith (2001).

3. Elsewhere Chisholm notes that:

> [*T*]he usual approach to the traditional questions of the theory of knowledge is properly called 'internal' or 'internalistic'. The internalist assumes that merely by reflecting upon his own conscious state, he can formulate a set of epistemic principles that will enable him to find out, with respect to any possible belief he has, whether he is *justified* in having that belief. The epistemic principles that he formulates are principles that one may come upon and apply merely by sitting in one's armchair, so to speak, and without calling to any outside assistance. In a word, one need only consider one's own state of mind. (Chisholm 1989: 77)

4. For an externalist account of justification that focuses on the reliability of the process by which the agent's belief is formed, see the early process reliabilist theory advocated by Goldman (1986) and developed by Talbott (1990). Process reliabilism is further discussed in §7.2.

5. Indeed, some externalists are happy to grant that the notion of justification is essentially an internalist notion and thereby concede that the justification-type concept that they are elucidating is not, strictly speaking, a concept of justification at all. For these externalists, the focus of the debate will not be on the concept of justification but rather on the concept of knowledge, and thus their view will essentially incorporate a rejection of the putative centrality of the internalist conception of justification to the theory of knowledge. Consider, for example, Dretske's remarks in the following passage:

> Those who think knowledge requires something other than, or at least more than, reliably produced true belief, something (usually) in the way of justification for the belief that one's reliably produced beliefs are being reliably produced, have, it seems to me, an obligation to say what benefits this justification is supposed to confer. ... Who needs it, and why? If an animal inherits a perfectly reliable belief-generating mechanism, and it also inherits a disposition, everything being equal, to act on the basis of the belief so generated, what additional benefits are conferred by a justification that the beliefs are being produced in some reliable way? If there are no additional benefits, what good is this justification? Why should we insist that no one can have knowledge without it? (Dretske 1981: 95)

Similarly, Lewis (1996: 551) denies that internalist justification is either sufficient (with true belief) or necessary for knowledge. In a related vein, there are also those, such as Foley (1987), who think that the project of elucidating the concept of justification and the project of elucidating the concept of knowledge, whilst both central to epistemology, are two largely distinct projects in that knowledge, unlike justification, is an essentially externalist notion. Thus, on this view, there is no essential connection between (internalist) justification and knowledge, though not because justification is in some sense a secondary epistemological concept.

6. I discuss this point in more detail in Pritchard (2001*e*). This conception of the externalism–internalism distinction as it applies to knowledge is common in the literature. It is, for example, a recurrent *motif* of BonJour and Sosa (2003). See also, Brandom (1998).

7. For further discussion of the chicken-sexer example, see Foley (1987: 168–9), Lewis (1996), Zagzebski (1996: §§2.1 & 4.1), and Brandom (1998). See also the exchange between Sainsbury (1996) and Wright (1996). I return to consider the chicken-sexer example in more detail later in Part I and in Part II. Another example that is often cited in the literature instead of the chicken-sexer example is that of face recognition (e.g. Lewis 1996: 551). Like the chicken-sexer case, this skill also involves a natural and highly reliable way of forming beliefs about a certain subject matter where the agents who employ this skill typically lack good reflectively accessible grounds in support of their beliefs.

8. Note that this way of characterizing the internalist thesis doesn't leave it straightforwardly open to Gettier-style counter-examples. For whilst such examples attack the sufficiency of an internalist notion of justification for knowledge, they do not obviously undermine the view that such justification must be at least necessary. Gettier counter-examples are discussed further in Part II.

9. One way in which the internalist might try to respond to this line of argument could be to maintain that we have good *abductive* grounds for believing in the denials of sceptical hypotheses because their falsity forms part of the best possible explanation of the empirical data. Accordingly, we do have an internalist justification, of sorts, for believing these propositions and thus the tension regarding closure does not arise. It is far from clear, however, just how this line of thought can help the internalist in this respect because it is not obvious that this use of inference to the best explanation presents us with *epistemic* grounds for our antisceptical beliefs as opposed to merely *pragmatic* grounds, such as that our belief in the denial of sceptical hypotheses accords us a simpler and more conservative belief-system. And if this line of argument is not offering us epistemic grounds, then it is not going to be able to provide us with grounds that can support an internalist justification for our beliefs in these antisceptical propositions. For a presentation of an antisceptical thesis that is primarily based on abductive reasoning of this sort, see Vogel (1990).

10. A further contention that Klein makes in this regard (e.g. Klein 1995: 226–8) is that the argument for the claim that agents are unable to have an internalist justification for their beliefs in the denials of sceptical hypotheses (and are thus unable to know the denials of sceptical hypotheses) itself *assumes* the failure of the closure principle and thus is question-begging. Whilst it is certainly true that one *could* argue for this claim in this way, it is far from obvious that this is the *only* way to motivate it. Indeed, it seems to directly follow from the (fairly standard) rendering of internalism that we have offered here.

11. Two other apparently internalist antisceptical theories which retain closure have recently been proposed by Pryor (2000) and Wright (2000, 2002, 2003a, 2003b, 2004; cf. Davies 1998, 2000, 2003, 2004). In both cases, however, the view presented is unstable. This is because in order to retain closure these theses end up allowing certain beliefs a 'default' or 'basic' epistemic status even though they do not meet the usual epistemic rubric demanded by internalists for basicality, such as being self-evident or incorrigible. In the case of Wright the default epistemic status is conferred on our antisceptical beliefs, such as our beliefs in the denials of sceptical hypotheses, whilst in the case of Pryor it is our perceptual beliefs in world-involving propositions such as that one has two hands which are accorded a default epistemic status. The trouble is that such proposals conflict with the avowed internalism of the theses since by internalist lights such beliefs are not basic or self-justifying at all, and nor can their epistemic status be adequately traced back to other beliefs which the agent holds in any way that would satisfy the internalist. I offer an extended discussion of Wright's response to the sceptic which develops this point in Pritchard (2002a, 2005e).

12. Note that the principle must be restricted to contingent propositions because there is no possible world (nearby or otherwise) in which a necessary truth is false. Moreover, it is important to recognize that this formulation of sensitivity simplifies Dretske's position somewhat. For example, one key component of the Dretskean view is a relativisation of this principle to the 'epistemic credential' that gave rise to the belief in the actual world. I will be setting this, and other, complications aside for now because they are not relevant to the present discussion (they will be considered in their own right in Part II).

13. Or, at least, nothing needs to be added as regards further *epistemic* conditions on knowledge at any rate. (Indeed, in places Dretske takes his formulation of sensitivity to entail the truth and belief conditions for knowledge as well, so even these extra conditions on knowledge might be unnecessary given the sensitivity condition.)

14. See the quotation from Dretske in note 5 above. Nozick (1981) adds a further 'tracking' condition that we will discuss below, though this principle is not directly relevant to the discussion concerning closure because even in Nozick's account it is the sensitivity principle that is doing the work as regards motivating the denial of closure.

15. This line of objection is usually associated with Craig (1989) who directed an argument of this sort against Nozick's antisceptical account. For discussion of Craig's argument, see Brueckner (1991) and Pritchard (2000*d*).

16. For an argument against the sensitivity-based approach to scepticism (again, as expressed by Nozick) that is largely directed at its commitment to epistemological externalism, see Bonjour (1987).

17. Of course, there can be non-everyday conversational contexts which are not thereby *sceptical* conversational contexts (i.e. conversational contexts in which sceptical error-possibilities are at issue). For our purposes here, however, we can take it that non-everyday conversational contexts are always, unless otherwise specified, sceptical conversational contexts.

18. Indeed, a number of commentators have noted that externalism, far from leading to the rejection of closure, actually seems to license it. See, e.g., Stine (1976), Klein (1987), and Pritchard (2002*b*). We will return to this issue below.

19. The same general problem will emerge, *mutatis mutandis*, for any development of the Dretskean line. In particular, it applies to the influential version of this type of antisceptical thesis that is put forward by Nozick (1981). Nozick establishes the sceptical problem in terms of the challenge of how it is that we could know the denials of sceptical hypotheses given that there is, *ex hypothesi*, nothing reflectively accessible to us which could indicate to us that this is the case (167). He then goes on to develop a theory of knowledge based around a sensitivity-type principle (172–8). Finally, he argues that this theory of knowledge explains how it could be that we could know everyday propositions whilst failing to know the denials of sceptical hypotheses, and thus why closure fails (204–11). However, it is only on the internalist supposition that a lack of reflectively accessible grounds for believing that we are not the victims of sceptical hypotheses entails that we thereby lack knowledge that we are not the victims of sceptical hypotheses that there is any 'datum' for his theory to explain in the first place. Indeed, since Nozick's theory is allied to epistemological externalism in much the same way as Dretske's, there is the same tension in this view regarding whether such an intuition should take the form of a 'datum' at all (one could thus just as well regard the denial of closure as an awkward consequence of the position rather than as a happy 'result'). So although Nozick puts the dialectic in a different order to Dretske, he is nevertheless subject to essentially the same criticisms.

20. Attributer contextualists have been notoriously unforthcoming about just what is involved in a conversational context. Whilst the paradigm case of a conversational context will involve a conversation about a certain topic, a conversational context could, it seems, also be a context in which nothing is said at all, perhaps because the communication is non-verbal, or because it is a 'conversation' that one is having with oneself 'in one's own head', as it were. To keep matters as simple as possible in this regard, I will henceforth only deal with examples of conversational contexts where an explicit conversation is taking place.

21. At the very least, attributer contextualists are able to retain the *sceptic's* use of the closure principle. Some attributer contextualists—most notably Heller (1999*a*)—have argued that one should reject the closure principle anyway, but on grounds that have no impact on the use of this principle in the sceptical debate. For discussion of this proposal, see Pritchard (2000*a*).

22. One must tread carefully here, however, in that most attributer contextualists hold that actually asserting such an ascription sentence would change the conversational context to a sceptical context and thereby raise the epistemic standards in such a way as to make what is expressed by the assertion in question false. Given this feature of the attributer contextualist's position, it is thus a vexed question what we mean when we say that what *would* be expressed by the assertion of this ascription sentence would have been true relative to the epistemic standards at issue in everyday conversational contexts given that one can never actually make such an assertion in an everyday conversational context, and therefore never truly assert such an ascription sentence. (Lewis (1996: 566) compares the situation to asserting 'It is silent now', an assertion which is always false but which, if unasserted, would seem to have expressed something true in a conversational context where nothing is being said.)

    It is worth noting that it is in this sense that attributer contextualism is wedded to a theory of meaning that is radically different from that espoused by rival 'contextualist' antisceptical theories which argue on broadly Wittgensteinian grounds that the assertions made by both the sceptic and the antisceptic lack meaning because they are not appropriately embedded within a context. For some of the key discussions of this alternative contextualist thesis, see Wittgenstein (1969), Cavell (1979), McGinn (1989), and Travis (1989). See also the exchange between Conant (1998) and McGinn (2002). For further discussion of this form of Wittgensteinian contextualism in the light of the contemporary literature on scepticism, see Pritchard (2005*e*).

23. Of the three main attributer contextualist antisceptical theories—as advanced by Cohen, DeRose, and Lewis—the main distinction is between epistemologically internalist (Cohen) and epistemologically externalist (DeRose and Lewis) construals of this thesis. I briefly remark on Cohen's internalist version of attributer contextualism below. Even between DeRose and Lewis, however, there are important differences. In particular, whilst DeRose gives a sophisticated and unified contextualist theory of knowledge, Lewis instead offers merely a series of 'rules' which govern the manner in which different epistemic standards are relevant to each conversational context. Williams (2001*a*) offers a perceptive criticism of Lewis's antisceptical thesis on the basis of this issue, to which Williamson (2001) responds. It should also be noted that not all contextualist theories in the recent literature are construed along attributer contextualist lines, nor are they all motivated specifically in response to the problem of scepticism. Annis (1978) presents an influential version of a contextualist epistemology that is developed in a way that is largely independent of the sceptical problem, and Williams (1991) is a good example of a contextualist antisceptical theory that is not (at least not primarily) understood along attributer lines. The literature on epistemological contextualism is now vast, but a good place to start would be Norman (1999) and Black (2003). See also Pritchard (2002*e*; cf. Pritchard 2002*c*: §§5–7) for a critical comparison of Williams's version of contextualism with its attributer contextualist rival theories.

24. A further problem affecting Cohen's defence of our knowledge of the denials of sceptical hypotheses in terms of our belief in these propositions being a priori rational is that the rationality in question here seems to be non-epistemic. That is, the reason why we seem

to be entitled to hold such beliefs concerns the *pragmatic* benefits of retaining such beliefs rather than relating to any grounds we might have for thinking that such beliefs are true. It thus appears that Cohen's approach, even by his own lights, is unable to explain why we should treat agents as having knowledge of these propositions.

This theme of accounting for an agent's putative knowledge of the denials of sceptical hypotheses in a priori terms is picked up by DeRose (2000), who argues that one could (in a very qualified sense) regard the warrant agents have for believing these propositions as being gained in this fashion. He motivates this move on content externalist grounds, though he sharply distinguishes his view from alternative antisceptical positions that are *entirely* grounded on a content externalist thesis. Crucially for our purposes, however, his explanation of how agents know the denials of sceptical hypotheses is primarily in terms of an epistemologically externalist thesis. We will return to the issue of how epistemological externalists are to account for knowledge of this antisceptical sort below. For further discussion of DeRose's proposal, see Williamson (2000b). The relationship between scepticism and content externalism is further explored in §9.2.

25. More recently, Neta (2002, 2003) has put forward a slightly different antisceptical proposal which shares some key similarities with the attributer contextualist approach and which, he argues, is an instance of epistemological internalism. Roughly speaking, the basic idea is that what is sensitive to the conversational context is what is allowed to count as evidence, so that beliefs regarding the external world, such as one's perceptual beliefs regarding how the world is, are allowed to count as part of my evidence in everyday conversational contexts, but not in sceptical conversational contexts. When the sceptic raises the epistemic standards what she does is therefore raise the standards for what counts as evidence, thereby denying one the evidential support that one had for one's beliefs in the everyday conversational context and hence undermining one's knowledge. By the lights of this ingenious proposal, we can thus claim, it seems, that agents have adequate evidential support for their beliefs in everyday conversational contexts (including their beliefs in the denials of sceptical hypotheses which they know are entailed by their everyday beliefs), even whilst granting that they lack evidential support for these same beliefs in sceptical conversational contexts. Even setting aside the issue of whether this theory is consistent with epistemological internalism, however, the problem with this strategy is that it is difficult to see how it can enable us to resist the sceptical conclusion that, *strictly speaking*, our beliefs are not evidentially supported at all and only seem to enjoy such support because we arbitrarily do not consider sceptical hypotheses in everyday conversational contexts. Moreover, if the evidential support that we have for our beliefs in everyday conversational contexts really is legitimate, then why should we endorse a contextualist thesis of this sort at all, rather than simply denying the relevance of sceptical hypotheses? I discuss the evidential dimension to the sceptical challenge in more detail in Chapter 4.

3

Neo-Mooreanism

3.0. Introduction

In the last chapter we saw just what is, at root, problematic about responses to scepticism that work either by denying closure or by adopting attributer contextualism—namely, their ambivalent attachment to epistemological externalism. The issue then becomes whether there is a consistent epistemologically externalist response to scepticism available that can evade this problem. In the last chapter we saw the first inklings of such a view, and the goal of this chapter is to examine this position in greater depth. In the recent literature this proposal is known as 'neo-Mooreanism' and, as we will see, neo-Mooreanism does have considerable advantages over the two main rival antisceptical theories that we looked at in Chapter 2. As we will discover in Chapter 4, however, such a result is small comfort once one reflects that even if one of these three lines of argument were, in their own light, successful, they would still not be intellectually satisfying antisceptical theories. And as we will also discover in Part 2, that these theories are problematic in this way is a result of their failure to understand the way in which the sceptical problem rests upon a very specific issue regarding epistemic luck. That the neo-Moorean argument is the most plausible of the three main antisceptical theories in the contemporary literature is meant to bring this point into clear focus.

3.1. Neo-Moorean Antiscepticism

So far we have seen that both the Dretskean and the attributer contextualist proposals each essentially incorporate a commitment to epistemological externalism but that, with this commitment made explicit, it is no longer clear that either view is adequately motivated. We have also seen, however, that the prospects for an epistemologically internalist response to scepticism are dim indeed. The focus therefore falls on the possibility of an epistemologically externalist response to scepticism that can avoid attributer contextualism whilst retaining the closure principle. In the contemporary literature this position is known as 'neo-Mooreanism'.

Of course, there is going to be an issue in this regard as to whether adopting epistemological externalism is ever a legitimate move to make in response to scepticism, especially since the tenor of the sceptical attack is internalist. I am sympathetic to this concern, and will discuss it in more detail below. For now, we will take the legitimacy of this type of move for granted since it is, after all, a move that is being made by the main protagonists of this debate anyway, whether they are fully explicit about this fact or not.

We saw above that Fred Dretske was led to his account of knowledge in terms of sensitivity by reflecting on what he took to be the failure of the closure principle for knowledge. The role of sensitivity was thus to explain what Dretske regarded as being the epistemological datum that closure failed. We also saw, however, that a sensitivity-based epistemological theory of this sort was essentially externalist but that Dretske's argument against closure turned upon an *internalist* construal of that principle. That is, what Dretske was object-ing to, it turned out, was not the bare closure principle that we formulated above, and which says nothing about what specific demands we are to put on the knowledge at issue in that principle, but rather a sister principle which specifically understands knowledge possession as demanding internalist justification—i.e. a principle which is explicitly formulated in terms of an *internalist* conception of knowledge. It was only by understanding the principle in this way that Dretske was able to motivate his initial claim that closure must fail in terms of our inability to have an internalist justification for believing certain propositions (such as antisceptical propositions) which we know to be entailed by other propositions which we take ourselves to know.

We can formulate this 'internalized' version of closure as follows:

The closure principle for internalist knowledge
For all agents, φ, ψ, if an agent has internalist knowledge that φ, and has (internalist) knowledge that φ entails ψ, then that agent has internalist knowledge that ψ.

Of course, for epistemological internalists there will be no difference at all between this internalized version of closure and the basic closure principle formulated in §1.2. For epistemological externalists, in contrast, there will be a difference, in that a lack of internalist knowledge on this view will not entail a lack of knowledge *simpliciter* (in particular, a lack of internalist justification will not entail a lack of knowledge *simpliciter*).[1] Accordingly, it could be the case that internalist closure fails and yet closure itself is unaffected, in that although knowledge *simpliciter* is 'closed' under known entailment it is not thereby true that knowledge of a specifically internalist sort is closed under known entailment as well (in particular, without it thereby being true that internalist justification is closed under known entailment).

As we saw in the last chapter, there is clearly a problem regarding closure if the internalized version of the principle is under consideration, since closure-type inferences will take us from internalist knowledge of everyday propositions (which, recall, even proponents of modest externalist theses would wish to allow), to internalist knowledge of what is known to be entailed by these everyday propositions—the denials of sceptical hypotheses. And as we noted, it is highly implausible to suppose that we could ever have internalist knowledge of these antisceptical propositions because we are unable to have an internalist justification for our beliefs in them. Nevertheless, that we are unable to have internalist knowledge of the denials of sceptical hypotheses does not in itself entail that we are unable to know them at all, either internalistically or externalistically. Thus, it could be that closure holds even in such antisceptical cases, but that the knowledge that transfers across the entailment does not remain of the same type. In this way, we can know everyday propositions internalistically whilst only knowing the (known to be entailed) denials of sceptical hypotheses externalistically.

Of course, allowing that we might be able to know such antisceptical propositions at all, externalistically or otherwise, is still a fairly radical move to make, and amounts to a denial of the minor premiss of the template closure-based sceptical argument (C2). Provided that the rejection of this premiss is adequately motivated, however, then this represents one way in which the closure-based template argument can be blocked without adopting attributer contextualism and with closure intact. We noted above that attributer contextualists deny this premiss too, albeit only in everyday contexts in which the epistemic standards are sufficiently low. This raises the interesting possibility that perhaps in the relevant sense the epistemic standards are always of this 'low' sort.

In order to see how this thesis might function, one needs to disentangle the different ways in which one can respond to the kind of anti-infallibilist 'relevant alternatives' intuition that we noted above. In essence, this is just the claim that we need not consider *every* error-possibility to be relevant to the determination of knowledge, and thus that infallibilism is false. In particular, far-fetched sceptical error-possibilities cannot have the relevance for knowledge possession that the infallibilist (and thus the sceptic) takes them to have. The particular spin that Dretske put on this thesis was to argue for a position that only saw sceptical error-possibilities as relevant to the determination of our knowledge of the denials of sceptical hypotheses. Otherwise, one could gain knowledge without needing to know that one was not the victim of a sceptical error-possibility. In this way, closure could be rejected and the sensitivity principle then adduced as a constraint on knowledge in order to explain this fact. In contrast, the attributer contextualist responds to the basic relevant alternatives thesis by arguing that what counts as relevant is itself a variable matter. So Dretske is not only wrong to think that sceptical error-possibilities are relevant to the determination of knowledge of the denials of sceptical hypotheses in normal conversational contexts (this is why we can know the denials of sceptical hypotheses in everyday contexts), he is also wrong to think that they are always irrelevant to the determination of our knowledge of everyday propositions. In particular, sceptical error-possibilities are relevant to our knowledge of everyday propositions in sceptical conversational contexts in which the epistemic standards have been raised.

There is, however, a third way of interpreting the core relevant alternatives thesis that incorporates key features from both of these views. This third interpretation simply takes the intuition at face-value and argues that far-fetched error-possibilities—and thus, putatively, *sceptical* error-possibilities—are not relevant to the possession of *any* knowledge in *any* conversational context. On this view, in so far as sceptical hypotheses do indeed concern far-fetched error-possibilities, then they are not relevant to the determination of any knowledge, even (*contra* Dretske) one's knowledge that one is not the victim of a sceptical scenario. Moreover, the thought is that conversational context alone can do nothing to alter the truth-value of what is expressed by an assertion of an ascription sentence, and thus that if such an assertion expresses a truth, then (*contra* attributer contextualism) it expresses a truth relative to *all* conversational contexts of ascription.

This interpretation of the relevant alternatives thesis is more motivated than its two counterparts because, as we saw above, the other two views are predicated upon diverse and, ultimately, incompatible intuitions. In particular, Dretske is only led to the non-closure view that he advocates because he is impressed by the failure of internalist closure, even though, as an externalist, Dretske can accept this conclusion without thereby denying closure. Moreover, attributer contextualists were led to their adoption of contextualism on the grounds that closure must hold and thus that it must be the epistemic standards that are shifting when we move from everyday conversational contexts to sceptical conversational contexts. But adopting this position requires them to accept that agents do have knowledge of the denials of sceptical hypotheses relative to the low epistemic standards in operation in quotidian conversational contexts, and once that much is conceded it is no longer obvious why we should adduce the contextualist theoretical machinery at all. After all, the tension with closure only came about because we were uncritically accepting the minor premiss of the sceptical argument, (C2), which maintains that knowledge of the denials of sceptical hypotheses is impossible. If, however, we have reason to reject this premiss, as the attributer contextualist claims, then we also have grounds that are sufficient to meet the sceptical argument, regardless of whether we supplement the rejection of this premiss with attributer contextualism. Moreover, it should be clear that this interpretation of the relevant alternatives thesis is also committed to epistemological externalism, since we have already noted that epistemological internalists must grant the minor premiss of the sceptical argument. Thus, the thought is that in so far as we are going to allow the move to epistemological externalism here, and in so far as we want to be true to the core relevant alternatives intuition, then the most direct response is not to deny closure (since this tactic trades on internalist intuitions that have already been disavowed), or to go attributer contextualist (which requires denying the minor premiss of the sceptical argument anyhow), but to simply deny the minor premiss of the sceptical argument (and thus maintain that we can know the denials of sceptical hypotheses).

The onus now falls upon the proponent of such a view to be able to offer an epistemological theory that can do justice to these intuitions. What is required is an account of knowledge that primarily understands knowledge in terms of a 'safety' condition. In essence, we can understand this condition in terms of the following principle:

The safety principle
For all agents, φ, if an agent knows a contingent proposition φ, then, in most nearby possible worlds, that agent only believes that φ when φ is true.[2]

What is significant about this principle is that, whilst it offers a broadly modal condition on knowledge of the sort proposed by Dretske and Robert Nozick, unlike the Dretske–Nozick proposal it does not take far-off possible worlds to be relevant to the determination of knowledge (at least as regards meeting this condition at any rate). Accordingly, it allows not only knowledge of everyday propositions, but also knowledge of the denials of sceptical hypotheses as well. Moreover, *contra* attributer contextualism, this principle makes no mention of conversational contexts.

Take an instance of putative everyday knowledge, such as that I am currently seated. By the lights of this condition, knowing this proposition largely consists in having a true belief in this proposition in the actual world and only believing this proposition in nearby possible worlds where it remains true. Intuitively, of course, this is just what we are able to do across a wide range of everyday cases. That I know that I am currently seated manifests itself (at least in part) in the way in which I not only truly believe this to be the case in the actual world, but also would only believe this to be the case in most worlds that are like the actual world in which this remains true—e.g. those nearby possible worlds in which I remain seated, but other things are different, such as where I am looking out of my office window rather than at my computer screen. Moreover, where my beliefs do not match the truth in nearby worlds in this way then, intuitively, I lack knowledge. If my car was, unbeknownst to me, very nearly just stolen from my driveway, then whilst I might truly believe that my car is parked outside in the actual world, there will be a wide class of nearby possible worlds in which I retain this belief but my belief is false because my car has just been driven away by thieves. Accordingly, my belief is not safe and hence I lack knowledge.

Of course, an initial condition that needs to obtain if one is to be in a position to have such everyday knowledge in the first place is that there are no sceptical possible worlds near to the actual world (i.e. worlds where sceptical hypotheses are true), since if there were such worlds then this would undoubtedly affect one's ability to have a safe belief in everyday propositions. For example, suppose there are sceptical possible worlds close to the actual world, in the sense that at present one is only narrowly avoiding being captured by neuro-scientists who aim to remove one's brain and turn one into a BIV. If this is right, then whilst one's belief that, say, one is currently seated is true (in the actual world), there will be a wide class of nearby possible worlds in which one continues to believe this proposition and yet this proposition is false—such as those worlds in which one is being 'fed' the experience that one is standing up. Safety thus allows the possibility of everyday knowledge just so long as sceptical possible worlds are, as a matter of fact, modally remote.

One question that might be asked about this principle is why it asks us to consider a *range* of close possible worlds, rather than (as with the formulation of sensitivity that we considered in §2.3) just the *nearest* possible world or worlds? The reason for this is that one can formulate examples where what undermines knowledge is a possibility that obtains in a near, but non-nearest, possible world. Consider the following example, adapted from one adduced by Alvin Goldman (1986: 45). Suppose that there are a number of thermometers in Sue's medicine cabinet, and that all but a few of them are reliable. Furthermore, suppose that Sue is unable to tell the difference between a reliable and an unreliable thermometer just by looking at them. The unreliable thermometers are towards the back of the medicine cabinet and Sue is marginally less likely to take a thermometer from the back of the cabinet rather than the front. Finally, suppose that Sue in fact chooses one of the reliable thermometers and so accurately finds out her son's temperature. Plausibly, the nearest possible world to the actual world will be one in which Sue also chooses a reliable thermometer and so forms a true belief as a result, and so if we restrict the range of possible worlds to the nearest possible worlds then Sue will (on this formulation of safety) have a safe belief and therefore (potentially) have knowledge also. Nevertheless, intuitively at least, Sue does not have knowledge in this case because she could just as easily have opted for one of the unreliable thermometers and formed a false belief as a result. This intuition is captured by the safety principle as formulated above, in that there is a wide class of nearby but non-nearest possible worlds in which Sue uses one of the unreliable thermometers and so forms a false belief as a consequence.[3]

We will consider in more detail various problems that might be raised for the safety principle in Chapter 6, and also look at some of the ways in which this principle can be modified to deal with these problems. For now, however, it is enough to note that there is at least a prima facie plausibility in the idea that knowledge requires that one's beliefs should be safe in the way that we have just described.

Any theory of knowledge that was entirely based on the safety principle—in that it treated the safety principle as completely capturing the epistemic condition for knowledge—would be a paradigm example of an externalist account, at least when compared to the two main rival externalist theories of knowledge that we have considered here—the sensitivity-based theory and attributer contextualism. As regards the sensitivity-based view, the safety-based theory has the edge in this respect in that it accommodates the core externalist intuition common to both theories that knowing demands a counterfactual responsiveness to the truth without actually making the additional demand made by sensitivity theorists that this responsiveness should include, with respect to certain propositions, far-off possible worlds. Similarly, as regards attributer contextualist theories of knowledge that are understood along externalist lines, the safety-based view has the edge in that whilst both of them only allow nearby possible worlds to be relevant to knowledge (at least in everyday conversational contexts), the attributer contextualist goes further to also insist that there are some conversational contexts (i.e. sceptical contexts) in which far-off possible worlds are relevant to knowledge. Thus, we might say, as far as externalism goes an entirely safety-based view constitutes the *minimalist* alternative with respect to these competitor externalist accounts.

In order to see this point in more detail, consider again the 'chicken-sexer' example that we considered in §2.2. The core externalist reliabilist intuition in this regard is that this chicken-sexer can have knowledge of the sex of the chicks even though her beliefs in this respect fail to meet an internalist justification condition because those beliefs are formed via a reliable method. The safety principle can capture this intuition because the chicken-sexer's beliefs will be safe. If she really has this ability, then, in most nearby possible worlds in which she forms the same belief as she does in the actual world (e.g. that the two chicks before her are of different sexes), she will continue to form a true belief.[4]

Theories of knowledge that treat the epistemic condition on knowledge as being entirely captured by the sensitivity principle, or which interpret attributer contextualism along externalist lines, will tend to generate the same result. In the first case, the chicken-sexer will have knowledge because, given that she has this 'sexing' ability, in the nearest possible world in which what she believes is false (e.g. the world where she is looking at two chicks of the same sex), she will not form the same belief (but will rather form the belief that the chicks are of the same sex). Externalist attributer contextualist theories will concur in this regard, arguing that in this everyday conversational context the chicken-sexer can be appropriately ascribed knowledge because the epistemic standards are sufficiently low to make such an ascription true. The difference between the three theories thus does not emerge merely at the level of considering 'every-day' ascriptions of knowledge. Instead, it appears only when one considers 'sceptical' ascriptions of knowledge, either because the proposition in question is the denial of sceptical hypotheses (sensitivity-based views), or because the conversational context at issue is a sceptical conversational context (attributer contextualist views). In these cases, the knowledge that would be ascribed to the agent is denied by the other two theorists because on their view more is needed for the agent to have such knowledge. In particular, what is demanded in such cases is that agents be able to track the truth in far-off sceptical possible worlds. We can thus see that it is attributer contextualist and sensitivity-based views, as opposed to the safety-based view, which make additional demands on knowledge possession.[5]

This is not to say, of course, that any safety-based theory of knowledge is an externalist theory, since it is open to the internalist to combine the safety principle with a demand for internalist justification in order to get an internalist safety-based account of knowledge. The point is rather that the safety principle accommodates the core externalist intuition about knowledge such that any theory of knowledge that treated this principle as capturing the epistemic condition on knowledge could plausibly be regarded as a paradigm case of a (minimalist) externalist epistemology.

So the safety principle will suffice to ensure knowledge of everyday propositions provided that there are no sceptical possible worlds near to the actual world whilst also not being so inclusive as to credit agents with knowledge in cases where, intuitively, such ascriptions seem out of place. Given that agents do have knowledge of everyday propositions, however—and thus that the supposition that there are no sceptical possible worlds near to the actual world is true—then in light of this principle those agents will also be in a position to have knowledge of the denials of sceptical hypotheses as well, just as closure-type inferences predict. After all, the very antisceptical beliefs that are a necessary condition for knowledge of everyday propositions will also be safe, in that in all nearby possible worlds in which these beliefs are held (which one would expect to be all of them), they are true. That is, in all nearby possible worlds agents believe that they are not the victims of sceptical hypotheses and, as a matter of fact, they are not the victims of sceptical hypotheses.[6] So in light of this account which only focuses upon nearby possible worlds, there is no problem with the sceptic's (and the antisceptic's) use of closure.[7]

Moreover, since agents are able to know the denials of sceptical hypotheses (at least in so far as they know anything much of substance at all), it follows that there is no need for the attributer contextualist theoretical machinery. On this view, the problem with the sceptical argument is that it contends that agents are unable to know the denials of sceptical hypotheses, even in situations in which the possible worlds are ordered such that agents have a great deal of everyday knowledge and hence that sceptical hypotheses do indeed concern far-off sceptical scenarios.

Indeed, with this diagnosis in mind, it is worthwhile reconsidering how Dretske motivates his denial of closure. Recall that Dretske asks the question of whether the agent knows the entailed antisceptical proposition as if this were an issue that could be settled entirely independently of establishing whether or not the agent knows the original antisceptical proposition. With the question so construed it is unsurprising that our intuitions are inconclusive. The relevant question to ask as far as the status of closure is concerned, however, is whether agents can know the denials of sceptical hypotheses *given* that we grant that they have knowledge of the everyday propositions which they know entail the denials of sceptical hypotheses. The reason why this shift of emphasis is so important is that, as we have seen, in so far as one grants that the agents in question have knowledge of everyday propositions then, on any plausible view of knowledge, sceptical possible worlds are, perforce, far-off possible worlds (since how could one know such an everyday proposition if sceptical possible worlds were in the modal neighbourhood?). Accordingly, by granting that the agents in question have knowledge of the relevant everyday propositions, the issue then becomes whether they have knowledge of the entailed antisceptical propositions *given* that the sceptical hypotheses that they concern are indeed far-off sceptical possibilities. And with the issue so understood, our intuitions are now, I take it, far more inclined towards ascribing knowledge of the antisceptical propositions to the agents concerned rather than denying such knowledge. Hence, not only does Dretske confuse the issue of whether internalist closure fails with the issue of whether externalist closure fails, he also motivates the denial of closure in a way that fails to adequately capture what is at issue.

Nevertheless, this does not mean that a safety-based antisceptical theory is home and dry, since it needs to do a great deal more work in order to make the position plausible. (Moreover, as we will see in Part 2, we also need to qualify our understanding of safety in certain key respects.) What is interesting, but also potentially troubling, about the view is that it bears a certain similarity to the notorious 'common-sense' response to the sceptic offered by G. E. Moore (1925, 1939). In essence, Moore responded to the sceptic by arguing that he did have the knowledge that was being contested (in particular, that he knew an everyday proposition, in this case that he had two hands), and thus that he must know the denial of the sceptical hypothesis under consideration (in particular, that he must know that there is an external world). At the very least, he contended, he had as much right to the premisses of this argument as the sceptic has for her premisses. The safety-based approach just sketched bears the key hallmarks of this Moorean stance in that it allows knowledge of every-day propositions and seems to argue on this basis (via a closure-type inference) to knowledge of the denials of sceptical hypotheses. And yet there is almost universal agreement that there is something seriously amiss with the Moorean antisceptical strategy (though little agreement on just what). So is the approach described here tantamount to a Moorean strategy (at least in its problematic respects)?

Clearly there are a number of parallels between the antisceptical strategy that Moore proposes and the neo-Moorean stance, but there are also a number of key differences. In particular, one crucial difference between the neo-Moorean antisceptical strategy and that put forward by Moore himself, is that Moore actually tried to *argue for* his antisceptical conclusion. In contrast, the neo-Moorean contents herself merely with the claim that, in so far as certain conditions obtain, then agents are able to know everyday propositions and the denials of sceptical hypotheses (thus, closure is preserved). That this is so, however, does not mean that one can legitimately employ one's knowledge of an everyday proposition as part of an argument to the conclusion that one knows the denials of sceptical hypotheses, as Moore attempts to do.

There are, in essence, two interrelated reasons for this. The first concerns how although closure itself is maintained on this view, internalist closure is rejected. The second concerns the predominantly internalist grounds that are typically needed if one is to be able to properly claim knowledge. Take the former point first (we will consider the second point in the next section). We noted earlier that it is highly implausible to suppose that one can have an internalist justification for one's belief in the denials of sceptical hypotheses, and thus have internalist knowledge of them, which means that the kind of knowledge of these propositions that is being rescued from the sceptic's grasp by the neo-Moorean is, perforce, of an externalist nature. In itself, this does not mean that internalist closure should fail, since it could just be that all knowledge is of this externalist sort, and thus that there are no possible counterexamples available to the internalist closure principle because there is no such knowledge (even knowledge of everyday propositions) that meets the internalist rubric in the first place. This would be a very extreme externalist thesis, however, and one that would be very unattractive since it would mean that even in good cognitive conditions and as regards everyday propositions agents were unable to offer sufficient reflectively accessible grounds to support an internalist justification for their beliefs in these propositions.

Of course, one motivation for adopting such an austere externalism might be the very sceptical argument that we have been considering, though here interpreted so that it undermines the possibility of specifically internalist knowledge rather than knowledge *simpliciter*. The thought would be that in order to meet the internalist condition for internalist knowledge of even everyday propositions, one must be able to meet the relevant internalist condition for internalist knowledge of the denials of sceptical hypotheses. Since this isn't possible, it follows that one never has internalist knowledge of everyday propositions. It is difficult to see, however, why meeting the internalist condition for knowledge of everyday propositions should require one to also meet the internalist condition as regards one's belief in the denials of sceptical hypotheses (at least, provided one doesn't simply assume the truth of the closure principle for internalist knowledge from the outset). After all, even though one lacks any good reflectively accessible reasons for believing that one is not the victim of a sceptical scenario, one can have excellent reflectively accessible reasons for thinking that one is, say, currently seated. Of course, these reasons are not decisive, and part of their defeasibility is precisely the fact that they are unable by themselves to rule out sceptical error-possibilities. Intuitively, however, epistemological internalism about justification merely demands good reflectively accessible grounds that suffice to support internalist justification for the belief in question, it does not demand *decisive* reflectively accessible grounds.

Accordingly, whilst the obtaining of the kind of external conditions that need to obtain if I am to know everyday propositions ensures that I must have externalist knowledge of the denials of sceptical hypotheses, this does not mean that the excellent reflectively accessible grounds which support my belief in the everyday propositions will transmit through a known entailment to be excellent reflectively accessible grounds which support my belief that I am not the victim of a sceptical hypothesis. According to epistemological internalism, this presents us with a problem since it seems to undermine the reflectively accessible grounds that I have for belief in everyday propositions. This is not the case when it comes to epistemological externalism, however, since if the relevant external conditions do obtain (so that I do have knowledge of the everyday propositions), then this means that the world is pretty much as I take it to be, in which case the reflectively accessible grounds that I can offer in favour of my belief in the everyday propositions are excellent even despite the fact that they fail to exclude sceptical error-possibilities. One could put the point by noting that whilst on an internalist theory of knowledge our putative internalist knowledge of everyday propositions seems to merely presuppose the *falsity* of the sceptical hypotheses (since we can never know them to be false on this account), in light of the externalist theory of knowledge under consideration here our internalist knowledge of everyday propositions can rest on our *knowledge* of the denials of sceptical hypotheses, albeit only our *externalist* knowledge of these antisceptical propositions.[8]

This is not to suggest that there is *nothing* problematic about the suggestion that internalist knowledge might rest upon externalist knowledge of what is known to be entailed by that internalist knowledge, only that there is no problem which immediately arises on the externalism–internalism picture that we sketched above and which is standard throughout contemporary epistemology. Later on, I will argue that the dissatisfaction one might feel with a response of this sort is misplaced in that the real focus of the difficulty is not with this understanding of internalist knowledge but elsewhere. For now, however, we will stick with the characterization of the debate as it is here understood.

So on any plausible externalist view of knowledge, internalist knowledge of everyday propositions should be possible, and thus, in light of the specific safety-based externalist model of knowledge under consideration here, internalist knowledge of everyday propositions is consistent with mere externalist knowledge of the denials of sceptical hypotheses. So whilst closure is maintained, internalist closure fails. This consequence has ramifications for any argument of a general Moorean form because it undermines our ability to always employ internalist knowledge in a dialectical context, particularly where that dialectical context concerns the problem of scepticism. In order to properly locate these ramifications in the wider sceptical debate, it is first necessary to consider the second problem that faces the Moorean—as opposed to the *neo*-Moorean—antisceptical thesis, which is the way that knowledge in this account is *claimed*. As we will see, reflecting on the conditions under which it is appropriate to claim knowledge will also point to a way in which we can account for the contextualist intuitions which drive attributer contextualism without actually advancing the problematic attributer contextualist thesis.

3.2. Claiming Knowledge

When Moore claims his knowledge he does so explicitly by using locutions of the form 'I know that P'. Typically, of course, one does not convey what one knows via assertions of this sort at all, but rather by simply asserting the embedded sentence, 'P'. Indeed, it may well be that it is a general rule of assertion that one should only assert what one knows, but for our purposes we can retreat to the less contentious principle that one typically conveys one's knowledge that P via the assertion that P.[9] In what follows, we will for convenience treat all assertions—even those that do not explicitly employ the term 'know' or its cognates—as being knowledge-conveying. These two ways of self-ascribing knowledge (via assertions of 'I know that P' and 'P') need to be further distinguished from the kinds of assertions used to ascribe knowledge to others. Typically, this will involve assertions of sentences of the form, 'S knows that P'. We thus have three sorts of *ascription sentences*, a first category of locutions of the form 'I know that P' used to explicitly self-ascribe knowledge (*explicit self-ascription sentences*), a second category of locutions of the form 'P' used to non-explicitly self-ascribe knowledge (*simple self-ascription sentences*), and a third category of locutions of the form 'S knows that P' used to ascribe knowledge to others (*third-person ascription sentences*). Since the standard way to self-ascribe knowledge is via assertions of simple self-ascription sentences, we will begin by looking at the propriety conditions for these assertions.

The conversational propriety of our assertions is context-sensitive in the straightforward sense that our assertions ought, *ceteris paribus*, to be relevant to the conversational context in which they are entered. Paul Grice famously formulated this constraint on proper assertion in terms of the following over-arching conversational principle (or supermaxim):

Make your conversational contribution such as is required, at the stage at which it occurs by the accepted purpose or direction of the talk exchange in which you are engaged. One might label this the *Cooperative Principle*. (Grice 1989: 25–6)

Imagine that one is at the airport and is asked what the time is. In general, co-operation within this conversational context will demand that one relates what the time is, if one knows. More specifically, as Grice points out, cooperation demands that one's contribution to this exchange be as informative as required, and be accurate, relevant, and clear.

Of these further sub-demands of cooperation—the need to be informative, accurate, relevant, and clear—the most interesting for our purposes is the requirement of accuracy. This requirement was formulated by Grice in terms of the 'sub-principle' that one's assertions should be supported by adequate evidence—the so-called conversational maxim of evidence (Grice 1989: 26). Suppose, for example, that one communicates one's knowledge of the time in this case by the simple assertion 'It's eleven o'clock'. In doing so, one is clearly cooperating with the other participant in this conversational context by offering the required information. This cooperation presupposes, however, that one has adequate grounds for believing that this is the right time, and in hearing one's assertion the other participant in this conversational exchange will certainly reasonably infer that this is the case. That is, this assertion will generate the *conversational implicature* that one has adequate grounds that can support this assertion, where a conversational implicature is, roughly, any inference which one is entitled to make upon hearing an assertion (but which is not entailed by the proposition asserted) given that one is allowed to make certain reasonable assumptions about the agent making that assertion—that she is, for instance, honest, cooperative, and (at least otherwise) rational. If one makes an assertion whilst knowing that this assertion will generate what one believes is a false conversational implicature, then that assertion is, *ceteris paribus*, conversation-ally inappropriate, even if it is true. In this case, for example, if one were to assert that the time is eleven o'clock whilst having no grounds for thinking that this is the case (one hadn't just looked at one's watch for instance), then this assertion would be conversationally inappropriate, regardless of whether the time actually is eleven o'clock.[10]

Crucially, however, given that the general role of assertion involves the agent's cooperation with the other members of the conversational context, the kind of evidence that is demanded by an assertion will be sensitive to the conversational context. Often, this will merely involve *different* evidence being required by an assertion, but it can also mean that *more demanding* evidence can sometimes be relevant as well. For example, suppose the conversational context changes to one in which a lot hangs on the correctness of your answer (e.g. your friend informs you that if she is late for this plane then she will miss her only daughter's wedding). Plausibly, in this new conversational context the evidential demands on proper assertion will rise. In this context, making an assertion about the time will generate the implicature that you have made *special* checks on the accuracy of what you say (that you have looked for verification of the time that your watch says, for example). If one lacks such special grounds, then one ought not to make an assertion about what one believes the time to be, at least not without qualifying this assertion with a disclaimer of some sort (e.g. '*My watch says* it's eleven o'clock'). Thus, an assertion that is entirely proper in one conversational context can be inappropriate (because it generates what the agent believes are false conversational implicatures) in another conversational context, even though all that might have changed in the interim are conversational factors.

Notice, however, that in the example just offered it is not as if the raising of the evidential constraints on assertion in response to conversational factors led to the agent *reversing* her assertion. That is, in response to the change in conversational context, the agent no longer asserted what she previously asserted (or asserted it with a rider attached), but we would not plausibly regard her as being inclined to assert the *opposite* of what she previously asserted (i.e. 'It is *not* eleven o'clock'). Part of the reason for this is that making an assertion implies a commitment to the proposition asserted such that there is a presumption that one will retain that commitment in all subsequent conversational contexts, at least in so far as none of the salient facts change (a fortiori, at least in so far as it is only conversational factors that change). Of course, if the agent becomes convinced by arguments or considerations offered in a subsequent conversational context then this might well change her assertion, but this is a case where the agent has *changed her mind* and thus incurred a new commitment to the opposing proposition. In general, the (unqualified) assertion of a proposition will generate the conversational implicature that one is committed to that proposition and this means that one will, *ceteris paribus*, retain that commitment regardless of mere changes in the conversational context. Call this the '*commitment principle*'.[11] The example given above bears this out, for whilst agents might withdraw what they assert in response to mere changes in the conversational context, they do not lose their commitment to what is asserted (the agent still believes, for example, that the time is eleven o'clock) and thus they do not reverse their assertions.

The maxim of evidence thus entails a certain context-sensitivity in the propriety conditions for assertions, but this is held in check by the commitment principle that constrains the extent to which agents can properly alter their assertions in response to mere changes in the conversational context. When these two factors are highlighted they offer an alternative pragmatic explanation of the linguistic data that is very different from the semantic account that we saw attributer contextualists offering above. For note that on this view the constraints on appropriate assertion that led to agents withdrawing, rather than reversing, assertions in response to mere changes in the conversational context will imply that agents should also withdraw rather than reverse their assertions of ascription sentences that involve the term 'knows' in response to mere changes in the conversational context (i.e. assertions of explicit self-ascription sentences and third-person ascription sentences).

For one thing, if the assertibility, but not the truth, of the 'simple' sentence 'P' is responsive to mere changes in the conversational context, then one would expect that likewise the assertibility, but not the truth, of the 'complex' sentence 'S knows that P' (or 'I know that P') should be responsive to mere changes in the conversational context as well since the proposition which is expressed by an assertion of this sentence entails the truth of the proposition expressed by an assertion of the embedded simple sentence. Accordingly, just as agents do not reverse their assertions of simple self-ascription sentences in response to mere changes in the conversational context, so we would not expect them to reverse their assertions of third-person ascription sentences and explicit self-ascription sentences in response to mere changes in the conversational context.

That is, given that agents do not reverse their assertions of a simple self-ascription sentence like 'It's eleven o'clock' when they enter more epistemically demanding conversational contexts, but only withdraw or qualify such an assertion, then this suggests that assertions of the corresponding (and logically stronger) explicit self-ascription sentence and third-person ascriptions sentence (i.e. 'I know that it's eleven o'clock' and 'She knows that it's eleven o'clock', respectively) should also only be withdrawn or qualified as one enters more epistemically demanding conversational contexts. Since attributer contextualists are committed to holding that agents will actually *reverse* their assertions of explicit self-ascription sentences and third-person self-ascription sentences in the light of a move to a conversational context that is epistemically more demanding, this raises a prima facie problem for the view.[12]

Moreover, the evidence maxim and the commitment principle get a grip even as regards assertions of explicit self-ascription sentences and third-person ascription sentences. The evidence maxim explains why an assertion of the very same ascription sentence of this sort could be conversationally appropriate in one conversational context and yet inappropriate in a second conversational context where the epistemic standards are higher. After all, if one lacks sufficient grounds to support one's assertion of 'P', then one is clearly going to also lack adequate grounds to support one's assertion of the logically stronger sentences, 'I know that P' and 'S knows that P'.[13] Furthermore, the commitment principle explains why agents do not simply reverse their assertions of these sorts of ascription sentences in response to mere changes in the conversational context. With this principle in mind, a raising of the epistemic standards brought about by a shift in the conversational context merely has the potential to undermine the appropriateness of repeating an assertion that was previously (and appropriately) entered. It does not mean that what was once properly assertable and true is now not properly assertable *and false*.[14]

When these two considerations are put together, they imply that all that is shifting as one moves from conversational context to conversational context is the conversational propriety of the assertion in question, not the truth of what is being expressed by that assertion. At the very least, the interplay of the evidence maxim and the commitment principle puts pressure on the idea that the context-sensitivity of the propriety of assertions of ascription sentences should be thought to indicate that the term 'know' is itself a context-sensitive term.

Indeed, a closer inspection of the linguistic data when it comes to our engagement with the problem of radical scepticism lends further support to this claim. Agents do not respond to sceptical arguments by reversing their assertions of ascription sentences regarding everyday propositions and claiming instead that, for example, they do *not* know the propositions they previously claimed to know. Rather, they are simply reluctant to assert any ascription sentence (at least unless they have changed their minds, but that agents sometimes change their minds is of no help to the contextualist cause). That is, an agent who was previously willing to assert a complex ascription sentence regarding an everyday proposition, such as 'I know that I am currently seated',[15] or 'She knows that she is currently seated', and who does not change her mind in her assessment of the relevant agent's epistemic position, will not be inclined to reverse her assertion in response to moving into a sceptical conversational context and assert the negation of what she previously asserted. Instead, she will tend to either assert nothing at all, or else continue to assert what she previously asserted but in a qualified manner (e.g. 'I know that I am currently seated, in so far as I know anything'). The linguistic data thus seem to favour a pragmatic explanation of the content-sensitivity of the propriety conditions for our assertions of ascription sentences over a semantic explanation.

Of course, the contextualist will respond to this line of argument by contending that it begs the question against contextualism by presupposing that it is the *same* proposition that is being asserted when one asserts an ascription sentence involving the term 'know' in two different conversational contexts. That is, more specifically, the presupposition is that in asserting an explicit self-ascription sentence like 'I know that I am seated' in an everyday conversational context and asserting the (apparent) negation of this sentence ('I do not know that I am seated') in a sceptical conversational context, the agent in question is contradicting herself. By the lights of an attributer contextualist view of how the term 'knows' functions, however, the proposition being asserted in the everyday conversational context (and which the agent thereby incurs a commitment to) is not the same proposition that is being denied by asserting the opposing sentence in the sceptical conversational context. Thus, the attributer contextualist can offer an interpretation of the linguistic data that is entirely compatible with the conversational principles that we have laid down.

That the attributer contextualist will understand the commitment principle in a very different way to the non-contextualist is quite right of course. Nevertheless, the non-contextualist can allow this point without thereby conceding anything of substance to the contextualist. Recall that the original claim that the attributer contextualist made was that the linguistic data spoke directly in favour of a contextualist understanding of the term 'knows', at least provided we were willing to take the data at face value. The situation now, however, is entirely different, since it seems that all the contextualist is offering is a kind of stand-off with the non-contextualist. That is, even by the contextualist's lights, the situation now is one of an *impasse* between the two interpretations of the linguistic data, with both camps granting that, in terms of the linguistic data alone, the issue of whether we should prefer a contextualist and semantic explanation of the context-sensitivity of the propriety conditions of assertions of ascription sentences over a non-contextualist and pragmatic explanation is underdetermined. Such a stand-off is to the neo-Moorean's benefit, however, given that such a view has, as we have seen, considerable theoretical advantages over its contextualist rival. In particular, since the neo-Moorean can account for our epistemological intuitions in this regard without needing to employ a contentious attributer contextualist account of the term 'knows', such an *impasse* between the two views puts the burden of explanation squarely in the contextualist's court.[16]

With this in mind, we will return to consider the pragmatic account on offer of the shifting propriety conditions for assertions of ascription sentences. We noted above that we would expect simple self-ascription sentences to become unassertable as one moves into more demanding conversational contexts. This feature of the pragmatic account will explain why assertions of simple ascription sentences which concern 'everyday' propositions, such as the sentence 'My car is parked outside', are conversationally appropriate in everyday conversational contexts but not in sceptical conversational contexts. In everyday conversational contexts, we would (*ceteris paribus*) treat assertions of 'everyday sentences' as conversationally appropriate just so long as the agent making the assertion was able to offer relevant evidence in favour of this assertion (such as that she parked her car in the driveway herself earlier on in the day, and has no reason for thinking that it has moved).

If such an assertion were made in a sceptical conversational context, however—a context in which sceptical error-possibilities were actively being considered— then this same assertion would not be conversationally appropriate. For example, in the sceptical conversational context in which the BIV sceptical hypothesis is actively being considered, the evidential burden incurred by making an assertion of this sort would be far greater than in the everyday conversational context. For now the agent's assertion is generating the conversational implicature that she can offer grounds in favour of this assertion that can discount the error-possibilities under consideration (i.e. grounds for thinking that her car is parked outside that discount even the truth of the BIV sceptical hypothesis). Crucially, of course, no one has grounds of this sort in favour of their assertions, and thus the assertion would be conversationally inappropriate. And note, the same considerations apply to assertions of the contrary sentence, 'My car is *not* parked outside'. This means that agents will not reverse their assertions in response to a mere change in the conversational context, but rather merely withdraw their assertions (i.e. be reluctant to assert them). Furthermore, note that the impropriety or propriety of these assertions has no obvious impact upon the issue of whether or not they express truths. Intuitively, either the assertion is true or it isn't, with the correct verdict being applicable in *both* conversational contexts.

Given that sceptical conversational contexts will be those contexts in which participants actively consider the truth of sceptical hypotheses, it follows that assertions of simple self-ascription sentences that involve sceptical hypotheses will always be conversationally inappropriate since they will, perforce, always be entered in a sceptical conversational context. This thus explains our reluctance to assert sentences such as 'I am not a BIV' (or, indeed, 'I *am* a BIV') since such assertions will always be insufficiently supported by evidence and thus be conversationally inappropriate, even though what is asserted may well be true.

There is thus a pragmatic account available of our use of epistemic terms that can help us to avoid the need for attributer contextualism. It does so by highlighting the sense in which knowledge that can be properly claimed or ascribed in one conversational context cannot be properly claimed or ascribed in another conversational context, even though all that might have changed in the interim are conversational factors. The apparent context-sensitivity of our use of the term 'know' is thus accounted for without actually treating 'know' as a context-sensitive term.

Such an account also speaks against Moore's method of claiming knowledge in the face of the sceptical challenge, in that on this view his claims to know were manifestly inappropriate. There are two immediate reasons for this. First, because he claimed to know the denial of a sceptical hypothesis (the hypothesis that there is, undetectably, no external world), and, as we have seen, a claim to know of this sort is always inappropriate.[17] Second, because he claimed to know a proposition which was not the denial of a sceptical hypothesis, but did so in a conversational context in which sceptical hypotheses were at issue. Again, as we have seen, entering almost any claim to know in a sceptical conversational context is inappropriate.

This isn't the full story of what is wrong with the Moorean antisceptical strategy in this respect, however, since there are a few further complications that we need to consider. To do this, we need to look at Wittgenstein's famous critique of Moore's claims to know.

3.3. Wittgenstein *contra* Moore on the Propriety of Claims to Know

Interestingly, there will also be claims to know that involve everyday propositions that will typically be unassertable for the same reason as claims to know regarding the denials of sceptical hypotheses, even though they make no mention of sceptical hypotheses. The kinds of propositions that are at issue here are what Wittgenstein (1969) calls 'hinge propositions'. These are everyday propositions that are so taken as given in normal circumstances that a conversational context in which the truth of these propositions is at issue will, perforce, be a sceptical conversational context.[18] Suppose, to use a Moorean example (one which, moreover, Wittgenstein also focuses upon), one asserts the sentence 'I have two hands'. Since in normal circumstances nothing is more certain than the proposition expressed by this sentence, it follows that if there is an issue about the truth of this proposition which demands that one assert it, then this can only be because we are now in a sceptical conversational context where the bulk of what we believe to be true is open to question. In a sceptical conversational context, however, this sentence is unassertable.

Wittgenstein often puts this point in terms of how our practice of offering evidence in favour of our assertions takes it as given that these hinge propositions are what 'stand fast'. For example, he writes:

My having two hands is, in normal circumstances, as certain as anything that I could produce in evidence for it.
  That is why I am not in a position to take the sight of my hand as evidence for it. (Wittgenstein 1969: §250)

Similarly, elsewhere he argues:

If a blind man were to ask me 'Have you got two hands?' I should not make sure by looking. If I were to have any doubt of it, then I don't see why I should trust my eyes. For why shouldn't I test my *eyes* by looking to find out whether I see my two hands? *What* is to be tested by *what*? (Wittgenstein 1969: §125)

The principle in play here is that in order to coherently offer grounds in favour of an assertion, the grounds in question need to be more certain than the proposition asserted. Accordingly, when it comes to propositions which are as certain as anything, in that context, it makes no sense to offer grounds in favour of them. For this reason, in normal circumstances there is no evidence that one can offer in favour of one's assertion of 'I have two hands'. Indeed, if the truth of this proposition is, in this context, in question, then *nothing* is certain. Of course, this does not mean that there are no abnormal circumstances in which this sentence cannot be properly asserted, but only that these circumstances will have different hinge propositions in play (for example, upon stumbling from the wreckage of a car explosion one might properly assert that one has two hands, but here the evidence gained by one's sight is more certain that the belief that one has two hands). In general, then, it is always conversationally inappropriate to assert simple ascription sentences involving hinge propositions because one will inevitably lack adequate grounds to back up this assertion. And if assertions of simple ascription sentences involving hinge propositions are conversationally inappropriate for this reason then, a fortiori, so too will be assertions of the logically stronger explicit self-ascription sentences and third-person ascription sentences involving hinge propositions.

This line of reasoning clearly immediately counts against the conversational propriety of Moore's assertion of the explicit self-ascription sentence, 'I know that I have two hands'. Of course, this is not to say that Moore's assertion was false, but only that it was conversationally inappropriate. The same goes for his assertion of an explicit self-ascription sentence that concerns the denial of a sceptical hypothesis, 'I know that there is an external world'. Given that agents necessarily lack the required evidential grounds to back up antisceptical assertions of this sort—and that, in any case, such assertions are necessarily entered in sceptical conversational contexts—this assertion will also be conversationally inappropriate. Again, though, this does not mean that what is asserted isn't true. Furthermore, as we have seen in our discussion of the neo-Moorean view, there are reasons for thinking that what Moore says is true, despite the impropriety of his saying it. Indeed, Wittgenstein seems to give expression to this diagnosis of the Moorean strategy when he writes: 'Moore's mistake lies in this—countering the assertion that *one cannot know* that, by *saying* "I do know it" ' (Wittgenstein 1969: §521, *my italics*).

A key mistake that Moore makes is thus to respond to the sceptic with contrary assertions, since whatever one's stance as regards the truth of what he says, all should be agreed that his assertions are conversationally inappropriate. The neo-Moorean view should thus differ from the Moorean view in at least this respect.[19]

Moreover, given the commitment principle, it follows that neither should Moore respond to the sceptical argument by *reversing* his assertion—i.e. by claiming that he does *not* know that he has two hands, which is what the attributer contextualist would recommend—since he is still committed to holding that he has this knowledge in this new conversational context. Rather, the shifting evidential demands on assertion mean that he should retain this commitment but do so only tacitly in order to avoid making an assertion that generates false conversational implicatures.

Similar remarks will apply to assertions of third-person ascription sentences. Since these assertions are also logically stronger than assertions of simple self-ascription sentences, the evidential demands incurred will be greater, as, accordingly, will be the tendency for these assertions to be conversationally inappropriate because the agent lacks the required grounds to back up the assertion. In conversational contexts in which an assertion of 'P' is conversationally inappropriate, an assertion of 'S knows that P' will, a fortiori, also be conversationally inappropriate. Furthermore, that agents should not assert such third-person ascription sentences in sceptical conversational contexts does not mean that they should assert the contrary sentence (i.e. that 'S does *not* know P'), which is what the contextualist recommends. In asserting the third-person ascription sentence they incur a commitment to the proposition expressed which should survive a mere change in the conversational context.[20]

Indeed, this feature of the pragmatic constraints on assertions of third-person ascription sentences also accounts for one of the key claims that we saw motivating infallibilism above, which was David Lewis's contention that it seems incoherent to ascribe knowledge to an agent whilst explicitly mentioning an error-possibility that the agent is unable to know is false. On this view, such assertions seem incoherent because by making an error-possibility explicit in a conversational context one is thereby altering the evidential constraints on proper assertion so that an assertion of a third-person ascription sentence in that context will tend to generate the conversational implicature that the agent in question knows that the error-possibility in question is false. It is little wonder then that such assertions sound incoherent, since the agent making the assertion is raising the evidential constraints on assertion of the relevant third-person ascription sentence in such a way as to make the assertion in question conversationally inappropriate whilst simultaneously making that assertion. So once one makes the pragmatic constraints on assertions of ascription sentences explicit, the conversational impropriety of such assertions gives us no overriding reason to think that knowledge must be understood along infallibilist lines as being inconsistent with the possibility of *any* error.[21]

3.4. Claiming Knowledge and the Externalism–Internalism Distinction

So far we have seen that there are reasons for preferring a pragmatic account of the shifting-propriety conditions for assertions of ascription sentences over a contextualist account. That this is so, however, only lends support to a non-contextualism (an 'invariantism') of some sort, it does not thereby lend support to a *neo-Moorean* version of this invariantism, one that has antisceptical implications. In particular, the natural question to ask at this juncture is why we shouldn't adopt a *sceptical* version of invariantism, one that explains our apparent willingness to assert ascription sentences in terms of the propriety, but not the truth, of those assertions (for example, the kind of account that we saw Unger arguing for above). In terms of the linguistic data alone, this issue will be underdetermined, although our intuitions will inevitably be on the side of an antisceptical version of invariantism because scepticism generates such counter-intuitive consequences. Nevertheless, once one factors-in the kinds of theoretical claims that we have argued for so far, then an antisceptical neo-Moorean version of invariantism does have significant advantages over its sceptical invariantist rival.

Recall that we are accepting epistemological externalism here, the view standardly endorsed by neo-Mooreans, Dretskeans, and attributer contextualists alike. With this in mind, it is significant that there is a close correlation between the propriety conditions for knowledge claims and the possession conditions for knowledge imposed by the internalist. This is because the evidential constraint on proper assertion will demand that, *ceteris paribus*, in order to properly claim to know a proposition (especially where this is done via the assertion of an explicit self-ascription sentence), one should be able to offer adequate evidence in support of one's assertion. If one is able to do this, then such evidence must be reflectively available to one, and this would tend to indicate that one thereby has an internalist justification for what one believes. Accordingly, since internalist knowledge is defined as knowledge that has met an internalist justification condition, where one does properly and truly claim to know a proposition one will also tend to have specifically internalist knowledge of the proposition claimed. Indeed, given that we have noted that agents need to be able to offer supporting evidence not only for the proposition asserted but also, in the cases of assertions of third-person ascription sentences, for the proposition embedded in that assertion, this will imply that in those cases where the agent speaks properly and truly she will tend to have met the internalist rubric not only for the proposition asserted but also for the embedded proposition. For example, an agent's proper and true assertion of 'John knows that he is in his study' will tend to imply not only that she has internalist knowledge of the 'complex' proposition asserted, but also that she has internalist knowledge of the embedded 'simple' proposition (that John is in his study).[22]

In general, one can put the point here more specifically by saying that meeting the evidential constraint in such a way that one is able to properly assert an ascription sentence will tend to imply that one is internalistically justified in believing the proposition which one asserts (and the embedded proposition, in the case of third-person ascription sentences). Accordingly, since internalist justification is a necessary condition for knowledge by the lights of the internalist rubric, it follows that there will be a close connection between meeting the propriety conditions for knowledge claims and meeting the internalist possession conditions for knowledge such that in so far as an agent has met the former conditions, then she will tend to also meet the latter conditions and, a fortiori, in so far as the agent has met the latter conditions, then she will tend to also meet the former conditions. On the internalist account of knowledge, then, that an agent is unable to properly claim to know a proposition would be a good indication that the agent lacks the knowledge in question.

In contrast, this will not be the case in light of the externalist account of knowledge, since on this view an agent could have knowledge without meeting a justification condition and therefore without, *ceteris paribus*, being able to meet the evidential constraint on proper assertion of self-ascription sentences. Indeed, the paradigm case of 'mere' externalist knowledge that we noted above—the chicken-sexer—would be a situation in which the agent concerned has knowledge in light of the externalist rubric and yet cannot properly claim to have that knowledge (whether via an explicit self-ascription sentence or otherwise) because she lacks the necessary reflectively accessible grounds to back up that assertion.

Externalists will thus be suspicious of drawing any strong conclusions about whether or not an agent has knowledge from the fact that the agent is unable to properly claim that knowledge. Indeed, a partial diagnosis of the prima facie attractiveness of scepticism is now available to the externalist on the grounds that scepticism *seems* intuitive because it focuses upon the denials of radical a sceptical hypotheses, which we can't claim to know, and thereby takes us in to sceptical conversational context where all our claims to know are conversationally inappropriate. That such claims to know are conversationally inappropriate need not indicate that we lack the knowledge in question, however, and since the externalist has an account of knowledge available that can explain how knowledge is possible (i.e. the safety-based account employed by the neo-Moorean), they are therefore in a position to 'explain away' these sceptical intuitions.

This point also has important ramifications for how we assess the adequacy of the externalist antisceptical theories that are competing with the neo-Moorean account—the Dretskean and contextualist views. Take the Dretskean view first. We saw earlier that when it comes to evaluating whether or not agents have knowledge of antisceptical propositions—whether this be the denial of a radical sceptical hypothesis, such as the BIV hypothesis, or a local sceptical hypothesis, such that the zebra before one is not a cleverly disguised mule—Dretske's focus was on the issue of whether the agent concerned could properly claim to know this proposition. But this shouldn't be relevant on the externalist account since of course agents can't claim to know such propositions, especially if, as with the zebra case, the agent is in a conversational context where the evidential demands on proper assertion have been raised by the introduction of a new error-possibility. In general, externalists should not be persuaded purely by the fact that it is never conversationally appropriate to claim knowledge of the denials of sceptical hypotheses that such knowledge is never possessed.

By paying close attention to the gap between the propriety conditions for knowledge claims and the possession conditions for knowledge on the externalist account, neo-Mooreans can thus diagnose part of the attraction behind the intuition that we lack knowledge of the denials of sceptical hypotheses, and thus also the related Dretskean intuition that closure must be rejected. The problem arises from a failure to distinguish between what we know and what we can properly claim to know, a distinction that is very important on the externalist theory of knowledge.

This point also impacts on the attributer contextualist account since as we have seen above they seem to move too quickly from the claim that agents are unable to properly assert certain self-ascription sentences in certain conversational contexts to the claim that these assertions express falsehoods in that context, even though assertions of the same sentences in other conversational contexts expressed truths. On the externalist view, it is far more plausible to suppose that what it is appropriate to say about the epistemic status of one's beliefs can be very different from what that epistemic status is, such that a claim to know, whilst expressing a truth in all conversational contexts, will be conversationally inappropriate in some of them for purely pragmatic reasons. Accordingly, one should be suspicious of the general contextualist line in this respect. That we cannot say that we know that we are not BIVs does not mean that, in this conversational context, such an assertion is no longer true, but only that in making such an assertion we raise the conversational standards in such a way that this assertion, whilst still true, is no longer conversationally appropriate.

Putting these points together implies that perhaps some of our ambivalence towards the epistemic luck platitude—i.e. the fact that we sometimes understand it very strongly so that it excludes any degree of epistemic luck, and yet we sometimes also understand it concessively such that it allows a significant degree of epistemic luck—might be due to how the extent to which we want our knowledge to be immune to epistemic luck depends upon the kind of knowledge that we have in mind. If, for example, it is mere externalist knowledge that is in question, then our inclination is to be relatively permissive as regards epistemic luck. Alternatively, however, if it is the kind of internalist knowledge that is being put to use in a conversational context (especially in the dialectical fashion that Moore tries to employ his 'knowledge') then our inclination to be permissive in this fashion dwindles. Moreover, it dwindles depending upon the epistemic standards at issue in that conversational context, where these epistemic standards are in turn dictated by the shifting evidential demands on proper assertion.

As we will see in Part 2, this picture of how our understanding of the epistemic luck platitude varies in response to the kinds of knowledge that we are interested in in different contexts is not quite right. Nevertheless, it contains within it an important truth.

3.5. The Structure of Reasons

Given the close relationship between the propriety conditions for proper knowledge claims and the internalist conditions for knowledge possession, it should be unsurprising that this point about epistemological externalism dovetails with the claim made earlier regarding the distinction between internalist closure and closure *simpliciter*. Recall that we observed that it does not follow from the fact that agents who are able to meet the internalist conditions for knowledge as regards an everyday proposition are unable to meet the internalist conditions for knowledge as regards a known to be entailed antisceptical proposition that closure must fail, since all that directly follows from this is the failure of an internalized version of closure. This has ramifications for the propriety of knowledge claims, in that an agent might meet the relevant internal epistemic condition as regards one proposition in such a way as to be in a position to properly claim to know that proposition, might know that this proposition entails a second proposition, and yet fail to be in a position to properly claim to know the entailed proposition because she is unable to meet an internal epistemic condition as regards this entailed proposition in such a way as to be in a position to properly claim to know it. We thus get what we might loosely call a failure of closure for the propriety of knowledge claims.

The Moorean argument is not an instance of this sort of failure of closure because, as we saw above, Moore cannot even properly claim to know the antecedent proposition that he knows he has two hands. Nevertheless, there are such arguments available that exemplify this phenomenon which employ everyday but non-hinge propositions as antecedents and antisceptical propositions as consequents. A possible example might be an assertion of the self-ascription sentence 'I'm wearing my black shoes today', which could clearly be properly claimed in the appropriate circumstances (the same goes for the corresponding explicit self-ascription sentence 'I know that I'm wearing my black shoes today'). The proposition expressed by this sentence clearly entails (and is typically known to entail), however, the falsity of the BIV sceptical hypothesis, and yet it would be conversationally inappropriate to assert a self-ascription sentence (especially an explicit self-ascription sentence) regarding this antisceptical proposition.

This has important consequences for how we understand arguments. After all, the argument in question here is entirely valid (even when the premises and the conclusion are supplemented with the knowledge operator), and yet one cannot properly argue for the conclusion on the basis of the premises without making an assertion that is conversationally improper. The failure of internalist closure—and the related failure of closure for the propriety of knowledge claims—indicates that we need to distinguish between a conclusion which is entailed by a valid argument and a conclusion that one can actually *argue for* via a valid argument. It seems that an 'argument' can meet the first conception of an argument without thereby meeting the second.

Often this contrast is put in terms of how certain arguments, whilst valid, are nevertheless in some sense 'question-begging' and therefore cannot be thought to be able to persuade anyone of the conclusion. For example, Crispin Wright has expressed this contrast in terms of the distinction between what he calls 'transmission' and closure. Transmission is held to be a stronger principle because it makes the extra demand that the knowledge that transfers across the known entailment should also preserve what Wright refers to as the 'cogency' of the argument, which is its aptitude to produce *rational conviction*.[23] Here is Wright: 'A *cogent* argument is one whereby someone could be moved to rational conviction of the truth of its conclusion' (Wright 2000: 140).

This distinction certainly seems to be applicable to the cases that we are interested in. One could not hope to persuade someone of the truth of the claim that one is not a BIV via one's assertions (even if they are true) of the premises that one knows that one is wearing black shoes and one knows that this entails that one must not be a BIV. This indicates something important about the structure of reasons that has ramifications for the dialectical use that we can make of valid arguments. On the neo-Moorean account, if one is able to know that one is currently wearing black shoes (and the relevant entailment), then one is able to know that one is not a BIV, but this does not mean that one can properly argue for that conclusion on that basis. The reasons that one has for one's beliefs in everyday propositions which enable one to have internalist justification for (and thus internalist knowledge of) them—and which enable one to make proper assertions of them—do not transfer across known entailments to being grounds in support of one's beliefs in what is entailed by those propositions where the entailed propositions are the denials of sceptical hypotheses. Scepticism may be false in the sense that knowledge is possible, but this does not mean that one can *argue* one's way out of the sceptical problem as Moore attempts to do by claiming knowledge of the contested propositions since such claims will always be conversationally inappropriate.

The initial moral that we can draw from our engagement with the sceptical argument is thus that we should recognize this fact about the structure of reasons whilst also noting that an externalist epistemology of a safety-based variety allows knowledge to be consistent with the lack of reasons in such a way that closure is retained and attributer contextualism is avoided. The sceptical puzzle works by drawing us into a very special kind of conversational context and inviting us to respond by making certain knowledge claims. In this context, however, our claims to know are inappropriate because they lack the required evidential support and the sceptic convinces us that our inability to properly claim knowledge in this context indicates that we do not really possess this knowledge after all. The trick is to recognize that one can possess knowledge even without being able to offer grounds, and that therefore one can consistently allow that one's knowledge is not always properly claimable. Moreover, one also needs to realize that the evidential burdens that apply to assertions in sceptical conversational contexts are specific to that context, and thus that our necessarily mute response to the sceptic in the specific conversational context that she creates does not entail that assertions of ascription sentences are *always* conversationally inappropriate, in *all* conversational contexts. This at any rate is the neo-Moorean way of responding to the sceptical argument.[24]

3.6. Concluding Remarks

In this chapter we have seen that of the three dominant antisceptical arguments that have been put forward in the recent literature—the arguments for non-closure, for attributer contextualism, and for neo-Mooreanism—the neo-Moorean line is the most plausible. The reason for this is that it is the only antisceptical thesis that is consistently epistemologically externalist in its motivation, and so avoids the problems regarding the diverse motivation of the other two theories. We have also noted that the non-dialectical aspect of the neo-Moorean strategy which distinguishes it from its Moorean counterpart is grounded in a conception of the structure of reasons and of the pragmatics of assertion which further favours the neo-Moorean account over its main rival antisceptical theories. As we will see in the next chapter, however, the advantages that neo-Mooreanism holds over its competitor views are little cause for celebration once one considers that there is something inherently problematic about all epistemologically externalist responses to scepticism. Moreover, as we will discover in Part II, the reason why such antisceptical strategies do not get to grips with the sceptical problem is because of a failure to understand the sense in which the problem of scepticism is ultimately concerned with a specific variety of epistemic luck.

Notes

1. Recall that externalists can consistently allow that some knowledge is internalist knowledge (i.e. knowledge which meets the relevant internalist epistemic conditions). What they deny is only that *all* knowledge is internalist knowledge.
2. Of course, as with sensitivity, this principle will need to be complicated in a number of ways if it is to avoid being subject to some fairly straightforward counter-examples. In particular, in common with sensitivity, it will be necessary to adduce some sort of condition that indexes the agent's belief to the manner in which the agent forms her belief in the actual world. We will set these complications aside for now (the safety principle is discussed further in Part II). Principles of this sort have been proposed by Sosa (1999, 2000, 2002), Sainsbury (1997), and Williamson (2000a, 2000c: ch. 8). I outline some of the antisceptical advantages of a safety-based approach to knowledge in Pritchard (2002d). Black (2002; cf. Williams 1991: ch. 8) offers an account of Nozick's counterfactual conditions on knowledge that ends up construing them much like the safety principle. For three recent, and critical, discussions of the safety principle, see DeRose (2002b), Greco (2002), and Kvanvig (2004).
3. For further discussion of examples of this sort, see Heller (1999b) and Pritchard (2003c).
4. As we will see in Part II, there are good grounds available for thinking that the notion of reliability at issue in reliabilist theories of knowledge is best understood in terms of the safety principle.
5. The relationship between the safety and the sensitivity principle is further explored below in §6.3.
6. It is, of course, an interesting question whether rational agents have to believe such antisceptical propositions, or whether they could genuinely and rationally believe otherwise. The crux of the matter in this respect is, I take it, the issue of just what it is that gives rise to such a belief, especially since these beliefs are not adequately grounded by an internalist justification. I return to consider this issue in Part II.
7. I develop this point in more detail in Pritchard (2002b). Note that all I am defending here are *sceptical* and *antisceptical* closure-type inferences, rather than closure *simpliciter*. Whilst I think that a safety-based view can be made consistent with closure, as it stands there are potential counter-examples that can be generated, albeit not ones that will have any effect on the use of closure in the sceptical debate. We will return to consider some potential counter-examples to closure on the safety-based account in §6.3.
8. I discuss this point, including the issue of just what epistemological internalism about knowledge demands in this regard, in more detail below.
9. The more radical conception of assertion—the so-called 'knowledge' account of assertion—is these days most often associated with the work of Williamson (1996b, 2000c: ch. 11). Williamson cites Unger (1975: 250–65) and Slote (1979) as offering earlier (and slightly qualified) versions of this view.
10. This is perhaps a broader construal of conversational implicature than that offered by Grice himself since he tended to reserve the notion for those implicatures that were not trivially generated by the cooperative principle and the associated conversational maxims. See, e.g., Grice (1989: 41–2), although his position in this regard wasn't always consistent. A related issue here is that a conversational implicature can always be 'cancelled' by the agent making the assertion offering some sort of explicit disclaimer or *caveat*. It should be noted, however, that whilst non-trivial conversational implicatures

can usually be cancelled quite comfortably, conversational implicatures that are more directly inferred from the assertion are not so easily cancelled. Since I work with the broader conception of implicature here, I will thus not take the issue of whether a putative conversational implicature can be comfortably cancelled as determining whether or not it is a genuine conversational implicature, as some commentators do. I am not alone in this with even Grice (1989: 46) allowing certain conversational implicatures to be bona fide conversational implicatures even though they cannot be comfortably cancelled. For further discussion of this point, see DeRose and Grandy (1999: notes 13 & 19) and Rysiew (2001: §7).

11. The commitment principle is closely bound up with the conversational maxim that one should only assert what one believes to be true (though note that, for Grice (1989: 26), this maxim is understood as the slightly weaker 'Do not say what you believe to be false'). Since believing that P is itself a form of commitment to P—and moreover a commitment which, if genuine at all, is not easily lost—then arguably one could just as well focus on the close relationship between belief and assertion. Indeed, in a recent book, Williams (2002: ch. 4) has argued that the close ties between belief, truth, and the role of assertion ensure that something like the commitment principle must hold. See especially, Williams (2002: 80–1). For another influential, and recent, discussion of this general commitment that is incurred by assertion, see Brandom (1994: ch. 4; cf. Brandom 1995).

12. DeRose is one contextualist who is aware of this difficulty, which he labels the 'Generality Problem'. His response is to tie contextualism to the Williamsonian account of assertion which holds that in asserting that P one represents oneself as knowing P (such that one should only assert that P if one knows that P—the so-called 'knowledge rule' for assertion). As a result, he can explain the shifting propriety conditions of assertions of simple self-ascription sentences in terms of how agents implicitly recognize that they lack their erstwhile knowledge of the relevant proposition in sceptical conversational contexts. Although this is an ingenious suggestion, it does face the problem that the correctness of the controversial attributer contextualist thesis now hinges on an equally controversial thesis about assertion. After all, as we have just seen, there is a Gricean account of assertion available that is not committed to so strong a thesis about assertion but which is nevertheless consistent with the intuition that we typically convey knowledge via assertions of 'simple' sentences, such as 'P'. Moreover, as we will see below, epistemic externalists, like DeRose (and Williamson as well, as it happens), are committed to allowing cases in which an agent possesses knowledge but where she cannot properly claim that knowledge. Since DeRose also holds that the knowledge rule is the only rule governing how well positioned one must be in order to properly assert a proposition, it is not obvious how he is going to deal with such cases whilst retaining his externalism. Moreover, if the further considerations that DeRose adduces to account for these cases are of a broadly Gricean type then this will inevitably weaken the appeal of the view relative to the Gricean alternative. For DeRose's key discussion of the Generality Problem, see DeRose (2002a; cf. DeRose 1996). DeRose further considers the issue of whether there is an alternative non-contextualist pragmatic explanation of the linguistic data available in DeRose (1999: §§8–11). I discuss DeRose's proposal at length in Pritchard (2005a). For further discussions of DeRose's proposal, see Rysiew (2001), Bach (2004), and Brown (2005).

13. I comment further on this point as it relates to third-person ascription sentences below. One finds this claim about how assertions of explicit self-ascription sentences raise the

evidential stakes in a number of writers. Wittgenstein (1969: §591) notes that one will say 'I know' if '. . . one wants especially to emphasize certainty; perhaps to anticipate being contradicted.' He goes on, '. . . one might begin with the observation "that's a . . . ", and then, when this is contradicted, counter by saying: "I know . . . ", and by this means lay emphasis on being sure.' Elsewhere he writes: 'One says "I know" when one is ready to give compelling grounds. "I know" relates to a possibility of demonstrating the truth' (Wittgenstein 1969: §243).

This contention is echoed by Austin. Consider, for example, the following passages:

> When I say, 'I know', I give others my word: I *give* others *my authority for saying* that 'S is P'. . . .
>
> 'If you say you know something, the most immediate challenge takes the form of asking, 'Are you in a position to know?': that is, you must undertake to show not merely that you are sure of it, but that it is within your cognisance.' (Austin 1961: 99–100, *italics in the original*)

See also, Ayer (1956: ch. 1). It should be noted, however, that for Austin the evidential demands on assertion are not simply raised as one moves from an assertion that P to an assertion that one knows that P. Instead, he argues that a claim to know P is, in this respect, different in *kind* from the weaker assertion that P. For more on this point, see Austin (1961). For an excellent overview of Austin's position as regards knowledge (and much more besides), see Travis (2005).

14. I develop these points in more detail in Pritchard (2005*a*).
15. As I discuss in a moment, it is actually difficult to imagine a conversational context in which an agent could coherently assert an everyday proposition like this, but we will let this issue pass for now.
16. Indeed, the situation for the contextualist is even worse once one starts to factor-in further elements of the pragmatic story to explain why, apparently, agents might be inclined to reverse their assertions of ascription sentences in response to mere changes in the conversational context. Since an *impasse* will suffice for my purposes here, however, I won't explore this possibility further.
17. There is actually a further complication when it comes to the external world sceptical hypothesis, which is that it is far from obvious that the sentence 'There is an external world' expresses a proposition at all (more specifically, it does not seem to be a *fact-stating* proposition). This certainly seemed to be Wittgenstein's view. For our purposes, however, we can just treat this sentence as representative of the denials of sceptical hypotheses in general, since most of the sentences which express these denials *will* be fact-stating. For more on Wittgenstein's treatment of scepticism about the external world, see Williams (2003*b*).
18. Consider the following passage:

> . . . the *questions* that we raise and our *doubts* depend upon the fact that some propositions are exempt from doubt, are as it were like hinges on which those turn.
>
> That is to say, it belongs to the logic of our scientific investigations that certain things are *in deed* not doubted.
>
> But it isn't that the situation is like this: We just *can't* investigate everything, and for that reason we are forced to rest content with assumption. If I want the door to turn, the hinges must stay put. (Wittgenstein 1969: §§341–3)

Although the 'hinge' metaphor is the dominant symbolism in *On Certainty*, it is accompanied by various other metaphors such as the following: that these propositions constitute the 'scaffolding' of our thoughts (§211); that they form the 'foundations of our language-games' (§§401–3); and also that they represent the implicit 'world-picture' from within which we inquire, the 'inherited background against which [*we*] distinguish between true and false' (§§94–5). For two of the key recent discussions of Wittgenstein's account of hinge propositions, see Wright (2003*b*; cf. Wright 1985, 1991, 2004) and Williams (2003*b*; cf. Williams 1991). I critically contrast these two readings of the hinge proposition thesis in Pritchard (2005*e*).

19. I am not here suggesting that we should interpret Wittgenstein's *On Certainty* along neo-Moorean lines, though I do think that there are echoes of such a view in this text. Indeed, given that *On Certainty* is merely a series of unedited notes on the subject of knowledge and certainty, it would be problematic, I think, to argue that *any* consistent interpretation of this text is available. Nevertheless, it should be noted that most attempts at an interpretation of Wittgenstein's remarks in this respect do not offer a neo-Moorean reading.

20. Brandom (1994: ch. 4) puts the point about the greater evidential demands involved in asserting explicit self-ascription sentences and asserting third-person ascription sentences in terms of the interplay between the agent's commitments and her 'entitlements' (which in this context roughly corresponds to the evidential constraints on assertion). He notes that in claiming knowledge one incurs a commitment to the proposition claimed as known and represents oneself as being entitled to this commitment. Similarly, the ascription of knowledge to others not only implies that one has a commitment and an entitlement to the proposition expressed, but also that the agent concerned has a commitment and a corresponding entitlement to the known proposition.

21. This point highlights the issue of how on a broad sense of 'conversational implicature' an implicature cannot always be comfortably cancelled. As noted above (in note 10), when it comes to conversational implicatures that follow very directly from the assertion in question, the attempt to cancel those implicatures raises the issue of why the original assertion was ever made in the first place. In terms of the example that Lewis offers of an agent asserting the sentence 'S knows that P, but cannot eliminate a specific possibility in which not-P', if this unelimated error-possibility is here relevant to whether or not we should assert that the agent in question has knowledge, then why say that she has knowledge at all?

22. Or at least, it will imply that she has knowledge of the embedded proposition *under that description*. This qualification is important because of locutions such as 'John knows that the third sentence on the page before him expresses a truth'. Clearly, demanding that the agent who properly makes this assertion internalistically knows that the embedded proposition, under that description, is true, is very different from demanding that the agent internalistically knows this proposition under a different description. After all, the agent might not know which sentence is being referred to in this embedded proposition.

23. Elsewhere, Wright (e.g. 1985, 2002) uses the term 'transmission' in a more specific sense to indicate that the warrant that supports the conclusion of the argument is the very same warrant that supports the premises. This is because he thinks that this way of understanding the notion explains why some arguments preserve cogency whilst others merely preserve knowledge or truth. Our interest here, however, is the more general understanding of transmission rather than this specific rendering. For some of the key recent discussions on Wright's distinction between closure and transmission, see Nuccetelli (2003) and the exchange between Davies (2004) and Wright (2004). I discuss this contrast at length in Pritchard (2002*a*, 2005*e*).

24. I develop the neo-Moorean strategy in a number of articles. For an overview of the position, see Pritchard (2002*d*, 2002*c*: §8). I argue that one can reinterpret DeRose's version of attributer contextualism as a pragmatic thesis that can accommodate some of the key neo-Moorean intuitions in Pritchard (2001*a*). See also Pritchard (2004*d*, 2005*b*) in which I critically contrast neo-Mooreanism with contextualism more generally. I argue that the neo-Moorean distinction between internalist closure and closure *simpliciter* can accommodate the distinction between transmission and closure in Pritchard (2002*a*). Finally, in Pritchard (2001*c*), I show how one can interpret Wittgenstein's *On Certainty* along lines that are broadly compatible with the neo-Moorean strategy, and indicate how this interpretation can accommodate certain features of the kind of contextualism advocated in Williams (1991). Whilst other commentators, most notably Sosa (1999), Black (2002), and Greco (2003), have also described their position as Moorean, none of them has offered the theoretical support that is needed for a thesis of this sort. Instead, the claim is simply that there is a plausible counterfactual analysis of knowledge available that is consistent with the possession of knowledge of the denials of sceptical hypotheses (and which is thus consistent with closure without requiring attributer contextualism).

4

The Source of Scepticism

4.0. Introduction

In the last two chapters we have seen how the neo-Moorean response to the sceptic is the most plausible of the three main antisceptical theses in the contemporary literature, and that the reason why this is so is because it is the only one of the three theses that presents a consistent epistemologically externalist response to scepticism. In this chapter we will be using the relative success of the neo-Moorean account in this respect to highlight that there is something problematic about *any* epistemologically externalist response to scepticism. The way this will be done is by comparing the closure-based template sceptical argument that we considered in Chapter 1 with an alternative sceptical argument that is based on the so-called 'underdetermination' principle. As we will see, the closure-based argument, far from displaying the underlying logical structure of the sceptical argument, in fact disguises the true source of scepticism. As we will discover in Part II, once the core motivation for scepticism is properly understood it becomes apparent that it is concerned with a very specific problem regarding epistemic luck.

4.1. Disillusionment

So far we have witnessed the success of the neo-Moorean antisceptical strategy relative to its two main competitor theses—the Dretskean account which denies closure and attributer contextualism. It is important to remember, however, that the cogency of the neo-Moorean strategy in this respect is dependent upon the acceptability of epistemic externalism (or at least externalism of this form), not only as a general epistemological thesis, but more specifically as a thesis that can be effectively employed in a response to scepticism. We haven't as yet considered any arguments in defence of employing externalism in a response to scepticism, except the purely negative argument that, unlike epistemological internalism, externalism does at least seem to offer us the *possibility* of blocking the sceptical argument. We will return to the issue of whether one can appropriately employ externalism in a response to scepticism in a moment. First, we will reconsider some of the considerations that have been offered so far in favour of the plausibility of an externalist theory of knowledge in general.

There are two types of support that have been offered for epistemological externalism. The first concerns cases (contentious though they are) of 'chicken-sexer' type examples where it seems appropriate to ascribe knowledge to the agent even though that agent has failed to meet the relevant internal epistemic condition. A second and related consideration in favour of externalism is that we have noted that we sometimes allow that agents can possess knowledge even though they are unable to properly claim that knowledge. Again, 'chicken-sexer' type cases are the obvious examples in this respect. Given the close correlation that we have observed between meeting the constraints on proper assertion and meeting the epistemic conditions imposed by the internalist, this presents us with prima facie grounds for thinking that sometimes knowledge is possessed even though the agent concerned has not met an internal epistemic condition.

Indeed, the grounds presented in favour of epistemological externalism by these two considerations are mutually supporting. On the one hand, we can explain a possible reluctance to consider the chicken-sexer as possessing knowledge in terms of how we would think it inappropriate for her to claim to possess that knowledge. On the other, we can explain certain cases in which agents cannot properly claim knowledge but where we would be happy to ascribe that knowledge to them in terms of how the agent's belief has merely met the kinds of external epistemic conditions that the chicken-sexer's belief has met.

We might also add a third element of support to the externalist epistemological thesis in that endorsing externalism (at least of a certain form) seems to enable us to meet the sceptical puzzle, and this is certainly positive grounds in favour of the thesis given the counter-intuitiveness of the sceptical conclusion (although, as noted above, this consideration doesn't offer us much in the way of support for the more specific thesis that externalism can be an appropriate part of an *antisceptical* theory of knowledge). Relatedly, we might also add that externalism does seem to offer us at least one way of responding to the epistemic luck platitude that we identified in Chapter 1 in that a belief that meets an external epistemic condition—such as, in this case, the safety principle—is not obviously a belief the truth of which is lucky (though we shall look more deeply into this claim in Part 2). If the sceptical problem arises from the intuition that the truth of even our most certain beliefs is in an important sense epistemically lucky, then externalism seems to offer a prima facie case for responding to that problem. And given that we have seen that the neo-Moorean proposal is the most coherent and least revisionistic externalist antisceptical thesis on offer, then any grounds available in support of epistemic externalism will in this regard be grounds in favour of neo-Mooreanism.

Nevertheless, one might feel a certain sense of disillusionment with the neo-Moorean reply to the sceptic, and I think that such a response would be entirely reasonable. This is because we began by considering how scepticism attacks our sense that our epistemic relationship to the world is as secure as we suppose it to be, and yet this particular 'resolution' of the sceptical problem does not appear to return us back to our state of innocence in which we took it for granted that we knew more or less what we took ourselves to know.

This disillusionment is closely related to the externalist element of the neo-Moorean response to scepticism. Consider again how the sceptical problem emerges in the contemporary debate. We begin by noticing that there are indistinguishable sceptical error-possibilities that we cannot discount, and then realize that this appears to undermine our knowledge of even everyday propositions. Ideally, we would like to discover some account of knowledge which could explain how we can nevertheless retain our knowledge of everyday propositions and this seems to demand that we are able to discount the sceptical error-possibilities after all (i.e. know them to be false). Epistemological internalism is no help to us in this regard, since it is unable to accommodate any sense in which we might know the denials of sceptical hypotheses. It thus leaves us, at best, with a situation in which we are putatively able to know everyday propositions even whilst lacking knowledge of the denials of sceptical hypotheses, and there is small comfort in that. Externalist responses that deny closure are subject to the same fate, and adopting attributer contextualism merely heightens the sense of epistemic contingency in play here because it makes knowledge possession far too dependent on the arbitrary epistemic standards employed by the attributer.

This leaves us with neo-Mooreanism. One might think that neo-Mooreanism has one major advantage over all the other views in that it *can* allow that we do indeed (unrestrictedly) know the denials of sceptical hypotheses after all, at least in so far as we know everyday propositions. And wasn't that the ideal solution to the problem that we desired?

The problem is, however, that the kind of knowledge of the denials of sceptical hypotheses that is being rescued from the sceptic's grasp is very different from the knowledge that we originally sought. Furthermore, since our knowledge of everyday propositions presupposes this antisceptical knowledge, this also impacts on our knowledge of everyday propositions as well. The problem is that our knowledge of the denials of sceptical hypotheses on the neo-Moorean account is not only externalist but is, more specifically, externalist in a very peculiar and 'brute' fashion which is never accompanied by an internalist justification.

To begin with, note that unlike many other forms of externalist knowledge (such as that putatively possessed by the chicken-sexer), this particular sort of externalist knowledge admits of *no* adequate reflectively accessible grounding since, *ex hypothesi*, grounds of this sort are lacking when it comes to belief in propositions such as these. Whereas chicken-sexers are only *incidentally* lacking in reflectively accessible grounds for their beliefs, in that they could acquire such grounds if need be, the lack of evidential grounds in favour of our belief in the denials of sceptical hypotheses is a matter of principle. Unlike the chicken-sexer, there is *nothing* that we could do to improve our epistemic position in this respect. What we have here, then, is more than just the usual externalist knowledge where the agent has not, as it happens, met an internal epistemic condition; it is rather 'pure' externalist knowledge. Indeed, since this knowledge cannot be the result of an entirely empirical process (again, unlike the chicken-sexer's knowledge), there has been a certain amount of debate about just how we can make sense of it at all without granting it an oddly a priori status (as we saw above, some attributer contextualists have bitten the bullet on this point and simply argued that it is a priori knowledge).

Indeed, what precedents there are for this sort of (non-a priori) knowledge are not encouraging. For in so far as we can make sense of this sort of knowledge at all, then we need to understand it along the lines of the kind of 'brute' knowledge that we ascribe to 'agents' (the reason for the scare quotes will become apparent in a moment) who are *in principle* unable to offer the reflective grounds necessary for meeting the internalist condition on internalist knowledge. Small children are the obvious example in this respect, since we do have a practice of ascribing, for instance, very basic perceptual knowledge to young children even though we grant that they are not in a position to offer anything like sufficient reflectively accessible grounds in support of that knowledge (and, accordingly, we would thus regard any claim to know on their part as being improper). Some higher-order mammals—such as clever chimpanzees—are another possible example in this respect.

The problem with this parallel with the basic perceptual belief of 'brutes', however, is that, whilst it does lend independent support to the idea that such antisceptical knowledge is possible, it does so at the expense of highlighting just how controversial and basic this 'knowledge' is. For one thing, many find ascriptions of knowledge to small children (let alone animals) on externalist grounds as being, if anything, a *reductio* of the position. But even if one is willing to grant that such knowledge is possible, the worry remains that it is of a mere 'brute' variety. Could we really answer the sceptic by offering knowledge of this sort? This worry is accentuated once one reflects that whilst small children can develop their reflective capacities and come to offer the kind of reflective support for their perceptual beliefs that they erstwhile lacked (if only in principle), there is no possible incremental improvement in our reflective capacities that would enable us to have internalist knowledge of the denials of sceptical hypotheses. We are thus forever trapped in an 'infantile' epistemic state as regards these propositions.[1]

The real force of this concern is brought to the fore once one reflects on the second key feature of the neo-Moorean view, which is the manner in which it allows our internalist knowledge to be dependent upon this special variety of externalist knowledge. This result was achieved by denying internalist closure whilst keeping closure itself intact. This ensured that, provided agents did indeed have externalist knowledge of the denials of sceptical hypotheses, then there was no in principle problem with them having internalist knowledge of everyday propositions as well. As we saw, this is a coherent position for an externalist to hold, but, again, it is a position that undermines the ultimate antisceptical appeal of the view. For of what use is it to rescue in principle internalist knowledge of everyday propositions if it is still reflectively inaccessible to us whether or not we have externalist knowledge of the denials of sceptical hypotheses, and thus whether one of the key preconditions for such internalist knowledge has obtained?

It is important to emphasize here that the point is *not* that the neo-Moorean position is an inadequate response to the closure-based sceptical argument that we saw above, since nothing that I have just said weakens the contention made in the previous sections that this view is the best antisceptical thesis available to respond to this argument. Rather, the point is that the closure-based template sceptical argument does not seem to be the right way to capture what is most fundamentally at issue in the sceptical argument in the first place. What the success of the neo-Moorean strategy reveals to us is that once one understands scepticism in this way simply in terms of the possibility of knowledge, then externalism ought to be a viable response to scepticism and, in so far as we are entitled to offer an externalist account of knowledge, the fuss about denying closure or adopting attributer contextualism is simply a red herring. That is, the neo-Moorean antisceptical view just *is* what an epistemologically externalist antisceptical response to this construal of the sceptical problem amounts to, with arguments for non-closure and attributer contextualism merely confused expressions of this core idea. Whilst this might be a resolution of the particular formulation of the sceptical argument under consideration here, however, its success merely reveals the inadequacy of understanding the general sceptical puzzle in this closure-based fashion.

In Part 2, I will be explaining exactly how epistemologically externalist antisceptical theories miss the point of scepticism by showing how they respond to the epistemic luck-based challenge posed by the sceptic by eliminating a very different sort of epistemic luck to that which the sceptic has in mind. Before I do that, however, it is first helpful to return to the closure-based formulation of the sceptical argument and identify exactly where it goes wrong as an expression of the sceptical problem.

4.2. Underdetermination and Closure

One might think that the way to recapture what is at issue in the sceptical argument would be to simply rephrase the closure-based template sceptical argument that we considered above so that it was specifically directed at internalist knowledge. We would thus have something like the following:

The template internalist closure-based radical sceptical argument

(C1) If one is to have internalist knowledge of a wide range of everyday propositions, then one must have internalist knowledge of the denials of all radical sceptical hypotheses that one knows to be incompatible with the relevant everyday propositions.

(C2) One cannot have internalist knowledge of the denials of radical sceptical hypotheses.

(CC) One cannot have internalist knowledge of a wide range of everyday propositions.

If this conclusion went through, then it would mean that all of our knowledge, even our knowledge of everyday propositions, would be on a par with our externalist knowledge of the denials of sceptical hypotheses, and thus be of a brute externalist sort. The problem, however, is that we have rejected the closure principle for internalist knowledge on which this argument turns.

Indeed, more specifically, we have rejected the analogue closure principle for internalist justification on which the closure principle for internalist knowledge depends, which can be formulated as follows:

The closure principle for internalist justification
For all S, φ, ψ, if S is internalistically justified in believing φ, and S knows that φ entails ψ, then S is internalistically justified in believing ψ.

That is, we have denied the claim that an internalist justification in one proposition need transfer across a known entailment to be an internalist justification in a known to be entailed proposition, especially when the entailed proposition is the denial of a radical sceptical hypothesis. Accordingly, this argument is blocked by the neo-Moorean response to scepticism just as much as the original template closure-based argument was.

Nevertheless, as we have seen in the previous section, whilst there does not seem to be any direct way to show that the neo-Moorean response to scepticism merely provides us with brute externalist knowledge of everyday propositions, it remains that we have a very strong intuition that this is in fact the case. That is, the manner in which the neo-Moorean strategy allows our knowledge of everyday propositions to rest upon brute externalist knowledge of the denials of sceptical hypotheses strongly suggests that our everyday knowledge can be no better than the brute knowledge that it rests upon. One way in which I think we can begin to express what is at issue here is to move away from the closure-based formulation of the sceptical argument altogether and consider a different formulation of the problem that is based on a different epistemic principle entirely.

Whilst the closure-based version of the sceptical argument has been the accepted interpretation of the sceptical challenge in the recent literature, there have been a few lone voices who have contested its importance to capturing this challenge. In particular, in an influential paper Anthony Brueckner (1994) has argued that one could just as well run the argument in terms of a different epistemic principle which he terms the 'underdetermination' principle, a version of which can plausibly be found in ancient Pyrrhonian sceptical writings.[2] Although he contends that the underdetermination principle and the corresponding closure principle are logically equivalent, he also maintains that the former is more fundamental in the sense that any adequate explanation of why the corresponding closure principle fails need not thereby be an adequate explanation of why the underdetermination principle fails (but that an explanation of why the underdetermination principle is false *would* thereby be an adequate explanation of why the corresponding closure principle is false).

Scepticism

We can characterize the underdetermination principle as follows:

The underdetermination principle
For all S, φ, ψ, if S's evidence for believing φ does not favour φ over some hypothesis ψ that S knows to be incompatible with φ, then S is not internalistically justified in believing φ.[3]

One can see the attraction of this principle and the support that it offers for sceptical arguments. If I am internalistically justified in believing a proposition (say, that I am currently in the town's Odeon cinema), then, intuitively, I must have evidence that prefers this hypothesis over any known to be incompatible hypothesis (such as that I am not in the town's other cinema, the Multiplex). Conversely, if I lack such relative evidential support, then I lack the original internalist justification that I took myself to have.[4] Crucially, however, the sceptic maintains that our evidence is of its nature inconclusive as regards sceptical hypotheses, since there is nothing to tell between the circumstances that I take myself to be in and being, say, a BIV. Accordingly, the sceptic can use the underdetermination principle to argue directly for her radical sceptical doubt as follows:

The template underdetermination-based sceptical argument

(U1) If my evidence does not favour my belief in everyday propositions over the known to be incompatible sceptical hypotheses, then I am not internalistically justified in believing everyday propositions.
(U2) My evidence does not favour my belief in everyday propositions over the known to be incompatible sceptical hypotheses.
(UC) I am not internalistically justified in believing everyday propositions (and thus I lack internalist knowledge of everyday propositions).

And this argument does seem to establish that we lack internalist knowledge even of everyday propositions without making any essential reference to the disputed closure principles for internalist justification and knowledge.

Furthermore, one can see why Brueckner regards the underdetermination-based sceptical argument as capturing what is at issue in the sceptical argument in a way that the internalist closure-based argument does not, since it makes explicit what is only implicit in the closure-based argument. For the point the sceptic makes is not simply that we cannot have internalist knowledge of, or form internalistically justified beliefs in, the denials of sceptical hypotheses (and thus, given closure, that we cannot have internalist knowledge of everyday propositions either), but that the reason for this lack of internalist knowledge is a lack of evidential support for our beliefs in the denials of radical sceptical hypotheses. And if we do lack this evidential support, then how can this not fail to infect the evidential support that we take ourselves to have for everyday propositions as well? It is thus the underdetermination principle that explains what is plausible about the sceptic's use of the closure principle by highlighting the evidential basis of the sceptical argument. Even if the two principles are logically equivalent, then, as Brueckner contends, a diagnosis of what is wrong with scepticism is not thereby given simply by offering a diagnosis of what is wrong with the closure principle for internalist justification or knowledge, or the internalist closure-based sceptical argument. Such an antisceptical strategy must do more, and this means engaging with the underdetermination principle (and thus the underdetermination-based sceptical argument) as well.

We will return to look at the underdetermination principle and the sceptical argument that it supports in more detail in a moment. First, I want to examine Brueckner's claim that the underdetermination principle is equivalent to the closure principle. Since the underdetermination principle is specified in terms of justification, if we are to compare it to the closure principle then the relevant closure principle will be the closure principle for internalist justification outlined above. As we will now see, however, Brueckner is wrong to contend that these two principles are equivalent, since the underdetermination principle is in fact logically weaker than the closure principle for internalist justification.

In order to simplify the discussion here, we will focus on instances of these two principles. We will also take it as given in each case that the entailment in question is known by the agent, and stipulate that the notion of justification at issue is specifically internalist. With this in mind, we can take the following conditional to be a relevant instance of the closure principle for (internalist) justification, where 'E' is the everyday proposition that the agent is presently seated, and 'SH' is a relevant sceptical hypothesis (one that is inconsistent with E, such as the BIV sceptical hypothesis):

(A) If S is justified in believing E, then S is justified in believing $\neg$ SH.

A parallel conditional for the underdetermination principle could then be the following:

If S's evidence does not favour E over SH, then S is not justified in believing E.

Contraposed, this becomes conditional (B):

(B) If S is justified in believing E, then S's evidence favours E over SH.

109

Scepticism

With these two conditionals in mind as representatives of the closure principle for justification and the underdetermination principle, we can assess the logical relationships between the two principles.

First, the putative entailment from the closure principle for justification to the underdetermination principle. We will begin by assuming the common antecedent of conditionals (A) and (B):

(1) S is justified in believing E.

Using conditional (A), we can infer (2):

(2) S is justified in believing ¬ SH.

All one now needs to do is assume the uncontentious principle that the possession of a justification for belief in a proposition entails that you *lack* a justification for belief in the *negation* of that proposition.[5] If that principle is granted, then S's *possession* of a justification for believing that she is *not* the victim of a sceptical hypothesis entails that she *lacks* a justification for believing that she *is* the victim of a sceptical hypothesis:

(3) S is not justified in believing SH.

Since the notion of justification here is specifically internalist, and since one's beliefs in ordinary (non-foundational) empirical propositions on this view need to be evidentially grounded (we will return to consider this claim in more detail below), it follows from the fact that S is justified in believing E—(1)—but is not justified in believing the known to be incompatible sceptical hypothesis—(3)— that S's evidence supports a justification for her belief in E but not for her belief in SH. That is, it supports the conclusion that S's evidence favours the hypothesis E, that she is sitting here now, over the alternative sceptical hypothesis SH. We can thus infer (4):

(4) S's evidence favours E over SH.

From the assumption that S is justified in believing E we can thus infer, using conditional (A) and a further uncontentious principle regarding the notion of justification, that she has evidence which favours E over SH. We are thus entitled to conclude (5):

(5) If S is justified in believing E, then S's evidence favours E over SH.

Crucially, of course, (5) is just the simplified version of the underdetermination principle that we formulated above as conditional (B). Closure for justification thus (relatively) straightforwardly entails the underdetermination principle.

Next, consider the other direction of fit, from the underdetermination principle to the closure principle for justification. This time we will not only make use of the conditional (B), but also (for reasons that will become apparent in a moment) the following conditional, (B*), which is a variation on (B):

(B*) If S is justified in believing SH, then S's evidence favours SH over E.

As before, we will begin by assuming the common antecedent of both (A) and (B):

(1) S is justified in believing E.

Using conditional (B), we can infer (2):

(2) S's evidence favours E over SH.

That S's evidence favours belief in E over SH must entail that her evidence does *not* favour belief in SH over E:

(3) S's evidence does not favour SH over E.

Using conditional (B*), however, we can only conclude from this that S is not justified in believing SH:

(4) S is not justified in believing SH.

This is a much weaker conclusion than the one that we were looking for, however, in that a *lack* of a justification for believing that one is the victim of a sceptical hypothesis is much weaker than the *possession* of a justification for believing the *negation* of this proposition—that one is *not* the victim of a sceptical hypotheses—and it is the latter conclusion that is licensed by the closure principle for justification.[6]

Simply put, given the uncontentious principle employed above that if one is justified in believing a proposition then one is not justified in believing the negation of that proposition, then that one is justified in believing the negation of SH—as the closure principle for justification licenses—entails that one is not justified in believing SH—which is what the underdetermination principle licenses. Crucially, however, it does not follow from the fact that one is not justified in believing SH that one is justified in believing the negation of SH. Indeed, it is entirely possible that one both lacks a justification for believing SH *and* lacks a justification for believing the negation of SH. Accordingly, the closure principle for justification is logically stronger than the underdetermination principle, and thus, *contra* Brueckner, the two principles are not logically equivalent. In short, all the underdetermination principle gets you is relative evidential supremacy when what closure for justification demands is a supremacy of justifications and, pending further argumentation, the latter claim is much stronger than the former.

The importance of this result is that it accounts for why simply denying closure for internalist justification won't suffice to undermine the sceptical contention that an epistemically externalist response to the sceptic will always end up debasing one's everyday knowledge, even in the best case. Perhaps we can make sense of the idea that an internalist justification for believing an everyday proposition can coexist with an inability to possess an internalist justification for believing the denial of a sceptical hypothesis which one knows is entailed by the everyday proposition, but this doesn't alter the fact that such a justification must coexist with one's evidence failing to prefer the everyday belief over belief in known sceptical alternatives. It is only if one can make sense of this further claim—that, *contra* the underdetermination principle, one can be internalistically justified in believing a proposition even whilst lacking evidence that favours this belief over belief in a known alternative—that one can block the sceptical argument that concludes in the debasement of our everyday knowledge. But this is a tough claim to make. How could it be that one possesses such a justification if one lacks such evidential support? For isn't the concession that the 'evidence' one has in favour of one's everyday beliefs doesn't favour those beliefs over belief in known sceptical alternatives simply the concession that one doesn't really have any evidence of substance in favour of one's everyday beliefs?

4.3. Arguing against Underdetermination

It isn't at all clear how the antisceptical strategies that we have considered could be developed to deal with this further sceptical challenge. Take the Dretskean strategy of denying closure first. Since the underdetermination principle is locally weaker than closure for internalist justification, even if it were true that closure for knowledge *simpliciter* entailed closure for internalist justification (which it isn't), it still wouldn't follow that a principled rejection of closure for knowledge *simpliciter* would thereby offer grounds for rejecting the underdetermination principle. Furthermore, there seems to be nothing in the Dretskean account of why closure fails which would explain why the underdetermination principle fails. On this view, our inability to recognize that our knowledge of everyday propositions could be consistent with a failure to know the (known to be entailed) denials of sceptical hypotheses—and thus, by parity of reasoning, our inability to recognize that our internalist justification for belief in everyday propositions could be consistent with a failure to possess an internalist justification for belief in the (known to be entailed) denials of sceptical hypotheses—simply reflects the fact that we let the sceptic put the epistemic standards too high. Properly understood, our fallibilist everyday knowledge is consistent with some (known) alternatives not being known to be false, and thus with a lack of internalist justification for belief in the denials of those alternatives. But this account of the sceptical problem doesn't explain at all why we should credit agents with internalist justification, and thus with internalist knowledge, when it comes to their everyday beliefs, given that they fail to meet the epistemic rubric set down by the underdetermination principle. After all, the problem here is not that the epistemic standards for internalist justification/knowledge are being set too high, as if the epistemic support agents have for their beliefs approximate to, but do not meet, those standards. Rather, the sceptical point that is raised by the underdetermination argument is that the epistemic support that agents have for their beliefs does not even approximate to the epistemic standards in question since, strictly speaking, they have no evidential support for their beliefs at all.

Again, the attributer contextualist response to scepticism makes no essential reference to the underdetermination-based formulation of the sceptical argument, so this antisceptical strategy will not be directly applicable to this logically distinct sceptical challenge. Presumably, the analogue of the attributer contextualist response to scepticism as regards the underdetermination-based sceptical argument will be to argue that whilst an agent's evidence will prefer everyday propositions over sceptical error-possibilities in everyday conversational contexts where the epistemic standards are low, this will not happen in sceptical conversational contexts where the epistemic standards are much higher. The problem with this line of response should be immediately obvious, since aren't the relations of evidential superiority simply *facts* which are unaltered by mere changes in the conversational standards? That is, whilst it might be possible to make a case for supposing that the standards for the correct application of epistemic terms might fluctuate relative to conversational standards, it is unclear how this same argument can be applied to a simple statement of fact regarding the evidential superiority of one belief over another. After all, *ex hypothesi*, the 'evidence' at issue in each conversational context should remain exactly the same. Accordingly, my evidence in favour of my everyday beliefs fails to prefer this belief over belief in known sceptical alternatives in *all* conversational contexts, and hence attributer contextualism is unable to explain why the lowering of epistemic standards as one enters an everyday conversational context could enable me to meet the underdetermination principle and thereby possesses an internalist justification for my everyday beliefs (and thus have internalist knowledge of what I believe).[7]

A slightly different way of applying attributer contextualism in this case that might have a little more plausibility would be to contend that whilst a principle such as the underdetermination principle is applicable in sceptical conversational contexts where the epistemic standards are high, it is not applicable in everyday conversational contexts where the epistemic standards are much lower. Accordingly, the underdetermination principle can legitimately support a sceptical argument in sceptical conversational contexts, but not in everyday conversational contexts.

Although this version of attributer contextualism is more plausible, in that it does not directly lead into difficulties, it still lacks cogency. For whereas the contextualist claim we considered above was simply that standards were fluctuating from context to context as if on a linear scale of epistemic 'toughness', this new proposal brings to the fore the sense in which the epistemic standards in play in the sceptical conversational context are not simply different in degree from those at issue in the everyday conversational context, but are rather different in kind. What this interpretation of the attributer contextualist position makes explicit is the fact that as we move from everyday contexts to sceptical contexts we are not merely demanding more of the same—such as more evidence— rather, we are demanding something very different entirely. For example, on this approach one could imagine two non-sceptical conversational contexts that employed different epistemic standards, and which therefore required that beliefs should have different levels of epistemic support before they counted as internalistically justified. The sceptical conversational context, in contrast, is not merely asking for *more* evidential support, but rather asking for evidential support of a different kind—support that meets the underdetermination principle. Accordingly, this suggestion, though superficially compatible with the attributer contextualist approach, is in fact antithetical in spirit.[8]

We are thus left with the neo-Moorean response to scepticism which, like the Dretskean and attributer contextualist strategies, makes no essential reference to the underdetermination-based sceptical argument. How might this view be developed to meet this further sceptical challenge? Presumably, proponents of such a position will try to simply embrace the consequences of their (perhaps implicit) commitment to epistemological externalism and contend that although an internalist conception of justification demands relative evidential support for the beliefs in question, an externalist reading of this notion need make no such demand. And since externalists do not hold that internalist justification is necessary for knowledge, so an agent might have knowledge—and, indeed, 'justified' beliefs in one sense of that term—without meeting the constraints imposed by the underdetermination principle at all.

Note, however, that this response is far more radical than the neo-Moorean strategy that we saw being applied to the closure-based sceptical argument above, since whilst that proposal allowed that one could have internalist knowledge of everyday propositions, this proposal in effect denies even that by arguing that as regards everyday propositions agents are unable to offer reflectively accessible evidence. This means that *all* knowledge is now of a brute externalist nature, and this is not an attractive conception of our epistemic position.

In effect, what this point highlights is the underlying awkwardness of the neo-Moorean denial of internalist closure whilst attempting to keep closure itself intact. If one sets the issue of evidential support to one side, then there is no immediate problem with the idea that one could have internalist knowledge of everyday propositions even though one knows that this knowledge entails the denial of sceptical hypotheses and that one is only able to have externalist knowledge of these propositions. The reason why no immediate problem arises at the level of knowledge is that there is no in principle difficulty with the idea that agents can have internalist knowledge by meeting both internal *and* external epistemic conditions and thus that there are epistemic conditions which they need to meet in order to know but which are not reflectively accessible to them.

Once one descends to the level of evidential justification, however, and thereby focuses on the underdetermination principle, it becomes clear just what is problematic about this strategy. For how can one meet the relevant internal epistemic condition at all, as regards *any* belief, if, *ex hypothesi*, one's evidence cannot meet the demands set out by the underdetermination principle? In terms of the evidence that one has reflective access to, there are no good grounds for believing everyday propositions over sceptical propositions, and thus one is unable to meet an internal epistemic condition as regards even one's beliefs in everyday propositions. Shifting the focus from closure to underdetermination thus highlights what is problematic about the neo-Moorean contention that internalist knowledge of everyday propositions could ultimately rest upon externalist knowledge of the denials of sceptical hypotheses.

There are various other ways of responding to the underdetermination-based sceptical challenge which are all, in effect, tantamount to the neo-Moorean strategy. I will here discuss two of the main arguments that might be offered of this sort.

One style of response that one might be tempted to employ in this regard is to adduce the kind of anti-evidentialist arguments that have been put forward in other areas of epistemology in order to motivate a rejection of the underdetermination principle. The idea would be that there are independent reasons for supposing that one can have internalist justification, and thus internalist knowledge, of some non-foundational propositions (i.e. propositions which are not self-justifying in any way, by being self-evident, or incorrigible and so forth) without having any evidence at all.[9] Accordingly, the underdetermination principle cannot be allowed to stand as it is since on this view it *is* possible to be internalistically justified in believing a proposition even whilst lacking evidence in favour of that belief that supports that belief over known to be incompatible alternatives.

Now it is certainly plausible to suppose that one can have justification and knowledge without being able to adduce evidence in certain cases, because there are all sorts of beliefs which we are willing to grant a 'default' positive epistemic status such that, in the right conditions at least, they are justified (and so the proposition believed can be known), even though the agent is not in a position to offer evidence in support of that belief. Basic perceptual beliefs are an obvious candidate here, since it seems that, scepticism aside at least, in normal circumstances one might form justified perceptual beliefs simply by having cognitive faculties (good eyesight and so forth) that are functioning correctly. That said, however, it is far less plausible that the kind of justification that we would be willing to ascribe here would be of an internalist variety, and thus that the resultant knowledge, if it is possessed at all, would meet the internalist rubric. After all, the kind of knowledge and justification at issue in these basic perceptual cases seems to be on a part with the 'brute' externalist knowledge that we considered above.

Even setting this concern to one side, however, it still remains that denying an evidentialism that objected to allowing such 'default' epistemic status to basic perceptual beliefs is very different from denying the kind of evidentialism at issue in the underdetermination-based sceptical argument. For what is different in the two cases is that one can, in principle at least (and, recall, setting sceptical issues to one side for the moment), offer the evidence that is needed in the perceptual case. Indeed, the standard construal of the 'default' line requires agents to seek such evidence if there are defeaters present which indicate possible problems with their cognitive faculties or that there is something amiss regarding the environmental conditions. In contrast, the evidential lack at issue in the sceptical employment of the underdetermination principle is not merely one of practical cognitive limitations but rather represents an in principle difficulty. As noted above, there is no possible incremental improvement in our epistemic position that could accord us with evidence that would support our beliefs in everyday propositions over known to be incompatible sceptical hypotheses. Intuitively, we are content to allow such 'default' states of positive epistemic status only because we do not want to deny (non-internalist) justification to beliefs whose pedigree, whilst excellent, is not a pedigree that the subject can vouch for via the evidence she has. In the sceptical case, in contrast, the very issue of the pedigree of the belief is open to question and, moreover, the lack of evidential support is one of principle rather than of mere practice. (Indeed, in so far as 'pedigree' relates here to the purely empirical process by which the belief is formed, then our beliefs in the denials of sceptical hypotheses do not obviously have any pedigree.) The cases are thus disanalogous in the very respects that make anti-evidentialism an otherwise plausible thesis.

Besides, whilst the standard non-evidentialist thesis merely allows a restricted class of beliefs in non-foundational propositions to enjoy a default epistemic status, the proposal on offer here seems to extend this compliment to an unduly wide range of beliefs. All-in-all, then, even if we grant that non-evidentialist arguments have an impact on issues regarding internalist justification (which is highly implausible), it remains that the most a non-evidentialist attack on the underdetermination principle is going to achieve is to merely restrict the application of this principle in some peripheral respect. Crucially, however, this restriction will have little, if any, impact on the use of this principle in sceptical arguments.

A second style of response to the underdetermination-based challenge that one might be tempted to employ, and which is tantamount to that just sketched, is to 'externalize' the notion of evidence in such a way that there *is* a difference between the evidence that is available to a BIV relative to her undeceived counterpart. In order to make this move plausible, of course, it is necessary to understand evidence here such that one's 'evidence' is not the evidence that is reflectively available to one since, *ex hypothesi*, the two cases are described so that what is reflectively available to the subject is the same in each case. The problem facing this proposal, however, is that the sense of 'evidence' that is at issue in the underdetermination-based sceptical argument is precisely that sense in which one's evidence is, by its nature, reflectively available. In particular, the sense of 'evidence' that is at issue is one that is relevant to the possession of *internalist* justification, and that can only be evidence that is reflectively accessible to the agent. Thus, to say that there is a sense of 'evidence' in which there may well be an evidential difference that escapes the underdetermination-based sceptical argument, but that it is a difference which is in principle reflectively inaccessible to an agent, is just to grant that in the sense of evidence that *we* are concerned with agents have no evidence at all for their beliefs (regardless of whether those beliefs are concerned with the denials of sceptical hypotheses or with everyday propositions). It is thus a distinction which, in this regard, makes no difference.[10,11]

So although the neo-Moorean response to the sceptic is adequate to the challenge in so far as we understand scepticism in terms of the closure-based template argument, once one recognizes that it is the underdetermination principle, and not the closure principle, which is the underlying force behind sceptical arguments, even this theory falls out of consideration as an intellectually satisfying response to the sceptic. Moreover, since the other main anti-sceptical theories that we have considered cannot be adapted to deal with the underdetermination-based sceptical argument, the sceptic is still alive and kicking, despite the many well-publicized claims to the contrary.

4.4. The Source of Scepticism

So what moral should we draw from this discussion of the inadequacy of recent antisceptical theories? The general point is that they fail because they *misdiagnose* what the focus of scepticism is. Recall that we began with the infallibilism-based sceptical argument that was closely allied to a demand for absolute certainty. This challenge then transmuted itself into a closure-based challenge that focused on knowledge. The move to knowledge here was significant, for whilst it does seem prima facie plausible to suppose that the relevant sense in which we should 'rule out' sceptical error-possibilities in the way that the infallibilist demanded could be captured in terms of knowledge, the foregoing discussion reveals what was problematic about this construal. For what Peter Unger had in mind when he talked of 'ruling out' sceptical error-possibilities was clearly not going to be captured in terms of the agent having mere externalist knowledge of the denials of sceptical hypotheses, which is what the best response to the closure-based sceptical problem—the neo-Moorean strategy— offers us. Instead, he clearly had an internalist evidentialist construal of this notion in mind, one that was closely associated with one's subjective certainty in believing the proposition in question, and which could therefore support appropriate claims to know.

The move to the closure-based sceptical template thus masks the distinctively internalist focus of the sceptical challenge. We return internalism back to the heart of the sceptical problem by shifting the focus away from closure and towards the underdetermination principle, since now evidential support is what counts, and the only coherent understanding of evidence available in this regard is an internalistic one (the evidence that is reflectively accessible to one).

Crucially, however, the underdetermination principle does not validate the infallibilism advocated by Unger, still less his related demand for absolute certainty. The way that Unger expresses the matter gives the impression that sceptical challenges are simply more demanding than everyday challenges to know, as if there were a continuum of epistemic standards with scepticism at one extreme of that continuum. As we saw above, this superficially attractive picture of the sceptical problem led to the Dretskean and attributer contextualist antisceptical theories, since they both, in their different ways, try to respond to the sceptic by limiting her capacity to adduce the standards in play at her extreme end of the spectrum (the Dretskean theory does this by straightforwardly outlawing the sceptical standards, at least as regards everyday propositions, whilst the contextualist theory does this by disallowing them in everyday conversational contexts).

Underdetermination does not license this construal of the sceptical problem, however, for the simple reason that in light of this principle scepticism is not a demand for an impossible *degree* of evidence, but rather a demand for a *kind* of evidence that is in principle unavailable, *viz.* reflectively accessible evidence that favours one's everyday beliefs over their sceptical alternatives. It is not then plausible to suppose that we could meet the sceptic by simply allowing knowledge to be based on a weaker degree of evidence, since the point of the sceptical argument is that there is an important sense in which our beliefs are not evidentially based at all.

4.5. Concluding Remarks

The underdetermination principle thus highlights two key features about what is essential to the sceptical argument. First, that it is a challenge to our *internalist* and evidentialist conception of knowledge. Responding to scepticism with externalist knowledge alone as the neo-Moorean ultimately does is thus beside the point. Second, that scepticism is not a challenge that only emerges at the *highest* epistemic standards. Instead, it employs general epistemic principles that are constitutive of *any* notion of epistemic standards.

As we will see in Part II, the deeper problem that afflicts the closure-based responses to scepticism is that they in effect respond to the sceptical problem by outlawing only one way in which luck can infect knowledge. In doing so they leave untouched a second variety of epistemic luck that is epistemically problematic and which is what motivates the sceptical argument. The core inadequacy of contemporary responses to scepticism—a problem that has defined much of the direction of recent epistemological theorizing—thus exposes an underlying confusion regarding the relationship between luck and knowledge. Identifying just what is wrong with the recent responses to scepticism is thus essential to the project of elucidating this relationship.

Notes

1. For the sake of argument here I am assuming that small children and clever chimpanzees (and the like) do possess the relevant conceptual capacities necessary if they are to genuinely form a belief in the target proposition, since I take it that the possession of such capacities is not in question in the case of the chicken-sexer example. The problem that I am focusing upon here is thus not that ascribing brute knowledge to these agents is problematic because they lack the relevant conceptual capacities, but rather because they lack the specifically reflective capacities needed to justify their beliefs. Whilst it is of course contentious to ascribe conceptual capacities to the non-human higher mammals and to very small children, all camps will surely agree that there is a developmental stage at which small children have the conceptual capacities necessary to genuinely form beliefs whilst lacking the reflective capabilities needed to gain an internalist justification for those beliefs. Such cases will thus be potential instances of 'brute' knowledge on the externalist account in the manner just described.
2. See also, Yalçin (1992) and Vogel (1993). The Pyrrhonian sceptical challenge is discussed in its own right below in §8.3.
3. The reader should note that I have made two minor modifications to UP (and subsequent formulations of this principle). The first is that I have incorporated the claim that the incompatibility in question should be *known* (Brueckner makes no such demand). Since the examples that both Brueckner and I focus upon are such that the agent might reasonably be thought to know the incompatibility in question anyhow, this ought to be an uncontroversial addition to make. The second is that I have made explicit, in a way that is only implicit in Brueckner's formulation of the principle, that the notion of justification at issue here is specifically internalist.
4. It is interesting to note the parallel between the underdetermination principle and the underdetermination of theory thesis discussed (primarily, at any rate) by philosophers of science. Roughly, this latter principle states that, for any finite set of evidence, there is always more than one (logically incompatible) theory that is consistent with that set of evidence. Although the principles are structurally equivalent, the challenge that the underdetermination thesis poses for the philosophy of science is very different from that facing us here. The difference relates to how in the scientific case each particular instance of underdetermination can be met by conducting more experiments and thereby extending one's set of evidence. Of course, for each incremental change in the evidence-base, there will always be a further underdetermination problem arising, so although one can, in principle at least, always meet the 'local' underdetermination problem in this way, a 'global' underdetermination challenge will always remain. Crucially, however, there is no analogue to this 'local' resolution in the sceptical case because, according to the sceptic, there is, *ex hypothesi*, no possible way of responding to a specific underdetermination challenge

by enlarging one's evidence base. In this sense, then, the underdetermination-based sceptical challenge is more demanding than the analogue challenge that is at issue in the philosophy of science. The *locus classicus* for discussion of the underdetermination of theory thesis in contemporary debate is, of course, Quine (1953). Vogel (2004) notes the relationship between the two principles and briefly discusses the parallels.

5. Intuitively, any notion of justification worthy of the name must satisfy this principle. As I argue in Pritchard (2005*d*), there are in fact some interesting logical connections between various versions of this principle and the two epistemic principles currently under discussion, though it would take us too far away from the present discussion to explore them in detail here.

6. Cohen (1998*b*) argues against Brueckner on similar grounds. Intriguingly, Cohen further argues that this logical difference between the two principles is ultimately irrelevant because, in any case, the two premises of the underdetermination-based sceptical argument entail the major premiss of the closure-based sceptical argument (i.e. (C1), though where it is internalist justification rather than knowledge that is at issue). Accordingly, effective logical parity between the two principles is resorted. As I show in Pritchard (2005*d*), however, Cohen's reasoning here is based on a fairly elementary error. Accordingly, it poses no challenge to the claim just made that the underdetermination principle is logically weaker than the closure principle for internalist justification (even in effect).

7. As I discussed in note 25 of Chapter 2, Neta (2002, 2003) has an inspired go at defending a type of attributer contextualism that is similar to the view just described, in that it treats what counts as evidence as being a context-sensitive matter. On this view, one can have evidence which suffices to internalistically justify one's beliefs in everyday propositions in quotidian conversational contexts and thus, via closure for internalist justification, therefore have evidence which also supports an internalist justification for one's beliefs in the denials of sceptical hypotheses. As one moves into sceptical conversational contexts, in contrast, and the epistemic standards are raised, the evidence that one is allowed to cite in favour of one's beliefs becomes more restricted in such a way as to undermine one's internalist justification for believing both everyday and antisceptical propositions. As I noted in Chapter 2, however, it is far from clear that on this proposal we have sufficient grounds for regarding the supposed 'justification' for our beliefs in everyday conversational contexts as bona fide (much less as being of a standard that would meet the internalist rubric), since this view seems to implicitly allow that one's 'evidence' in these conversational contexts only stands provided one does not take sceptical error-possibilities seriously. Accordingly, the proper conclusion to be drawn is surely that, strictly speaking, our everyday (and antisceptical) beliefs are not evidentially supported at all (and so not internalistically justified), not that they enjoy some kind of quasi-evidential support (and thus a quasi-internalist justification).

8. It is interesting to note that the 'inferential' version of contextualism advanced by Williams (e.g. 1991) is sensitive to this point, since it is a key part of this view that the sceptic doesn't raise the epistemic standards at all by introducing her sceptical argument but instead merely attempts to change the rubric against which the epistemic status of beliefs is assessed. As I argue in Pritchard (2005*e*), however, this view faces fatal problems of its own.

9. One area of philosophy where anti-evidentialist arguments have received a lot of discussion recently is in the philosophy of religion regarding the issue of whether certain fundamental religious beliefs are, to use Plantinga's phrase, properly basic. Famously, so-called 'reformed' epistemologists, such as Plantinga, maintain that they are. The *locus classicus* in this respect is Plantinga (1993*b*). I discuss the reformed epistemological proposal in this

regard at some length in Pritchard (2003*b*; cf. Pritchard 2000*c*). As I note in a moment, however, such approaches are not obviously congenial to the neo-Moorean antisceptical strategy in this respect because they tend to understand the epistemic status of these beliefs along *externalist* lines.

10. For a sophisticated development of a view of evidence of this sort, see Williamson (1996*a*, 1997, 2000*a*, 2000*c*). The reader should note that I am only rejecting this thesis in so far as it is construed as a response to an underdetermination-based sceptical argument (something which Williamson himself never explicitly considers). In general, I am sympathetic to the idea that we need to clearly distinguish these two senses of 'evidence', I merely think that this distinction is of no help when dealing with this particular formulation of the sceptical problem. I discuss Williamson's view in this regard at some length in Pritchard (2006). A superficially similar account to Williamson's in this respect (though one that I think is in fact fundamentally different) is offered by McDowell (e.g. 1995). I critically discuss McDowell's proposal at length in Pritchard (2003*a*). His related conception of factive reasons is discussed below in §9.2.

11. A slightly different response to the underdetermination-based sceptical argument might be to argue that despite the lack of evidential superiority in favour of our everyday beliefs over their sceptical counterparts we are nevertheless epistemically entitled to our everyday beliefs because antisceptical hypotheses constitute better explanations of the evidence than sceptical hypotheses. It is not clear how this line of thought helps, however, in that it is far from obvious that this use of inference to the best explanation presents us with *epistemic* grounds for our everyday beliefs (as opposed to merely pragmatic grounds, such as that our belief in the denial of sceptical hypotheses accords us a simpler and more conservative belief-system). And if this line of argument is not offering us epistemic grounds, then it is not going to present us with the kind of response to the sceptical argument that we are seeking here. For a presentation of an antisceptical thesis that is primarily based on abductive grounds of this sort, see Vogel (1990).

Part Two

Epistemic Luck

5

Luck

5.0. Introduction

As we will see in this part of the book, the shift in focus from a closure-based sceptical argument to one that is based on the underdetermination principle that we argued for in Chapter 4 represents a recognition that the kind of epistemic luck that is at issue in the sceptical debate is very different from that which many in the contemporary literature suppose. More precisely, what guides the contemporary debate regarding scepticism is the supposition that there is just *one* problematic variety of epistemic luck at issue, when there are in fact *two* varieties.

We begin in this chapter with an analysis, albeit a partial one, of luck itself, something that is noticeably lacking in the contemporary literature, and then distinguish (with Peter Unger's help) several types of luck that might reasonably be called 'epistemic'. A number of these varieties are irrelevant to knowledge possession, and the reason why is clarified via consideration of our rough analysis of luck. The aim of this chapter is thus to clear the ground so that we can get to grips with the problematic varieties of luck in Chapters 6 and 7 and relate them back to the sceptical problem in Chapters 8 and 9.

5.1. Luck

One of the difficulties that has afflicted attempts to get a handle on the notion of epistemic luck is that many of the discussions on this topic have tended to take the notion of luck itself as either an undefined primitive or else merely gesture at a loose conceptual characterization.[1] Nevertheless, a closer inspection of these partial conceptual elucidations of the notion—along with the main problems that they face—is useful to help us understand what luck is.

accident, chance, lack of control

Epistemic Luck

One of the most standard accounts of luck offered in the literature involves defining it in terms of the notion of an accident. William Harper (1996), for instance, notes that ' "luck" overlaps both with "accident" and "chance" ', and Unger (1968: 158) cashes out his anti-luck epistemology in terms of a clause which states that it is 'not at all an accident that the man is right about its being the case that p'. Carolyn Morillo (1984) seems to adopt a similar line because throughout her discussion of the topic she uses the notions of luck and accident interchangeably. For example, she notes (1984: 109), that knowledge precludes luck and then immediately goes on to say that it is for this reason that some analyses of knowledge demand that the truth of the belief in question should not be accidental.[2]

The relationship between the notions of luck and accident is not nearly so straightforward as these commentators appear to believe, however. Consider, for example, the paradigm case of luck—the lottery win. In such a case, it is a matter of luck (given the odds) that one wins the lottery, but it need not thereby be an *accident* that one wins (at least absent some further details about the scenario). If one deliberately bought the ticket in question and, say, one self-consciously chose the winning numbers, then it would be odd to refer to the resulting outcome as being accidental.

Interestingly, Harper, in the quotation just cited, does not just group the concept 'luck' with the concept 'accident', but also with the concept 'chance'. This too is a common way of characterizing the notion of luck, with Nicholas Rescher being one of the foremost exponents of a version of this thesis.[3] Again, however, although there is manifestly a close conceptual connection between the concepts, it is far from clear exactly how they relate. After all, intuitively at least, chance events can occur without anyone's lives being affected by them, and yet it is only events which are significant to agents in some way that are counted as being lucky.[4] For example, it may be a matter of chance that a landslide occurs when it does (or occurs at all), but if no one is affected by this event (either adversely or otherwise), then it is hard to see why we would class this occurrence as lucky (or, indeed, unlucky for that matter).[5]

This issue is further complicated once one reflects upon what the relevant understanding of chance is in this context. After all, events that have a low probability of occurring from the agent's point of view (such as a lottery win) are nevertheless plausibly regarded as predetermined to occur given the initial conditions of the situation and the relevant fundamental physical laws. With this in mind, it is not transparent that the relevant sense of chance at issue here should be understood in terms of low probability. Moreover, identifying chance with indeterminacy would fare little better since it ought to be uncontroversial that at least some lucky events are not brought about by indeterminate factors. It thus appears that a more subtle account of what is meant by 'chance' in this regard is needed.[6]

Another common way of characterizing luck is in terms of control, or rather the absence of it. If one were to say that, for example, 'I discovered the buried treasure by luck', one would be naturally understood as implying that one did nothing to ensure that one discovered what one did—that the discovery itself was out of one's control in some way. This is, perhaps, the most common account given of the notion in the philosophical literature and its influence is probably due to the fact that in his influential paper on the specific topic of moral luck Thomas Nagel defines this species of luck in just these terms.[7] Here is Nagel:

> Where a significant aspect of what someone does depends on factors beyond his control, yet we continue to treat him in that respect as an object of moral judgement, it can be called moral luck. (Nagel 1979: 25)

Following Nagel, a number of writers have adopted this line as regards luck in general.[8] Daniel Statman, for example, offers the following account of good and bad luck:

> Let us start by explaining what we usually mean by the term 'luck'. Good luck occurs when something good happens to an agent P, its occurrence being beyond P's control. Similarly, bad luck occurs when something bad happens to an agent P, its occurrence being beyond his control. (Statman 1991: 146)

And a similar account is offered by Michael Zimmerman (1993) and John Greco (1995).[9] Nevertheless, as Statman (1991: 146) acknowledges, in a foot-note, lack of control could only plausibly be regarded as a *necessary* condition for luck. After all, as Andrew Latus (2000: 167) neatly points out, the rising of the sun this morning was an event the occurrence of which was out of one's control. But would we really want to say that it was *lucky* that the sun rose this morning? Moreover, the issue of control is particularly problematic when it comes to epistemic luck, because (on most views at least) belief is a component of knowledge, and it is certainly common to regard the formation of at least one's most basic perceptual beliefs as not being within one's immediate control. Nevertheless, it seems odd to argue on this basis that basic perceptual belief is inherently 'lucky'.

So although there is clearly something intuitive about thinking of luck in terms of the notions of accidentality, chance, or the absence of control, there is no straightforward way available of accounting for luck in these terms.

Unfortunately, the philosophical literature does not go further to offer any deeper analysis of the concept of luck that goes beyond these suggestive equivalences. Nevertheless, a plausible (though rough) modal account of luck can be offered, one which can meet the main intuitions in play in the philosophical discussion.

The account comes in two parts. The first, which captures the specifically modal dimension to luck, can be expressed as follows, where, recall, possible worlds are to be understood, in the standard way, as ordered in terms of their similarity to the actual world (i.e. so that 'distant' possible worlds are very unlike the actual world, whilst 'nearby' possible words are very alike the actual world):

(L1) If an event is lucky, then it is an event that occurs in the actual world but which does not occur in a wide class of the nearest possible worlds where the relevant initial conditions for that event are the same as in the actual world.

With (L1) in mind, consider how it captures two of the paradigm cases of luck mentioned above, the lottery win and the lucky discovery of treasure. In the former case, we have a lucky event which, true to (L1), occurs in the actual world but which—so long as, of course, the lottery was both fair and sufficiently demanding—does not occur in a wide class of the nearby possible worlds where the relevant initial conditions for that event are the same (i.e. where the agent continues to buy a lottery ticket, where the lottery is still free and fair, and so on). Although the agent has a winning ticket in the actual world, in most (if not all) of the nearest possible worlds at issue she will be in possession of a losing ticket.

One advantage of understanding luck in terms of a similarity ordering of possible worlds is that it explains why agents would be willing to take part in lotteries given the low odds of success. This is because the very attraction of a fair lottery lies in the fact that the possible world in which one wins is very like the actual world, even though it is in fact unlikely that such a possible world should be the actual world. This point highlights the sense in which the similarity ordering of possible worlds is not tantamount to an ordering in terms of probability. For although it is highly unlikely that one should win the lottery, it is nevertheless true that there is a nearby possible world in which one does win the lottery because very little needs to be different to turn the actual (non-lottery-winning) world into the appropriate (lottery-winning) possible world (for example, a few numbered balls just need to fall into slightly different holes on the machine that draws the lottery numbers).[10] (L1) thus explains our first paradigm case of luck, in that the lucky event of a lottery win is clearly an event which, on this conception of possible worlds, obtains in the actual world but not in a wide class of nearby possible worlds where the relevant initial conditions for that event are the same as in the actual world.

Similarly, (L1) can also account for the case of the lucky discovery. According to (L1), this event can count as lucky because, although it occurred in the actual world, it does not occur in a wide class of the possible worlds that are most alike the actual world where the relevant initial conditions for that event are the same (where, for example, the agent continues to have no particular reason for thinking that he would find the buried treasure where he did). And, indeed, this conforms to our intuitions concerning this case. To say that the discovery is lucky is to say that, in a wide class of possible worlds similar to the actual one in the relevant respects, one would not have made the discovery that one did. Accordingly, it follows that although the treasure was found in the actual world, it would not have been found in a wide class of the relevant nearby possible worlds, just as (L1) demands.

Significantly, this condition on luck can also accommodate examples which aren't, intuitively, cases of luck. For example, it is not lucky that the sun rose this morning, on this view, because although this is an event that is out of one's control, it is nonetheless also true that the sun rises in most (if not all) of the nearest possible worlds to the actual world.

What is interesting about cases like the buried treasure example and, especially, the lottery case is that not only does the event in question not obtain in a wide class of the relevant nearest possible worlds, but in fact doesn't obtain in most of them (indeed, in the case of the lottery win, it doesn't obtain in nearly all of them). This raises the issue of just how 'wide' this wide class of worlds needs to be. Typically, as we have seen with the two examples just cited, lucky events will be events which do not obtain in most of the nearby possible worlds. Crucially, however, there do seem to be cases in which luck is genuinely involved but where it does not seem to be quite true that most of the relevant nearby worlds are worlds in which the event does not obtain.

Consider, for example, the case of a contestant on a gameshow who must choose between two possible answers to the winning question. Imagine that this contestant has not got the faintest clue which answer is right, but happens to win anyway because she guesses the right answer. I think our intuition here is clearly that she is lucky to win the prize given that she is simply guessing the answer, but it would seem that it isn't true to say that she gets this question wrong in most of the relevant nearby possible worlds (the actual figure is more likely to be in the region of half of them). Indeed, cases like this suggest that as the width of worlds in which the event in question does not obtain recedes then our intuition that luck is involved recedes with it. Suppose, for example, that the contestant had to simply choose a 'winning' answer from a batch of four, where only one of the answers on offer was a 'losing' answer. If the contestant guessed correctly in this case then I think it would be unlikely that we would put this down to luck since the odds were squarely in her favour. After all, in most nearby possible worlds where she chose her option solely on the basis of a guess we would expect her to be a winner. This suggests that the correct reading of 'wide class' in (L1) is as at least approaching half of the relevant nearby possible worlds, and that typically events which are *clearly* lucky will be events which do not obtain in most nearby possible worlds.

A further motivation for employing (L1) as a condition on luck is that it can explain why accidentality and lack of control are both closely related to, but not sufficient for, luck. This is because if one has control over a certain event, such that one is able to (typically) determine that a certain outcome obtains, then that is naturally understood as implying that in a wide class of relevant nearby possible worlds that outcome is realized and therefore not lucky (just as (L1) would predict).

Consider the example of a fair 100-m race between an amateur athlete and an Olympic gold medallist at this distance, both of whom want to win. Presumably, we would say that if the gold medallist wins then that win will not be due to luck, whilst if the amateur athlete wins then (all other things being equal) it *will* be due to luck (because it will be due, for example, to the gold medallist falling over or succumbing to some similar fate). Moreover, this is reflected in the fact that it is only the Olympic gold medallist who has significant control over the outcome in this respect. Thanks to her prodigious skill, coupled with her strict training schedules and heightened levels of concentration and so forth, she is able to not only ensure that she wins in the actual world, but also in most of the nearby possible worlds as well where the relevant initial conditions for that event are the same as in the actual world (where she continues to try to win, for example). Indeed, the only worlds where she fails to win are those where something goes wrong, such as those worlds where she stumbles and falls before the winning line. Accordingly, should the other runner win the race, then this win will be lucky because in most of the relevant nearest possible worlds she loses. The lucky race winner thus lacks the kind of control over this event that is present in the case of the Olympic gold medallist. Control over events is thus a good determinant of whether or not luck is involved.

Similar remarks apply to accidentality. Intuitively, when we describe an event as an accident we thereby typically imply that in a wide class of the relevant nearby possible worlds it doesn't occur. For example, when we say that the agent found the buried treasure by 'accident' this is naturally taken to mean that in a wide class (if not most) of the relevant nearby possible worlds the agent in question doesn't find the treasure and thus that her discovery is due to luck. Similarly, if we were to say that this discovery was not accidental, perhaps because the agent knew where to look, then this would be reflected in the fact that the agent finds the treasure not just in the actual world but also in most of the relevant nearby possible worlds as well. Accordingly, on the rough modal analysis of luck offered above, it would follow that accidental events will tend to be lucky events, just as the informal elucidations of luck we considered earlier supposed.

(L1) is also able to capture the relevant sense of 'chance' that we saw commentators trying to identify above. The chief concern raised regarding accounts of luck formulated in terms of chance was that it was unclear how one is to understand the notion of chance in this context. In particular, it was noted that two plausible ways of understanding this notion—in terms of low probabilities or indeterminacy—were highly unsatisfactory since there were paradigm cases of luck where the event in question was, at least in one sense, neither indeterminate nor of a low probability. By employing (L1) we can evade this concern by noting that the sense of chance in play is merely that modal notion of how the event in question, though it occurs, does not occur in a wide class of the relevant possible worlds similar to the actual world. On this view, the temptation to identify chance with indeterminacy, low probabilities, or some other factor is simply a red herring.[11]

There are, of course, problems with this partial specification of luck, one of which is the inherent vagueness involved in the demand that the relevant initial conditions of the event should be the same in all the nearby possible worlds under consideration. I think we have an intuitive grasp of what this involves (such as the purchase of a lottery ticket in the 'lottery' example, or the lack of any special grounds to begin digging at that particular location in the 'discovery' example), but as it stands it is an uncomfortably open-ended constraint on the condition. For example, if one includes in the initial conditions for the event the demand that the balls fall into the lottery machine in a certain way, then one will no longer generate the desired result that the event is lucky in light of (L1) because the specification of the initial conditions will *determine* the event in question across all the relevant nearby worlds. What we have in mind by this clause is thus some conception of the initial conditions which does not understand them in such a way that, individually or collectively, they determine the event in question. The problem, however, is to specify this 'non-determining' feature of the clause in a manner that doesn't ensure in advance that the event in question is 'chancy' in just the respect that is needed if it is to be regarded as a lucky event, for otherwise (L1) will be trivially true in virtue of having this clause.

One way around this problem could be to drop this clause and simply consider the (unrestricted) class of nearby possible worlds, on the grounds that this class of worlds will tend to be dominated by worlds in which the 'relevant initial conditions' as we intuitively understand them are the same. After all, given the kind of sophisticated deception that needs to be in place in order for a national lottery to be fixed, it is plausible to suppose that most, if not all, nearby possible worlds will be worlds in which the lottery continues to be fair. Moreover, the possible worlds in which the agent wins the lottery without having purchased a ticket are clearly going to be very unlike the actual world! Given this possible escape route, the objection is no longer fatal. Nevertheless, since this clause does do some explanatory work in clarifying how we understand luck, in what follows we will keep it as part of (L1) and let our intuitions guide us as to what it should be read as demanding as regards particular scenarios. In any case, since the examples we will be using are fairly clear-cut cases in which luck either is or is not involved, I don't think we will find our intuitions being unduly indeterminate on this matter.[12]

(L1) alone does not capture the core elements of what is involved in the notion of luck, however, because, as noted earlier, we also need to say something about the significance that the agent in question attaches to the target event, since it is only significant events that are counted as lucky or unlucky. The example cited to illustrate this above was that of the landslide which did not affect anyone, either positively or adversely. Clearly, such an event is neither lucky nor unlucky. Nevertheless, it might still be an event that meets the condition outlined in (L1), and hence this example serves to illustrate that (L1) alone is not sufficient to capture the core notion of luck.

We thus need a second condition that captures the 'significance' element of luck. Here is one possible formulation:

(L2) If an event is lucky, then it is an event that is significant to the agent concerned (or would be significant, were the agent to be availed of the relevant facts).

Though vague, this condition should suffice to capture the basic contours of the 'subjective' element of luck, and thus also capture the sense in which luck can be either good or bad. Take the landslide example just noted, for instance. (L2) rules this event out as being an example of luck on the grounds that it is not an event that is of any significance to anyone. Moreover, by adapting this scenario, we can accommodate the manner in which whether or not an event is judged to be lucky can depend upon the significance attached to the event by the agent concerned. For example, if only one person was affected in a significant way by the landslide, then this event would be lucky (or unlucky) for them only. Furthermore, the manner in which the event affects the agent will determine the type of luck that is involved. For example, if the landslide has adverse effects on the agent (as one would expect)—such as if it destroyed her house—then we would expect this agent to regard this event as being unlucky. Conversely, however, if the landslide has positive effects—if, for example, it levelled the hillside that she was about to pay a small fortune to have levelled artificially—then we would expect the agent to regard this event as lucky. The type of luck, and its very existence from that agent's point of view, thus depends upon the significance that the agent attaches to the event in question.[13]

We need to add the *caveat* regarding the significance that the agent would attach to the event were she to be availed of all the relevant facts in order to deal with cases where agents do not count an event as being lucky simply because they are not aware of certain features of the event. For example, one might have narrowly avoided being hit by a thunderbolt which would have meant losing one's life, and yet simply fail to notice that one had had such a lucky escape. Accordingly, the event would not be significant even though it was manifestly lucky. Clearly, the way to deal with such an example is to widen our understanding of significance so that it includes what the agent would find significant were she to be availed of all the relevant facts.[14]

Of course, there will be considerable room for manoeuvre regarding how one is to interpret the notion of 'significance' in this account, though, typically, one would expect the context to fix the appropriate reading. Nevertheless, the conjunction of (L1) and (L2) is clearly able to accommodate a number of our basic intuitions about luck. Accordingly, whilst this account of luck is admittedly vague, it should suffice to aid us in our discussion of the phenomenon of epistemic luck.[15,16]

5.2. Three Benign Varieties of Luck

Perhaps the subtlest account of the notion of epistemic luck in the literature is that offered by Unger (1968) who presents a 'non-accidental' theory of knowledge (where, recall, for 'accident' read 'luck'). What makes Unger's analysis particularly interesting is that he is one of the few commentators

Epistemic Luck

to give at least a passing attempt at distinguishing between epistemically significant and epistemically insignificant varieties of luck. Consider the following passage:

In my analysis of human knowledge, a complete absence of the accidental is claimed, not regarding the occurrence or existence of the fact known nor regarding the existence or abilities of the man who knows, but only as regards a certain relation concerning the man and the fact. (Unger 1968: 159)

Unger here distinguishes two harmless ways in which luck can have an influence on knowledge. We will refer to the first harmless type of luck that he mentions—concerning the 'occurrence or existence of the fact known'—as 'content epistemic luck'. It can roughly be summarized as follows:

Content epistemic luck
It is lucky that the proposition is true.

The second harmless type of luck—'regarding the existence or abilities of the man who knows'—we will call 'capacity epistemic luck'. We can roughly characterize this type of luck as follows:

Capacity epistemic luck
It is lucky that the agent is capable of knowledge.

In what follows we will take it as given that to say that an agent is lucky to be capable of knowledge can include not just the luck that might be involved in the agent having the cognitive capacities that enable her to know (the luck regarding her 'abilities'), but also the luck that she is alive in the first place (the luck regarding her 'existence').

The example that Unger gives to illustrate the first type of epistemic luck is of someone who happens to witness a paradigm case of an accidental event—a car accident. Unger (1968: 159) notes that even though it is an accident that this event should have occurred, and thus that it is in this sense an accident that the proposition which says that it has occurred is true, nevertheless an agent can know that proposition just so long as 'it is not accidental that he is right about its being the case' that the accidental event happened. Unger is surely right here, in that there seems no reason why the content of the proposition at issue should affect an agent's knowledge of that proposition provided that all the usual conditions for knowledge have been met (i.e. truth, belief, and whatever epistemic conditions are needed to transform true belief into knowledge). Moreover, note that Unger's example of an accident conforms to the account of luck offered above. For a car accident is naturally understood as being an event which

134

occurs in the actual world, but which does not occur in a wide class of the relevant nearby possible worlds (for then it wouldn't be an accident), and which is of some significance, both to the person concerned and, in this case, to the witness to the event.

As regards the second type of epistemic luck, there is an ambiguity regarding what Unger has in mind. He talks of how it is 'largely accidental' that one exists when one does (or even at all), though this claim is far from obviously true (unless he is illicitly identifying 'accidental' with 'contingent', though even this claim is far from uncontentious). The example he offers to illustrate his main point, however, is more straightforward. He speaks of how an agent may be looking at a turtle and, as luck would have it (and unbeknownst to him), he has at that moment narrowly avoided being smashed to pieces by a rock that would have ordinarily fallen onto him by now (Unger 1968: 160). Here we clearly have a case of good luck since, *ex hypothesi*, in most relevant nearby possible worlds our protagonist would be dead (and his existence is, we might reasonably suppose, something which is highly significant to him). Nevertheless, Unger argues that although

it is indeed quite an accident that the turtle watcher is alive at the time he sees the turtle crawling on the ground before him . . . it is not at all accidental that he is right about its being the case that there is a turtle on the ground. [Thus . . .] the turtle watcher knows that there is a turtle crawling there upon the ground. (Unger 1968: 160)

The luck that the agent is alive and therefore in a position to know anything at all entails that it is also a matter of luck that he is able to make this observation of the turtle. After all, in most nearby possible worlds he does not make this observation, and this event is clearly of significance to him. Nevertheless, that he is lucky to have made this observation does not count against him gaining knowledge about the turtle before him because, as Unger points out, it is not a matter of luck that he is right in this matter. Accordingly, genuine knowledge possession is not undermined merely by the fact that it is a matter of luck that the agent is in a position to know anything at all at that moment.

Moreover, with this example in mind we can easily think of further examples which can illustrate a case where, whilst it is not a matter of luck that the agent is alive, it is a matter of luck that he has the required cognitive capacities to gain knowledge in this case. Imagine, for example, that the counterfactual danger does not come from a heavy rock overhead, but from a sturdy branch that is caught (at eye-level) behind another branch so that, were someone to move the other branch, they would almost certainly get thwacked in the face by the branch behind with enough force to be permanently blinded. Suppose, however, that moments prior to seeing the turtle, the agent moves the second branch, thereby releasing the caught branch behind, but, as it happens, does not get hit because he happens to duck at that very moment to tie his shoelaces. That he is not blinded by the force of the branch hitting him in the face is clearly a lucky event, since whilst it obtains in the actual world it does not obtain in a wide class of nearby possible worlds where the relevant initial conditions are the same as in the actual world, and it is obviously an event that is of significance to him. Furthermore, that it is a matter of luck that the agent is not blind at that moment entails that it is also a matter of luck that he is in a position to observe the turtle (again, in a wide class of nearby possible worlds he cannot see the turtle right now, and that he can see the turtle is clearly an event that is of significant to him). Nevertheless, this is obviously consistent with the agent having knowledge that there is a turtle before him because, as before, it is not a matter of luck that he is right in this matter.[17]

Although Unger only explicitly lists the above two types of harmless epistemic luck, one can discern two other varieties of epistemic luck if one pays careful attention to the text. For example, Unger makes the following remark:

[A] man may overhear his employer say that he will be fired and he may do so quite by accident, not intending to be near his employer's office or to gain any information from his employer. Though it may be an accident that the man came to know that he will be fired, and it may be somewhat accidental that he knows this to be so, nevertheless, from the time that he hears and onwards, it may well be not at all accidental that the man is right about its being the case that he will be fired. Thus, he may know, whether by accident or not. (Unger 1968: 159)

Curiously, however, although this example is found within the account given of the first type of benign epistemic luck, it does not conform to either of the types distinguished above. After all, this is not a scenario in which the agent is lucky to be able to possess knowledge in the first place nor is it even a case in which the proposition known is only luckily true. It would seem, then, that Unger has stumbled across another form of harmless epistemic luck. We will call this type of luck 'evidential epistemic luck', and characterize it as follows:

Evidential epistemic luck
It is lucky that the agent acquires the evidence that she has in favour of her belief.

As Unger points out, we would be quite willing to ascribe knowledge to the unfortunate man in this example even though it was entirely lucky that he came across the evidence which supports his knowledge (in a wide class of the relevant nearby possible worlds he does not acquire this evidence, and that he does acquire this evidence is clearly something which is of significance to him). We have thus identified a third variety of innocuous epistemic luck.

Indeed, such cases of evidential epistemic luck are common in the contemporary epistemological literature, although they are rarely explicitly understood in these terms. For instance, consider the following example offered by Robert Nozick (1981) in his discussion of his modal theory of knowledge, where he asks us to imagine a situation where the bank robber's mask slips off as he is escaping and the bystander sees it is Jesse James (Nozick 1981: 193).

On this basis, argues Nozick, the bystander can come to 'know that Jesse James is robbing the bank' (193) even though it is purely a matter of luck that the bystander is in the position that she is when James's mask happens to slip. This is clearly a case of evidential epistemic luck in that it is lucky that the agent should acquire the evidence that supports her true belief in the identity of the bank robber. After all, this is an event (the gaining of the evidence in question via the sight of James's face) that is significant enough to the agent for her to form the relevant belief. Moreover, in a wide class of nearby possible worlds where the relevant initial conditions are the same as in the actual world (where, for example, she is not making any special effort to get a glimpse of the bank robber, such as by confronting him and attempting to remove his mask herself) she will not gain the evidence that she does in the actual world. Accordingly, the agent would not form this belief in these worlds (because she would not see James's face).

One might think, however, that this way of putting the matter runs two distinct forms of innocuous epistemic luck together—that is, an evidential luck regarding the evidence that one has in favour of one's belief and a *doxastic* luck regarding the formation of one's belief. The reason for this is that these cases happen to be cases in which it is both lucky that the agent has the evidence that she does *and* lucky that she forms the belief that she does. We have already remarked on the evidential aspect of this luck, so let us pause for a moment to consider the doxastic aspect.

Take Unger's example of the employee overhearing that he will be fired. Upon receiving this information, this agent will form a belief that he will be fired where the formation of this belief will be lucky by the lights of our characterization of luck. That is, he will form this belief in the actual world but, in a wide class nearby possible worlds where the relevant initial conditions are the same as in the actual world—where, for example, he isn't given any reason to be suspicious in this regard, and so does not attempt to find out the information in question—he won't overhear this conversation and so won't form this belief that he is to be fired. Moreover, the event at issue, that he forms this belief that he will be fired, is clearly an event which is of significance to him. That he forms this belief is thus a matter of luck.

The same goes for Nozick's example regarding Jesse James. The agent forms his belief that the robber is Jesse James in the actual world but, in a wide class of nearby possible worlds where the relevant initial conditions are the same as in the actual world—where, for example, she has no further grounds available which would lead her to form this belief, such as one of the other members of the gang referring to Jesse James by name within earshot—she will not form this belief. Moreover, that she forms this belief is clearly something that is of significance to her. Again, then, we can see that this is a case where the agent is lucky to form the belief that she does.

In general, we can characterize this notion of doxastic epistemic luck as follows:

Doxastic epistemic luck
It is lucky that the agent believes the proposition.

Given that it is both doxastic and evidential luck that is at issue in these cases, the natural question to ask is whether there could not be cases where these types of luck came apart so that the one sort of luck was present without the other also being present.

Since evidential luck is defined in terms of the evidence that supports the agent's belief in the target proposition, this rules out a possible epistemologically trivial sense in which doxastic and evidential luck can come apart. This would be where an agent's evidence is gained in an evidentially lucky fashion even though her belief isn't gained in a way that is doxastically lucky because the agent doesn't believe the proposition in question at all (perhaps because the agent has independent grounds for discounting this 'lucky' evidence). Given that belief in the target proposition is a necessary condition for knowledge of that proposition, however, the agent in this case is not even going to be in the market for knowledge in the first place, and this severely undermines any epistemological significance that this observation might have. Since our formulation of evidential epistemic luck stipulates that the agent has the belief in question, however, we can ignore such a case without further ado.

Nevertheless, our formulations of evidential and doxastic epistemic luck do not rule out cases where doxastic luck and evidential luck come apart where the agent's belief is gained in a doxastically lucky fashion but his evidence is not gained in an evidentially lucky manner because he has no evidence. Indeed, it is important that this possibility is not ruled out by our formulations of evidential and doxastic epistemic luck since such cases will be epistemologically significant provided that one allows (as we allowed in Part I) the possibility that agents can sometimes gain knowledge without having any evidence in favour of their beliefs. Such cases might be basic perceptual beliefs where an agent spontaneously forms a perceptual belief in response to a certain stimuli but where she is lucky to see what she does, and so lucky to form the belief in question. In such cases it is at least plausible to suppose that the agent concerned lacks evidence in favour of her belief in the epistemically internalist sense of that term that we outlined in Part I, and yet that this is so does not prevent her from gaining knowledge of the target proposition.

These types of examples are contentious, however, since one has to subscribe to an externalist theory of knowledge in order to be able to make sense of them. Accordingly, it would be better to rest our case for the epistemological significance of this distinction between these two types of epistemic luck on examples which are less controversial. Unfortunately, this is easier said than done. Perhaps the most natural cases that come to mind in this respect concern scenarios where the time at which the belief is formed is different from the time at which the evidence is acquired, thus allowing for the possibility that luck was involved in the one case but not in the other. For example, an agent might gain the evidence that supports her belief in an evidentially lucky fashion and yet not form the belief at issue in a doxastically lucky fashion because she already held the belief prior to gaining the lucky evidence. For example, imagine a jury member who, because of prejudice, already believes (truly as it happens) that the defendant is guilty even before gaining any evidence that would indicate her guilt. Now imagine that our juror subsequently gains the evidence that will support this belief in a lucky fashion, perhaps because she accidentally overhears forensic information that is crucial to the case being discussed by the prosecution counsel which, due to a point of law, was withheld from the jury. We thus have a case of evidential luck but not doxastic luck. Moreover, the agent is clearly in the market for knowledge given that she has a true belief supported by impeccable evidence.

Of course, one issue with cases like this is that the very reason given for thinking that we have a case of evidential luck that is not thereby a case of doxastic luck is also a reason for thinking that the agent in question should not be ascribed knowledge in the first place. In this case, for example, that the agent would believe what she does anyhow, regardless of having any evidence in favour of that belief, is a reason to question whether we should ascribe knowledge to her of the proposition in question. Indeed, as we will see in the next section, there are good reasons for this, in that beliefs formed outwith supporting evidence will tend to be only luckily true in a way that undermines knowledge possession. So even though we may well ultimately ascribe knowledge in such cases, it remains true that there are prima facie grounds for thinking that cases where the agent is evidentially lucky and yet not doxastically lucky are, *ipso facto*, cases where the agent is not even in the market for knowledge in the first place. Accordingly, this undermines the epistemological significance of such examples.

Examples where the agent is doxastically lucky and yet not evidentially lucky because the evidence was acquired prior to the belief are even more controversial. Such a case might be a scientist who had the supporting evidence all along but who did not appreciate its significance until, by luck, a further (non-evidential) stimulus came along to make her see how this evidence fitted together to support the target belief (what we might call a scientific 'gestalt switch'). And since she only came across this further stimulus to her belief by luck, we might naturally suppose that her belief is formed in a doxastically lucky fashion. The problem with this case is that it is hard to understand what is meant by 'evidence' in this regard given that the agent had it without appreciating its significance. In effect, this seems to mean—in light of any epistemically internalist construal of 'evidence' at any rate—that the agent didn't really have the evidence in question after all (it was, we might say, 'potential' or 'proto-'evidence, rather than evidence *simpliciter*). Thus one can't get an uncontroversial case of doxastic luck which is not also evidential luck either.

So although there are clearly two types of luck at issue here, in that it is at least logically possible that the one might be present whilst the other is absent, it is nevertheless the case that they will tend to always be co-applicable. Moreover, although there do seem to be possible cases where the one variety of luck is present without the other, such examples are by their nature controversial, with their very existence dependent upon further contentious epistemological claims. Given that both of these types of luck are compatible with knowledge possession, we can sidestep this problem by simply confining our attention to those situations where, uncontroversially, these two sorts of luck are both applicable. In doing so, we will need to be conscious of the fact that these varieties of luck could in principle come apart, and thus be wary of ambiguities in the details of examples that might be relevant in this regard. Henceforth, unless there is special reason to distinguish between these two types of epistemic luck, when I talk about 'evidential' epistemic luck I will take this to cover doxastic epistemic luck as well.

We have thus identified four possible types of epistemic luck, all of which are consistent with the possession of knowledge. As we will see, the importance of distinguishing these types of epistemic luck is that the kinds of cases in which there is a genuine tension between luck and knowledge can easily be confused with cases in which there is no tension at all. Distinguishing between those types of luck that undermine knowledge possession and those that do not is thus essential if we are to capture the source of the supposed tension between luck and knowledge.

5.3. Concluding Remarks

We have seen in this chapter that a general rough account of what is involved in the notion of luck can be given, and have applied this account in order to identify, with Unger's help, several varieties of epistemic luck that are compatible with knowledge possession. The task in hand is now to delimit these unproblematic varieties of epistemic luck from the other types of epistemic luck that do pose problems for a theory of knowledge. This is the topic of the next chapter.

Notes

1. Ravitch (1976), Foley (1984), Gjelsvik (1991), Hall (1994), Heller (1999b), Axtell (2001), and Vahid (2001) are all representatives of the former camp, since none of them offers an account of luck at all. Moreover, some writers who do offer at least a loose conceptual characterization of the notion fare little better. Engel (1992: 59), e.g., describes the notion of epistemic luck in terms of 'situations where a person has a true belief which is in some sense fortuitous or coincidental', which is hardly illuminating. Indeed, in general, there is no real developed account of luck available in the literature, perhaps the closest thing being Rescher (1995). The reader should note that, henceforth, and unless specified otherwise, when I talk about 'luck' I will not be taking this to imply *good* luck (as it often does in ordinary language), but rather to be compatible with the luck in question being either good or bad.
2. It should be noted that there is a broader sense of 'accident' which applies even if the event in question was not, strictly speaking, an accident at all. Such a case might be where someone deliberately drives into the oncoming traffic. The subsequent news reports would no doubt still refer to the ensuing carnage as being a traffic 'accident' even though there was nothing at all accidental about this event. Henceforth, when I talk about the notion of an accident I will have the stricter meaning in mind that excludes this non-standard usage.
3. See, e.g., Rescher (1995: 19).
4. This point has been made by experimenters who have studied the psychology of luck. For a survey of the key treatments of luck in the psychological literature, see Pritchard & Smith (2004).

5. Indeed, intuitively, the very same event can coherently (and simultaneously) be judged to be lucky by one person, unlucky by another, and neither lucky nor unlucky by a third person. (See, e.g., the example of the sinking of the Spanish Armada offered by Rescher (1995: 20).) Relatedly, Teigen—a psychologist—has noted that accident victims often describe themselves as extremely lucky one minute and then extremely *un*lucky the next. He gives the following example to illustrate this:

> Anat Ben-Tov, survivor of two Tel Aviv bus bomb attacks, expressed this [*point*] succinctly in an interview, given from her hospital bed: 'I have no luck, or I have all the luck—I am not sure which'. (Teigen 2003: 1)

Note that it is clear from the context of this statement that in saying that she has 'no luck' this woman means that she is *un*lucky. Accordingly, the issue here is the variability in the type of luck that is in question, not its existence.

6. Rescher (1995) is actually sensitive to these issues (though not others). His view is discussed in more detail below.

7. Although it is with the debates regarding moral and epistemic luck that one finds the most explicit discussions of luck in the philosophical literature, one can also find discussions of this notion in the philosophy of religion (e.g. Zagzebski 1994*a*), the philosophy of logic (Sorenson 1998), and the debate regarding free will (e.g. Dennett 1984), to cite just three examples.

8. For more on the debate regarding moral luck, see the papers collected in the anthology edited by Statman (1993*b*), and in particular the exchange between Nagel (1979; cf. Nagel 1976) and Williams (1981*b*; cf. Williams 1976) that is reprinted in that volume.

9. Consider these passages from Zimmerman (1993) and Greco (1995):

> '[S]omething which occurs as a matter of luck with respect to someone P is something which occurs beyond P's control.' (Zimmerman 1993: 231)
> '[T]o say that something occurs as a matter of luck is just to say that it is not under my control.' (Greco 1995: 83)

See also Latus (2000). Latus (2003: 446) also offers the following examples of this type of view about luck:

> ' "As a matter of luck" here means: in a way that is beyond our control.' (Moore 1990: 301)
> 'By "luck" I mean factors, good or bad, beyond the control of the affected agent.' (Card 1990: 199)

10. This is encapsulated in the slogan for the British National Lottery: 'It Could be You'. Clearly the 'could' here is not the could of probability, since in this sense it *couldn't* be you (the odds are astronomically against your favour). Instead, it is the could of counterfactual similarity. The world in which one wins the lottery is very much like the actual world in which (as yet) one hasn't won.

11. A further advantage to (L1) is that it can incorporate our intuition that some events are luckier than others. It is certainly the case that sometimes events occur which are so fortuitous that they appear to constitute a greater degree of luck than is usual. For example, that one happens to find one's wallet, replete with its contents, in the street the day after losing it is clearly lucky, but it is not nearly as lucky as losing one's wallet and then finding it again, replete with its contents untouched and unharmed, a year later. A plausible explanation of why we think the second event is luckier than the first is that there are far fewer nearby possible worlds where the second event occurs. (L1) thus captures the sense

in which extremely unusual events can be regarded as luckier than just plain unusual events. There are complications here, however, in that a number of psychological studies of luck seem to suggest that the degree of luck attributed by an agent is, at least in part, a function of the particular counterfactual circumstances that are being focused upon by that agent. I discuss this issue further in note 13 below. For more discussion of this point, see the literature surveys in Teigen (2003) and Pritchard and Smith (2004).

12. Our concept of luck is, in any case, vague—in that there will be events where it is just not clear whether or not they are lucky—so it is pointless trying to find a characterization of luck that completely eliminates this vagueness. For instance, to return to an example employed in the last note, does dropping one's wallet and finding it (untampered with) ten minutes later when one retraces one's steps (and knowing that one has only just dropped it) count as lucky? Possibly, though, equally, possibly not. Our confusion here relates to the fact that such an event is part of the wide range of penumbral cases where it is simply not transparent that luck is involved. (L1) captures this aspect of luck because it will likewise be a vague matter whether or not the event does not occur in a wide class of the nearby possible worlds. In general, possible worlds are not well suited to drawing sharp boundaries because it isn't always straightforward how one is to accurately 'measure' the nearness of the relevant possible world or (relatedly) to 'count' possible worlds in the required manner. (This is the so-called 'world order' problem for possible worlds.) Since our notion of luck is not sharp either, however, the vagueness inherent in measuring or counting possible worlds is all to the good. For further discussion of some of the issues related to possible worlds, see the papers collected in Loux (1979).

13. There are complications here, however, in that a number of psychological studies have shown that sometimes agents describe positive lucky events as instances of bad luck, and vice versa. This typically occurs when the conversational context is such as to prompt the agent to focus on a specific counterfactual possibility which is, respectively, either much better or much worse than the actual outcome. For example, a lottery winner could be made to describe her substantial lottery win as an instance of bad luck (even whilst granting that the outcome was positive) if the specified counterfactual contrast is winning the lottery when there is a far bigger jackpot. Conversely, an agent can be made to describe her car accident as an instance of good luck (even whilst granting that this outcome was negative) if the specified counterfactual contrast is being involved in a car accident and being seriously harmed as a result. (The example of the survivor of the Tel Aviv bus bomb attacks given in note 5 above is a good illustration of this second type of case.) For our purposes here we can stick to the basic cases where agents are not being asked to focus on any specific counterfactual possibility, and thus where there will be a correlation between positive lucky events and the agent regarding those events as instances of good luck and negative lucky events and the agent regarding those events as instances of bad luck. I discuss the way in which this account of luck should be adapted to deal with this element of the psychological literature in more detail in Pritchard and Smith (2004). For more on the psychological literature in this regard, which includes a proposed development of the account of luck that I offer here along lines that can accommodate this difficulty, see Teigen (2003).

14. There are further issues here, of course. What should we do, e.g., with those agents who are (counterfactually) unresponsive to the relevant facts? Should we maintain that in these cases the event just is not lucky or tighten our *caveat* so that it involves some claim about what the agent *ought* to regard as significant were she to be availed of all the relevant facts? My inclination here is towards the former alternative, on the grounds that when it comes to meeting (L2), luck is, in the relevant sense, in the eye of the beholder.

This raises a further issue, however, of what to do with cases where the agent in question does not regard the event as lucky but others do (such as, e.g., a scenario in which a devoutly religious person who regards all events as predestined and so does not believe that any event is lucky is regarded by others as being 'lucky' to survive a plane crash in which everyone else was killed). In these cases our intuitions are not, I think, all that clear, and I will be setting this problem to one side. In any case, this rough account of luck should be informative enough to suffice for our purposes here.

15. A challenge to this model of luck is posed by those, such as Rescher, who argue that luck is inextricably tied to what the agent can rationally expect to occur. On this view, an event could be lucky for an agent even though it occurred in most nearby possible worlds just so long as the agent could not be rationally expected to have predicted such an event. Fortunately, the examples that Rescher offers to support this line are unpersuasive. Here is one of them:

> [A] happy or unhappy development can be a matter of luck from the recipient's point of view even if its eventuation is the result of a deliberate contrivance by others. (Your secret benefactor's sending you that big check represents a stroke of good luck for *you* even if it is something that he has been planning for years.) Thus even if someone else— different from the person affected—is able to predict that unexpected development, the eventuation at issue may still be lucky for those who are involved. (Rescher 1995: 35)

It is far from clear that this is a case of luck, however, no matter how much the agent may regard it as such. Indeed, the example seems more accurately to be an instance of good fortune rather than luck, where fortune relates to those cases where certain events that one has no control over count in one's favour (where 'fortune smiles' on one) rather than cases where luck is specifically involved. (On this view of fortune, one could regard positively lucky events as being part of a more general class of fortunate events. Interestingly, Rescher (1995: *passim*) also makes this distinction between luck and fortune, though he does not draw the same consequences from it.) In order to see this, one need only note that if the agent were to discover that this event had been carefully planned all along, then he would plausibly no longer regard it as a lucky event. Indeed, once he discovered that this event was always due to occur, it seems natural to suppose that he would regard himself as no more lucky than a favoured son is 'lucky' to have received a vast inheritance from his rich father (i.e. not lucky at all, but merely fortunate). The moral to be drawn from such cases is thus not that lack of information on the part of the agent is a determinant of luck (which is the moral that Rescher draws), but rather that lack of information can seriously affect the agent's ability to correctly determine whether or not an event is lucky in the first place. Similar remarks apply to the other examples that Rescher (1995: §2.5) offers to support his case in this regard. For further discussion of Rescher's account of luck, see Pritchard (2004b) and Pritchard and Smith (2004).

16. Since writing this chapter I have come across Latus's (2003) intriguing new article on luck in which he sketches an account of the notion. Although I have not the space to explore this proposal in depth here, it is worth noting that it bears a number of similarities with the view just described in that Latus rejects a conception of luck which simply identifies this notion with lack of control or chance, and seeks instead what he calls a 'hybrid' view that incorporates features of both these conditions and applies them only to significant events. In broad outline, then, Latus's position may thus be equivalent to the one set out here (though expressed in different terms).

17. For further discussion of Unger's account of epistemic luck in this respect, see Harper (1996).

144

6

Two Varieties of Epistemic Luck

6.0. Introduction

In the last chapter we saw a general account of what is involved in the notion of luck, and used it to identify several varieties of epistemic luck that were clearly compatible with knowledge possession. With these less interesting types of epistemic luck set to one side, the focus for this chapter will be on those two varieties of epistemic luck—what I term 'veritic' epistemic luck and 'reflective' epistemic luck—that are problematic.

It is argued that a safety-based account of knowledge can eliminate veritic epistemic luck, which is the type of epistemic luck that is at issue in the Gettier-style counter-examples to the classical tripartite account of knowledge. Furthermore, it is also claimed that it is the elimination of this sort of epistemic luck that is the primary motivation of the core externalist response to the closure-based radical sceptical challenge—i.e. neo-Mooreanism—which, as we saw in Chapter 3, is also understood along safety-based lines. Nevertheless, I further argue that a safety-based account of knowledge alone cannot deal with the problem posed by reflective epistemic luck, and that this presents us with a prima facie motivation for epistemological internalism. The scene is thus set for the next chapter in which we examine the relationship between reflective epistemic luck and cognitive responsibility.

6.1. Veritic Epistemic Luck and the Gettier Counter-examples

As we saw Peter Unger putting the point in the last chapter, the issue about epistemically problematic examples of epistemic luck is that they impair the epistemic 'relation concerning the man and the fact', and the types of epistemic luck that we have examined so far do not have this effect. Instead, the varieties of epistemic luck that we have identified as being epistemically harmless concern luck in the 'preconditions' for knowledge, rather than luck that infects the core epistemic relation between an agent and a true proposition which is pivotal to knowledge possession. We must thus look more specifically at the sort of epistemic luck that affects this epistemic relationship between the knowing subject and the fact known.

As we will see, the key type of epistemic luck that is relevant here is that which concerns the truth of the belief in question, what we will call 'veritic' epistemic luck:[1]

Veritic epistemic luck
It is a matter of luck that the agent's belief is true.

In terms of our account of luck, this demands that the agent's belief is true in the actual world, but that in a wide class of nearby possible worlds in which the relevant initial conditions are the same as in the actual world—and this will mean, in the basic case, that the agent at the very least forms the same belief in the same way as in the actual world (we will examine a little more what this clause means in a moment)—the belief is false.[2]

For example, consider again the case of 'Gullible John' that we looked at in §2.3. Gullible John is a very trusting individual who tends to believe any testimony he receives without ever pausing to think whether it really is true (whether he has grounds to support, or at least not undermine, what he is being told, or for thinking that the informant is reliable in this respect). Now suppose that, knowing about Gullible John's trusting nature, his friends decide, for a joke, to tell him that his house is on fire, and that John forms a belief that this is the case on this basis and accordingly he runs home to deal with the blaze. Finally, imagine that John's belief in this respect is, as it happens, true, in that at that very moment an electrical fault triggers a small fire at John's house which he discovers on his return and puts out.

Clearly, upon hearing the testimony of his so-called 'friends', John does not know that his house is on fire, even though this belief is in fact true, and we can account for this lack of knowledge in terms of how his belief in this respect is veritically lucky. That is, in most nearby possible worlds in which John forms the same belief about his house being on fire on the basis of his mischievous pals' testimony, his belief will be false. After all, in most of these worlds his house will not have happened to have burst into flames at that moment and John returns to his house to find, to his surprise, that there is nothing to be concerned about. Knowledge, it seems, is incompatible with veritic luck.

Indeed, it is useful to compare John's belief formed on the basis of testimony that is meant to be false, and which does not qualify as knowledge, with that same belief held by John which is formed solely on the basis of seeing the fire. Intuitively, in the second case John *does* know that his house is on fire since this is an appropriate way of forming one's beliefs about this subject matter. Crucially, this intuition is compatible with the thesis that knowledge is inconsistent with veritic luck because of how the belief in this case is *not* veritically lucky. After all, in most nearby possible worlds where John forms his belief that his house is on fire as a result of seeing his house alight his belief will tend to correspond with the truth. In those worlds where there are no flames to be seen John will not believe that his house is on fire, whilst in those worlds in which there are he'll believe that it is.

What about the case in which John initially forms his belief that his house is on fire on the basis of dishonest testimony, and then later sees that his house is on fire? We have already seen that he lacks knowledge in the former case, so the key question is whether this veritic luck extends over to the latter case to continue to undermine his knowledge. The issue here will be whether John alters his belief in response to the changing circumstances. For example, let's suppose that John, like most people I take it, allows what he sees to 'trump' what he's told so that if he arrives at his house and discovers that there's no fire, then he will cease to believe that his house is on fire regardless of the fact that he has been told that this is the case by his pals. If this is right, then I think that our intuition is that John does have knowledge in the latter case, even despite his lack of knowledge in the former case. This result is consistent with the idea that knowledge is incompatible with veritic luck, however, for the simple reason that with the example so described John's belief at the later time is based on what he sees and not on what he has been told, and thus his true belief is not veritically lucky at the later time in the way that it was at the former time.

Suppose, however, that John is not only gullible but also rather insensitive in his belief formation, such that he will not change his testimony-based belief in response to what he sees, and hence will continue (somewhat bizarrely) to believe that his house is on fire because this is what he has been told even despite the fact that he can see no such fire when he arrives home. In this case, our intuition is clearly that John lacks knowledge at both the earlier and the later times, and this is accounted for in terms of the thesis that knowledge is incompatible with veritic luck because of how with the details so described this example constitutes a case in which John's belief, even at the later time, continues to be based on dishonest testimony and so continues to be veritically lucky. Again, then, the thesis that knowledge is incompatible with veritic luck accords with our intuitions in this case.

So the hypothesis that knowledge is incompatible with veritic luck receives a lot of intuitive support, both from cases in which agents lack knowledge and seem to do so because their beliefs are veritically lucky, and from cases in which agents have knowledge and seem to do so because (at least in part) their beliefs are not veritically lucky. Further support for this hypothesis comes from the fact that it is veritic luck that is at issue in the counter-examples to the classical tripartite account of knowledge that were famously advanced by Edmund Gettier (1963). According to the tripartite account of knowledge, the relevant epistemic condition that transforms true belief into knowledge is understood as an internalist justification condition. Gettier's point, set out in terms of veritic epistemic luck, was that an agent could have a true belief which met this internalist epistemic condition but which was not knowledge because the true belief was veritically lucky. These days it is pretty much taken as given that Gettier's examples were successful in this regard, and thus that the classical tripartite account of knowledge is a non-starter. Here, for example, is how Jonathan Dancy describes the point:

[K]nowledge must somehow not depend on coincidence or luck. *This was just the point* of the Gettier counter-examples; nothing in the tripartite definition excluded knowledge by luck. (Dancy 1985: 134, *my italics*)

That examples which highlight the presence of this type of epistemic luck are widely thought to decisively refute a certain epistemological theory indicates just how intuitive it is to suppose that this particular species of epistemic luck is incompatible with knowledge possession.[3]

Consider the following Gettier-style example adapted from one given (though in a different regard) by Bertrand Russell (1948: 170–1). Our hero comes downstairs every morning around about the same time and looks at the time on the old clock in her hall. The clock tells her that it is 8.22, and as a result our agent forms the belief that this is the time. Furthermore, the clock is right, because it *is* 8.22 a.m. Nevertheless, unbeknownst to our protagonist, the clock has in fact broken down (it broke down 12 hours before). This is clearly a case where our agent's belief is only luckily true, since in most of the nearest possible worlds where the agent forms her belief about this matter and the relevant initial conditions for this event are the same as in the actual world—e.g. such that she forms her belief in the same way as in the actual world, by looking at this clock—her belief will be false. We thus have an example of veritic epistemic luck.

Moreover, this is also a Gettier-style counter-example to the classical tripartite account of knowledge, in that the presence of this veritic epistemic luck is not ruled out by the agent meeting the relevant epistemic condition—in this case the internalist justification condition. We can suppose, for example, that the agent has good reflectively accessible grounds in support of her true belief, such as grounds for thinking that the clock is a highly reliable timepiece and that there is no reason for thinking that it is not working normally this morning, perhaps because the agent has independent evidence for thinking that this is roughly the right time. Nevertheless, the presence of this internalist justification for her belief is compatible with the belief being only luckily true. After all, no matter how good the agent's reflectively accessible grounds are, they will not be grounds which *entail* that the clock has not stopped, and in so far as the agent is forming her belief via a stopped clock then there will be a significant degree of veritic epistemic luck involved, enough to undermine an ascription of knowledge to the agent.[4]

As Linda Zagzebski (1994*b*, 1999) points out, there is a systematic method for generating Gettier-style examples. First, take a belief that has met the relevant epistemic condition or conditions demanded by the epistemological theory at issue. Next, introduce a dose of bad epistemic luck that would usually prevent the agent from having a true belief. So, to return to our example of the stopped clock, although the clock is broken in the actual world, given that we have stipulated that it is generally a reliable clock (and provided that we keep the initial conditions for this event fixed), in most nearby possible worlds it won't be broken right now. And, typically, finding out what the time is by looking at a stopped clock will lead to one gaining a false belief. Finally, stipulate a further case of good epistemic luck that cancels out the bad luck and which ensures that the agent's belief is true. The good epistemic luck in this example concerns the fact that the agent just happens to look at the clock at the one point at which it is displaying the right time. Although this occurs in the actual world, it will not happen in most of the nearby possible worlds in which the relevant initial conditions for this event remain the same—instead, the agent will be looking at the clock at a point at which it is displaying the wrong time. In summary, the bad epistemic luck that (despite the general reliability of the clock and all the good reasons the agent has for thinking the contrary) the clock is broken is cancelled out by the good epistemic luck that the agent happens to look at the clock at the time that she did so that she forms a true belief regardless.

The standard diagnosis of these examples is that they show that merely true belief supported by good reflectively accessible reasons will not suffice to ensure knowledge because such reasons will not be sufficient to rule out epistemic luck. More specifically, we can note that the problem is not the presence of epistemic luck per se, but rather the presence of veritic epistemic luck. Mylan Engel (1992) concludes from this that the problem of veritic epistemic luck cannot be dealt with by internalist epistemological theories (and thus that those theories are inadequate) on the grounds that whatever internal conditions are adduced by such theories, they will not incorporate the kind of external relationship to the truth that would eliminate this sort of epistemic luck. Engel doesn't offer a fully-fledged account of what he has in mind regarding epistemological internalism here, but his comments seem to fit the standard conception of this position as described above in §2.2. Recall that this understanding of epistemological internalism treated internalist knowledge as being essentially composed of internalist justification, and, in turn, characterized internalist justification as demanding that an agent is only justified provided that she is able to know the facts which determine that justification by reflection alone. On this conception of internalism, one can see why any austere internalist theory of knowledge that merely held that knowledge was justified true belief would be hostage to veritic epistemic luck. After all, there is no fact that one could know by reflection alone that would ensure that one's justified true belief was not 'Gettiered'.

For example, the facts that the agent in the 'stopped clock' example above knows by reflection alone could also be known by a counterpart agent who is in exactly the same circumstances except that she is forming her true belief by looking at a clock that has *not* stopped. That is, the difference between the agent whose putative knowledge is subject to a significant and undermining degree of veritic epistemic luck and the counterpart agent whose (bona fide) knowledge is not influenced by veritic epistemic luck is not one that can be captured in terms of the facts that the agent is able to know by reflection alone. Accordingly, knowledge cannot just be true belief that is justified by the lights of the internalist account.

Nevertheless, Engel is wrong to conclude on this basis that there is some essential problem in *all* internalist theories of knowledge, even renderings of this thesis that are not as austere. This is because it is entirely open to internalists to advocate extra epistemic conditions in addition to an internalist conception of justification in their account of knowledge. Recall that the characteristic claim made by epistemological internalists is that meeting an internalist justification condition is *necessary* for knowledge possession, not that it is (with true belief) *sufficient*. Accordingly, epistemological internalists can consistently allow that agents need to meet external epistemic conditions over and above the internalist justification condition without undermining their view.

So whilst veritic epistemic luck is indeed epistemically significant—in that it is inconsistent with knowledge possession such that its elimination is an adequacy condition on any theory of knowledge—its ramifications for contemporary epistemological discussion are not quite as direct and dramatic as Engel claims. At best, all that is ruled out by this incompatibility between veritic epistemic luck and knowledge possession is an extreme version of epistemological internalism which held that knowledge was nothing other than internalistically justified true belief.[5]

The way to eliminate veritic epistemic luck from one's theory of knowledge — and therefore evade the Gettier counter-examples—is thus to identify an external epistemic condition which ensures that the agent's true belief cannot be acquired in a veritically lucky fashion. More specifically, one needs to identify an external condition that makes it such that meeting the relevant epistemic conditions entails not only the truth of the target proposition but also ensures that the belief in question tracks the truth across most of the relevant nearby possible worlds to ensure that veritic epistemic luck is unable to intervene.[6]

One easy, but unilluminating, way of doing this would be to simply specify that knowledge is justified true belief that arises in a 'Gettier-free' fashion, where the latter condition is an 'external' epistemic condition in the sense that its obtaining concerns facts that the agent will not be able to know by reflection alone (such as that the clock which the agent uses to form her belief about the time is working). Indeed, Unger's (1968) theory of knowledge in terms of 'non-accidental' true belief is along these lines. A more plausible theory would, of course, specify what it means for an agent's justification to be Gettier-free. Such theories as the 'indefeasibility' thesis propounded by Keith Lehrer and Tom Paxson (1969) could be construed as attempts to offer such a specification.[7]

With our characterization of epistemic luck in terms of (L1) and (L2) in mind, however, we can offer a more general account of what is required to eliminate veritic epistemic luck. Recall that what is needed is a theory of knowledge that ensures that it is not a matter of epistemic luck that the agent's belief is true given that she meets all the relevant epistemic conditions. It must thus be part of what is involved in meeting the epistemic conditions that one not only forms a true belief in the actual world, but that in most nearby possible worlds where the relevant initial conditions for that belief are the same as in the actual world (e.g. where the agent forms her belief in the same way as she did in the actual world), the agent also forms a true belief in the target proposition. It should be clear by now just what is needed in this respect, namely the sort of 'safety' principle that we looked at in §3.1, and which we saw was independently motivated by the core relevant alternatives intuition that knowledge requires one's beliefs to be responsive to relevant nearby possibilities, and *only* nearby possibilities. After all, as we saw in §3.1, this principle is *defined* in such a way that it excludes the possibility that the agent's belief fails to match the truth in a wide class of relevant nearby possible worlds. It is thus able to deal with the problem posed by veritic epistemic luck—and thus with Gettier counter-examples—directly, and hence offer a good first approximation of what is required by an 'anti-luck' epistemology.

Before we can consider how the safety principle is able to deal with the problem posed by veritic epistemic luck, however, we need to look a little deeper at how this principle needs to be understood if it is to achieve this end.

6.2. Refining the Safety Principle (Part One)—The Relevant Initial Conditions

We have already noted in our characterisation of luck, and thus in our specific characterisation of veritic epistemic luck, that the relevant possible worlds need to be understood such that the initial conditions for the target event are fixed. Moreover, we have noted that this restriction is going to mean, in the basic case (we will consider a non-basic case in a moment), that the nearby possible worlds that are at issue are specifically those worlds where at the very least the agent forms her belief in the same way as she does in the actual world. Intuitively, this is just how safety will be understood anyway in that possible worlds in which the agent forms her belief in a different way from how it is formed in the actual world will tend to be further out than those worlds in which what gave rise to the belief stays the same. Nevertheless, it is worthwhile extracting this element of our implicit understanding of safety in order to get a better grip on what this principle involves. Moreover, as we will see, adding this detail to the principle also enables us to get clearer about the differences between two key types of epistemic luck.

To begin with, we need to note that the 'way' in which the belief is actually formed needs to be individuated *externally* rather than *internally*, where by this I mean that what the agent believes is the way in which she forms her belief is not necessarily the way in which it is formed. I take it that this is relatively uncontroversial, but a couple of illustrative examples of why we need to understand the way in which the belief is formed in this manner won't do any harm.

First, consider the following case—adapted from one given by D. M. Armstrong (1973: 209), and which he in turn attributes to Gregory O'Hair—in which a mother believes that the way in which she formed her (true) belief about her son's innocence of a murder charge was via the excellent evidence she has acquired which indicates that this is the case (e.g. by hearing the forensic evidence about the cause of the victim's death which backs-up the son's story). To tighten up our intuitions in this regard, we will stipulate that whilst her son was not in fact the murderer, he very nearly was (we will consider an example in which the target event is not 'lucky' in this way below in §6.4). Perhaps, for example, he intended to murder her, but she died of a heart attack before he had a chance. Knowing what we do about the mother's psychology, however, we know that her belief was actually formed as a result of her love for her son, and thus that she would have retained her belief in his innocence even if the relevant evidence had not come to light.

If we allowed the way in which the belief is formed to be individuated by what the agent believes gave rise to her belief, then this would mean that only those nearby possible worlds where she has the same good evidence in favour of her belief as she has in the actual world would be relevant to whether or not she has knowledge (i.e. where she hears the forensic evidence which supports her son's story). Since the nearby possible worlds in which the excellent evidence for her son's innocence remains will tend to be almost exclusively worlds in which he is innocent, hence the mother will, on this construal of what gave rise to her belief, have a safe (non-veritically lucky) belief in the target proposition and (depending on the details of the theory of knowledge at issue) will therefore have knowledge of this proposition.

Given the actual pedigree of the mother's belief, however, this ascription of knowledge is clearly dubious, and being clear about what actually gave rise to the belief in question reveals why. In this case, for example, the class of relevant possible worlds is not that where she continues to receive the excellent forensic evidence which supports her son's story, but rather those nearby worlds where she retains her love for her son (i.e. *regardless* of whether she hears the forensic evidence which counts in favour of her son's innocence, or indeed *any* evidence in favour of his innocence). Crucially, however, a wide class of these worlds will be worlds in which her son is guilty, and thus where she forms a false belief. Accordingly, her belief is veritically lucky. The mother's belief in her son's innocence is thus not safe and hence she lacks knowledge of this proposition, just as intuition would predict. So provided that we identify the way in which the belief was actually formed correctly, then we get the right result.

We can also manipulate the details of this example so as to formulate a case study which illustrates how individuating the way in which the belief is formed internally can lead one to deny knowledge to agents who, plausibly, have such knowledge. Imagine, for instance, that our protagonist thinks that she believes what she does about her son's innocence not because of the evidence she has in favour of this hypothesis but because of her unconditional love for him. Suppose further, however, that she is in fact self-deceived on this point, in that her belief in her son's innocence is actually due to the evidence she has in favour of this hypothesis. Nevertheless, and here is the twist in the tale, this doesn't mean that in all nearby possible worlds in which she lacks this evidence she will lose her belief in his innocence, since there are some nearby possible worlds where her son's predicament is so desperate—he is suicidal at the prospect of jail, for example—that her maternal love for him overrides her respect for the evidence and she believes in his innocence regardless.

Although the details when it comes to cases like this are admittedly somewhat convoluted, there does seem to be a prima facie case for thinking that the mother nevertheless has knowledge of her son's innocence even though she has a mistaken conception about what has given rise to the belief at issue. After all, she is forming her true belief in the right kind of way (i.e. because of the evidence that she has for his innocence). Crucially, however, were we to individuate the way in which she formed her belief in terms of what she believes gave rise to her belief, then the relevant range of nearby possible worlds would be restricted to those worlds where she retains her love for her son rather than those worlds where she continues to have evidence in favour of her son's innocence. On this 'internal' reading, however, and unlike the 'external' reading, there will be a wide class of nearby possible worlds where although the evidence in favour of her son's innocence is lacking, she nevertheless believes that he is innocent anyway because of the desperate nature of his situation. Moreover, given the further hypothesis that the son could very easily have committed the murder in question, it follows that a large number of these possible worlds where the evidence is lacking will be worlds where he did commit the crime and thus where the mother's belief is false (indeed, that he committed the crime would be a good explanation of why the evidence is lacking in these worlds). She thus has a belief which fails to match the truth across a wide class of the relevant nearby possible worlds, and hence her belief is veritically lucky. Thus, on this understanding of the way in which the mother formed her belief, she comes out as not having a safe belief in the target proposition and hence as lacking knowledge of her son's innocence even though, by hypothesis, she does know that her son is innocent. Again, then, we see that being clear about the way in which the belief is actually formed is crucial to generating the right result from our theory.

One final point that we need to make here concerns those 'non-basic' cases in which what gave rise to the original belief is not what sustains that belief at a later point in time. We saw a case of this sort above when we considered the example of Gullible John who originally forms his belief that the house is on fire on the basis of misleading testimony but later retains that belief on the basis of what he sees. It was important in this case that we evaluated John's belief relative to the two different ways in which the belief was sustained at the earlier and later points in time, since this generated the required difference in epistemic evaluation.

Returning to our example of the mother who has a son who is accused of murder, one could imagine, for example, a situation in which the mother initially believed in her son's innocence solely because of her love for him, but went on to discover the evidence that indicated his guilt. In order to sharpen our intuitions here, let us suppose that the evidence which she discovers that decisively indicates her son's innocence reveals him to be such a generally debauched and wicked individual that in discovering the evidence she loses her love for her son (perhaps the evidence indicates that he is innocent of this crime because it reveals that he was in fact committing a far more heinous crime at the time). We thus have a case in which the agent in question retains her belief in the target proposition throughout, but where what is sustaining the belief at a later point in time is entirely different from what gave rise to the belief in the first place.

With this in mind, consider how the epistemic status of the mother's belief changes as we shift our focus from the moment that she formed the belief to the point at which she retains that belief, but on a different basis. In the former case, she lacks knowledge because her belief is subject to a substantive degree of veritic epistemic luck. In a wide class of nearby possible worlds in which she forms her belief in the same way as in the actual world (i.e. because of her love for her son), she continues to believe what she does even though her son is guilty of the crime. She thus lacks a safe belief in this proposition and is therefore not in a position to have knowledge of this proposition. In contrast, at the later point in time in which her belief solely rests on the evidence that she has for believing in her son's innocence, her belief is not only true in the actual world but remains true in most nearby possible worlds in which she forms her belief in the same way as in the actual world. At the later point in time, then, her belief is safe and hence a candidate for knowledge. So although the 'basic case' will be one in which we understand the relevant initial conditions in terms of what originally gave rise to the belief, we need to be wary of non-basic cases like this where the belief remains but is sustained by something entirely different.[8]

We thus get a formulation of safety along the following lines:

Safety II
For all agents, φ, if an agent knows a contingent proposition φ, then, in most nearby possible worlds in which she forms her belief about φ in the same way as she forms her belief in the actual world, that agent only believes that φ when φ is true.

Consider how this principle deals with the paradigm Gettier-style counter-example that we have been considering—the stopped-clock example. Part of the problem with this case, and which leads us to conclude that it is not a genuine instance of knowledge, is that the relationship between the agent's belief and the truth is such that, in a wide range of nearby possible worlds, forming a belief in the way that the agent did in the actual world would lead to false beliefs. For consider, if the clock really has stopped in the actual world, then there will be a wide class of nearby possible worlds in which looking at the clock will be a very poor way of finding out the time because it will lead to the formation of false beliefs. It is thus essential to the example that there is a wide range of nearby possible worlds where the agent forms her belief in the same way that she does in the actual world, but forms a false belief instead of a true one. Crucially, however, the safety principle disallows this possibility and thus excludes the kind of veritic epistemic luck that is in play in the Gettier counter-examples. If one meets the safety principle, then it is not a matter of epistemic luck that one's belief is true since, in most nearby possible worlds in which one forms the same belief in the same way, it remains true.

Note that a further advantage of specifying that the possible worlds that are at issue in the determination of knowledge are those where the agent forms her belief on the same basis as in the actual world is that it enables us to distinguish the type of veritic epistemic luck from the sort of evidential epistemic luck discussed above where agents are only lucky to have the evidence that they do (or, in the specific case of doxastic epistemic luck, to form the belief that they do). Without this constraint, there could be a wide range of nearby possible worlds where the agent forms a false belief even though the agent does have the knowledge in question. For instance, consider Robert Nozick's example concerning Jesse James described in §5.2. If we had not added this extra condition to the safety principle, then the agent concerned might end up lacking knowledge on the grounds that there is a wide range of nearby possible worlds where she forms her belief on a different evidential basis (via testimony, say, rather than by the lucky sighting of Jesse James's face) and forms a false belief as a result. An unmodified safety principle would thus be in danger of classing the agent as lacking knowledge even though, as we saw above, knowledge possession is compatible with the lucky acquisition of evidence (and, in the case of doxastic epistemic luck, with the lucky formation of a belief).[9] In contrast, by the lights of the modified safety principle the agent's knowledge is secure since in most nearby possible worlds where she forms her belief in the same way as in the actual world (i.e. by seeing the robber's face), she will form a true belief as a result. The move from the basic safety principle outlined in §3.1 to the modified safety principle just formulated thus allows us to respond to the veritic epistemic luck at issue in the Gettier counter-examples in a way that is sensitive to the fact that evidential epistemic luck is compatible with knowledge possession. What we have, then, is an independently motivated constraint on knowledge that eliminates veritic epistemic luck (and thus handles the Gettier counter-examples) in such a way as to be compatible with evidential epistemic luck.[10]

Moreover, note that this principle is consistent with epistemological internalism because merely adding this constraint on knowledge possession does not prejudice the issue of whether the internalist conception of justification is a necessary component of knowledge. More specifically, this principle is consistent with epistemological internalism in the sense that non-austere renderings of the internalist thesis could coherently incorporate this principle into their view.

6.3. Interlude—Safety *versus* Sensitivity

In the next section we will consider one further way in which we need to modify our understanding of the safety principle, and also examine a range of examples that are often cited in epistemology in order to test this new formulation. Before we do, however, it is worthwhile returning to look at the relationship between the safety principle as it is now formulated and the sensitivity principle that we looked at in §2.3.

Recall that the sensitivity principle demanded that the agent's belief not only be true in the actual world, but that in the nearest possible worlds in which the proposition believed is false the agent does not continue to believe it. More specifically, bringing the formulation up to date in line with Safety II, we need to add that the class of possible worlds that are relevant will be further constrained by the proviso that these possible worlds are worlds in which the agent forms her belief about the target proposition in the same way as in the actual world. We noted in §3.1 that the sensitivity principle is, at least in one respect, much stronger than the safety principle in that it allows far-off possible worlds to be relevant to an agent's knowledge. It is for this reason that sceptical possible worlds are relevant, on this account, to the issue of whether or not an agent has knowledge of the denials of sceptical hypotheses, even if such worlds are in fact far removed from the actual world. We also noted, however, that the motivation for endorsing such a demanding principle came from epistemologically internalist intuitions to which the proponents of such a thesis, being externalists, should not have accorded much theoretical weight.

It ought to be clear that sensitivity-based approaches to knowledge, like safety-based approaches, will also have no difficulty dealing with the Gettier-type cases that we have considered, but that the manner in which they do so is entirely captured by the weaker safety principle. Consider again the stopped-clock example. Here the agent has a true belief but it is also a belief which fails to be sensitive to the truth in the sense that, in the nearest possible world in which what is believed is false (i.e. the world where the clock is displaying the wrong time) the agent will continue to form the same belief (which is now false) in the same way as she formed her belief in the actual world.

The appeal of Gettier cases largely resides, however, in the fact that the possible worlds in which the agent is in error are *nearby* worlds, and it is this counterfactual nearness of error that gives us the sense that the agent's true belief is just too lucky to count as knowledge. Given this feature of the examples, however, and thus given that sensitivity only deals with Gettier cases by considering the relevant nearest possible worlds in which what is believed is false, it should be clear that the safety principle is all that is needed here. For as we saw in Chapter 2, it is only if one thinks that sometimes far-off possible worlds can be relevant to knowledge possession—as in the sceptical case, according to Fred Dretske, Nozick et al.—that there is a motivation for adducing a modal principle along sensitivity-based rather than safety-based lines.

Moreover, although the safety principle is in one sense weaker than the sensitivity principle because it doesn't allow far-off possible worlds to be relevant to the determination of knowledge, it is in another sense—one that is more salient here—*stronger* than sensitivity in that it considers a *range* of nearby possible worlds rather than just the nearest relevant possible worlds. We would thus expect safety to be more effective than sensitivity at dealing with our intuitions about knowledge in cases where it is clear that only nearby possible worlds are at issue.

For example, one can imagine a Gettier-style case in which the agent forms her true belief by looking at a stopped clock in the manner described above, but where in the nearest possible world in which the target proposition is false, the agent doesn't, as it happens, form a false belief in this way but rather a true one. It could be, for instance, that there is an epistemic 'guardian angel' at work who is ensuring that the stopped clock is telling the right time in the actual world, but who is not particularly robust in her desire to ensure that the agent has a true belief in this respect.[11] Accordingly, whilst she will still be altering the clock to match up with the truth in the nearest possible worlds to the actual world, in nearby but non-nearest worlds she will be leaving the stopped clock alone, thereby causing the agent to form false beliefs. On the sensitivity-based view, and contrary to intuition, the agent ought to be in the market for knowledge in this case, even despite the fact that her belief is subject to a substantive degree of veritic epistemic luck (and so is not in the market for knowledge in light of a safety-based view).

Moreover, it is not as if simply widening the range of possible worlds at issue will help the sensitivity-based view, for whilst it will enable the account to deal with these sorts of cases it will then not be clear what there is to be gained by advancing sensitivity as opposed to safety. After all, with sensitivity so construed it seems that the principle is, roughly speaking, simply the contraposition of safety. Recall that the principles didn't contrapose before, and so were clearly different, because they potentially led to a different range of possible worlds being relevant in each case. Now, however, it seems that it will, at least roughly at any rate, be the same range of worlds at issue. After all, a counterexample to sensitivity as we are now construing that principle would involve a wide class of nearby (but not necessarily nearest) possible worlds in which the target proposition is false and yet the agent continues to believe it in the same way as in the actual world. Similarly, a counter-example to safety is a wide class of nearby possible worlds in which the agent continues to believe the target proposition in the same way as in the actual world, and yet forms a false belief as a result. In both cases, then, the relevant class of worlds is that in which the agent still believes the target proposition on the same basis but the belief is false. So what does adducing sensitivity give you over and above safety?

There is also a further reason for preferring safety over sensitivity, one that we can only make explicit now that we have highlighted the necessity of restricting the class of possible worlds at issue to the manner in which the agent formed her belief in the actual world. Recall the way in which the Dretske–Nozick endorsement of sensitivity led to the breakdown of closure by enabling us to have knowledge of everyday propositions whilst lacking knowledge of the denials of sceptical hypotheses which we know are entailed by these propositions. This result was achieved because, intuitively, in the nearest possible worlds in which a sceptical hypothesis is true—such as the world in which one is a BIV—one continues to believe that one is not the victim of this hypothesis and thus one's belief is not sensitive (hence, on this view, it is not a candidate for knowledge). The problem, however, is that now that we have restricted the range of relevant possible worlds to those where the agent forms her belief in the same way as in the actual world, it is far from clear that this result is still generated by the sensitivity principle because it is not at all obvious that the world in which one is the victim of a sceptical hypothesis one forms one's belief in the same way as in the actual world.

Take the case of the BIV. Here it seems that the manner of belief formation regarding my belief that I am not a BIV in the actual (non-sceptical) world, if it is prompted by anything specific at all, will be, at least in major part, via perception (i.e. by looking at my apparently unenvatted environment). In the world in which I am a BIV, however, my perceptual faculties are no longer available to me as a means of belief formation since I'm now forming my beliefs as a result of being 'fed' experiences by the neuroscientists. Accordingly, such a world should not be relevant to whether or not I know this proposition. But if that's the case, then why is the sensitivity-based theorist so sure that we lack knowledge of this proposition, and thus that closure fails? If far-off sceptical worlds are not relevant to whether or not I have knowledge of this antisceptical proposition, then it seems that I *could* know this proposition after all, even in light of the sensitivity-based view. One of the key motivations that is cited for adopting a sensitivity-based view is thus potentially neutralized.

Moreover, it is worth emphasizing that the way to deal with this problem is not to simply internalize one's conception of what counts as the manner in which one forms one's beliefs, so that what gave rise to one's belief was simply what one believes gave rise to it. Whilst this might resolve this particular difficulty—in that the method of belief formation under this description is, plausibly, the same in both the non-sceptical and the sceptical (BIV) world—as we saw above, this manoeuvre will generate counter-intuitive consequences elsewhere in one's epistemology. So once we understand the way in which an agent's belief is formed in the appropriate manner, then it ceases to be clear that we can always sensibly treat far-off sceptical possible worlds as relevant to knowledge possession because the way in which the belief was actually formed is, it seems, unavailable to the agent in these worlds. This gives us further motivation to stick to nearby worlds as the safety-based model enjoins us to do, since on this model this problem about how our actual method of belief formation manifests itself in far-off worlds that are completely different from the actual world does not arise.[12]

Of course, there are issues here as to just what gives rise to our antisceptical beliefs, since it is not entirely uncontentious to suppose that they are formed via one's perception. As we have noted at a number of junctures, one of the problems posed by these beliefs is that it is not obvious that they are empirical beliefs at all (which is why some attributer contextualists, as we saw in §2.4, try to understand their epistemic status along a priori lines). This, however, is a problem shared by all epistemologists who try to offer an account of the epistemic status of our beliefs in this propositions, and what is clear is that those theorists who offer a sensitivity-based account are in no better position than other theorists to make any headway on this point (indeed, given the problems that we have just noted with the view, they are surely in a *worse* position).

So provided that it is only those nearby possible worlds in which the agent formed her belief in the same way as in the actual world that are at issue, then safety is the natural choice. Moreover, now that we have highlighted the sense in which Gettier cases are instances of veritic epistemic luck, and that safety is the antidote to veritic epistemic luck, the theoretical grounds for advancing the stronger sensitivity principle to deal with Gettier cases completely evaporates.[13]

6.4. Refining the Safety Principle (Part Two)—Some Examples and Potential Counter-examples

In order to see the safety-based (and so anti-veritic epistemic luck) account of knowledge in more detail, we will look at how it deals with some of the standard examples offered in epistemology and examine whether it accords with our epistemological intuitions.

First, consider the 'barn façade' scenario, a version of which was first advanced (in print)[14] by Alvin Goldman (1976). In this example we are asked to consider the epistemic status of Henry's true belief that there is a barn before him. The twist in the tale is that although Henry happens to be looking at a genuine barn, he is currently in 'Barn Façade County' where, unbeknownst to him, all the other barns are fake. Furthermore, the 'fake' barns are such good fakes that Henry would not have been able to tell the difference simply by looking at them in the way that he looked at the real barn. Hence, had he happened to have looked at one of the many fake barns surrounding him rather than the real one, then he would have a formed a false belief in this regard rather than a true one. Intuitively, although Henry has a true belief based (by hypothesis) on impeccable evidence, it is not an instance of knowledge.

We can explain this intuition in terms of our account of veritic epistemic luck by noting that there are going to be a great many nearby possible worlds where Henry forms the same belief on the same basis (by simply looking at the 'barns') and yet his belief is false. As a result, Henry's true belief is veritically lucky and this means that it fails to meet the safety condition. Our safety-based account of knowledge that excludes veritic epistemic luck can thus explain why Henry's belief is not an instance of knowledge.

Reflection on other key examples employed in the epistemological literature enables us to further refine our understanding of the safety principle. In particular, it highlights the sense in which when it comes to knowledge the agent's belief must not only be true in *most* of the nearby possible worlds where she forms her belief in the same way as in the actual world, but in *nearly all* (if not all) of them. Though initially surprising, this result is not nearly as unexpected once one reflects that being a knower involves a specific kind of cognitive achievement, and that this will undoubtedly tighten up the sense in which one's belief has a met an epistemic condition which ensures that the belief is *clearly* not infected with veritic epistemic luck. In order to clarify this point, we will consider the famous 'lottery' puzzle.

We have already noted that winning a free and fair lottery that has long odds is a paradigm case of a lucky event and also that, true to our account of luck, it is also (thereby) an event that obtains in the actual world but not in most nearby possible worlds where the relevant initial conditions are met (such as worlds in which the agent buys a ticket). Now one might accordingly think that provided one's belief that one will lose the lottery is true in most nearby possible worlds in which one forms one's belief in the same way as in the actual world, then this will suffice to meet the safety principle, and thus eliminate veritic epistemic luck, and hence (in this respect at least) suffice for knowledge. As we will see, however, this is not the case.

The so-called 'lottery' puzzle relates to the fact that forming a true belief that one has lost a free and fair lottery with extremely long odds purely on the basis of the probabilities involved will not suffice for knowledge, and yet forming a true belief that one has lost purely on the basis of, say, reading the result in a normally reliable newspaper *will* (usually at least) suffice for knowledge, *even though the possibility that one is mistaken is far less in the former case than in the latter*. This is a puzzle because, pre-theoretically at any rate, we tend to think that knowledge is in some sense a function of the strength of the evidence that one has for one's true beliefs such that the greater the probability in favour of one's true belief then the greater the likelihood that one has knowledge. If this were correct, however, then it would follow that forming one's true belief that one has lost a lottery by considering the odds involved would be far more likely to yield one knowledge than forming that same true belief by reading the result in the newspaper, and this is clearly contrary to intuition.[15]

In contrast to any account of knowledge that regarded knowledge as a function of the strength of evidence that one has for one's true belief, the account under consideration here focuses on the sense in which one's true belief must (at the very least) not be veritically lucky. In terms of the safety principle as it is understood above (Safety II), however, the belief that one will lose the lottery based on the odds involved *isn't* veritically lucky and thus it shouldn't be counted as failing to be knowledge purely because it does not meet this epistemic condition. Moreover, it is not as if the moral to be drawn from this is simply that the agent needs to meet an extra internal justification condition before she can be counting as knowing, as an epistemological internalist would argue, since the agent in this case who has weighed up the probabilities is, plausibly, internalistically justified in forming her belief as well.

The problem seems to be that the agent's belief, whilst meeting the safety principle as we understood it above, is still veritically lucky since, given the nearness of the possible worlds in which the agent wins the lottery (and thus where forming her belief on the basis of the odds leads her astray), it is still a matter of luck that her belief happens to be true. It thus appears that when it comes to knowledge what is demanded is not just safety as it is understood above, but the stronger principle that nearly all (if not all) nearby possible worlds are relevant to knowledge. We will formulate this principle as follows:

Safety III
For all agents, φ, if an agent knows a contingent proposition φ, then, in nearly all (if not all) nearby possible worlds in which she forms her belief about φ in the same way as she forms her belief in the actual world, that agent only believes that φ when φ is true.

Safety III can deal with the lottery puzzle. The agent who forms her belief that she has lost the lottery purely on the basis of the odds involved lacks knowledge because her belief, whilst true and matching the truth in most nearby possible worlds in which she forms her belief in the same way as in the actual world, does not match the truth in a small cluster of nearby possible worlds in which what she believes is false (i.e. where she wins the lottery). Her belief is thus veritically lucky in this stronger sense of veritic epistemic luck that is at issue in Safety III and thus does not count as an instance of knowledge.

Of course, the natural reaction to this line of argument might well be to claim that with the standards for veritic epistemic luck set so high hardly *any* putative instance of knowledge will count as bona fide knowledge because there will always be some small set of nearby possible worlds in which the agent forms her belief in the same way as in the actual world and yet that belief is false. Consider, for example, the case of the rubbish chute that Ernest Sosa offers when expounding his theory of knowledge in terms of a safety-type principle:

> On my way down to the elevator I release a trash bag down the chute from my high rise condo. Presumably, I know my bag will soon be in the basement. But what if, having been released, it still (incredibly) were not to arrive there? That presumably would be because it had been snagged somehow in the chute on the way down (an incredibly rare occurrence), or some such happenstance. (Sosa 2000: 13)

Safety-based views can apparently explain our intuition that the agent has knowledge in this case since the agent's belief is true in most nearby possible worlds where she forms her belief in the same way as in the actual world. One might think, however, that such an example only works because we are implicitly working with the weaker reading of safety offered in Safety II rather than the stricter version at issue in Safety III. After all, isn't there a fairly large class of relevant nearby possible worlds in which the bag snags but where the agent's belief remains the same as in the actual world? If this is so then, given that we opt for Safety III over Safety II, it would follow that, contrary to intuition, the agent in this example in fact lacks knowledge.

I think that cases like this are ambiguous in that they trade on diverse readings of the example at issue. As Sosa describes it above, there clearly *isn't* meant to be a nearby possible world where the bag snags on the way down, which is why he talks of how such an eventuality would be an 'incredibly rare occurrence'. If this is so, then one ought to be able to say that the agent's belief meets not only Safety II but also the stricter Safety III. Nevertheless, we also have the intuition that even rare occurrences can happen in nearby possible worlds, and this explains our reluctance to think that Safety III, rather than Safety II, is applicable here as an explanation of why the agent has knowledge.

I think that the way to get a grip on what is going on here is to actually stipulate just what is happening in the modal neighbourhood, rather than, as Sosa does, simply note that the possibility in question is rare. After all, rare possibilities could still be possibilities that are modally near (the lottery win is a classic example in this respect). For instance, it could be that there is a snag on the chute which, as it happens, has never caught any of the trash bags that have been sent down. In such a case, although the snagging of the bag would be a (statistically) rare occurrence, it would nevertheless be an event that obtains in a nearby possible world. Given that this is so, however, then even though the possibility at issue is rare, our intuition is, I take it, that the agent *doesn't* know that the trash bag is now in the basement because it could so very easily have not been. Moreover, on this construal of the example, this is what *both* formulations of safety would predict.

In contrast, a rare possibility could also be one that is modally far off (this is the standard implication, and certainly the one that Sosa seems to have in mind), such that there is no nearby possible world where the bag snags because a lot would have to be different for this particular bag to get caught on the way down (for example, there would have to be differences to the shaft, the bag would need to fall in a very peculiar way, and so forth). If this is what is at issue here, then our intuitions are clear that the agent *does* have knowledge that the bag is in the basement. Moreover, the conclusion that she has this knowledge is permitted by *both* construals of the safety principle because there are no (or at least hardly any) nearby possible worlds in which she believes that the bag is in the basement and yet it is still caught in the rubbish chute. Properly understood, then, we don't need to choose between a weaker version of the safety principle that can deal with most putative cases of knowledge and a stricter formulation that can deal with the lottery puzzle, since the stricter understanding of safety generates conclusions in accord with intuition in both cases.[16]

This stricter construal of safety also enables us to resolve certain other problems that have been raised for the view. For example, Jonathan Kvanvig (2004) has argued that safety-based views have problems dealing with certain kinds of perceptual knowledge. The case he gives to illustrate this is of an agent who is colour-blind in such a way that everything she sees looks brown. Fortunately, however, everything in her environment is, as it happens, coloured brown, and thus this perceptual impediment does not prevent her from forming true beliefs about the colour of her environment. Kvanvig argues that such an agent has a safe belief in the perception-based propositions in question even though she also clearly lacks knowledge of these propositions because her true beliefs are only gained via luck. Safety-based theories of knowledge are thus in trouble.

Once one specifies the detail involved in this example, however, it ceases to be quite so plausible as a potential counter-example to safety-based views. First, in order to make the example more cogent, we will suppose that the agent can only see *two* colours—brown and green, say—and that everything in the environment happens to be brown and green. This alteration to the example is needed because it is not clear what a colour judgement would be that something is brown if it wasn't made in contrast to a different colour judgement. Furthermore, let us take a concrete proposition which the agent believes, such as that everything is either green or brown. Finally, in order to keep matters simple, let us stipulate that this belief is entirely perception-based, so that nothing else was involved in the formation of this belief, such as testimony, memory, and so forth. With these points in mind, we'll return to the example.

It is clearly important to the example that it is an incidental matter that the environment only contains brown and green things since if this were a stable fact about one's environment then there would be no worry about knowledge here (at least provided that we allow, as we have done here, the prima facie plausibility of externalist treatments of knowledge). If there are no other colours to see, nothing to discriminate brown and green things from, then it can hardly matter to one's perceptual knowledge that one lacks the discriminative capacities that would enable one to identify colours other than brown and green. Moreover, with the details of the example so construed, it is clearly not a matter of luck that the agent's belief that everything is either green or brown is true, since this is something that is true not just in the actual world but also in nearly all nearby possible worlds as well.

Given that it is an incidental matter that the environment is set up in this way, however, then it seems that there must be a wide class of nearby possible worlds in which an object which is coloured other than green or brown becomes part of the agent's environment and so leads the agent to form a false belief. Accordingly, there will be a fairly substantial class of nearby possible worlds in which the agent forms her belief in the same way as in the actual world and yet forms a false belief as a result. Hence, the agent's belief is subject to a substantive degree of veritic epistemic luck and this ensures that the belief is not safe after all. Contrary to what Kvanvig claims, then, the example he offers does not present a fatal difficulty for safety-based views.

Similarly, understanding the safety-based view along these lines also enables us to deal with other types of problem cases in which the belief concerns an event which is fairly stable across nearby worlds and which is matched by a stable true belief, albeit one that is formed in the wrong kind of way. In order to see this, consider again our example of the mother who believes in her son's innocence of a murder charge purely on the basis of her love for him which we considered in the last section. This time, however, suppose that we *don't* stipulate that the son could *very* easily have committed the murder. Of course, it is crucial to the example that the son is charged with murder by a reputable law enforcement agency, and thus that there are good reasons available for thinking that he committed the crime, for otherwise it would not be thought problematic that the mother continues to believe in her son's innocence on the basis of her maternal love for him (*ceteris paribus*, mothers are surely entitled to treat the fact that their sons are not murderers as a default position to take!). Accordingly, it cannot be an altogether absurd proposition that the son committed the crime and hence there must be *some* nearby possible worlds in which the son is guilty. What is crucial, however, is that this class need not be very large at all. By the lights of Safety II this poses a problem, since it seems that the agent would count as having knowledge in this case, even though she is forming a true belief via an epistemically poor method. By the lights of Safety III, however, the problem disappears, since there will be a large enough class of nearby possible worlds where the mother continues to believe in her son's innocence even despite the fact that this belief is false in these worlds. We thus have further grounds for moving to this more austere rendering of the safety-based view of knowledge.

A second problem that Kvanvig (2004) raises for safety-based views is the charge that they are unable to retain closure. We have already seen in §3.1 that safety-based views are consistent with sceptical and antisceptical uses of the closure principle, but we have not yet defended the general point that closure holds unrestrictedly on the safety-based view except to note that there seems to be a strong presumption in favour of thinking this to be so. The counterexample that Kvanvig cites—and which he in turn attributes to Saul Kripke, from his notorious (and unpublished) 'Nozick-bashing' lectures at Princeton in 1980s—is a variant on the barn façade example and goes as follows. First we suppose that an agent is driving through Barn Façade County which is full of fake barns, though with the added twist that all the fake barns are painted red, with the one solitary real barn in the county painted green. Kvanvig then asks us to image an agent who looks at the one real (green) barn and forms a true belief that this is a green barn. This belief is, claims Kvanvig, safe. The agent also knows that a logical consequence of the proposition that this artifice before him is a green barn is that it is a barn, and so he forms the belief that this is a barn. The problem, however, is that the agent's belief that he is looking at a barn is not, it seems, safe (because of the presence of so many barn façades in the vicinity), and thus safety does not transfer across known entailments in such a way as to preserve closure for knowledge.

The trouble with examples such as this is that it is far from plausible that the agent has knowledge of the antecedent proposition—in this case that this is a green barn—in the first place. Kvanvig motivates this thought by understanding safety in such a way that one's beliefs need only match the truth in the *nearest* possible world or worlds in which the proposition in question remains true.

If this were all that safety demanded, then it would be plausible to suppose that the agent's belief in this proposition is safe, since it is true that in the nearest possible world or worlds in which it remains true that the barn is green (e.g. where the barn is moved five inches to the left) the agent continues to believe that it is green. As we have seen, however, safety demands much more than this. Even on a weak construal it demands that one's belief matches the truth across a wide range of nearby possible worlds, and we have just seen that in fact a stronger reading is preferable which demands that one's belief matches the truth across nearly all, if not all, nearby possible worlds.

With this in mind it seems that the agent in this example does not have a safe belief in the target proposition, since in an environment where there is barn-deception going on there will be a wide class of nearby possible worlds where, for example, the agent is looking at a green barn façade and yet is nevertheless forming a belief that she is looking at a green barn (it could be, for instance, that this is one of the barn façades that the townsfolk haven't got around to painting red yet). Indeed, this result is entirely in accord with intuition, since surely we would be uncomfortable about ascribing knowledge to an agent who formed a 'barn' belief of this sort in an environment where there was such widespread barn deception taking place, and the explanation for this is surely that there is too much veritic epistemic luck involved in the agent's belief being true. Properly understood, therefore, Kvanvig's example poses no challenge to the claim that a safety-based conception of knowledge is consistent with closure.

Of course, that this counter-example fails does not ensure that there could be no counter-example to the thesis that safety is consistent with closure. It should be clear, however, that with safety understood as it is here it is hard to see how such a counter-example could possibly work. How could it be that one's belief in the antecedent proposition matches the truth in nearly all nearby possible worlds and yet one's belief in the known to be entailed consequent proposition does not? The onus is thus on detractors of the safety principle to explain how such an example might work. In the meantime, the default position is surely that closure and safety, properly understood, are compatible.

Finally, we will consider another famous example often discussed in the epistemological literature—the 'assassination' case offered by Gilbert Harman (1973: 142–54). In this scenario we are asked to consider the epistemic status of Jill's true belief that the president has been assassinated, a belief that she has formed on the basis of reading the morning edition of a newspaper. The twist in this story comes from the fact that subsequent editions of the paper retract the story on the orders from powerful figures in the present administration who fear that a coup will be attempted if this information becomes widely known.

Moreover, had Jill read the retractions, which she doesn't because she falls ill and retires to her bedroom, she would no longer have believed that the president had been assassinated and would believe instead that he was still alive. This is meant to be a Gettier-style example, in that the agent concerned has a justified true belief and yet, the thought runs, our intuition is that there is a substantive degree of luck in play here which is enough to prevent her from having knowledge.

I think it is right that we typically do have the intuition that Jill lacks knowledge in this case, though I think that this is in fact the result of the further collateral information that we implicitly build into this rather underdescribed scenario. If different collateral information were added, then we might well have different intuitions. In order to see this, we will consider two 'extreme' ways in which the details of this case might be understood. On the first reading Jill is in an epistemically 'unfriendly' situation and that is why she lacks knowledge. On the second reading, in contrast, she is in an epistemically 'friendly' situation, and therefore possesses knowledge despite the luck that is involved. Since these are 'extreme' readings, there will, of course, be cases which trade on elements from both the epistemically friendly and the epistemically unfriendly scenario, and these interpretations will give rise to mixed intuitions about the example. Focusing on the extreme cases is useful, however, in that it highlights those features of the example that are doing the work in leading us to believe either that Jill has, or lacks, knowledge in this scenario. Since we typically have the intuition that Jill lacks knowledge in this case, we will begin by describing the epistemically unfriendly scenario.

On this reading we implicitly suppose that Jill is in some sort of 'tinpot' dictatorship in which there is a tendency for the state to interfere with the media, especially regarding reports of this nature. This reading is suggested by the example because of how assassinations, state interference in the media, and fears about coups do not seem to be hallmarks of stable liberal democracies. So understood, the scenario is epistemically unfriendly because of how in this kind of situation the media is not generally a reliable source of information about this kind of subject matter. A difficulty immediately arises on this reading, however, which is that it is now problematic that Jill should form the belief that she does in the first place, given that she ought to be expected to know that the media in such a state will not be a reliable source of information about matters like this. Relatedly, it is even more implausible to suppose that Jill would have *reversed* her belief in the light of the subsequent retractions had she heard them, as opposed to simply reserving judgement on the grounds that something questionable was clearly taking place. This is problematic because the example clearly invites us to regard Jill as generally intellectually virtuous such that the issue raised by this scenario is not her lack of intellectual virtue but rather that she has formed her belief in such epistemically unfriendly circumstances.

In any case, with this reading of the scenario in mind, let us focus on Jill's belief that the president has been assassinated at the point at which she reads the newspaper (we will return to consider how the epistemic status of Jill's belief might be affected by the passage of time in this case in a moment). Clearly, on this interpretation of the example, Jill lacks knowledge. Moreover, we can offer a straightforward explanation of why this is so in terms of the presence of a substantive degree of veritic epistemic luck, and thus in terms of how Jill's belief is not safe. After all, there is clearly a wide class of nearby possible worlds in which Jill forms her belief in the same way as in the actual world (i.e. by reading a newspaper) and yet forms a false belief as a result, such as, for example, those worlds in which the political powers that are intent on hiding the death of the president get to the newspapers in time to prevent them from printing the original news story regarding the assassination and force them instead to print that the president is still alive. Given that Jill does form beliefs about this subject matter on the basis of what she reads in the newspapers (problematically so, as we have just noted), then her belief in this respect is thus subject (as in all Gettier-style examples) to a substantive degree of veritic epistemic luck, which means that it is not safe and thus that she does not know what she believes.

If the details of the example were spelt out in a different way, however, then it would cease to be quite so intuitive that Jill lacks knowledge in this case. For example, let us suppose that it is not a tinpot dictatorship in which this situation is occurring, but rather a stable liberal democracy where state interference in the media is highly unlikely and in which the newspapers are thus very reliable, especially about such an important subject matter. (In countries like this, we might suppose, if the state were to interfere with the media in this way then they would typically opt to simply shut down the newspapers, at least in the short-term, rather than engage in the difficult and messy business of attempting to coerce them into giving false reports.) That Jill is in a situation like this would explain why she forms her belief about the death of the president in the first place, and would also explain why she would at least withdraw such a belief in the light of subsequent retractions (though even here we might expect her to be a little suspicious of how events are proceeding, and thus not to directly form the belief that the president is alive after all). With this in mind, we will focus, as before, on the question of whether, at the point at which she read the newspaper, Jill knows that the president has been assassinated.

With the example understood in this way it starts to become far more plausible to regard Jill as possessing knowledge, and our account of safety backs up this claim. After all, given the general reliability of the news source in question, and the fact that it is highly unlikely that the state would interfere with the media in the way envisaged, then it appears that Jill not only has a true belief in this proposition at this time, but also that in nearly all nearby possible worlds in which Jill continues to believe this proposition at this time (and on the same basis) her belief remains true. This is because with the example so described there will be hardly any nearby possible worlds in which the political interference is able to affect the early edition of the newspapers. Indeed, if anything, the result would be that this newspaper does not get printed at all, or that some newspapers print the original story and some others the retraction, and in either case we would suppose that a generally intellectually virtuous agent like Jill would refrain from forming her belief in the target proposition.

Of course, part of the appeal of the example is that it implicitly asks us to evaluate the epistemic status of Jill's belief not at the point at which she reads the newspaper but rather later in the day once the retractions have been published. Here we get the sense that there is information available that Jill should be taking account of, and would take account of if it were available to her, but which is unavailable to her and so undermines her putative knowledge. As we have just noted above, provided this example is not simply meant to be a case in which the agent is lacking in the intellectual virtues, then we need to suppose that Jill both correctly forms her belief in response to the early edition of the newspaper and also would correctly revise her belief in response to later editions. Given that this is so, however, then we need to understand the example so that Jill's environment is epistemically friendly in the manner described above. It is only with the example understood this way that we can make sense of why anyone possessing the normal intellectual virtues would be willing to form and then revise her beliefs about such a subject matter so readily in response to what she reads in the newspaper.

On this reading, however, Jill's belief remains unaffected by veritic epistemic luck even later on in the day when the retractions are published. After all, her belief is not only true in the actual world, but also in nearly all nearby possible worlds in which she continues to believe what she does on the same basis. In order to see this, note that the nearby possible worlds in which she hears the retractions are not worlds in which she forms a false belief about the target proposition, but rather worlds in which she become suspicious about the issue of whether or not the president has been assassinated and so no longer believes that proposition (preferring instead, in her intellectually virtuous way,

171

to reserve judgement). Her knowledge is, we might therefore say, unstable, in that there is a wide class of nearby possible worlds in which she lacks the relevant belief and so loses that knowledge. Nevertheless, this instability does not prevent it from being bona fide knowledge.

We can diagnose what is going on here in terms of our distinction between veritic and evidential epistemic luck. In the epistemically unfriendly understanding of the example we are dealing with an agent whose belief is infected by a substantial degree of veritic epistemic luck, and this is why she lacks knowledge. In the epistemically friendly understanding of the case, in contrast, we are either faced with knowledge that has not been infected by luck at all, or else we are faced with a case of evidential epistemic luck which is compatible with knowledge possession. In order to see this, consider Jill's belief just after she has read the newspaper and which is formed in the epistemically friendly environment. Here there is no luck involved, either veritic or evidential. Whilst we have already seen that here is no substantive degree of veritic epistemic luck involved, we haven't considered the possibility of evidential epistemic luck in this case. Clearly, however, Jill's belief is not evidentially lucky with the situation described in the epistemically friendly way since she will acquire this evidence in most nearby possible worlds in which the relevant initial conditions are the same (where, for example, she has no special reason to doubt what she reads). Given the way the actual world is, it is not a matter of luck that Jill gained the evidence that she did by looking at this newspaper.

In contrast, when we consider Jill's belief at the later time in which the retractions have been made public, it *is* now a matter of evidential epistemic luck that she has this supporting evidence for her belief. After all, in most nearby possible worlds in which the relevant initial conditions for her gaining this evidence are the same, she acquires counter-evidence at this later time which neutralizes the evidence gained at the earlier time. Accordingly, in most nearby possible worlds she lacks the relevant evidential support for her belief in the target proposition. Crucially, however, since evidential epistemic luck is compatible with knowledge possession, this does not undermine the epistemic status of her belief. Instead, her belief now becomes akin to the employee who overhears that he is to be sacked that we considered in §5.2. Like this hapless employee, she is lucky to have the supporting evidence for her belief that she does, but she has knowledge nonetheless.

This example is thus very slippery, in a number of different ways. First, the example is underdescribed and invites us to import details into the scenario that substantially affect how we assess the epistemic status of the agent's belief. As we have seen, one of the problems here is that the natural way to understand the example—so that the agent is in an epistemically unfriendly environment—seems to conflict with the natural way to understand the epistemic qualities of the agent, in that in such a scenario it is puzzling why she is forming her beliefs in the way that she does given that we don't further suppose that she is lacking in intellectual virtue. The second way in which the example is slippery is that it equivocates between asking us to consider the epistemic status of the agent's belief before and after the retractions are considered. As we have seen, this shift in focus can have an impact on the way in which we assess the agent's belief. Finally, the example is also ambiguous in that, depending on how one fills out the details, it can be thought to describe one of at least three scenarios. The first is a case in which no substantial degree of epistemic luck is involved, and thus where the agent has knowledge. The second is a situation in which only evidential epistemic luck is involved, and thus where, again, the agent has knowledge. And, finally, the third possible scenario is one where there is a substantial degree of veritic epistemic luck present and thus where the agent *lacks* knowledge. This type of example thus highlights the importance of being clear about the details involved, and also illustrates the importance of distinguishing veritic luck from evidential epistemic luck.[17]

The safety principle, suitably understood, is thus able to accommodate some of the main epistemological examples discussed in the contemporary literature. Moreover, it is worthwhile noting that we were able to account for these examples without making any reference to a further epistemic condition, such as, crucially, an internalist justification condition. Whilst this obviously does not determine the issue of whether we should be epistemological internalists, it does lend prima facie support to the thought that all that is needed from a theory of knowledge is an account of the epistemic condition which eliminates veritic epistemic luck. Since safety can do this all by itself, this suggests that all that is needed is a safety-based externalist theory of knowledge.

6.5. Reflective Epistemic Luck

Crucially, however, eliminating veritic epistemic luck from one's epistemology will not suffice to evade the tension between epistemic luck and knowledge. This is because even with veritic epistemic luck eliminated, another form of epistemic luck remains that is potentially just as epistemologically significant, if not more so. This type of epistemic luck concerns the manner in which, *from that agent's reflective position*, it is a matter of luck that her belief is true. Significantly, this type of luck can remain even if we stipulate that the agent in question has a true belief that is safe. Thus, in light of a safety-based theory of knowledge which understands the epistemic condition entirely in terms of the safety principle, it could be the case that the agent has knowledge and yet, from that agent's reflective position, it is still a matter of luck that her belief is true, where the presence of this type of epistemic luck makes the original attribution of knowledge questionable.

In order to get a handle on this type of epistemic luck, suppose for a moment that one defined knowledge purely in terms of some formulation of the safety principle, such as Safety III. In so doing, one would eliminate veritic epistemic luck and thereby meet the Gettier problem, and, as we saw above, one would also be able to deal with a number of key examples that are discussed by epistemologists. Still, however, one might feel very uneasy about such a theory of knowledge, and the reason for this is that it allows agents to have knowledge even though the agent lacks good reflectively accessible grounds in support of her true beliefs. Recall the example of the chicken-sexer, an agent who has a highly reliable ability to determine the sex of chicks but who has false beliefs about how this ability works and, let us stipulate, even lacks evidence which would indicate that this 'ability' she has is reliable. The problem is that our chicken-sexer's beliefs, whilst clearly lacking in *something* epistemically important, *will* meet the safety principle and so are not subject to veritic epistemic luck. Given that the agent really does have this ability, then in so far as she forms a true belief about the subject matter at issue in the actual world then, in nearly all nearby possible worlds in which she forms her belief in the same way as the actual world, her belief will continue to be true. Nevertheless, the point is often made that the chicken-sexer's beliefs are still in some substantive and troubling way *lucky*.

For example, Zagzebski, in commenting on examples such as this, remarks:

The value of the truth obtained by a reliable process in the absence of any conscious awareness of a connection between the behaviour of the agent and the truth he thereby acquires is no better than the value of the lucky guess. (Zagzebski 1996: 304)

And there is clearly something right about this—we do have a very strong intuition that the agent in this example is forming beliefs that are only luckily true, even despite the fact that her beliefs are reliable in such a fashion as to meet the safety principle and so not be subject to veritic epistemic luck. Moreover, what appears to be lacking, and which gives rise to this form of epistemic luck, is just the kind of 'conscious awareness of a connection between the [*agent's*] behaviour ... and the truth [s]he thereby acquires' that Zagzebski seizes upon. After all, for all the chicken-sexer can tell, it *is* a matter of luck that her belief is true. The problem, however, is that since this type of epistemic luck is manifestly not of a veritic variety, we need to distinguish a second way in which knowledge can be problematically associated with epistemic luck.

I will call this type of epistemic luck 'reflective' epistemic luck, and characterize it as follows:

Reflective epistemic luck
Given only what the agent is able to know by reflection alone, it is a matter of luck that her belief is true.

In essence, what is at issue in this type of epistemic luck is not that the agent's belief fails to match the truth across a wide range of the relevant nearest possible worlds, where these worlds are ordered in the usual way in terms of the facts of the situation, but rather that the agent's belief fails to match the truth across a wide range of the relevant nearest possible worlds where these worlds are ordered in a non-standard way *solely in terms of what the agent is able to know by reflection alone in the actual world.*

Furthermore, given the way that we are understanding the ordering of the possible worlds in this respect, it should be clear that the range of nearby possible worlds that are relevant will be restricted in terms of the way in which the agent *believes* (or would believe)[18] she formed her belief in the actual world, rather than (as with veritic epistemic luck) in terms of the way she *in fact* formed her belief. We will return to this point in a moment.

Consider again our chicken-sexer and compare her with an 'enlightened' counterpart chicken-sexer who is exactly alike except that she possesses the reflectively accessible grounds to back up her beliefs about the sex of the chick that her 'naïve' counterpart lacks—i.e. good reflectively accessible grounds that indicate, for example, that she has this reliable ability, that it works in such-and-such a way, and so on. As we noted above, neither of these chicken-sexers will be forming true beliefs in ways that are veritically epistemically lucky since in so far as they genuinely have this ability then they will not only be forming true beliefs in this regard in the actual world but also in nearly all nearby possible worlds where they are forming their beliefs in the same way as in the actual world.[19] In assessing whether or not these two counterpart chicken-sexers are forming beliefs that are veritically lucky, however, we are focusing on possible worlds that are ordered in the usual way in terms of the facts of the situation. Thus, that we know that both these agents do indeed have this ability has an impact on this ordering in such a way as to ensure that neither of them are forming beliefs that are veritically lucky.

However, when we are trying to capture the sense in which the naïve chicken-sexer, as opposed to the enlightened chicken-sexer, is forming a true belief in a *reflectively* epistemically lucky way, we have to consider the possible worlds ordered solely in terms of what that agent can know by reflection alone in the actual world. In terms of the enlightened chicken-sexer who has a great deal of reflectively accessible evidence in support of her true belief, the possible worlds will tend to be ordered much as we ordered them from our 'external' perspective. She is in possession of good reflectively accessible grounds, for example, for thinking that she continues to have this ability in most nearby possible worlds. And on this ordering of the possible worlds, she will tend to have beliefs that match the truth of the matter in most of the relevant nearby possible worlds. Contrast this with the belief of the naïve chicken-sexer. Since she has next to no relevant reflectively accessible knowledge in support of her belief, just about any possible world can count as a nearby possible world on this ordering. In particular, she is not in possession of any reflectively accessible grounds which would require us to order the possible worlds in such a way that she tends to retain this ability in nearby possible worlds, and so we would expect her to fail to track the truth across most of the relevant nearby possible worlds. The naïve chicken-sexer's beliefs are thus epistemically lucky in a reflective way that is not applicable to the enlightened chicken-sexer.[20]

Notice that it is crucial to our understanding of the relevant possible worlds in this respect that it is restricted in terms of how the agent believes (or would believe) she formed her belief in the actual world, rather than in terms of how she in fact formed her belief in the actual world. After all, the actual way in which the naïve chicken-sexer formed her belief was via her sense of smell, not (as she believed) via her senses of sight and touch. If the range of nearby possible worlds was restricted in terms of how the naïve chicken-sexer in fact formed her belief, then this would rule out worlds in which she received the same stimuli from her senses of sight and touch as she received in the actual world, even though such worlds will clearly be relevant to whether or not her belief is infected by a substantive degree of reflective epistemic luck.

In order to see this, recall that the naïve chicken-sexer lacks good reflectively accessible grounds for believing that she has this chicken-sexing ability, and thus in most nearby possible worlds on the reflective ordering she will lack this ability. With this ability absent, however, the way in which she will form her belief about the sex of the chicks will clearly be via her senses of touch and sight rather than by her sense of smell. It would be counter-intuitive, therefore, to restrict the range of possible worlds to those worlds where she continues to have the same olfactory stimulus that she received in the actual world, since on any plausible conception of what would count as a nearby possible world on the reflective ordering her sense of smell plays no substantive role in the formation of her belief in this respect at all.

It ought to be clear that the naïve chicken-sexer's beliefs are lucky in a way that is epistemically problematic, in that we naturally think that there is some-thing epistemically lacking about her beliefs in comparison to the correspond-ing beliefs held by her enlightened counterpart. At the very least, it is certainly true to say that, given the choice, we would opt to be in the epistemic position of the enlightened chicken-sexer rather than her naïve counterpart. It seems then that whilst advancing an externalist epistemology (such as a safety-based view) which can deal with the problem posed by veritic epistemic luck will eliminate one problematic variety of epistemic luck, the problem posed by epis-temic luck is not thereby eliminated entirely. Indeed, this point seems to be what Zagzebski is getting at in accusing 'pure' externalist knowledge of being epistemically lucky. The issue is not that such knowledge is epistemically lucky in, say, the way that the true beliefs at issue in the Gettier cases are epistemic-ally lucky (i.e. veritically lucky), but, more specifically, that externalist accounts of knowledge allow knowledge possession to coexist with a certain type of reflective epistemic luck that is epistemically problematic. We therefore seem to have identified a strong motivation for preferring a certain type of internalist theory of knowledge that insists that agents not only have safe beliefs but that they also have internalistically justified beliefs, since this appears to be the only way of ensuring that one's knowledge is not subject to epistemic luck, whether veritic or reflective.[21]

6.6. Concluding Remarks

We have thus disambiguated two ways in which epistemic luck can be epistemologically problematic. First there is the veritic epistemic luck which is the kind of epistemic luck that is at issue in the Gettier-style counter-examples to the tripartite account. It is the elimination of this variety of epistemic luck that is the focus of externalist epistemological accounts (*especially* the safety-based neo-Moorean thesis). This type of epistemic luck is clearly incompatible with knowledge possession (this is the immediate moral of the post-Gettier literature), and hence it is an adequacy condition on any theory of knowledge that it offers an account of the epistemic condition(s) such that they are able to eliminate this type of epistemic luck. As we have seen, however, there is also a reflective variety of epistemic luck, and we have noted that when some commentators complain about how externalist accounts of knowledge allow an undue degree of epistemic luck what they have in mind is specifically this notion. The issue of whether or not it is a goal of any theory of knowledge that it is able to eliminate reflective epistemic luck is at present still moot, though we saw above that a prima facie case can be made for this contention, and that this thus counts in favour of *internalist* safety-based theories of knowledge which insist on the necessity of the internalist justification condition.

In the next chapter we will examine this particular motivation for epistemological internalism in more detail by looking at the issue of cognitive responsibility. In particular, we will be discussing the related topic of what the status is of the two main types of virtue epistemology that have been proposed in the recent literature, and which are explicitly designed to capture the required sense in which knowledge demands cognitive responsibility.

Notes

1. I borrow the term from Engel (1992), who argues for a similar characterization of epistemic luck, although he specifically puts the point in terms of evidence.
2. In order to simplify matters in what follows, henceforth when I discuss possible examples of epistemic luck I will simply assume that the event in question is of some significance to the agent, and thus that the significance condition, (L2), is met. Indeed, since we are talking here about events which the agent has already formed a belief about, it is clear that these events must have had some impact on the agent concerned.
3. As far as I know, the only prominent epistemologist to reject the Gettier counter-examples to the classical tripartite account is Hetherington (1998). I briefly remark on where I think Hetherington goes wrong in this respect in note 17.
4. This is not to deny, of course, that an agent who has an internalist justification in support of her belief will tend to have a true belief that is *less* veritically lucky than any counterpart agent who lacks an internalist justification, since the internalist justification will enable her to be sensitive to certain changes in the facts in counterfactual situations in ways that her counterpart agent will not be. Nevertheless, since the belief is still being formed via a stopped clock, this internalist justification for her belief won't prevent her from forming a false belief in this proposition in most nearby possible worlds in which she forms her belief in the same way as in the actual world, and thus will not prevent her from forming a veritically lucky true belief.
5. Vahid (2001) also notes that Engel is mistaken in this regard, although for slightly different reasons than those offered here.
6. For further discussion of the thesis that any epistemic condition which suffices to transform true belief into knowledge must at the very least entail that the belief in the target proposition is true, see Plantinga (1993*a*; cf. Greene and Blamert 1997, Plantinga 1997), Zagzebski (1994*b*, 1999), and Merricks (1995; cf. Ryan 1996, Merricks 1997).

7. This theory holds, roughly, that knowledge is internalistically justified true belief where there is no other truth such that the agent's believing it would have destroyed her justification. See also Swain (1974).

8. Of course, it is often very difficult to get a sharp individuation of the way in which a belief is formed in real life situations where (unlike in philosophy examples) one cannot stipulate the details of the scenario (indeed, there is a related vagueness regarding just how we are to individuate actual beliefs in the first place). Nevertheless, such individuation is not in principle impossible since we can imagine tests that could be carried out to determine such facts, or at least identify what further information would settle the matter (the cognitive theory literature is full of case studies where theorists were able to at least give an approximate account of what gave rise to an agent's belief). There is a fairly vast philosophical literature on this issue of how we should individuate the way in which beliefs are formed, though much of it is exclusively focused on the specifically Nozickean conception of methods (see Nozick 1981: 179–85). For a good survey of some of the issues in this regard, along with further references, see Williamson (2000c: §§7.4–5).

9. Whether or not an unmodified conception of safety would have this consequence would ultimately depend upon what weight one put on the actual method of belief-formation in determining the closeness of possible worlds.

10. We will consider another case in which evidential epistemic luck is confused with veritic epistemic luck, and vice versa, below in § 6.4.

11. We don't need to take the description of this epistemic helper as a 'guardian angel' literally of course—i.e. as involving a supernatural being—since one of the agent's pals would suffice to fill this role.

12. For further discussion of this problem for sensitivity-based theories, see Williams (1991: ch. 8) and Black (2002).

13. There are actually a number of other good reasons to prefer safety over sensitivity, but it would take us too far afield to survey them all here. As a taster, though, consider the following two propositions:

    (1) I don't falsely believe that I have two hands.
    (2) I am not an intelligent dog who is always incorrectly believing that I have two hands.

    In both cases, I take it, we would tend to suppose that we do have knowledge of these propositions. Crucially, however, such knowledge is excluded by a sensitivity-based approach because one's beliefs in these propositions clearly cannot be sensitive. By definition, it cannot be that in the nearest possible world in which I *do* falsely believe that I have hands my belief continues to track the truth, and the same goes as regards proposition (2). Safety can deal with these cases, however, in that if I do know these propositions then in the nearby possible worlds in which they remain true I will continue to believe them. These counter-examples to the sensitivity-based approach are presented and discussed in DeRose (1995). For a subtle discussion of examples of this sort and the challenge they pose to the sensitivity-based view, see Williamson (2000c: ch. 7).

14. The example is often attributed to Carl Ginet. See, e.g., Stine (1971: 252).

15. Note that for this example to work, we have to suppose that the agent who forms her belief that she has lost the lottery by reading the result in the newspaper does not reflect upon the probabilities involved, and thus that these poor odds of winning play no part in the formation of her belief. If this were not the case, then the apparent puzzle here could easily be explained in terms of the agent who reads the newspaper having *additional* evidence in favour of her true belief. Most discussions of the lottery puzzle fail to be clear

about this point. For some of the key recent discussions of the lottery puzzle, see DeRose (1996), Lewis (1996), Cohen (1998a), Williamson (2000c: ch. 11) and Hawthorne (2004).

16. For the contrary position in this regard, see Greco (2002).

17. See Hetherington (1998) for an argument to the effect that, despite our first intuitions in this regard, agents *do* have knowledge in the Gettier, barn façade and assassination cases. Hetherington's mistake results from noticing that sometimes epistemic luck is compatible with knowledge (e.g. as in cases of evidential/doxastic epistemic luck), and concluding on this basis that epistemic luck is *always* compatible with knowledge, even when the epistemic luck, as in some of the cases under discussion here, is veritic.

18. We need this qualification because the agent might be so unreflective as to have never actually thought about how it is that she is forming her belief in the target proposition. Note that if the agent does not have even this counterfactual 'belief' about how her belief was formed, this does not pose a problem for the view. All this would mean is that *no* restriction is placed on the range of nearby possible worlds that can count as relevant in this respect.

19. Though we would of course expect the enlightened chicken-sexer to be forming beliefs that matched the truth across a broader range of possible worlds than her naïve counterpart. Her beliefs will, for example, tend to track the truth in worlds where she has a cold and therefore loses her sense of smell. In these worlds she will not form beliefs about the sex of the chicks because, unlike the naïve chicken-sexer, she will be conscious of the fact that her ability works via her sense of smell and thus, since (she is aware) having a cold impairs one's sense of smell, she will know that she is not in a position to form reliable beliefs about this subject matter via this process.

20. As we will see in § 8.1, however, this contrast between the enlightened and unenlightened chicken-sexer is only as stark as it is presented here because we are implicitly bracketing sceptical possible worlds (i.e. worlds in which sceptical hypotheses are true). As far as our present discussion is concerned—which is not directly concerned with the problem of scepticism—we can set this issue to one side. It will, however, become important later on in the book.

21. I further discuss the distinction between veritic and reflective epistemic luck in Pritchard (2004b, 2005c).

7

Cognitive Responsibility and the Epistemic Virtues

7.0. Introduction

In the last chapter we identified two varieties of epistemic luck that pose problems for any theory of knowledge. The first variety—veritic epistemic luck—is the type of epistemic luck that is at issue in the Gettier-style counter-examples to the classical tripartite account of knowledge. It is the elimination of this kind of luck that is the focus of externalist epistemologies—particularly the paradigm case of an externalist epistemology, the safety-based neo-Moorean account. We also saw that there was another epistemologically problematic variety of epistemic luck—reflective epistemic luck—and that when commentators charged externalist epistemologies with being far too concessive in their treatment of epistemic luck, it was specifically this variety of luck that they had in mind. Given that externalist accounts of knowledge are unable to eliminate reflective epistemic luck, this presents us with prima facie grounds in favour of an internalist safety-based epistemological theory.

One explanation that might be offered for thinking that we need an epistemology that is able to eliminate reflective epistemic luck—and which would further support the case for adopting a safety-based internalist theory of knowledge—is that it is only by proposing an epistemological theory that can eliminate reflective epistemic luck that one can adequately capture a conception of cognitive responsibility that is central to knowledge possession. In essence, the thought is that what is epistemically problematic about the knowledge putatively possessed by the (unenlightened) chicken-sexer is that she is unable to take cognitive responsibility for the truth of her beliefs in the kind of robust way that is at issue when we ascribe knowledge to agents.

Crucially, for example, the naïve chicken-sexer is unable to properly *claim* her brute externalist knowledge.

The goal of this chapter is to examine this relationship between reflective epistemic luck and cognitive responsibility in more detail and, in so doing, look a little deeper into the issue of just what is involved in the idea of cognitive responsibility. To this end, we will be discussing the 'virtue-theoretic' challenge that has recently been directed against early externalist accounts of knowledge and justification, and which has been used to motivate the kind of virtue epistemic theories that are currently popular in the literature. As I explain, this challenge largely concerns the difficulty that these externalist accounts have in eliminating epistemic luck and therefore in capturing the kind of cognitive responsibility that is necessary for knowledge. So understood, however, this complaint is ambiguous, and this explains why there are two very divergent types of virtue epistemology currently on offer in the literature—an epistemologically externalist version that models itself on process reliabilism, and an epistemologically internalist 'neo-Aristotelian' version. Disentangling the various threads of motivation for virtue epistemology thus not only throws light on the issue of why we should seek to eliminate reflective luck from our knowledge (and hence on the epistemological externalist–internalist distinction), but also on the issue of the status of virtue epistemology itself. Indeed, as we will see, by factoring our discussion of epistemic luck into the debate regarding virtue epistemology we are able to identify a core problem facing all such theories of knowledge.

7.1. Epistemological Internalism and Cognitive Responsibility

What we have then are *two* epistemically problematic varieties of luck. It is important to note, however, that in granting that these types of luck are both - epistemically problematic one does not *thereby* concede the truth of epistemological internalism, since there may be ways in which an agent's beliefs, whilst epistemically undesirable in some fashion, are nevertheless able to meet the standards for knowledge. That is, whilst it is clear that both of these types of luck are epistemically undesirable, and that veritic luck is incompatible with knowledge possession (such is the immediate moral of the post-Gettier literature), the further question of whether reflective luck is incompatible with knowledge is moot. There is certainly *something* epistemically deficient about the naïve chicken-sexer's beliefs, but it is not clear that this means that she lacks knowledge.

Indeed, it is important to remember that whilst no one seriously thinks that the agents in the Gettier-type cases whose beliefs are infected with veritic epistemic luck have knowledge, there *are* people—epistemological externalists— who think that the unenlightened chicken-sexer has knowledge, despite the presence of reflective epistemic luck. Indeed, such externalists will no doubt even grant that there is something epistemically lacking about the naïve chicken-sexer's beliefs. Nevertheless, they will contend that there is nothing epistemically lacking which is essential to knowledge possession. Accordingly, we cannot straightforwardly take the conclusion generated by our observations on reflective epistemic luck that there is something epistemically amiss with pure externalist knowledge and convert this into a knock-down argument for epistemological internalism.

We have thus returned to the debate between epistemological externalism and internalism, in that the issue is whether the kind of internalist justification that would be needed to eliminate reflective luck should be made a necessary condition for knowledge. If you think that it should—that only 'enlightened' chicken-sexers can have knowledge—then your intuitions side with the intern- alists, whilst if you think that it shouldn't, then your intuitions side with the externalists. We shouldn't expect an easy resolution to this issue. The endurance of the debate between the internalists and the externalists in the recent literature is evidence, if evidence were needed, that our intuitions about such examples are divided.

Nevertheless, the observation that epistemological internalists are more concerned about reflective epistemic luck than externalists does add something substantive to our understanding of this debate. In the first instance, it identifies one area about which internalists and externalists have managed to speak past one another. In §6.3, we quoted Linda Zagzebski arguing that the problem with pure externalist knowledge was that it was no better than a lucky guess. Although, as we saw, there was *some* truth in this, it wasn't altogether an accurate description of the situation given that even the unenlightened chicken-sexer was forming beliefs that were safe, and hence which were not veritically lucky.

This failure to recognize the subtleties involved in the way that externalists and internalists respond to the problem posed by epistemic luck is common in the literature. Consider the following quotation, again from Zagzebski:

The dispute between externalists and internalists looms large mostly because of ambiva- lence over the place of luck in normative theory. Theorists who resist the idea that knowledge ... is vulnerable to luck are pulled in the direction of internalism. ... Externalists are more sanguine about luck. ... There is lots of room for luck in externalist theories since the conditions that make it the case that the knower is in a state of knowledge are independent of her conscious access. (1996: 39)

Whilst superficially persuasive, this interpretation of the internalism–externalism debate is at best misleading. After all, it is just not true that externalists are sanguine about epistemic luck, since, like all post-Gettier epistemologists, they make the elimination of veritic epistemic luck an adequacy condition on their theory of knowledge. What they are sanguine about (if that's the right word) is only the presence of reflective epistemic luck, and even then it is entirely consistent with their position to concede that such luck is epistemically undesirable, if ultimately compatible with knowledge possession. (Indeed, I would suggest that any modest externalist epistemological theory would be inclined to allow that the naïve chicken-sexer's beliefs are epistemically problematic.)[1] In any case, the issue about conscious access is itself misleading, since even internalists will want to eliminate veritic epistemic luck and this goal, as we have seen, will have the consequence that they are obliged to incorporate an external epistemic condition into their theory, a condition which the agent lacks 'conscious access' to. Thus, internalists are also in an important sense 'sanguine' about epistemic luck as well (we will return to this point). So whilst Zagzebski's way of viewing the debate emphasizes the differences between the positions, focusing on the role of the two types of epistemically problematic luck in this debate brings out the common ground.[2]

My sympathies here are with the externalist, but I doubt that any definitive considerations can be offered which will decide the matter one way or the other. What is important for present purposes, however, is the issue of what is it about reflective epistemic luck that makes it an epistemically undesirable feature of one's beliefs. That is, why is it that we value beliefs that are internalistically justified, even if we don't also insist that meeting this constraint is necessary for knowledge? I think that the answer to this question relates to the fact that we tend to want beliefs that are more than just safe. That is, we don't just want agents to be forming beliefs in such a way that we can rely on the truth of those beliefs, we also want agents to be *cognitively responsible* for their beliefs, and this is only possible if they form beliefs in ways that are responsive to the reflectively accessible grounds that they have in favour of their beliefs. The naïve chicken-sexer may well be a reliable indicator of the truth regarding the subject matter at issue, but she is not in a position to take any credit for this reliability. Another way of putting this point is to say that whilst her safe true beliefs are in some minimal sense an achievement of hers, in that it is *her* cognitive trait that is giving rise to them, the achievement here is entirely at the sub-personal level.

So whilst we might think that her chicken-sexing capacity is a good cognitive trait to have—it does, after all, enable one to form safe true beliefs about the subject matter in question—we would not think that the naïve chicken-sexer herself is deserving of any epistemic credit for forming beliefs in this way because in the relevant sense the safety of her beliefs has nothing to do with any epistemic act of hers. In contrast, the enlightened chicken-sexer is deserving of epistemic credit because by forming beliefs in response to the reflectively accessible evidence that she possesses she has acted in a way that is epistemically responsible.[3]

I think that this point becomes clearer once one considers how the enlightened chicken-sexer is in a position to properly claim knowledge of what she believes whereas this is not the case for her naïve counterpart. We noted in §3.4 that agents who do not meet internal epistemic conditions will typically be unable to properly claim to possess knowledge, even if one grants that what the agent would be asserting in making such a claim would be true. The reason for this is that a claim to know—especially one that is made explicitly via a locution of the form 'I know that...'—carries the conversational implicature that one is able to offer relevant reflectively accessible grounds in support of that claim, and this is just what agents who don't meet internal epistemic conditions, such as naïve chicken-sexers, cannot do. The ability to properly claim the knowledge that one has is, however, a very desirable epistemic capacity. For whilst it might be useful to us to know that the naïve chicken-sexer is forming safe true beliefs, and thus know that she is a reliable indicator when it comes to the subject matter in question, she herself is not able to perform the role of being a reliable *informant* in this respect, since from her point of view she lacks any reason for thinking that she is forming beliefs in a safe fashion. But the ability to be a reliable informant, to put our knowledge to use in this way, is clearly something of tremendous value to us and thus it is little wonder that we find the kind of 'knowledge' (if that's what it is) that the naïve chicken-sexer has as being so intellectually dissatisfying.

7.2. Process Reliabilism, Agent Reliabilism, and Virtue Epistemology

This intuition that the possession of knowledge demands that the agent should in some way be able to take credit for the truth of her belief gets expression in recent work by virtue epistemologists, as does the more fine-grained thought that there are different ways in which an agent's belief can be of credit to the agent.[4] In essence, what virtue epistemologists contend is that knowledge should actually be *defined* in terms of the epistemic virtues—such as conscientiousness or open-mindedness—and perhaps also in terms of our cognitive faculties as well, such as our perceptual faculties. What is radical about this proposal is that we would ordinarily identify a trait as being an epistemic virtue or a cognitive faculty by noting that it is knowledge-conducive, and thus we would be presupposing a prior theory of knowledge. Indeed, whilst it is part of the recent epistemological tradition to regard any adequate epistemology as needing to include some account of how it is that agents such as ourselves come to have knowledge—a story which will undoubtedly make essential reference to the epistemic virtues and the cognitive faculties—it does not normally *define* knowledge in terms of the epistemic virtues and cognitive faculties. Nevertheless, given the widespread intuition that we have noted concerning how the cognitive achievement involved in knowledge possession excludes luck (in some sense), if a virtue epistemology is able to do this then it will be one way (if not the only way) of capturing what is involved in an anti-luck epistemology. As we will see, I am sceptical that we need to endorse the radical claim that virtue epistemologists make—i.e. that knowledge must actually be *defined* in terms of the epistemic virtues and cognitive faculties. Nevertheless, tracing the motivations for the development of the view will cast some light upon the distinction we have made here between veritic and reflective epistemic luck.

The early forms of virtue epistemology that have been developed in the recent literature were generally modelled along reliabilist lines and grew out of a certain kind of dissatisfaction with process reliabilism. Consider a crude process reliabilist account of knowledge as being one which simply demanded, in essence, that one has knowledge if, and only if, one forms one's true belief via a reliable process (a process which ensures a high ratio of true beliefs relative to false beliefs). In terms of rather 'low-grade' knowledge, such as basic perceptual knowledge, this is a fairly plausible account.[5] Intuitively, such beliefs count as knowledge just so long as they are formed in reliable ways which, as the products of our perceptual faculties in normal circumstances, we would expect them to be. Nothing more seems to be necessary to knowledge in this case than meeting such a condition. Such a view, however, at least if extended so that it applies to knowledge of contingent propositions in general, faces a number of difficulties.

For one thing, the position is clearly an externalist theory of knowledge that would allow ascriptions of knowledge to such agents as the naïve chicken-sexer, and we have already noted that there are those who would be unhappy about this consequence of the view. Moreover, there are notorious problems of formulation with process reliabilism, both in terms of the specification of reliability that is at issue and, relatedly, regarding the issue of how one individuates the relevant processes (the so-called 'generality problem').[6] Although the early virtue epistemologists were naturally concerned with these kinds of familiar difficulties for the process reliabilist position,[7] their focus was not on these objections facing the process reliabilist position but rather on the manner in which process reliabilism seemed to allow that agents could possess knowledge even though the reliability in question in no way reflected a cognitive achievement on their part.

Consider the following two problems. First, there is the difficulty of how process reliabilism as it stands seems to leave it open as to whether the reliability in question has anything to do with the agent's beliefs tracking the world. For example, suppose that there was a benevolent demon who ensured that every time our protagonist formed a belief the world was adjusted to make it such that the belief was true. Clearly, this would be a highly reliable way of forming beliefs since it would never fail to result in a true belief. Nevertheless, our intuition in such a case is that the agent lacks knowledge since her reliably formed true beliefs do not reflect a cognitive achievement on her part at all. John Greco describes just such an example as follows:

René thinks he can beat the roulette tables with a system he has devised. Reasoning according to the Gambler's Fallacy, he believes that numbers which have not come up for long strings are more likely to come up next. However, unlike Descartes' demon victim, our René has a demon helper. Acting as a kind of epistemic guardian, the demon arranges reality so as to make the belief come out as true. Given the ever present interventions of the helpful demon, René's belief forming process is highly reliable. But this is because the world is made to confirm to René's beliefs, rather than because René's beliefs conform to the world. (1999: 286)

Clearly here we would not regard René as having knowledge for the simple reason that the reliability that he is exhibiting in his beliefs is nothing to do with him, but rather reflects the interference of the demon helper.

Second, there is the problem that the process reliabilist account of knowledge seems to accord knowledge in cases where the reliability, whilst it might be 'to do with the agent' in some basic causal sense, is not related to the agent's cognitive character in quite the right fashion. A good way to bring this point out is via examples of reliable 'malfunctions'. This is where an agent forms a belief in a reliable manner despite the fact that this reliability is the product of a malfunction. An example, due to Alvin Plantinga, concerns a rare brain lesion that causes the victim to believe that he has a brain lesion. He describes this scenario as follows:

Suppose . . . that S suffers from this sort of disorder and accordingly believes that he suffers from a brain lesion. Add that he has no evidence at all for this belief: no symptoms of which he is aware, no testimony on the part of physicians or other expert witnesses, nothing. (Add if you like, that he has much evidence *against* it; but then add also that the malfunction induced by the lesion makes it impossible for him to take appropriate account of this evidence.) Then the relent [process] will certainly be reliable; but the resulting belief—that he has a brain lesion—will have little by way of warrant for S. (1993*a*, 1999)

We have a strong intuition that there is something epistemically amiss about forming true beliefs via malfunctions in this way, even where those malfunctions happen to support a process of forming beliefs which is reliable. Although malfunction examples like this are different from the helpful demon case in that the reliability at issue has at least *something* to do with the agent (it is *his* brain lesion after all), it is nevertheless the case that the agent's true belief cannot be considered a cognitive achievement on his part because it is *in spite of himself* that he formed a true belief. If his cognitive faculties had been functioning properly, and thus had not been malfunctioning, then we would not have expected him to have formed a true belief in this proposition.

In response to problems of this sort, early virtue epistemologists argued that process reliabilism should be rejected in favour of a kind of reliabilism that specifically focuses on the reliable traits of the agents. This view has come to be known as 'faculty' or 'agent' reliabilism.[8] The basic idea is that it is not reliability per se that epistemologists should be attending to, but rather the particular kind of reliability that represents a cognitive achievement on the part of the agent, and this means a reliability that is tied to stable belief-forming traits of the agent such as her intellectual faculties and epistemic virtues. In general, then, agent reliabilists advocate a thesis along the following lines:

Agent reliabilism
For all agents, φ, an agent has knowledge of a contingent proposition, φ, if, and only if, that agent forms a true belief that φ as a result of the stable and reliable dispositions that make up that agent's cognitive character.

For example, think about the range of stable dispositions involved in the formation of our beliefs about our immediate environment that make up our faculty of sight. If this faculty is working properly and applied in the right conditions, then the beliefs that it generates will be highly reliable. Moreover, since this reliability is keyed into our cognitive character, forming a true belief in this way is a cognitive achievement on our part and will thus tend to be regarded as an instance of knowledge (though we will consider some Gettier-style complications in a moment).

In contrast, the reliability that might attach itself to a cognitive malfunction will not count as knowledge-conducive on this view because the belief-forming process involved is not a stable feature of our cognitive character at all, and thus the reliable true beliefs that result are of no credit to us. Indeed, as we noted above, it is *in spite of* the stable cognitive dispositions that make up the agent's cognitive character that he is reliable in the malfunction case that we looked at earlier, not because of them. Similarly, forming beliefs in a reliable fashion where that reliability has nothing to do with one's cognitive character, as in the case in the 'benevolent demon' example, is also ruled out. The reliability at issue here cannot support knowledge because it represents no cognitive achievement at all on the part of the agent. Agent reliabilists are thus able to deal with a certain type of core objection that has been levelled against process reliabilism, and do so whilst staying within the general reliabilist framework.[9]

We noted above that these early virtue theorists were not primarily concerned with the problems of formulation facing process reliabilism, nor with its commitment to epistemological externalism, and this sketch of the agent reliabilist position should make it obvious why. To begin with, whilst we might have a better intuitive grasp of how we should individuate our intellectual faculties and our epistemic virtues than how we should individuate cognitive processes *simpliciter*, it remains that there will be still be issues of formulation left over here. Recall the brain lesion case, for example. Although this example is defined in such a way that it won't count as a stable and reliable cognitive disposition that makes up the agent's cognitive character—for one thing, it is *defined* as a cognitive malfunction—it doesn't take too much imagination to think of a way in which this example could be understood so that it did appear to meet the agent reliabilist rubric. As Greco himself concedes:

[I]t is not clear why the man with the brain lesion does not have a cognitive virtue, and it is therefore not clear how virtue reliabilism addresses the case. Put another way, it is not clear why the process associated with the brain lesion is not part of reliable cognitive character. Thus we can imagine that the lesion has been there since birth, and that the associated process is both stable and reliable in the relevant senses. (2003: 356–7)[10]

The problems of formulation associated with process reliabilism thus resurface—albeit perhaps in a more manageable form—with agent reliabilism.

Similarly—and these points are related—agent reliabilism is also clearly an externalist account of knowledge and so is subject, just like process reliabilism, to the counter-intuitions put forward by the epistemological internalist. Whatever one might want to say about reliable brain lesions, it is certainly true that the naïve chicken-sexer discussed above is forming her true beliefs via stable and reliable dispositions that make up her cognitive character. As a result, on the agent reliabilist view the chicken-sexer comes out as having knowledge, something which the epistemological internalist will find unacceptable. Again, the agent reliabilist can weaken this objection slightly by arguing that the externalism on offer here is tempered by the fact that the reliability in question must be essentially related to the agent's cognitive character. Accordingly, they can claim that by advocating epistemological externalism they are not thereby allowing knowledge to be completely unconnected with cognitive responsibility. Nevertheless, the issue remains that in these cases the cognitive achievement is entirely at a sub-personal level, and in this sense the agent proper is not cognitively responsible for her reliably formed true beliefs at all. So whilst agent reliabilist accounts of knowledge might ensure that agents are able to take a very minimal form of cognitive responsibility for their beliefs, what the epistemic internalist will demand is a more robust form of cognitive responsibility—a type of cognitive responsibility that could legitimate a claim to know, for example.[11]

Indeed, this point dovetails with the further issue that it sounds odd, to the modern ear at least, to describe agent reliabilism as a *virtue*-theoretic account of knowledge at all. After all, although there is, admittedly, a historical precedent for thinking of the cognitive faculties as being epistemic virtues, our contemporary understanding of the virtues, and thus of the intellectual virtues, tends to regard them as very different to cognitive faculties.[12] Indeed, in terms of the modern usage of the term 'virtue', I think the consensus would be to regard the naïve chicken-sexer as behaving in a way that exhibits an epistemic *vice* on the grounds that she is forming beliefs in the absence of any reflectively accessible evidence in favour of those beliefs. We will return to this point in the next section.

For now, the more pressing issue is how this account of knowledge ties in with the remarks we have made so far about epistemic luck. We have already noted the close relationship between cognitive achievement and the absence of epistemically problematic luck, so we should expect that the manner in which agent reliabilism constitutes an improvement on process reliabilism is directly related to how it eliminates luck of this sort. And, indeed, this is just what we find, since the counter-examples that the agent reliabilists direct against process reliabilism are all Gettier-style examples, in that they are instances of true belief where the agent has met the epistemic conditions demanded by the theory of knowledge in question, and yet the agent lacks knowledge because her belief is nevertheless veritically lucky.

Consider again the helpful demon example. Here we have an agent who would be forming beliefs in an unreliable fashion (via the Gambler's Fallacy) were it not for the fact that, as it happens, there is a helpful demon in town who not only has the capacity to ensure that any beliefs our agent forms in this regard are true, but also has the inclination to be helpful in this fashion. As a result, even though the agent has met the epistemic condition imposed by a basic form of process reliabilism—in that he is forming his true belief via a process which counts as reliable on this view—it is nevertheless also the case that his true belief is here being formed in a way that is subject to a substantive degree of veritic epistemic luck. That is, there will be a large class of nearby possible worlds in which this agent forms his belief in the same way as in the actual world—and this means in this case that he forms his belief via the Gambler's Fallacy—and his belief is false. After all, the class of possible worlds at issue here will include worlds where there is no demon, or where there is a demon but he is not being helpful, or where there is a demon who is being helpful, but who is not being helpful in this particular respect, and so on. Accordingly, since the belief in question is infected by veritic epistemic luck, it is therefore not safe, and so not an instance of knowledge in the light of a safety-based theory.

Next, consider the malfunction case. Again, as the example is described at any rate, we have a case of a true belief that is infected by a substantive degree of veritic epistemic luck. Whilst the agent has formed a true belief in the actual world via a causal process that meets the reliability condition imposed by a basic form of process reliabilism, in most nearby possible worlds we would expect the agent to form a false belief via this process. After all, if it is an incidental fact about the brain lesion that it supports a reliable belief-forming process about this subject matter in this way, then in most nearby possible worlds we would expect it to not be supporting a reliable belief-forming process and thus expect it to not lead the agent to true beliefs about whether or not he has a brain lesion. His belief is thus veritically lucky and hence not safe. Both these examples thus lend support to the Gettier-style contention that meeting the epistemic condition laid down by a basic process reliabilist account of knowledge does not suffice to eliminate veritic epistemic luck, and hence that such a theory of knowledge is highly questionable.

Of course, as we noted above, there is an added complication when it comes to the malfunction example in that there are alternative ways of understanding this case so that the reliability in question isn't incidental in the relevant way but is rather brought about by a stable cognitive disposition on the part of the agent. On this understanding of the example, the agent reliabilist response starts to look suspect, since now the agent *does* seem to be forming true beliefs as a result of stable and reliable traits that make up his cognitive character, at least given the agent reliabilist construal of 'cognitive character' as including the cognitive faculties. The brain lesion case now becomes akin to the naïve chicken-sexer example in that it is an instance of *merely* externalist knowledge—i.e. knowledge where the agent has met no relevant internal justification condition.

By the same token, the agent's true belief on this construal of the example is no longer (at least obviously) infected by veritic epistemic luck, and thus it will be, prima facie at least, in accordance with the demands laid down by a safety-based theory of knowledge. Of course (as in the naïve chicken-sexer example), we would not be happy with the agent making self-ascriptions of knowledge in this case and there is clearly something important epistemically lacking about this agent's belief (it is, as we saw above in our discussion of the naïve chicken-sexer, a true belief that is subject to a substantive degree of reflective epistemic luck). Nevertheless, depending on the details of the example, if we knew that the agent was forming beliefs about this subject matter in a safe way then we might be inclined to ascribe knowledge of a very brute sort to the agent even if we did not think that the agent should be ascribing this knowledge to himself.

It seems then that the objection raised by agent reliabilism against process reliabilism is much the same objection that the proponent of an anti-veritic-luck epistemology would make against process reliabilism—that it cannot capture even a minimal sense in which knowledge is a cognitive achievement on the part of the agent because the rubric it sets down for knowledge does not exclude veritic epistemic luck. The two theses are not complementary, however, in that they end up defining knowledge in very different ways. For whilst the safety-based theorist might no doubt wish to tell an explanatory story about how creatures such as ourselves come to have safe true beliefs that makes essential reference to the cognitive faculties and the epistemic virtues, she does not *define* knowledge in terms of these cognitive traits as the agent reliabilist does. Thus, despite being motivated by similar concerns, agent reliabilism, being a virtue-theoretic theory, is offering a much more radical epistemological thesis.

The issue is therefore whether we need to endorse such a radical view in order to eliminate veritic epistemic luck, or whether we can simply advocate a safety-based view that incorporates an explanatory story that makes essential use of the cognitive faculties and epistemic virtues. It seems that we can do the latter, and ought to, for two reasons. The first reason concerns how the agent reliabilist account of knowledge is not necessary for the elimination of veritic epistemic luck. As we have just seen, the examples of veritic epistemic luck that agent reliabilism claims to be able to deal with in a way that other theories cannot—such as the helpful demon and the brain lesion cases—are examples where a safety-based view has direct application.

As it stands, this observation alone merely puts the two views on a theoretical par in this respect, and thereby only leaves a mere safety-based approach as a live—rather than a preferred—option.[13] There is a further consideration, however, which motivates a safety-based approach over an agent reliabilist alternative, and this is that the agent reliabilist theory of knowledge, unlike the safety-based theory, is not only unnecessary to deal with the problem of veritic luck, but is also *insufficient*. Consider the following Gettier-style counter-example to agent reliabilism:

Mary has good eyesight, but it is not perfect. It is good enough to allow her to identify her husband sitting in his usual chair in the living room from a distance of fifteen feet in somewhat dim light. . . . Of course, her faculties may not be functioning perfectly, but they are functioning well enough that if she goes on to form the belief *My husband is sitting in the living room*, her belief has enough warrant to constitute knowledge when true. . . . Suppose Mary simply misidentifies the chair sitter, who is, we'll suppose, her husband's brother, who looks very much like him. . . . We can now easily amend the case as a Gettier example. Mary's husband could be sitting on the other side of the room, unseen by her. (Zagzebski 1996: 285–7)

What is the agent reliabilist to say about such a case? Clearly, Mary is forming a true belief which meets the epistemic conditions laid down by the agent reliabilist, in that her true belief is a result of the stable and reliable dispositions that make up her cognitive character. Crucially, however, the belief in this case is not an instance of knowledge because of the veritic epistemic luck involved. After all, there will be a wide class of nearby possible worlds in which Mary forms her belief in the same way as in the actual world and yet continues to form a false belief as a result because her husband is not, as it happens, in the room in these worlds.

What is crucial about the fact that agent reliabilist views can be 'Gettiered' in this way is that it completely undermines the agent reliabilist claim to be in a peculiarly good position to capture the sense in which knowledge is a cognitive achievement on the part of the agent. Whilst Mary is certainly deserving of some epistemic credit for forming the belief that she did, we would hardly regard it as a cognitive achievement on her part that she formed a true belief since the truth of her belief was largely due to luck. The inability of agent reliabilism to eliminate veritic epistemic luck means that it allows these Gettier-style cases where the agent meets the relevant epistemic rubric even whilst forming a veritically lucky true belief. Accordingly, the view legitimates a knowledge ascription even though the agent concerned is clearly not exhibiting anything like the kind of cognitive achievement (sub-personal or otherwise) that is necessary for knowledge.

Moreover, note that safety-based views will not have this problem since Mary's true belief, since it is veritically lucky, will not be safe and thus will not be accorded the status of knowledge by the lights of a safety-based thesis. The adoption of a safety-based view—unlike an agent reliabilist view—is thus sufficient for the elimination of veritic epistemic luck.

Furthermore, note that any safety-based account of knowledge that offered an explanatory story about how agents gain safe true beliefs—and thus are able to acquire knowledge—will no doubt make reference to the kinds of cognitive traits at issue in agent reliabilism. In this way, safety-based views can account for why Mary is deserving of some epistemic credit even though in this case she lacks knowledge because the cognitive faculties that she is employing in forming her belief are good ways in which to acquire safe beliefs. Nevertheless, since such a fully-fledged epistemological theory does not *define* knowledge in terms of the epistemic virtues and cognitive faculties, such an epistemology is still a safety-based theory rather than a virtue-theoretic account.

So whilst agent reliabilists are right to be troubled by veritic epistemic luck and thus to seek a theory of knowledge that eliminates such luck (thereby ensuring that knowing agents are able to take a minimal degree of cognitive responsibility for their beliefs), it remains that the way to achieve this is via a safety-based theory rather than via a virtue-theoretic account.

7.3. Neo-Aristotelian Virtue Epistemology

Not all virtue-theoretic accounts of knowledge are modelled along reliabilist lines, however, and more recent work on virtue epistemology has tended to move towards an epistemologically internalist version of the thesis which understands the epistemic virtues in a way that is more in keeping with our ordinary conception of them, and which thus does not treat mere cognitive faculties as epistemic virtues. Such views are often called 'responsibilist' or 'neo-Aristotelian' and stress that agents should not only exhibit reliable cognitive traits but that they should also be in a position to take the kind of robust reflective responsibility for their true beliefs that is noticeably lacking in externalist views of knowledge. Since epistemic virtues are reliable cognitive traits which also demand a certain level of reflective responsibility on the part of the agent, they fit the bill perfectly.

Perhaps the most prominent and well-developed version of a thesis of this sort is due to Zagzebski,[14] who argues that mere reliability is not enough and that agents should have to meet internal epistemic conditions as well. On her view, the kind of sub-personal cognitive achievement that is present in, for example, naïve chicken-sexer cases, will not suffice for knowledge. For whilst the naïve chicken-sexer might be forming belief in ways that are reliable, she is not forming beliefs in ways that are epistemically virtuous (at least in the modern sense of the term). She is not, for example, forming her beliefs in a way that is epistemically conscientious, or, indeed, in a way that is responsive to the reflectively accessible evidence that she has in favour of her beliefs at all. (In fact, as we noted above, the naïve chicken-sexer is, if anything, forming her beliefs via an epistemic vice rather than a virtue, at least provided we understand the epistemic 'virtues' in the standard way which excludes mere cognitive faculties.)

We saw above how Zagzebski also motivated her adoption of an internalist account of knowledge by claiming that such internalism was necessary to eliminate epistemic luck, but that the kind of epistemic luck that was at issue was, it turned out, specifically reflective epistemic luck rather than veritic epistemic luck. We would expect the motivation for most virtue epistemologies of this sort to be susceptible to the same diagnosis, in that their underlying concern regarding agent reliabilism is that whereas the reliabilist element of the view deals with veritic epistemic luck, and does so in a way that makes the reliability a product (in some sense) of the agent's cognitive character, since this form of 'virtue' theory allows sub-personal traits of the agent to count as knowledge-conducive, it won't capture the fuller sense in which knowledge is a cognitive achievement of the agent. This 'fuller sense' of cognitive achievement involves, of course, not just the elimination of veritic epistemic luck but also the elimination of reflective epistemic luck—hence the necessity of adding, via the focus on the epistemic virtues alone, an internal epistemic condition to the view.[15]

If one is persuaded by the general virtue-theoretic line and unpersuaded by the considerations in favour of epistemological externalism, then one will be inclined to adopt a virtue epistemology of this sort. As we will see in a moment, however, it is not at all clear that this new variant on the general virtue-theoretic approach adds anything which can help it evade the criticisms that we levelled against agent reliabilism above, since an internalized version of virtue epistemology doesn't appear to be in any better position to handle cases of veritic epistemic luck than an agent reliabilist view is. Accordingly, it appears that if one is troubled by the problem posed by reflective epistemic luck then one would be wiser to endorse an internalized version of a safety-based theory—i.e. a safety-based theory that also incorporated an internal epistemic condition—rather than a version of the more radical neo-Aristotelian virtue account.

In order to see this, consider again the Gettier-style example that we saw Zagzebski offering above which concerned an agent, Mary, who formed a true belief about whether or not her husband was in the room as a result of stable and reliable cognitive traits that made up her cognitive character, and yet who lacked knowledge because her belief was subject to a substantive degree of veritic epistemic luck (she was not looking at her husband, but her husband's brother). As it stands, this example doesn't demand that the agent should form her belief in a way that is epistemically virtuous rather than merely as a result of reliable and stable cognitive faculties, but we can easily understand the example along these lines. Suppose, for example, that Mary forms her belief in such a way that it is epistemically virtuous (she has been conscientious about forming her belief on the basis of adequate reflectively accessible evidence and so forth), and that the belief in question is therefore internalistically justified. Since her belief is true, and has been formed via the stable and reliable epistemic virtues that make up her cognitive character, we would expect Mary to have knowledge about what she believes. Nevertheless, all these conditions could be met and her belief still be 'Gettiered' because, as in the original example, she happens to be looking at her husband's brother whilst her husband is hidden from view elsewhere in the room. The belief is thus still veritically lucky and hence not a case of knowledge.

Interestingly, Zagzebski is quite willing to grant that she cannot meet the Gettier examples head-on via her theory of knowledge in this way. Instead, she tries to motivate a response to this problem by bringing additional resources to bear on the issue, albeit resources that are, she claims, consistent with her general virtue-theoretic approach. Essentially, her contention is that what is lacking about agents in Gettier cases is that whilst they have managed to acquire true beliefs by forming their beliefs in ways that are epistemically virtuous, they do not believe the truth *through* an act of epistemic virtue. Consider the following passage:

[I]n the case of Mary's belief that her husband is in the living room, she may exhibit all the relevant intellectual virtues and no intellectual vices in the process of forming the belief, but she is not lead to the truth through those virtuous processes or motives.

So even though Mary has the belief she has because of her virtues and the belief is true, she does not have the truth because of her virtues. (Zagzebski 1996: 297)

Zagzebski's claim is thus that it is not enough to merely form a true belief via one's stable and reliable epistemic virtues in order to have knowledge; rather one must form that true belief *because of* one's stable and reliable epistemic virtues.[16]

This distinction is obscure, however, since it is not at all clear what it involves. What is the difference between the case where Mary's belief hasn't been 'Gettiered', and where she thus has knowledge, and the case under discussion in which she has been 'Gettiered' and so lacks knowledge? Clearly, the difference does not relate to anything about Mary because, by hypothesis, Mary's cognitive character is exactly the same in both cases. Zagzebski thus seems to be implicitly supplementing her putatively virtue-theoretic account of knowledge with an extra non-virtue-theoretic condition that is able to rule out Gettier cases. Indeed, Zagzebski seems to have a modal claim in mind here. Not only should the agent form her true belief via her stable and reliable epistemic virtues, but she should also believe what she does *because* it is true where, intuitively, this means that were what is believed not true, then she would not form the belief that she did via her stable and reliable epistemic virtues. So construed, Zagzebski seems to be wanting to add a sensitivity condition to her virtue theory, such that the means by which the agent forms her true belief in the actual world should be via the epistemic virtues, and that in the nearest possible world or worlds in which the proposition in question is false the agent does not believe that proposition via this same method.

As we saw above in §6.3, adding a sensitivity condition will do the trick in Gettier-type cases like this, at least provided that the principle is understood in the right kind of way. But recall that we also noted that if any modal condition is applicable here, then it is the safety principle, not only because it directly defuses the veritic epistemic luck at issue in Gettier-type cases, but also because, unlike the sensitivity principle, it isn't committed to allowing far-off possible worlds to be relevant to knowledge. Moreover, we also saw that once sensitivity is modified so as to deal with Gettier-type cases—such that it is concerned with a range of nearby possible worlds—then it no longer differs from safety in any substantive respect, and thus there cannot be anything to gain by opting for the sensitivity principle over the safety principle.

Presumably, then, Zagzebski ought to be happy to construe her modal requirement on knowledge along safety-based lines, and thus argue that the knowing agent should form her true belief via her epistemic virtues, and that her belief should, in addition, be safe. However, if this is what her response to Gettier amounts to then one could just as well adopt a safety-based view that deals with veritic epistemic luck—and thus the Gettier-style examples—directly and then supplement it, if need be, with an internal justification condition to deal with the additional problem posed by reflective epistemic luck. Crucially, however, such a theory of knowledge need make no essential mention of the epistemic virtues, even if an account of how agents gain internalistically justified safe beliefs will no doubt incorporate a virtue-theoretic story. Again, then, we find that the case for the virtue-theoretic account of knowledge is moot.

The problem at issue here arises because even internalists need to advocate an external epistemic condition in order to eliminate veritic epistemic luck. The difficulty is that the only external epistemic condition that does the trick is a safety-type condition, and once one has made the crucial move to adopting a condition of this sort as part of one's theory of knowledge then one has thereby moved away from a virtue-theoretic account that defines knowledge in terms of the epistemic virtues because such a principle makes no essential reference to the epistemic virtues at all. It is not then as if Zagzebski is merely offering an internalized virtue-theoretic account that is supplemented by a safety-type condition, since the adoption of a safety-type condition makes the virtue-theoretic proposal obsolete. If one has externalist intuitions about knowledge, then one should seek a mere safety-based theory of knowledge that will, no doubt, be supplemented by a further explanatory story concerning the epistemic virtues and cognitive faculties that explains how agents gain safe beliefs that are not veritically lucky. Alternatively, if one has internalist intuitions about knowledge, then one should seek an internalist safety-based theory of knowledge that will, no doubt, be supplemented by a further explanatory story concerning the epistemic virtues that explains how agents gain safe and internalistically justified beliefs that are neither veritically nor reflectively lucky. Either way, one is left with a non-virtue-theoretic account of knowledge and, far from motivating the virtue-theoretic position in this regard, reflection on the role of epistemic luck merely highlights the juncture at which the virtue epistemological thesis goes awry.

One final point is in order. Recall that we saw Zagzebski arguing earlier that epistemological externalists, as opposed to internalists, were sanguine about epistemic luck, and we noted there that this was a misleading way of putting matters. This discussion of Zagzebski's response to the Gettier problem brings this point nicely to the fore. Zagzebski is just as concerned about the veritic epistemic luck that is at issue in the Gettier counter-examples as externalists are, and this is why she has a reliability condition in her account, one that is, moreover, implicitly coupled to a modal anti-veritic-luck condition for good measure. Moreover, we have also seen that an externalist theory of knowledge which eliminated veritic epistemic luck would capture one sense in which knowledge demands cognitive achievement, which is the minimal sense that the true belief in question is not gained via a matter of luck and so is, in this very limited sense, of credit to the agent.

Furthermore, it is worth emphasizing that it is not as if externalists are necessarily unconcerned about reflective epistemic luck either, since it is entirely consistent with their view that they regard such luck as being epistemically undesirable. What distinguishes epistemic internalists from externalists on this issue is thus not whether or not they are sanguine about epistemic luck *simpliciter*, but more specifically whether they think that the elimination of reflective epistemic luck should be a necessary condition for knowledge. The internalist thinks that it should be, and so adduces an internal epistemic condition, whereas the externalist disagrees.

7.4. Concluding Remarks

Epistemological externalists and epistemological internalists thus have a tendency to 'speak past' one another, and we have seen that this is caused, at least in part, by a failure to realize that they are each primarily concerned with advancing a theory of knowledge that is able to eliminate a *different* species of epistemic luck. Indeed, as we saw with our discussion of the two main types of virtue epistemology, this issue about eliminating epistemic luck also explains the different conceptions of cognitive responsibility that are at issue in debates between proponents of these two theses. Since we have already granted the internalist claim that the possession of an internalist justification for one's beliefs is epistemically desirable—where this epistemic desirability is reflected in how one is able to take cognitive responsibility for one's belief in a fuller sense than would be possible if such justification were lacking—it follows that we ought to be at least sympathetic to the theoretical aspirations of epistemological internalists. The issue therefore comes down to whether we are willing to allow that there are some instances in which agents might have knowledge in the 'brute' externalist sense where the agent's cognitive responsibility for her beliefs is, at best, entirely sub-personal.

As we will see in the next chapter, we cannot fully resolve this issue without returning to the problem of scepticism that we began this book with, since, as I shall explain, the sceptical problem is, first and foremost a challenge to the very sort of cognitive responsibility that epistemological internalists aspire to and which is downplayed by externalist theories of knowledge. The sceptical problem is thus, at root, concerned with the issue of eliminating reflective epistemic luck from our beliefs.

Notes

1. For example, Foley (1987) argues that we should seek beliefs that are both internalistically justified *and* reliable, but that it is only the satisfaction of external epistemic conditions that is necessary for knowledge. According to Foley, internalists and externalists are engaged in two distinct projects. Internalists are trying to identify the conditions under which an agent's beliefs are rational, whilst externalists are aiming to elucidate the conditions under which agents have knowledge. Crucially, according to Foley at any rate, one can meet the latter set of conditions without thereby having internalistically justified (and thus rational) true beliefs (and vice versa). As a result, the naïve chicken-sexer's beliefs are epistemically problematic, but not in a way that undermines her knowledge possession. See also Foley (1993).

2. It should be noted that Zagzebski characterizes the internalist–externalist distinction in a somewhat unorthodox fashion such that internalist epistemologies are theories that *only* advance internal epistemic conditions. In light of this understanding of the distinction, her own view comes out as being what she calls a 'mixed' externalist thesis because it incorporates both internal and external epistemic conditions, whereas it would be an internalist view in light of the more orthodox characterization of the distinction put forward here. There are a number of problems with the way in which Zagzebski draws the internalist–externalist distinction, but the most pressing is that on this understanding it is not clear who the opposition is supposed to be since hardly anyone in these post-Gettier days holds that knowledge is just internalistically justified true belief. The debate between internalists and externalists is thus trivialized.

3. Of course, agents might have reflectively accessible evidence and yet fail to take appropriate account of it, and it will be part of any theory of internalist justification to elucidate just what it means to take 'appropriate' account of the evidence that one has reflectively available to one. I ignore this complication in what follows.

4. Indeed, Zagzebski's remarks cited in the last section were taken from a context in which she was discussing her own version of virtue epistemology, a version which we will discuss further below.

5. And, indeed, process reliabilism was primarily aimed at perceptual belief. For discussion of process reliabilism, see Armstrong (1973), Goldman (1976, 1979, 1986), and Talbott (1990).

6. For more on the generality problem, see Brandom (1998) and Conee and Feldman (1998).

7. Indeed, as we will see below, they thought that their view could at least contribute towards a satisfactory resolution of them. A third sort of problem facing process reliabilism, and which a virtue-theoretic reliabilism might also hope to resolve, is its failure to deal with certain Gettier-style examples. Again, this is an issue that we will return to below.

8. Versions of this thesis have been proposed by Sosa (1985, 1991, 1993), Goldman (1993) and Greco (1993, 1999, 2000). A related view in this respect is Plantinga's (1988, 1993b, 1993c) 'proper functionalism', although he has explicitly resisted any virtue-based interpretation of his view. For an overview of proposals of this sort, see Axtell (1997: especially §2).

9. Although I'm willing to grant the general point that agent reliabilism constitutes an improvement on process reliabilism, I think that the issue is somewhat more complicated than proponents of agent reliabilism sometimes suppose. In particular, I would argue that they tend to achieve their victory over process reliabilism rather cheaply by working with a very underdeveloped formulation of the process reliabilist position. I discuss this issue in more detail in Pritchard (2003c), to which Axtell (2003) and Greco (2003) respond.

10. I develop this problem in Pritchard (2003c), and Greco was here responding to that objection. For more discussion of this issue, see the exchange between Plantinga (1993c) and Sosa (1993), and the references offered by Greco (2003: 357).

11. For an overview of the different ways in which the main virtue-theoretic forms of reliabilism try to meet the problems of formulation facing process reliabilism and deal with the more counter-intuitive aspects of its commitment to epistemological externalism, see Axtell (1997: §2).

12. Sosa defends his broad usage of the term 'virtue' in the following passage:

> For example, it may be one's faculty of sight operating in good light that generates one's belief in the whiteness and roundness of a facing snowball. Is possession of such a faculty a 'virtue'? Not in the narrow Aristotelian sense, of course, since it is no disposition to make deliberate choices. But there is a broader sense of 'virtue', still Greek, in which anything with a function—natural or artificial—does have virtues. The eye does, after all, have its virtues, and so does a knife. And if we include grasping the truth about one's environment among the proper ends of a human being, then the faculty of sight would seem in a broad sense a virtue in human beings; and if grasping the truth is an intellectual matter then that virtue is also in a straightforward sense an intellectual virtue. (1991: 271).

13. Though one might argue, of course, that the safety-based view is the more minimal of the two proposals, and thus that when one is faced with an *impasse* of this sort it should be preferred.

14. See especially Zagzebski (1996). Views of this general sort have also been offered by Code (1984, 1987), Montmarquet (1987, 1993), Kvanvig (1992), and Hookway (1994). For an overview of responsibilist virtue-theoretic theses in the recent literature (though one that invokes a broader understanding of this description than that employed here), see Axtell (1997: §4). For some of the recent literature on this topic that covers both this type of virtue theory and faculty-based accounts, see the papers collected in the following anthologies: Axtell (2000), Fairweather and Zagzebski (2001), DePaul and Zagzebski (2002), Steup (2002), and Brady and Pritchard (2003).

15. A secondary motivation that Zagzebski offers for preferring an internalist version of virtue-theory over an externalist version is that only the former can meet what she calls the 'value problem' which, essentially, is the claim that only an internalist virtue-theoretic account of knowledge can explain what is valuable about knowledge. She develops this line in Zagzebski (2003; cf. Percival 2003). For some of the key recent discussions of the value problem, see Jones (1997), Kvanvig (1998, 2003, 2004), Greco (2002), Riggs (2002), and Axtell (2003).

16. See also Zagzebski (1999). This idea has also gained expression in the work of a number of other proponents of virtue epistemology. See, e.g. Riggs (2002) and Greco (2002, 2003).

8

Scepticism and Epistemic Luck

8.0. Introduction

We saw in the last chapter that the issue which ultimately divides epistemological externalists and internalists concerns whether the possession of knowledge is consistent with one forming true beliefs in a way that is reflectively lucky, and which is thus lacking in a certain robust form of cognitive responsibility. Whilst externalists are content to offer a theory of knowledge which merely eliminates veritic epistemic luck—and which therefore only guarantees that knowers are able to take cognitive responsibility for their beliefs in a very weak 'sub-personal' sense—internalists opt for a more demanding theory of knowledge which also eliminates reflective epistemic luck and so ensures that only those who are able to take cognitive responsibility in this fuller sense for their beliefs are counted as knowers.

In this chapter we return to the sceptical problem that we began the book with, and consider this dispute between epistemological externalists and internalists in the light of this problem. As we will see, the sceptical challenge, properly understood, is not ultimately concerned with whether or not we are capable of possessing knowledge—where this is understood in terms of either an externalist or an internalist theory of knowledge—but is rather specifically directed at our conception of ourselves as agents who are able to take a robust form of cognitive responsibility for our knowledge. It is thus primarily concerned with the elimination of reflective epistemic luck and hence with *internalist* knowledge. This point is illustrated by examining the so-called 'metaepistemological' challenge that has recently been directed against epistemologically externalist theories of knowledge, and also by considering the classical Pyrrhonian sceptical techniques which purport to undermine 'dogmatic' belief.

8.1. Scepticism and Reflective Epistemic Luck

Recall that the characterization of the sceptical paradox that is the focus of the contemporary debate about scepticism is the following argument from ignorance formulated in terms of knowledge:

The template closure-based radical sceptical argument

(C1) If one is to have knowledge of a wide range of everyday propositions, then one must know the denials of all radical sceptical hypotheses that one knows to be incompatible with the relevant everyday propositions.

(C2) One cannot know the denials of radical sceptical hypotheses.

(CC) One cannot have knowledge of a wide range of everyday propositions.

With this kind of template sceptical argument in mind, we saw that there were three main antisceptical proposals that presented themselves. The first involved advocating some sort of sensitivity condition which demanded that one's true belief should be sensitive to the truth in the sense that in the nearest possible world or worlds in which what is believed is false one no longer believes it. This condition was supposed to entail that the closure principle which supports (C1) is false in that agents are able to have sensitive beliefs about everyday propositions (and thus knowledge of them) even though they lack sensitive beliefs (and thus knowledge) of the known to be entailed denials of sceptical hypotheses, though we have since seen that this conclusion is, at best, insecure.

The second antisceptical position involved offering an attributer contextualist understanding of the term 'knows' such that in different contexts of utterance the truth conditions of assertions of ascription sentences involving this term could change even though the agent's epistemic position and other relevant environmental facts stayed fixed. This ensured that premiss (C2) and the conclusion (CC) were false, in that there were some conversational contexts (everyday ones) where assertions of ascription sentences regarding the denials of sceptical hypotheses were true, and there were some conversational contexts (sceptical ones) where assertions of ascription sentences regarding everyday propositions were false. Whilst this was, like the sensitivity-based thesis, a somewhat revisionistic proposal, it did have the advantage of being consistent with closure. Within any particular conversational context, if an assertion of an ascription sentence expressed a truth, then the assertion of any ascription sentence regarding a proposition which the agent knew was entailed by that proposition would also express a truth (or, at least, the theory generates no reason for thinking otherwise).

We noted that it was in the nature of these proposals that they were allied to epistemological externalism, in that such views were incoherent unless they were understood along these lines. Crucially, however, we also saw that both of these antisceptical theses were illicitly motivated, at least in part, by epistemologically internalist intuitions, and that it was these internalist intuitions that led to the revisionistic aspect of the thesis in each case—the denial of closure in the case of the sensitivity-based theory, and the advocacy of a contextualist treatment of 'knows' in the case of the attributer contextualist theory. This led us to draw a rather startling conclusion—that in so far as endorsing epistemological externalism is legitimate in this regard, and in so far as we are right to focus on the closure-based characterization of the sceptical argument formulated above, then the appropriate response to scepticism is to endorse a thoroughgoing externalism that rejects arguments for both non-closure and attributer contextualism, and simply maintains that provided agents have knowledge of everyday propositions then they also have knowledge of the denials of sceptical hypotheses.

We called such a thesis 'neo-Mooreanism', in that it was, in outline at least, structurally similar to the 'common-sense' response to the sceptic offered by G. E. Moore. We also noted, however, that there were a number of differences between this thesis and the supposed analogue thesis that (on one reading at least) Moore himself advocated. For one thing, this proposal did something that Moore never did, and this was to offer an account of knowledge, albeit a partial one. This was done in terms of the safety principle that we have since explored in more detail. Moreover, neo-Mooreanism also incorporated a diagnosis of where the other antisceptical proposals went wrong in terms of the mixed (externalist and internalist) epistemological motivations that were leading to their views. Finally, the neo-Moorean approach distanced itself from the Moorean dialectical strategy of actually directly arguing against the sceptic—i.e. claiming to know everyday propositions and, on this basis, further claiming to know the denials of sceptical hypotheses. The neo-Moorean concedes to the sceptic the anti-Moorean point that such assertions are inappropriate, even though she does not thereby also concede to the sceptic that what is being asserted by these assertions is therefore false.

We have already seen that the safety-based theory of knowledge that is integral to the neo-Moorean strategy is further motivated by its ability to deal with the problem posed by veritic epistemic luck. It is thus able to handle Gettier-style counter-examples, not to mention other key examples discussed in contemporary epistemology, such as the lottery example. Moreover, we have noted that the moral of the post-Gettier literature is that any adequate epistemological theory—externalist or internalist, virtue-theoretic or non-virtue-theoretic—must incorporate a safety-type external epistemic condition on knowledge in order to evade veritic epistemic luck.

As we also saw in Chapter 4, however, whilst the neo-Moorean response to scepticism is preferable to its sensitivity-based and attributer contextualist rivals, it is still an intellectually unsatisfactory resolution of the problem. For as we noted there, all of these responses take it as given that epistemological externalism can be a legitimate part of an antisceptical proposal, and also that the template sceptical argument considered above captures what is fundamentally at issue in the sceptical argument. Both of these assumptions are highly contentious. The focus for this claim was the alternative formulation of the sceptical argument in terms of the underdetermination principle, a principle that we saw was logically weaker than its analogue closure principle, thus making the underdetermination-based sceptical argument prima facie resistant to antisceptical proposals that are primarily directed towards the closure-based template argument. Recall that we formulated this argument as follows:

The template underdetermination-based sceptical argument

(U1) If my evidence does not favour my belief in everyday propositions over the known to be incompatible sceptical hypotheses, then I am not internalistically justified in believing everyday propositions.

(U2) My evidence does not favour my belief in everyday propositions over the known to be incompatible sceptical hypotheses.

(UC) I am not internalistically justified in believing everyday propositions (and thus I lack internalist knowledge of everyday propositions).

It is the underdetermination principle that is motivating (U1), in that this principle demands that evidential superiority in one's beliefs relative to alternative hypotheses is needed if one is to have an internalist justification for those beliefs. Since the problem posed by sceptical hypotheses is that we are unable to have such relative evidential support for our beliefs, this way of formulating the sceptical argument exposes the manner in which a neo-Moorean response to scepticism—indeed, *any* epistemologically externalist response to scepticism—would only be able to rescue a very 'brute' form of externalist knowledge from the sceptic. In particular, it would not be able to salvage the kind of internalist knowledge which incorporates an internalist justification requirement that is the ultimate focus of the sceptical attack, and which is explicitly at issue in the underdetermination-based argument.

The reason why this is important is because any plausible externalist response to scepticism would need to ensure that a great deal, if not most, of our knowledge was supported by an internalist justification, and thus was 'internalist' knowledge. It is one thing to countenance, in isolated cases, the kind of unreflective 'brute' knowledge that, the externalist claims, is possessed by the naïve chicken-sexer, but quite another to suppose that most, if not all, of our knowledge is merely of this nature. As we have seen, even if one does not regard internalist justification as necessary for knowledge, it is still true that such a justification is highly epistemically desirable in that it enables us to properly claim the knowledge that we have and thereby take a more robust kind of cognitive responsibility for our beliefs. The problem is that all parties to the dispute agree that the evidence we have in favour of our everyday beliefs does not prefer those beliefs over their sceptical alternatives.[1] Given the underdetermination principle, however, this means that we necessarily lack an internalist justification for the bulk of our everyday beliefs (and hence lack internalist knowledge of the propositions believed).

Moreover, since the underdetermination principle is logically weaker than its closure-type counterpart, it follows that any principled rejection of the closure principle for internalist justification (or internalist knowledge) will not be in itself sufficient to meet the sceptical challenge raised by the underdetermination principle. It follows that if we are to engage with the sceptical problem then we need to get to grips with the underdetermination-based sceptical argument and thus with issues about justification and evidential support which the closure-based template argument, by being formulated in terms of knowledge, simply ignores.

So merely having an anti-luck epistemology in the sense of a safety-based neo-Moorean approach that treats the elimination of veritic epistemic luck as necessary for knowledge possession will not give us an easy way out of the sceptical problem. For whilst this is able to meet the closure-based sceptical paradox in a formal sense—in that it rescues knowledge *simpliciter* from the sceptic—the kind of knowledge that it rescues is not quite of the form that we wanted. It is mere brute externalist knowledge that is being saved, and what we wanted to rescue from the sceptic was something more substantial—knowledge that (at least on the whole) could be properly claimed and for which we could therefore take a robust degree of cognitive responsibility.

In terms of the contrast between reflective and veritic epistemic luck that has been explored here, the point becomes that the main antisceptical proposals in the literature merely focus on the elimination of veritic epistemic luck—and thus on rescuing externalist knowledge from the sceptic—without further recognizing that even if the elimination of reflective epistemic luck is not essential for knowledge possession, it is still epistemically desirable that it be eliminated. Unfortunately, the underdetermination-based sceptical argument highlights that this form of epistemic luck is ineliminable. Answering the closure-based sceptical argument is thus at best a first step towards answering the sceptical problem. What is also needed is a response to the underdetermination-based sceptical argument. In short, the sceptical problem, whilst apparently about knowledge possession *simpliciter*—and thus (given the plausibility of epistemological externalism) about veritic epistemic luck—is actually about a certain kind of knowledge possession, and, in particular, about reflective epistemic luck.

Now one might be puzzled at this juncture because didn't we show earlier on (in §6.5) that one *could* eliminate reflective epistemic luck? Recall our discussion of the enlightened chicken-sexer who had (we claimed) an internalist justification for her belief, in contrast to her counterpart, the naïve-chicken sexer, who was exactly alike except that she lacked an internalist justification. Both of these agents had a belief which was safe—and hence not veritically lucky—which meant that their beliefs were not only true in the actual world, but also true in nearly all nearby possible worlds in which they formed their beliefs in the same way as in the actual world. Nevertheless, since the naïve chicken-sexer lacked an internalist justification for her belief, it followed that, unlike her enlightened counterpart, she did not have a belief which was immune to reflective epistemic luck. More specifically, where the possible worlds were ordered solely in terms of what she knew by reflection alone (which wasn't very much when it came to the subject matter in question), her belief did not match the truth in most of the nearest possible worlds. In contrast, the putative internalist justification for her belief possessed by the enlightened chicken-sexer seemed to ensure that she did track the truth across nearly all of the possible worlds on the reflective ordering (indeed, recall that her internalist justification ensured that the 'objective' non-reflective ordering of possible worlds and the reflective ordering were essentially the same). But if the elimination of reflective epistemic luck—and thus the possession of internalist justification—is impossible, then how could this be?

The explanation lies in how when we ordinarily ascribe internalist justification to an agent we do so against a backdrop of further claims that we take as given. Typically, these further claims include the denials of sceptical hypotheses. We can see how this occurs in the case of the counterpart chicken-sexers by noting that in considering the reflective ordering of the possible worlds when it came to the enlightened chicken-sexer's knowledge we were implicitly bracketing sceptical possible worlds. Given that even the reflectively accessible grounds possessed by this chicken-sexer do not favour her belief over its sceptical alternatives (i.e. over belief in sceptical hypotheses), it follows that sceptical possible worlds *will* count as nearby possible worlds on the reflective ordering. After all, for them to count as far-off worlds on this ordering would require the agent to have reflectively accessible grounds in favour of her belief which preferred that belief over belief in sceptical hypotheses and, we have seen in our discussion of the underdetermination-based sceptical argument, no such grounds are available. Accordingly, provided that we do not bracket the sceptical possible worlds, then there will be a wide class of possible worlds that count as nearby worlds on this ordering, and this means that there will be a wide class of nearby worlds in which even the enlightened chicken-sexer's belief fails to match the truth. Her belief will thus be reflectively lucky even despite the reflectively accessible grounds that she has in favour of that belief.

As we will see below in our discussion of Pyrrhonian scepticism—and in the next chapter when we return to Wittgenstein's remarks on hinge propositions—it is part of our practice of ascribing knowledge, both to ourselves and others, that it takes place against a backdrop of ungrounded certainties. This is what disguises the force of scepticism where it is focused on our inability to eliminate reflective epistemic luck from our beliefs, since it leads us into thinking that there is a sufficient difference of degree regarding the epistemic status of the enlightened and the naïve agent's beliefs to enable the enlightened agent to have beliefs which are immune to reflective epistemic luck and thus resistant to this form of scepticism. There is a difference of degree here, but it does not suffice to support this conclusion, and this is because of the fact—highlighted to us by the underdetermination-based sceptical argument—that one's grounds can never favour one's everyday beliefs over their sceptical alternatives. Instead, the proper moral to be drawn is that, when the sceptical possibilities are not bracketed, our 'everyday' beliefs are never able to enjoy an internalist justification and are always ineliminably subject to reflective epistemic luck.

8.2. The Metaepistemological Sceptical Challenge

A number of writers in the recent philosophical literature have drawn attention to the inadequacy of the standard responses to the sceptical problem, although they haven't tended to make this point by raising the issue of epistemic luck. The focus for the attack is usually on the externalist element of the main anti-sceptical theses, the claim being that whilst externalist responses might in some sense rescue our knowledge from the sceptic, they do so in an intellectually unsatisfying way. Since this line of argument incorporates a kind of second-order doubt about the adequacy of antisceptical theories, it is often described as 'metaepistemological' scepticism.

If the diagnostic account regarding the underlying problem of scepticism sketched in the last section is right, however, then we ought to find that we can understand the motivation for metaepistemological scepticism in terms of the problem posed by reflective epistemic luck. As we will see, this suspicion is confirmed because what the metaepistemological complaint amounts to is the contention that externalist responses to scepticism *merely* eliminate the veritic epistemic luck that scepticism plays upon without also engaging with the second—and more fundamental—prong of sceptical attack that is directed at *reflective* epistemic luck.

Typically, of course, those propounding metaepistemological scepticism do not put the point in quite this fashion. The closest anyone comes to expressing the issue in these luck-based terms is Linda Zagzebski, whom we saw arguing in the last chapter that externalists were 'sanguine' about luck in a way that internalists were not, though she didn't make the connection in this respect to externalist treatments of scepticism. For others, the issue is simply that there is something lacking in externalist accounts of knowledge, and that this is brought to the fore once one considers externalist responses to scepticism. For example, Richard Fumerton makes the following point:

> It is *tempting* to think that externalist analyses of knowledge ... simply remove one *level* of the traditional problems of skepticism. When one reads the well-known externalists one is surely inclined to wonder why they are so sanguine about their supposition that our commonplace beliefs are, for the most part, ... knowledge. ... Perception, memory, and induction *may* be reliable processes (in Goldman's sense) and thus given his metaepistemological position we may [... have knowledge of] the beliefs they produce but, the skeptic can argue, we have no reason to believe that these processes are reliable and thus even if we accept reliabilism, we have no reason to think that the beliefs they produce [constitute knowledge]. (1990: 63)[2]

In effect, the complaint that Fumerton is giving expression to here is that externalism allows that there are certain conditions on knowledge that one is unable to reflectively know to have obtained. In particular, externalists' treatments of knowledge accord us with knowledge provided that (at the very least) sceptical error-possibilities are false, whilst also granting that we are unable to have adequate reflectively accessible grounds for believing that such hypotheses are false.

Indeed, Fumerton is more explicit about the focus of his objection when he goes on to write that

the main problem with externalist accounts, it seems to me, just is the fact that such accounts ... develop concepts of knowledge that are irrelevant. ... The philosopher doesn't just want true beliefs, or even reliably produced beliefs, or beliefs caused by the facts that make them true. The philosopher wants to have the relevant features of the world directly before consciousness. (1990: 64)

Presumably, to argue that externalist accounts of knowledge are problematic because they fail to demand that the relevant facts should be 'directly before consciousness' is simply to complain that such theories make the satisfaction of non-reflectively accessible external epistemic conditions essential to knowledge possession. And, intuitively, what is troubling about this is that it leaves these epistemological theories open to the kind of reflective epistemic luck that we saw earlier. That is, merely meeting the external conditions on knowledge does not give us any assurance that our knowledge is anything more substantial than that possessed by the naïve chicken-sexer.

Of course, Fumerton is here specifically talking about the need for the relevant facts to be reflectively available to the *philosopher* (i.e. the epistemologist), and this is of course consistent with the idea that such facts need not be reflectively available to agents in everyday life who do not seek philosophical accounts of their knowledge. But this simply serves to emphasize the point at issue here. If such facts are not reflectively available even to those who are in a better position than most to avail themselves of them, then this highlights their reflective inaccessibility. That is, it is not that the situation is akin to someone who knows all the relevant chicken-sexing facts passing a positive judgement on the epistemic status of the naïve chicken-sexer's beliefs, a positive epistemic assessment which coexists with that agent's lack of reflective knowledge of these facts. Rather, the situation is that there is no epistemically enhanced position from which we can positively determine what the epistemic status of an agent's belief is from which we, but not the agent, have reflective access to all the relevant facts. In the relevant respect, all of us are in an epistemic position which is on a par with the naïve chicken-sexer.

Another famous exponent of the metaepistemological challenge is Barry Stroud. He writes:

[S]uppose there are truths about the world and the human condition which link human perceptual states and cognitive mechanisms with further states of knowledge and reasonable belief, and which imply that human beings acquire their beliefs about the physical world through the operation of belief-forming mechanisms which are on the whole reliable in the sense of giving them mostly true beliefs. ... If there are truths of this kind ... that fact alone obviously will do us no good as theorists who want to understand human knowledge in this philosophical way. At the very least we must believe some such truths; their merely being true would not be enough to give us any illumination or satisfaction. But our merely happening to believe them would not be enough either. We seek understanding of certain aspects of the human condition, so we seek more than just a set of beliefs about it; we want to know or have good reasons for thinking that what we believe about it is true. (1994: 297)[3]

It is difficult to understand Stroud's objection here if it is not to be construed along similar lines to that found in the passages from Fumerton cited above. Stroud's thought seems to be that it is not enough merely to meet the epistemic conditions that (according to the externalist) give us knowledge; instead, we—that is, philosophers at any rate—should also be able to have reflective access to those conditions, the kind of access demanded by the internalist (and perhaps even more than that).

The implication of the Fumerton–Stroud line of argument is that what is needed is, at the very least, the introduction of an internal justification condition, thereby making the antisceptical positions under discussion epistemologically internalist. This is far too quick, however, for two reasons. The first is because, as we have noted at a number of junctures, we can allow that meeting an internal justification condition is epistemically desirable without thereby making it a necessary condition for knowledge possession—the two issues are, in principle at least, independent.

The second relates to the fact that the incorporation of an internal epistemic condition into one's theory would make one's view immediately susceptible to the sceptical challenge (at first-order). Everyone agrees that we lack internalist justification for believing in the denials of sceptical hypotheses and thus, given closure for internalist justification (let alone the underdetermination principle), it follows that we lack internalist justification for believing even everyday propositions as well, and this means on this view that we also lack knowledge of them as well. Of course, as we saw in Part I, there are considerations that can be brought to bear against closure for internalist justification, but these considerations only had force because a sister closure principle in terms of knowledge *simpliciter* was being retained, whereas on the internalist view closure for knowledge would automatically fall with closure for internalist justification (because, recall, knowledge *entails* internalist justification, according to the internalist).

This point is important because the internalist motivation for an internal epistemic condition in the case of non-sceptical instances of brute externalist knowledge—such as naïve chicken-sexer cases—is very different from that same motivation in the case of the putative sceptical challenge to externalist antisceptical theories. Adducing an internal condition can meet the problem of reflective epistemic luck in the former case precisely because we are here implicitly setting aside the sceptical problem. Scepticism apart, if the naïve chicken-sexer were to become 'enlightened' by gaining an internalist justification for her beliefs then she would no longer be forming true beliefs in a reflectively lucky fashion in the way that she did previously. Nevertheless, that this internalist justification would eliminate the reflective epistemic luck at issue in this case with the sceptical problem bracketed does not mean that the enlightened chicken-sexer's beliefs are not reflectively lucky once one factors the sceptical problem back into the equation. Indeed, this was just the point of the last section—that the moral of the underdetermination-based sceptical argument is that one's beliefs are always lacking in internalist justification and thus, provided we do not bracket the sceptical problem, they are always subject to a substantive degree of reflective epistemic luck as well.

The difference between the naïve chicken-sexer and her enlightened counterpart is thus, at best, a difference of degree, but we can only make sense of this difference of degree in such a way that it is extensive enough to support knowledge provided we bracket the sceptical problem. The moral is clear: adducing an internal condition only deals with the problem of reflective epistemic luck provided one is implicitly setting the sceptical problem aside. With the sceptical problem 'live', all our beliefs are akin, in the relevant respect, to the beliefs of the naïve chicken-sexer.[4]

One way of expressing this point is to say that whilst the challenge posed by Fumerton and Stroud is a *metaepistemological* sceptical challenge when it is directed at externalist antisceptical theories, it is simply a *sceptical* challenge when it is directed at internalist antisceptical theories. Since we can only make sense of our possessing internalist knowledge of a wide class of everyday propositions— and thus our having beliefs which, by being immune to any substantive degree of reflective epistemic luck, we can take a robust degree of cognitive responsibility for—provided that we already bracket the sceptical problem (and thus the sceptical error-possibilities), it follows that the solution to the metaepistemological challenge cannot simply be to present an internalist theory of knowledge. Instead, the Fumerton–Stroud complaint against externalist epistemologies presents us with a dilemma: either we adopt the alternative epistemologically internalist response to the sceptic, in which case we have no answer to scepticism at all; or else we continue to offer an epistemologically externalist response, in which case our antisceptical theory will be intellectually dissatisfying. Either way, there is no intellectually satisfying response to the sceptic.

This way of understanding the metaepistemological sceptical challenge is clearest in the work of Stroud. He argues that scepticism arises out of 'platitudes' that 'we would all accept' (Stroud 1984: 82). He therefore concludes that scepticism is at least conditionally correct:

I believe the [sceptical] problem has no solution; or rather that the only answer to the question as it is meant to be understood is that we can know nothing about the world around us. (1984: 1)

That is, for Stroud the alternatives are accepting scepticism or else questioning the way in which the sceptical argument is 'meant to be understood', where this means rejecting one of the 'platitudes that we would all accept' as a means of meeting the sceptical challenge. The choice is thus between a rock and a hard place: either we offer an intellectually unsatisfying response to the sceptic (such as an externalist response), or else we offer no response at all.

Ultimately, then, the metaepistemological challenge does not pose the specific problem for externalist theories of knowledge—and thus to externalist responses to scepticism—that it advertises, but simply reflects the general sceptical worry about reflective epistemic luck.[5]

8.3. The Pyrrhonian Problematic

Since the underdetermination-based sceptical argument owes its source to an ancient, rather than a modern, sceptical tradition, if we wish to gain a deeper understanding of what is involved in this type of scepticism it is worthwhile considering its original philosophical motivation in more detail.

It is often said that it is Cartesian scepticism which poses the more dramatic sceptical threat, and thus that earlier classical forms of scepticism—such as, in particular, Pyrrhonian scepticism—were constrained in comparison.[6] The former kind of scepticism consists of an *argument* that focuses on sceptical hypotheses as a means of generating the absurd conclusion that knowledge is impossible. In contrast, Pyrrhonian scepticism consists of a series of *techniques* that undermine any particular claim to know regarding a non-evident truth.[7] As a result, whereas Cartesian scepticism generates a paradoxical conclusion, the Pyrrhonian strategy merely creates what I will call an ongoing 'problematic', in that it holds within it the resources to 'problematize' any particular claim to know without going further to simultaneously show that knowledge is impossible. As one commentator has put it, Pyrrhonian scepticism is '*distributively* universal, but *collectively* non-universal' (Ribeiro 2002c, 325).[8]

There is good reason for this difference in emphasis between the two forms of scepticism. Cartesian scepticism is designed to serve the *methodological* goal of identifying certain general features of our epistemic position, which was why its paradoxical conclusion was not in itself a cause for alarm since it was never intended to be taken seriously *qua* conclusion.[9] Instead, the role of scepticism was more akin to the role that *reductio ad absurdum* can play in an argument, in that it was meant to motivate a further conclusion that was not paradoxical. The paradox only comes with the supposed realization that one cannot so easily discharge any of the assumptions that were leading to the *reductio*.[10]

In contrast, Pyrrhonian scepticism was, broadly, an *ethical* stance, in that it was meant to be a form of scepticism that could be 'lived' rather than one that is used merely to generate further non-sceptical conclusions.[11] It was largely for this reason that Pyrrhonian scepticism was constrained in the way that it was, since one could not properly 'live' a genuinely paradoxical conclusion (at least in so far as it has the required generality to qualify as a radical sceptical conclusion), but one could 'live' the kind of life of agnosticism that the Pyrrhonian techniques lead to. In any case, it was essential that Pyrrhonian scepticism was not understood as presenting a paradox because the Pyrrhonians demanded agnosticism on all non-evident matters, and yet to formulate this stance in the form of a paradox would involve incurring a commitment to the non-evident claims that make up that paradox, thereby making the stance self-refuting.[12] Pyrrhonian scepticism is thus meant to be a form of complete agnosticism about non-evident matters in a way that Cartesian scepticism would not allow.

As it stands, we have understood the sceptical arguments based on the closure and underdetermination principles as paradoxes, and noted that whilst we can evade the former fairly easily via a thoroughgoing externalist theory of knowledge, the same approach when applied to the latter highlights its inadequacies as an antisceptical strategy. We have also noted, however, that something like the underdetermination principle can be discerned from Pyrrhonian sceptical writings (although, being Pyrrhonians, they would never actually *endorse* such a thesis).[13] This should come as no surprise given that the focus for the Pyrrhonian attack was on the inadequacy of our grounds for belief in non-evident matters, especially when those beliefs were expressed in terms of a claim to know the proposition in question.

Consider, for example, 'Agrippa's trilemma'.[14] The idea behind this trilemma is that any challenge to a claim to know can only be responded to in one of three ways:

I.   Refuse to respond (i.e. make an undefended assumption).
II.   Repeat a claim made earlier in the argument (i.e. reason in a circle).
III. Keep trying to think of something new to say (i.e. embark on an infinite regress).

And given that there is no fourth option available, it follows that any attempt to justify one's claim to know will either be interminable (as with option III) or terminate in an epistemically unsatisfactory way (as with options I and II).[15]

What is significant here is that this sceptical technique is primarily directed at claims to know rather than at the possession of knowledge itself. There are, I think, good reasons for this. For one thing, as Sextus Empiricus (1933–49: I 3, *italics mine*) himself notes at the beginning of *Outlines of Pyrrhonism*, the Pyrrhonians are trying to situate themselves between, on the one hand, the Dogmatic philosophers—who 'have *claimed* to have discovered the truth'— and, on the other, the Academic sceptics—who 'have *asserted* that it cannot be apprehended'. In contrast, the Pyrrhonian claim is merely that we must 'go on inquiring'. As we have just noted, this distinction is important since to claim that knowledge is impossible in a general way would be to commit oneself, perversely, to a non-evident claim and Pyrrhonians are trying to avoid assertions of this sort. In any case, since the Pyrrhonian position is meant to be an ethical one, it should allow one to coherently live one's scepticism. This can be achieved by focusing on that form of belief that is tied to assent rather than to belief in general, since even the Pyrrhonians acknowledge that the force of nature is such that not all beliefs can be optional. Indeed, this is the reason why they focus upon beliefs—and in particular claims to know—regarding non-evident propositions, since (or so it was thought at any rate) this is where the force of nature is at its weakest.

There are varying interpretations of what 'non-evident' means in this context, from the contention that it is any claim about the way the world is (rather than simply about the way the world seems),[16] to the much weaker contention that it merely applies to theoretical claims.[17] I think that a middle path should be taken here, and that there is sufficient textual support to warrant such an interpretation. My claim is that the focus of Pyrrhonian scepticism is not on belief per se, but rather upon a certain *style* of belief that we might term *dogmatic assent*. As Michael Williams puts the point:

[T]he Pyrrhonian has a distinctive *style* of assent: spontaneous, involuntary submission to his unrationalised impulses. Assent is a *pathos*, something that comes over one. (It is tempting to see Sextus as ironically inverting the Stoic rule of overcoming the affections, *pathoi*, in order to live by reason, *logos*: Sextus neutralises reason in order to live by his affections.) Ordinary life, as Sextus sees it, is much more a matter of impulse and habit than of judgement properly so-called. (1988: 561–2)[18]

On this view, bare natural responses to the world (and thus 'ordinary life' where this does not lead to claims to know) are not the subject of scepticism. What is the subject of scepticism are merely those doxastic responses to the world which take on a more voluntary form and which thus give rise to a dogmatic assent to what is believed. Sextus Empiricus gives an indication that this is the focus for Pyrrhonian scepticism in the following passage, where he makes a distinction between 'dogma' and mere belief (in the sense simply of 'approval of a thing'):

[W]hen we say that the sceptic refrains from dogmatizing we do not use the term 'dogma' as some do, in the broader sense of 'approval of a thing' (for the Sceptic gives assent to the feelings which are the necessary results of sense-impressions, and he would not, for example, say when feeling hot or cold 'I believe that I am not hot or cold'); but we say that 'he does not dogmatize' using 'dogma' in the sense, which some give it, of 'assent to one of the non-evident objects of scientific inquiry'. (Sextus Empiricus 1933–49: I 13–4; cf. Sextus Empiricus 1933–49: I 16)

That is, the Pyrrhonians are willing to allow that agents might properly believe all sorts of propositions in so far as belief here merely consists in an involuntary brute response to the world (as occurs in response to 'sense impressions'). Indeed, *mere* assent to such involuntary brute responses would also be immune to the Pyrrhonian sceptical challenge (as when one shivers and mutters 'I'm cold'). The focus for Pyrrhonism is not belief in this brute sense, but only that sort of belief that generates a dogmatic assent, even when that assent concerns a proposition that takes an 'agnostic' form (such as 'I believe that I am not hot or cold').

One way of making sense of this point is to note that, intuitively at least, some beliefs—along with the corresponding style of assent to what is believed—are not, as it were, in the space of reasons.[19] No one seriously holds that one needs reasons to support one's spontaneous belief that one is cold, or to support one's spontaneous claim to be cold (indeed, it difficult to think of a situation in which the assertion of the sentence 'I'm cold' would be understood as a claim to know at all). This is in contrast to a great number of beliefs and the corresponding assertions of what is believed, where an implicit appeal to reasons is being made.

This point should remind us of our discussion of the rules governing the appropriate assertion of ascription sentences in §3.2. To assert that a tower is such-and-such a size is to make a claim that presupposes that one has reasons to support what one claims, and one would impose the same requirement on any responsible believer who held such a proposition to be true. In these cases the belief, along with the corresponding assent, is, in the relevant sense, dogmatic, and so is susceptible to the Pyrrhonian sceptical attack. Crucially, however, not all unqualified assertions generate the conversational implicature that one is claiming to know the proposition asserted, and thus that one is willing, and able, to back up that assertion with appropriate supporting grounds. Moreover, as we have seen in our discussion of epistemic externalism, it is plausible to suppose that not all beliefs which are (in one sense at least) rightly held presuppose such a rational grounding either, the exceptions being those beliefs that are the basic spontaneous product of our interaction with the world.

It is important that it is a style of assent that is the target of the scepticism, since, as we noted above, some have argued that Pyrrhonian scepticism is merely focused on assent as regards what is the case, and disregards assent when it is merely concerned with what *seems* to be the case, on the grounds that what seems to be the case is 'evident' in the relevant respect. This way of putting matters is confused, however. For whilst it is true that any claim about the way the world is can be undermined via the sceptical mode which identifies the relativity of experience, it is not as if any subsequently modified claim which merely stuck to what seemed to be the case would *thereby* be immune to sceptical attack. After all, Agrippa's trilemma would be just as applicable against this new claim as against the previous unmodified claim provided that this claim was made in a dogmatic fashion. That is, one can make a claim about the way the world appears that is in the space of reasons. For example, suppose an agent asserted that there *seems* to be a tower of such-and-such a size before her. One could legitimately respond to such an assertion by inquiring as to what reasons the agent has for thinking that what is being visually presented looks like a tower at all, much less a tower of a certain size. This indicates that even this sort of assertion, and hence the belief that gave rise to this assertion, is already in the space of reasons, despite its qualified form.[20] The focus of Pyrrhonian sceptical attack is thus on the type of assent that is at issue, rather than on the content of what is being assented to. Perhaps better put, it is directed against a kind of belief that generates dogmatic assertions, rather than on belief *simpliciter*.[21]

This distinction is especially important given our present purposes because it highlights the sense in which Pyrrhonian scepticism is, potentially at any rate, consistent with widespread brute externalist knowledge. This is because it allows a wide class of spontaneous 'natural' beliefs and at no point does it deny that such beliefs might in fact stand in the right kinds of 'external' relationships to the world.[22] What it attacks, at least primarily, is rather that kind of know-ledge that can be put into service in a claim to know (including, of course, the claim that our beliefs do stand in the required relationship to the world). Moreover, since it is only belief of a certain sort that is being attacked, so Pyrrhonian scepticism can be consistently 'lived' as an ethical stance.[23]

With this in mind, consider again Agrippa's trilemma. Since the focus in this trilemma is clearly upon specific claims to know, we can express what is happening here in terms of the sceptic creating a conversational context in which claims to know generate implicatures that are impossible to meet. We saw in §3.2 that claims to know generate the conversational implicature that one is able to offer contextually relevant evidential grounds in support of that claim. In the sceptical conversational context in which the Pyrrhonian tech-niques are being employed, however, the claims to know in question generate (amongst other things) the implicature that one is able to offer grounds that stop the regress dead, even though no such grounds are available (since claiming such grounds will lead to a further challenge to supply grounds, and so on). As a result, what this trilemma achieves is to highlight that our practices of offering evidential grounds must ultimately rest upon groundless foundations. We might think that the regress ends, but this is only because, typically, those in dispute about particular claims will eventually come to common sources of agreement. The Pyrrhonian sceptic will not allow these points of consensus to play a foundational role in our evidential practices, and in doing so they undermine our practice of claiming knowledge.

In quotidian conversational contexts, of course, claims to know do not generate such austere implicatures. A contextualist account of the pragmatics of language-games involving epistemic terms is thus able to partially contain the scepticism at issue here by restricting it to a certain conversational context. The problem, however, is that recognizing the force of Agrippa's trilemma in the scep-tical conversational context means recognizing that in everyday conversational contexts what stops the regress is not something evidential in form, but rather simply a kind of agreement between those engaged in the dispute. In particular, the agreement consists in a certain conception of how the world is which itself restrains our practices of seeking further evidential support (we will be discussing this point in more detail in the next chapter in the context of Wittgenstein's account of 'hinge' propositions). The ancient sceptical technique of employing Agrippa's trilemma thus highlights something important about our epistemic practices, and this moral is applicable in *all* conversational contexts.

Moreover, even if we argue (as an epistemic externalist no doubt would) that knowledge can coexist with a finite (and ultimately groundless) chain of supporting grounds (and even with no grounds at all), this will be beside the point in this regard. The issue is what knowledge can be *claimed* in certain contexts, not what the possession conditions for knowledge are. The Pyrrhonian can thus consistently grant that there may be certain beliefs—or at least a certain style of belief—which give rise to an assent that is non-dogmatic and so is not in the space of reasons. Accordingly, such beliefs, and such assent, will be outside the ambit of the Pyrrhonian sceptical techniques. Furthermore, the Pyrrhonian can consistently grant that these beliefs may be, in one sense at least, rightly held, in that they stand in the right kinds of external relationships with the world. But allowing this is not to allow that such knowledge, if that is what it is, can ever be put to any dialectical use. In particular, it does not license one in making a claim to know regarding the proposition known, since in entering such a claim one would thereby put it within the space of reasons and make it subject to the Pyrrhonian sceptical attack. Pyrrhonian scepticism may be consistent with widespread externalist knowledge, but it is consistent in such a way as to highlight how inadequate the defence of such knowledge is in the light of the sceptical challenge that Pyrrhonism poses.

Furthermore, although agents clearly lack internalist knowledge in sceptical conversational contexts, because in these contexts one cannot make use of the standard evidential orderings at all, the ability to coherently offer grounds in defence of one's claims in everyday conversational contexts does not mean that one has straightforward internalist knowledge of what one believes in these contexts. Since, as the Pyrrhonian sceptic highlights, the grounds one can adduce in favour of one's beliefs come to an end with wholesale assumptions which are not themselves grounded, so the 'knowledge' that one exhibits in everyday conversational contexts is only quasi-internalistic—it bears all the hallmarks of internalist knowledge up to, but not including, the underlying assumptions of that context.

Indeed, this point should remind us of the claim made at the beginning of this chapter that we can only make sense of the elimination of reflective epistemic luck on the internalist account by implicitly bracketing the sceptical possible worlds. For the point is that the stark contrast between agents who have internalist knowledge and those who do not disappears once one no longer arbitrarily excludes sceptical possible worlds from being at issue in the determination of internalist justification. And with this distinction deflated, the putative epistemological advantages of the possession of internalist knowledge—that it enables one to eliminate reflective epistemic luck, thereby putting one in a position to properly claim one's knowledge and take a robust degree of cognitive responsibility for it—disappear also.

It should be clear that the underdetermination principle is simply one way of going directly to the source of this inadequacy in the grounding of our beliefs. Since any regress can be made to come to a sceptical error-possibility at some point, and since we never have adequate grounds to prefer our everyday beliefs over the truth of such an hypothesis, it follows that this will be one juncture at which we will be faced with the unpalatable choice of either offering inadequate grounds in support of our beliefs or no grounds at all. Either way, our beliefs are insufficiently grounded and thus cannot be properly claimed as knowledge in that conversational context.

By focusing on claims to know Pyrrhonian sceptical techniques highlight the sense in which what is really problematic about our epistemic position is that we lack a certain kind of epistemic support for our beliefs. Even if, as the epistemic externalist claims, this specific kind of lack of support is in principle consistent with an externalist conception of knowledge, it still remains that there is something problematic about the epistemic status of our beliefs—namely, that their lack of an adequate internalist justification entails that they are ineliminably subject to reflective epistemic luck. Given that this is the case, and thus that we lack the required reflectively accessible grounds to neutralize this variety of epistemic luck, any claim to know can be called into question via the sceptical techniques that the Pyrrhonian sceptics have identified, and this highlights the ultimately 'brute' nature of our epistemic position.[24]

8.4. Concluding Remarks

The sceptical problem is thus, at root, not concerned with the possession of knowledge *simpliciter* at all, but rather with the possession of knowledge of a certain internalist form. As we have seen, the reason why this is the case is that it is only this sort of knowledge that eliminates reflective epistemic luck and thereby ensures that we are able to take a high degree of cognitive responsibility for our beliefs. It is little wonder then that the contemporary debate regarding scepticism, with its focus merely on knowledge possession, leads to responses to the sceptical problem that seem to bypass the crux of the problem entirely. The mistake lies in how a challenge to our evidential practices where the link between knowledge and a high degree of cognitive responsibility is strong is converted into a challenge to our possession of knowledge *simpliciter*. The problem is that the only plausible account of knowledge available that can respond to this challenge is one that breaks the link between epistemic status and cognitive responsibility, at least where such responsibility is understood in a robust sense. Thus, we are led astray by a certain formulation of the sceptical problematic.

Furthermore, we have also seen what the limits are of our putative internalist justifications for our beliefs. Although we can clearly make a distinction between beliefs that are grounded and beliefs that aren't, it remains that there are no grounds available in support of our beliefs that would suffice to favour those beliefs over sceptical alternatives. Accordingly, as the underdetermination-based sceptical argument highlights, we ultimately lack an internalist justification for our beliefs and, as a consequence, this means that our beliefs will also be ineliminably subject to reflective epistemic luck. This aspect of our epistemic position is disguised by the fact that we have a practice of offering grounds in a way that brackets the sceptical possibilities, thereby creating the illusion that our grounds can suffice to eliminate reflective luck and, correspondingly, can also suffice to support an internalist justification. The drama of the kinds of sceptical techniques employed by the Pyrrhonian sceptic is that they bring to the fore just how limited our grounds are in this respect, and thus make explicit (amongst other things) that we are bracketing the sceptical possibilities in our everyday epistemic practices.

By disentangling the two main types of epistemic luck we can thus make clear just what is missing from recent responses to scepticism—and which has therefore prompted the 'metaepistemological' sceptical complaint we considered above. This point is further highlighted by comparing the contemporary discussion of scepticism with its classical Pyrrhonian analogue, a species of sceptical doubt which, since it was largely directed at an agent's ability to properly claim knowledge, was clearly primarily focused on the issue of whether we are able to take a suitably high degree of cognitive responsibility for our beliefs.

As we will see in the next chapter, there *is* a way around such scepticism, though it is not quite the fully epistemic response to scepticism that we would wish.

Notes

1. Recall that we argued, in §4.3, that the relevant sense of 'evidence' in play here needs to be understood internalistically (such that, roughly, if there is no difference in what is reflectively available to the agent, then neither is there a difference in the evidence that the agent possesses, and *vice versa*).

2. Fumerton develops this line of argument at length in Fumerton (1995).
3. Stroud was explicitly responding here to Sosa (1994). See also Stroud (1996).
4. Indeed, these commentators—Fumerton especially—write as if what is needed is more than just an internal justification condition, but also the rejection of an external condition on knowledge, as if a pure internalist theory was the answer. But this is impossible since, as we have seen, no internal condition alone can eliminate veritic epistemic luck (this was, recall, the immediate moral of the Gettier counter-examples). At most, then, a weakened internalist thesis is required that has both an external and an internal condition, but even then it is worth remembering that there is no internal condition that could suffice to eliminate reflective epistemic luck given that one does not already bracket sceptical error-possibilities.
5. I further discuss the problem of metaepistemological scepticism in Pritchard (2000*b*, 2001*b*, 2005*c*).
6. Here, e.g., is Burnyeat:

   What he [Descartes] achieved was to bring about a permanent enlargement of our conception of the power and scope of skeptical doubt, with the result that Hume, for example, lists 'Cartesian doubt' as a species of skepticism alongside, and more fundamental than, Pyrrhonism. ... This was indeed a transformation of the ancient materials, but in a sense quite opposite to that which Descartes intended. (1983: 3)

   See also, Williams (1978: ch. 2; 1983) and Burnyeat (1982).
7. The claim to know need not be in the form of the assertion of an explicit self-ascription sentence, but could merely be an assertion of a simple self-ascription sentence. (Indeed, given that, as we noted in §3.2, assertions of second-person ascription sentences are also implicit claims to know, assertions of all ascription sentences could be affected by Pyrrhonian sceptical techniques. For the sake of simplicity, I will ignore this complication in what follows.)
8. Ribeiro (2002*c*: 30) in turn credits the phrase to Jeffrey Tlumak.
9. Indeed, Descartes explicitly notes at a number of junctures that to actually endorse the sceptical conclusion would be insane. He writes in the *Fifth Set of Replies*, for example, that when

   it is a question of organising our life, it would, of course, be foolish not to trust the senses, and the sceptics who neglected human affairs to the point where friends had to stop them falling off precipices deserved to be laughed at. Hence I pointed out in one passage that no sane person ever seriously doubts such things. (1984: 243)

10. Note that I am not here making an interpretative claim about Descartes's *Meditations*, but only about the general way that Descartes's sceptical arguments have been understood in the contemporary literature.
11. Sextus Empiricus (1933–49: I 19), for example, argues that 'the Sceptic's End is quietude in respect of matters of opinion and moderate feeling in respect of things unavoidable.' In general, Pyrrhonians argued that the 'dogmatic' stance of claiming knowledge with complete conviction should be opposed by offering a countervailing argument (*isosthenia*) which would engender a neutral attitude (*epoche*) and eventually lead to a tranquil and untroubled state of mind (*ataraxia*). The correct interpretation of 'non-evident' in this context is controversial and I return to this issue below.
12. That said, there are those, such as Gaukroger (1995), who argue that we should understand the Pyrrhonians as offering a philosophical *position* rather than a sceptical *stance*,

namely the philosophical position of relativism. On this interpretation it is part of the Pyrrhonian thesis that it involves the incurring of commitments to theoretical—and thus non-evident—claims. This interpretation is unorthodox, however, and in what follows I will keep to the standard readings of Pyrrhonian scepticism.

13. Sextus Empiricus is very clear about this point, since without it Pyrrhonism could be charged with straightforward inconsistency (though see the last footnote). He argues (Sextus Empiricus 1933–49: §1.202–5), for example, that the slogan 'To every argument an equal argument is opposed', which might sound like the endorsement of a general epistemic principle, should be understood as the injunction 'To every argument let us oppose an opposite argument!', which takes us back to a general technique designed to undermine belief in a piecemeal fashion.

14. See Sextus Empiricus (1933–49: I 95–101). See also Diogenes Laertius (1925: II 501), and the translation offered by Annas and Barnes (1985: app. C). The trilemma is actually presented as part of a collection of five 'modes' that lead to a suspension of judgement. The role that the other two modes play—'discrepancy' and 'relativity'—is, however, peripheral, and so I shall not discuss them here. For an excellent discussion of Agrippa's trilemma, from which I borrow the essentials of the above characterization, see Williams (1991: §2.4; cf. Williams 2001b: ch. 5).

15. Famously, of course, coherentists respond to this problem by allowing circular justifications, at least where the circle of justification is large enough. For what is, perhaps, the most developed account of coherentism available in the recent literature, see Bonjour (1985). BonJour has since recanted from coherentism, and one can get an overview of what he takes to be the definitive considerations that undermine coherentism in Bonjour and Sosa (2003: ch. 3). See also Williams (1991: ch. 6). For an intriguing and idiosyncratic suggestion of *how* we might respond to option III, see Klein (1998, 2003).

16. See, e.g. Burnyeat (1980) and Barnes (1982).

17. See, e.g. Frede (1987a, 1987b) and Fogelin (1994). For an intriguing development of Fogelin's position which has ramifications for this issue, see Sinnott-Armstrong (2004).

18. For Williams's opposing assessment of Cartesian scepticism, see Williams (1986).

19. It should be noted that this phrase, 'the space of reasons', is sometimes associated with the work of McDowell (e.g. 1994b). What McDowell has in mind is very different from what I am suggesting here, however, so the reader should set aside the specific use of this phrase made by McDowell. I discuss McDowell's view at length in the next chapter.

20. Others have noted this point. In a recent book, for example, Bailey writes that:

> Agrippa's five tropes ... are every bit as effective against first-person claims about the Pyrrhonist's present impressions as they are against claims about the objective properties of real objects. (2002: 247–8)

21. For further support for this distinction between dogma and mere belief, see Barnes (1982), Sedley (1983), and Burnyeat (1984). There is, of course, a Humean quality to Pyrrhonian scepticism on this interpretation, in that it distinguishes between beliefs that are grounded in reasons and 'natural' beliefs that are not grounded in reasons and which are therefore not susceptible to any sceptical argument that focuses on the supporting grounds for one's beliefs. Either way, one's beliefs lack a rational epistemic basis, since they are either (in this sense) natural, and hence ungrounded, or else non-natural, and so in need of the very rational support that, as the Pyrrhonian sceptical techniques highlight, is impossible.

22. I defend this externalism-friendly interpretation of Pyrrhonism in more detail in Pritchard (2000*b*).
23. For more discussion of the issue regarding the 'liveability' of Pyrrhonian scepticism, see Burnyeat (1980), Stough (1984), and Pritchard (2000*b*). Ribeiro (2002*c*) offers an interesting perspective on this problem. He claims that Pyrrhonism *was* directed at belief *simpliciter* (not just belief in the sense of dogmatic assent), whilst further arguing that complete non-belief is psychologically impossible. Nevertheless, he claims to rescue the thesis from absurdity by showing how the view is in effect merely 'aspirational', in that it is part of the Pyrrhonian conception of the sceptical challenge that the goal of such scepticism is, strictly speaking, non-realizable.
24. In some of his recent articles—especially Sosa (1997)—Sosa has responded to the Pyrrhonian problematic, as I call it, by contending that the way to avoid the problem is to recognize that there is a basic form of externalist ('animal') knowledge that is immune to the tribunal of reasons, and which can thus form as a foundation which enables one to develop a more refined 'reflective' knowledge—a type of knowledge which is subject to the tribunal of reasons—without fear of regress. Moreover, Sosa makes the intriguing suggestion that just such a line of argument can be found in Descartes's *Meditations*. I have not the space to consider Sosa's proposal in depth here, though its surface similarity in some respects to the view that I outline—though with different consequences as regards the sceptical problem, of course—means that I should say something about the point at which my position diverges from the view that Sosa recommends. The crux of the problem with Sosa's proposal relates to how we are to understand the supposed 'foundational' externalist knowledge. As Williams (2003*a*) points out, if such knowledge is not subject to the tribunal of reasons, then it is hard to see how it can possibly serve as a termination point to a regress of justification. Alternatively, if it *is* subject to the tribunal of reasons, then the antisceptical strategy that Sosa recommends simply collapses (by his *own* lights). Either way, Sosa's proposal does not seem to offer us a way out of the sceptical predicament as we have understood it here. Indeed, in terms of the way that I have characterized the sceptical debate, all Sosa manages to achieve is, at best, a validation of our widespread brute externalist knowledge, when what we seek is a validation also of our ability to have widespread internalist knowledge. Sosa responds to Williams's critique in Sosa (2003). For further discussion of Sosa's distinction between animal and reflective knowledge, see Grimm (2001; cf. Sosa 2001) and Greco (2003: 298–301).

9

Epistemic *Angst*

9.0. Introduction

In the last chapter we saw that the sceptical challenge, properly understood, is not ultimately concerned whether or not we are capable of possessing knowledge *simpliciter*, but is rather specifically directed at that sort of knowledge which we can take full cognitive responsibility for—*internalist* knowledge. This is the kind of knowledge that we can properly claim and which is also immune from reflective epistemic luck.

We also saw, however, that scepticism, so understood, is a problem without a solution since it is impossible to completely eliminate reflective epistemic luck from our beliefs. The difficulty posed by reflective epistemic luck is thus an unavoidable feature of our epistemic predicament, and I refer in this chapter to the recognition that this is the case as *epistemic angst*.

Moreover, we also noted that this point was 'hidden' by our everyday epistemic practices, in that such practices disguise the fact that the grounds that we present in favour of our beliefs themselves depend on further ungrounded assumptions. More specifically, we have a practice of offering grounds in favour of our beliefs which ungroundedly presupposes the falsity of sceptical hypotheses. It is the elaboration of this point that is the primary focus of this chapter, and it will be illustrated by considering in more detail the Wittgensteinian account of 'hinge' propositions and the structure of reasons—especially in contrast to the conception of reasons presented in the recent literature by John McDowell.

Nevertheless, it is also maintained that whilst there is no satisfactory *epistemic* response available to the sceptical problem posed by reflective epistemic luck, there is a *pragmatic* response, and that one can find the first inklings of how such a strategy might function in Wittgenstein's remarks on the limits of coherent doubt. The secondary focus of this chapter is thus to outline how such a pragmatic response might function.

9.1. Wittgenstein on 'Hinge' Propositions

In the last chapter we saw that classical Pyrrhonian scepticism was primarily directed not at our possession of knowledge *simpliciter*—where this was ambivalent between an externalist or an internalist account of knowledge—but rather at our ability to properly claim such knowledge and therefore take full cognitive responsibility for our beliefs. This picture of the Pyrrhonian problematic should remind us of our discussion in §3.3 of Wittgenstein's remarks on hinge propositions. Recall that these were propositions which were taken to be as certain as anything in that context, and included not only the denials of sceptical hypotheses, but also the most mundane of everyday propositions, such as (in normal circumstances) that one has two hands. The idea was that in order for a belief to act as a ground for another belief, it needed to be more certain than the belief it was grounding. But since hinge propositions were as certain as anything in that context, it followed that no other belief was ever able to ground belief in them, the supporting belief being itself more questionable than the belief in the hinge propositions that was being supported.

It follows that our practice of offering grounds takes place against a backdrop of claims which are of their nature ungroundedly held. Furthermore, Wittgenstein contended it is only if there is this backdrop of claims held fast that we could make sense of a belief playing a supporting role in the first place. As he argued, to doubt a hinge proposition is not to be more exacting or thorough in one's inquiries, but rather to give up the 'game' of doubting and offering grounds in the first place. For if what is most certain in that context is up for doubt then *everything* is now open to question (as Wittgenstein (1969: §613) puts it, a doubt about a hinge would 'drag everything with it and plunge it into chaos'). Indeed, given that supporting reasons need to be more certain than what they are reasons for, it follows that in such circumstances no reason could ever, even in principle, be offered in response to this doubt. It is in this sense that a doubt about whether or not one has hands is akin to a doubt about whether or not one is a BIV, since in both cases it is a general conception of one's relationship to the world—a conception which is needed if one is to make sense of the practice of offering reasons—that is being called into doubt. This is why Moore's assertion that he knows that he has two hands because he can see them strikes us as so odd. We do not normally make such assertions because the very act of offering reasons presupposes an antisceptical framework of certainties of which the belief that Moore is supporting with reasons is part. Accordingly, our practice of offering reasons in favour of our beliefs cannot be put into service against the sceptic as Moore proposes because such a practice already (ungroundedly) presupposes the very antisceptical claims that are in dispute.

As we saw in Chapter 3, these features of hinge propositions that Wittgenstein noted have interesting implications for the propriety of our knowledge claims. Whilst the impropriety of a knowledge claim involving the denial of a sceptical hypothesis is unsurprising given that we have no adequate reflectively accessible grounds in support of these beliefs, that we are unable to claim knowledge of apparently mundane propositions that seem on the surface to have nothing to do with scepticism, such as that one has two hands, *is* surprising. Nevertheless, since a claim to know carries with it the conversational implicature that one is able to supply supporting grounds in favour of that claim, the fact that the supporting grounds are in principle lacking in the case of a hinge proposition means that such assertions are improper. Indeed, the very act of asserting them takes one into a sceptical conversational context, since it implies that belief in this proposition should be treated the same as belief in any other non-hinge proposition and so susceptible to an epistemic grounding. Crucially, however, this is only the case in a sceptical context, and in this context our entire practice of offering grounds is under threat. Thus, it was not only Moore's assertion that he knew that there was an external world that was improper, but also his initial assertion that he knew that he had two hands.

Wittgenstein's reflections on our language games involving epistemic terms—and, in particular, regarding the propriety conditions for claims to know—thus highlight something important about the structure of reasons. In normal circumstances we proceed as if the grounds in favour of our beliefs go right down to the foundations, as if they were epistemic through and through. But this is not the case. Rather, the grounds that we have for our beliefs, and which support our (proper) claims to know, only go down far enough to reach the point of shared agreement, and this is encoded in the hinge propositions. That is, we unreflectively labour under the illusion that the grounds we have in support of our everyday beliefs are fully epistemic, but when we reflect on those grounds we discover that their basis is in fact simply a shared and ungrounded acceptance of certain claims and, in particular, a shared acceptance that the world is generally the way we take it to be—that (in normal circumstances at least) we have two hands, that we are not BIVs, and so forth.

We noted in Chapter 3 that this conclusion need not undermine our intuitions about closure, since an externalist account of knowledge could allow that in so far as we know everyday propositions then we will also know the known entailments of these propositions, even when they concern the denials of sceptical hypotheses.[1] Indeed, closure here is a red herring, since the knowledge that is transferring across the known entailment in this regard is not taking with it adequate reflectively accessible grounds for belief, and that is what is ultimately at issue in the sceptical challenge. If our most basic assumptions about the world are true, and thus our beliefs do stand in the right general relationships with the world, then we will (externalistically) know a great deal, but that does not mean that our reflectively accessible grounds in favour of our everyday beliefs are thereby reflectively accessible grounds in favour of believing our basic assumptions about the world. But this means that one does not have internalist knowledge—and so cannot properly claim to know—these basic assumptions. Moreover, as the underdetermination-based sceptical argument highlights, it also implies that one lacks internalist knowledge of every other proposition that one believes, including everyday propositions, and thus that we cannot claim knowledge of these propositions either.

Indeed, Wittgenstein seems entirely aware of this implication, contending that 'the difficulty is to realize the groundlessness of our believing' (Wittgenstein 1969: §166). Elsewhere, towards the end of *On Certainty*, he further remarks that '[i]t is always by favour of Nature that one knows something' (Wittgenstein 1969: §505), a comment which neatly encapsulates the recognition that our beliefs are ineliminably subject to reflective epistemic luck since it captures the sense in which even our beliefs which might meet the minimal externalist standards for knowledge are still subject to luck.[2]

This was also the moral, of course, of the Pyrrhonian attack on claims to know that we looked at in the last chapter. That is, that given this fundamental truth about the structure of reasons that the underdetermination-based sceptical argument captures—i.e. that the supporting grounds we have in favour of our beliefs only perform the role that they do provided we ungroundedly disregard certain alternative (sceptical) hypotheses—it is always possible for the Pyrrhonian to take us into a sceptical conversational context in which our claims to know are inappropriate—and this, note, is (pretty much) all of our claims to know, whether they are concerned with everyday or antisceptical propositions.

In terms of epistemic luck, the sceptical problem thus becomes the concern that whilst it might well be the case that our beliefs are not subject to veritic epistemic luck, they will always be (in the sense that the sceptic identifies) subject to reflective epistemic luck. Since there are no adequate reflectively accessible grounds available to us which suffice to indicate that the modal universe is ordered in the way that we take it to be with sceptical worlds 'far away' from the actual world, it follows that in terms of what we are able to know by reflection alone sceptical worlds could well be nearby possible worlds, and thus that our true beliefs in this world (if they are true), are true in a reflectively lucky fashion.

9.2. Wittgenstein *versus* McDowell on the Structure of Reasons

In order to see this claim in more detail, it is worthwhile contrasting Wittgenstein's account of hinge propositions with a very different conception of the structure of reasons offered by McDowell which is meant to form part of an effective antisceptical thesis. What is also useful about considering this contrast is that the McDowellian conception of reasons is meant to represent one way in which one can use content externalism to respond to the sceptical challenge. Since we have not considered the possibility of dealing with scepticism via an appeal to content externalism, this is thus an ideal opportunity to highlight what is involved in the Wittgensteinian picture whilst also explaining why the sceptical problem has nothing essentially to do with the status of the content externalist thesis.

At the very least, externalists about content will accept something like the following claim:

Content externalism
The content of at least some of an agent's mental states is determined, at least in part, by facts concerning that agent's environment.

This characterization of content externalism is very weak, in that most content externalists will want to be more robust—and, of course, more specific—in their construal of the role that environmental factors can play in determining the content of mental states, and will typically take environmental factors to be relevant to the determination of the content of just about *any* mental state. Nevertheless, the virtue of this formulation is that it highlights just what, at root, is being denied by content externalists, and this is the content internalist idea that the content of an agent's mental state is purely determined by non-environmental facts—that is, by facts that are only concerned with what is beneath the skin of the agent. As Hilary Putnam might have expressed the point (but didn't), content just ain't in the head.

Content externalism, if true, is clearly a thesis of vital philosophical importance. Moreover, one would expect content externalism to have *some* antisceptical ramifications. In particular, if content is at least sometimes determined, in part, by environmental factors, then it follows that in so far as we have mental states with 'externally' determined contents in this way then there must be an external world. Scepticism about whether there is such an external world is thus met.[3]

The more substantive issue, however—and the issue that we have been concerned with in this book—is whether content externalism is able to meet the sceptical challenge regarding whether it is possible for us to have *widespread knowledge* about the external world.[4] Clearly it will have some antisceptical import in this regard. For example, if content is at least sometimes determined, in part, by environmental factors, then this will impose a constraint on acceptable forms of sceptical argument of this type by restricting the kinds of sceptical hypotheses that the sceptic can use in such an argument (we will consider two examples in a moment). Nevertheless, it is generally accepted that whatever construal one might endorse of content externalism, it will inevitably lack the resources needed to offer a full resolution of the radical sceptical problem. That is, that whilst content externalist theses might be able to rule out a priori certain types of radical sceptical hypotheses—and thus certain types of sceptical argument which depend on those hypotheses—it won't be able to rule out a priori *all* sceptical hypotheses, and thus all sceptical arguments. Accordingly, one cannot answer the sceptical problem by adducing content externalism alone.

For example, Donald Davidson has presented a version of content externalism which licenses the conclusion that 'belief is in its nature veridical' (1986: 314), such that on any plausible interpretation of our beliefs they come out as being mostly true. Clearly, this particular version of content externalism has *some* antisceptical consequences, in that if it is true then it rules out a priori any sceptical hypothesis which entails that most of our beliefs are false. Nevertheless, it does not dispose of all radical sceptical arguments. In particular, it is consistent with a sceptical argument that allows widespread truth in one's beliefs but denies that such beliefs meet the relevant epistemic rubric that would suffice to make them instances of knowledge. After all, the sceptic's arguments are focused on denying us *knowledge*, and whilst denying that our beliefs are mostly true is one way of achieving this, it is not the only way.[5]

Similarly, even if one agrees with Putnam (1981: ch. 1) that it is a consequence of his content externalism that 'I am a BIV' is necessarily false, this only works on some very specific renderings of the BIV sceptical hypothesis, such as (for Putnam) where the agent has always been envatted and her vat-experiences are generated by supercomputers. Understand this hypothesis in a different way—such that the agent has only just been envatted, and it is neuroscientists who are generating her experiences (which is, in any case, the usual understanding of the BIV sceptical hypothesis and the one that we have adopted here)—and the antisceptical appeal of this form of content externalism is neutralized.[6]

So it seems that meeting the sceptical problem behoves us to do more than merely offer a content externalist account. And, indeed, this is to be expected. Scepticism is primarily an epistemological problem and it would be odd if there were any way to resolve this difficulty that bypassed serious epistemological analysis of the sceptical argument. Thus, the failure of content externalism to wholly dissolve the sceptical problem simply returns us to the status quo of regarding any resolution of the sceptical challenge as being primarily a task for epistemology.

Whilst this has been the conventional wisdom in much of the recent literature on this topic, there has been one prominent dissenting voice. In a series of publications, McDowell has argued that the key to the sceptical problem is an internalist view of content such that, with this internalist thesis rejected and his own externalist account put in its place, the sceptical problem disappears.[7]

Superficially, the epistemological position that McDowell develops is very orthodox, in that he grants that knowledge involves an appropriate 'standing in the space of reasons' (McDowell 1995: 877), a claim that he attributes to Wilfrid Sellars.[8] In doing so, McDowell distances himself from proponents of epistemological externalism who, as we have seen, allow that agents can have knowledge simply in virtue of their beliefs standing in a certain kind of relationship with the facts, and thus without having a belief that has a standing in the space of reasons at all. Nevertheless, this superficial orthodoxy masks an underlying radicalism because McDowell's ultimate aim is to reconfigure how we should understand the space of reasons. In particular, his claim is that the sceptical problem results from a certain philosophical picture which results in the 'interiorization of the space of reasons' and which generates a 'withdrawal from the external world' (ibid.). Once this withdrawal is effected, it then becomes a mystery how we are ever to have knowledge of that external world, just as the sceptic claims. The trick is thus to resist this 'interiorization' of the space of reasons in the first place.

According to McDowell, we are led to this interiorization of the space of reasons by holding that the visual appearance which gives rise to a perceptual belief could be present even though the belief in question is false. It might be claimed, for example, that one can believe that one is currently seeing a chair before one on the basis of the visual appearance of a chair, and yet this is consistent with the chair in fact being absent and the visual presentation in question being the result of an illusion. It is this train of thought which generates what McDowell (1982: 472) calls a 'highest common factor' (HCF) conception of perceptual experience which treats the content of perceptual experience as being what is common to the veridical case of perception and its non-veridical analogues. Accordingly, we conclude that the reasons which support our perceptual beliefs are always 'internal' in the sense that they are never able to entail the truth of what is believed. That is, what is given to us in perception that can count as a reason for believing that the chair is there is only what would have been there anyhow even if we were the victims of a perceptual illusion and the chair was in fact absent.

On this picture there are two epistemically distinct 'realms' which force a bifurcation in our epistemology. On the one hand, there is the 'inner' realm of ideas that bears no essential connection to the external world and from which our reasons for belief are forged. On the other, there is the 'outer' realm of external reality, knowledge of which can only be gained via a shaky inference from our 'inner' reasons. As a result, it is no surprise that the sceptical problem has the dialectical grip that it does, since our knowledge of the external world is now *of its nature* problematized. The theory of knowledge that this picture generates is what McDowell refers to as a 'hybrid' account. Knowing cannot, on this view, be itself an appropriate standing in the space of reasons, but must instead be a combination of an 'inner' justification, which is an appropriate standing in the space of reasons, and an 'outer' fact, which is the fact known.

McDowell thinks that it is this HCF conception of perceptual experience, and the interiorization of reasons that it generates, that should be rejected. Moreover, he claims that 'without the "highest common factor" conception of experience … the traditional problems [including scepticism] lapse' (McDowell 1982: 479). In its place McDowell offers an alternative conception of perceptual experience such that veridical perceptual experience has a different content to its non-veridical analogue. He writes:

But suppose we say—not at all unnaturally—that an appearance that such-and-such is the case can be *either* a mere appearance *or* the fact that such-and-such is the case making itself perceptually manifest to someone. As before, the object of experience in the deceptive cases is a mere appearance. But we are not to accept that in the non-deceptive cases too the object of experience is a mere appearance, and hence something that falls short of the fact itself. On the contrary, we are to insist that the appearance that is presented to one in those cases is a matter of the fact itself being disclosed to the experiencer. (1982: 472)

The content of the perceptual experience in the veridical case is thus different from the content of the analogue experience in the non-veridical case. Since McDowell holds that all experience is conceptual,[9] we thus have a robust form of content externalism being proposed here, in that the content of one's (conceptualised) perceptual experience is essentially dependent upon facts about one's environment. In particular, 'outer' facts about whether one's perceptual experience is veridical will determine the content of one's experience.

McDowell thinks that with this alternative content externalist account of perceptual experience in play we can evade the problems posed by the hybrid conception of knowledge, with its open invitation to scepticism. Knowledge is now an appropriate standing in the space of reasons in the full sense of it being *only* a standing in the space of reasons—there is no need to supplement such a standing with a truth condition. More specifically, the reasons that one has to support one's perceptual belief can be *factive* reasons regarding what one perceives. That I see a chair before me can be, for example, my reason for believing that there is a chair before me, where *seeing that P* is factive in the sense that it entails *P*. And in appropriate circumstances—in particular, in cases where one's perceptual experience is veridical—this can suffice for knowledge.

According to McDowell, this account of perceptual knowledge deals with the sceptical problem by denying a crucial element in the sceptical argument, which is that the reasons that we can offer in favour of our perceptual beliefs are only those reasons which we would have been able to cite anyway even if the beliefs in question were false. On the alternative picture that McDowell recommends, there is no epistemic gulf between our reasons for belief in the 'good' (i.e. non-deceived) cases and the elements of the external world that those beliefs are about. In the good cases, and *contra* the sceptic, that I see objects in the 'external' world can constitute good factive reasons for having the relevant perceptual beliefs, and thus I am able to have knowledge of what I believe. Accordingly, McDowell holds that he is able to explain how we can have widespread knowledge about the external world.

Finally, we need to comment on the oddly qualified way in which McDowell expresses his antisceptical account. In the quotation cited above, for example, he does not say that the traditional epistemological problems, such as the sceptical problem, are *answered* on his view, but only that they 'lapse'. Similarly, elsewhere he writes that the

considerations I have offered suggest a way to respond to skepticism about, for instance, perceptual knowledge; the thing to do is not to answer the skeptic's challenges, but to diagnose their seeming urgency as deriving from a misguided interiorization of reason. (1995: 890)

In general, McDowell's strategy is explicitly *not* to argue with the sceptic on her own terms, but rather to recommend a different philosophical picture that lacks the sceptical consequences of the traditional picture.

Presumably (McDowell is never altogether clear on this issue), the distinction that he has in mind here concerns whether we intend our antisceptical account to play a dialectical role in an (imagined) debate with the sceptic. Those offering a more robust response to scepticism would on this view be understood as presenting arguments which directly counter the sceptic's opposing arguments, with the net result that what is on offer are grounds for preferring the antisceptical account over the sceptical rival. The McDowellian antisceptical strategy, in contrast, appears to be stripped of this dialectical role, in that it merely presents a compelling way of looking at the issues so that the presuppositions which give rise to the sceptical problem are removed, but which does not pretend to offer independent grounds which would justify our accepting the scepticism-hostile philosophical picture over its scepticism-friendly alternative. As McDowell expresses the matter at one point, his antisceptical argument is 'not well cast as an *answer* to skeptical challenges; it is more like a justification of a refusal to bother with them' (McDowell 1995: 888).

Let us simply grant McDowell this weakened understanding of what is required of his response to the sceptic. Accordingly, all McDowell's antisceptical strategy needs to do to be successful is to show that the content externalist account that he offers, unlike the opposing content internalist account, does not generate the sceptical problem regarding our knowledge of the external world. As we will see, even on this restricted understanding of what counts as a successful antisceptical strategy, McDowell's account still fails to pass the test.

What is central to the McDowellian antisceptical picture is the idea that once we have rejected the content internalist presuppositions of traditional epistemological inquiry, then we can allow for the factivity of reasons and, in so doing, evade the sceptical problem. One of the key points in favour of McDowell's claim that reasons can be factive is the linguistic evidence that, outside of 'philosophical' conversational contexts at any rate, we do indeed adduce factive reasons in favour of our beliefs. If asked why I think the chair is in the room it seems perfectly acceptable to say that I can see that it is there, and, of course, seeing is factive in that I can only see that there is a chair before me provided that it is true that there is a chair before me. This linguistic data plays in McDowell's favour because it suggests that, just as he alleges, it is only when we are in the grip of a faulty philosophical picture that we find it necessary to 'revise' our intuitive—and partly factive—understanding of reasons and replace it with a non-factive construal.

234

This is only so, however, provided that we are entitled to take our everyday practice of offering factive reasons at face value, and this is where the McDowellian account gets into trouble. Indeed, as we have seen, Wittgenstein (not to mention the Pyrrhonian sceptic) offers us a compelling account of how our everyday reason-giving practices, factive or otherwise, disguise the ultimately ungrounded nature of our belief. The first thing to note in this regard is that whilst it is clearly *sometimes* acceptable to offer factive reasons in favour of one's beliefs, there are also cases where offering such factive reasons would be problematic. The obvious example in this respect is the sceptical case, where one is asked to support one's claims in a conversational context where the truth or otherwise of scepticism is at issue.

Consider, for example, the closure-based sceptical argument that we considered in §1.2. McDowell's rhetoric about offering a justification for not bothering with sceptical challenges might seem to suggest that he thinks the best way to respond to sceptical challenges of this sort is to simply ignore them. But, of course, McDowell cannot *simply* ignore such an argument because, as we noted above, it is incumbent upon his content externalist antisceptical account that it at least show that it doesn't, unlike the traditional content internalist account, generate the sceptical problem. Indeed, if one were entitled to *simply* ignore sceptical challenges then there would be no need to adduce McDowell's content externalism in order to meet the problem since one could do *that* within the traditional content internalist picture (this is, presumably, why McDowell talks of offering a *justification* for not bothering with sceptical arguments). It is thus necessary that McDowell explains just how his alternative account of content, and thus of reasons, is able to avoid the sceptical argument, even if he is not further able to present us with additional independent grounds for preferring his alternative account over the rival content internalist thesis that does lead to scepticism.

One can put this point into sharper relief by reminding ourselves that the sceptical argument under consideration is, properly understood, a *paradox*, in that it is a series of apparently uncontroversial premises which, taken independently, we would all be inclined to assent to, but which, taken collectively, entail an unacceptable conclusion. It is incumbent upon *any* philosophical proposal that it does not generate paradoxes in this way, and this alone places a burden on McDowell to explain just how his thesis avoids the sceptical conclusion by highlighting which particular premiss is being denied on his view. So whilst one might concede that a legitimate response to the sceptic need not offer supporting grounds which support the antisceptical thesis over its sceptical alternative, this does not preclude the proponent of such a response to scepticism from showing that the philosophical picture that they put forward does not generate the sceptical paradox. More precisely, whilst McDowell may not be attempting to advance grounds for rejecting one of the premises of the above argument which are more persuasive than the grounds the sceptic offers in favour of that premiss, he had better at least be presenting a philosophical picture which does not have as a consequence the set of problematic premises.

McDowell's response to this type of sceptical argument is to claim, *contra* the minor premiss of that argument, that we can know the denials of sceptical hypotheses after all, and indeed know them on the basis of our knowledge of everyday propositions. For example, consider McDowell's response to this formulation of the sceptical argument where it is the sceptical hypothesis that one might be dreaming that is at issue. He begins by noting an objection that Crispin Wright (1985: 443–4) makes to his antisceptical view:

Wright's ... reservation is that ' "lifting" the veil of perception' has no obvious bearing on a style of skeptical argument exemplified by the attempt to undermine perceptual knowledge, or even perceptually grounded reasonable belief, on the basis that ... one lacks sufficient reason to believe that one is not dreaming. (McDowell 1995: 888)

Here is how McDowell responds:

But I should have thought the bearing was quite obvious. Only if the veil is supposed to be in place can it seem that one would need to establish ... that one is not dreaming *before* one can be entitled to take one's apparent perceptions at face value. Once the veil is lifted, things can be the other way round; one's good reason to believe that one is not dreaming ... can reside in the knowledge of one's environment that one's senses are yielding one—something that does not happen when one is dreaming. (ibid.)[10]

So one can know that one is not dreaming—and thus, by implication, the denial of any sceptical hypothesis, such as the BIV hypothesis—in virtue of one's knowledge of the everyday propositions that make up one's knowledge of one's environment.

Let us grant to McDowell that one can, ordinarily at least, properly offer factive reasons in favour of at least some of one's most basic perceptual beliefs and that, as a result (and provided that one is as a matter of fact not subject to a deception), one can have knowledge (in some sense) of what one believes in this respect. In so doing one can concede that one can, for instance, know that there is a chair in the room because one sees that it is there without having to first establish that one is not the victim of a sceptical hypothesis, such as the dreaming hypothesis. The issue then solely rests on whether one can subsequently use such knowledge in order to establish that one is not the victim of a sceptical hypothesis. It is this last claim that is problematic. Whilst we do indeed have a practice of sometimes understanding the reasons that we offer in favour of our ordinary perceptual beliefs as factive, this doesn't extend to our beliefs in the denials of sceptical hypotheses. Instead, it seems altogether *inappropriate* to try to support one's beliefs about the denials of sceptical hypotheses by citing factive reasons about what, for example, one sees in one's environment.

We can illustrate this point with an example that Wittgenstein employs in *On Certainty* (see, e.g. §§182–92). In the context of a historical inquiry I can legitimately offer reasons in favour of my (non-hinge) beliefs in historical matters, such as concerning Napoleon's famous battle at Austerlitz. Some of these reasons will be factive in the relevant antisceptical respect in that they will entail that the universe did not undetectably come into existence in the last few minutes replete with the traces of a distant ancestry. Crucially, however, the factive antisceptical reasons that I can legitimately adduce in historical contexts of inquiry cannot be transferred to a philosophical context where the truth or otherwise of this sceptical hypothesis is at issue. And, indeed, this is entirely in accordance with intuition. Historians present reasons which support specific beliefs about past events, but they do not thereby offer grounds for thinking that there *is* a past in the first place, even though there can only be specific past events provided there is a past, and even though some of the reasons that they offer in favour of particular historical claims may well entail that there is a past.

Recall that this was just the point at which Moore's famous antisceptical assertions—which mirror the line that McDowell takes—go awry, in that Moore tries to make assertions as if he were in an ordinary conversational context when the type of assertions that he is making ensure that this context is in fact a sceptical conversational context and thus that the assertions in question are improper. Indeed, the parallels between the Moorean and the McDowellian use of antisceptical assertions, and thus of reasons, ensure that Wittgenstein's critique of Moore will have application to the parallel antisceptical account offered by McDowell. For whilst Wittgenstein grants that one can offer factive reasons in favour of one's beliefs, the manner in which he allows this deprives such reasons of having any antisceptical force. In ordinary contexts I can legitimately offer reasons regarding what I see in support of my beliefs about an external world, and such reasons can entail facts about that world. Nevertheless, this does not mean that one can respond to the sceptic with such factive reasons, either directly by offering factive reasons in support of one's beliefs in the denials of sceptical hypotheses, or indirectly by offering factive reasons in support of one's beliefs in other hinge certainties where doubt of these hinges in those circumstances would be tantamount to a radical sceptical doubt. This is because I am only able to coherently offer such reasons because in ordinary contexts one is (groundlessly) taking a framework of belief for granted which already excludes the truth of sceptical scenarios.[11] Thus, *contra* Moore (and hence McDowell), Wittgenstein reveals how what underlies the factivity of our reason-giving practices is something congenial, rather than hostile, to scepticism. As we cited in the last section, Wittgenstein remarks in this respect that 'the difficulty is to realize the groundlessness of our believing' (Wittgenstein 1969: §166).

McDowell is therefore in a bind. As we saw above, it is incumbent on him to at least show how his content externalist thesis and associated conception of reasons can evade the sceptical challenge, and this means that it must be a consequence of this thesis that he is able to reject one of the premises of the sceptical argument formulated above. Crucially, however, the very manner in which he tries to meet this sceptical argument reveals just what is implausible about the strategy that he advances. In particular, what we have seen is that the account of reasons which he claims is a consequence of his content externalism is unable to serve the antisceptical role that he sets out for it. Moreover, if McDowell's account of reasons is unable to meet the closure-based sceptical argument, then it is going to be even more ineffective when it comes to the underdetermination-based argument since what will be needed here are reasons for belief in everyday propositions which favour such beliefs over belief in alternative sceptical propositions, and no reasons of this sort will be available. Thus, there is no plausible route from the McDowellian account of content externalism to a general response to scepticism about our knowledge of the external world.[12]

Of course, McDowell could retreat at this point to an even weaker conception of what is required by an antisceptical proposal and simply claim that we just shouldn't take sceptical hypotheses seriously in the first place. But note that if this is the line that McDowell wishes to take then the conclusion we have just drawn from the previous discussion that his content externalism does not hold within it the resources to meet the sceptical problem is even more secure. After all, if one is simply entitled to disregard sceptical hypotheses then one could do that on *any* philosophical picture, even on the HCF conception of perceptual experience that McDowell rejects. Indeed, more specifically, if reasons do not play the antisceptical role that McDowell sets out for them (and it seems that they do not), then Wright's complaint was correct after all. The arguments regarding the need to lift the 'veil of perception' and offer a content externalism which allows us to offer factive reasons in favour of our beliefs have no obvious bearing on the sceptical problem.[13] Thus, despite the rhetoric, McDowell offers us no grounds for thinking that there is a route from content externalism to a one-size-fits-all response to external world scepticism.[14]

Before we leave McDowell's discussion of scepticism, it is worthwhile remarking on his related comments on the relationship between scepticism and epistemic luck, since they further reveal why the McDowellian antisceptical strategy is so impotent. McDowell grants that, at root, the sceptical worry that features as part of the traditional epistemological enterprise relates to how, since we cannot distinguish between veridical cases of perception and their sceptical counterparts, our perceptual 'knowledge' is inevitably subject to epistemic luck and thus not genuinely knowledge at all. McDowell thinks that this conception of the relationship between knowledge and epistemic luck leads to the very 'hybrid' account of knowledge that he rejects, in that it tempts us into thinking of knowledge as being composed of, on the one hand, reasons, which are immune to the influence of epistemic luck, and, on the other, a truth condition, which represents the 'cooperation' of the world. He writes:

The aim is to picture reason as having a proper province in which it can be immune to the effects of luck ... The idea is that reason can ensure that we have only acceptable standings in the space of reasons, without being indebted to the world for favours received; if we exercise reason properly, we cannot arrive at defective standings in the space of reasons, in a way that could only be explained in terms of the world's unkind-ness. The upshot of this interiorization is that knowledge of the external world cannot be completely constituted by standings in the space of reasons. (1995: 885)

Nevertheless, as McDowell notes, to endorse the hybrid conception of knowledge is still to allow luck a role in one's knowledge, since on this view two counterpart agents could have beliefs that have exactly the same standing in the space of reasons and yet, because of the non-factivity of reasons, one of the agents is in the 'good' non-deceived case whilst her counterpart is in the 'bad' deceived case. So despite the headline claim to be offering an epistemology that is luck-free, on the hybrid view luck is returned to the picture via the back door, as it were, and thus the tension with scepticism re-emerges. No matter what the standing of my beliefs in the space of reasons is, and even if those beliefs happen to be true, this is consistent with the truth of a sceptical scenario and thus the sceptical problem is not evaded at all.

Clearly the kind of luck that McDowell has in mind here is reflective epistemic luck, since the problem concerns our inability to possess grounds in favour of our everyday beliefs which prefer those beliefs over sceptical hypo-theses. According to McDowell, however, that the hybrid account is unable to fully eliminate such luck from one's acquisition of knowledge is not the source of the problem with the view. Rather, the failing in this regard is not recognising that there is *no* element of the epistemological realm that is immune to (reflective) epistemic luck—that is, of not allowing the concession to epistemic luck to go far enough. McDowell writes:

It seems clear where our suspicions should attach themselves. ... The hybrid view's concession to luck, tagged on to a picture of reason as self-sufficient within its own proper province, comes too late; the very idea of reason as having a sphere of operation within which it is capable of ensuring, without being beholden to the world, that one's postures are all right ... has the look of a fantasy, something we spin to console ourselves for the palpable limits on our powers. (1995: 886)

Removing this fantasy means, for McDowell, allowing epistemic luck to be all-pervasive in our epistemology, such that knowledge is irredeemably lucky through and through (i.e. it is not just that one component of knowledge is prone to epistemic luck), though it is none the less knowledge because of this.

What is odd about these remarks is that McDowell ends up allowing that reflective epistemic luck plays essentially the same role in our acquisition of knowledge as it did on the hybrid conception, with only the terms of reference having changed in the interim. On the hybrid view one's knowledge is subject to reflective epistemic luck because it demands cooperation from the world in the form of an external condition being met that the agent's reasons do not entail. Similarly, on the McDowellian view knowledge is subject to reflective epistemic luck because it demands cooperation from the world, the only difference being that on the alternative *factive* conception of what constitutes a reason that McDowell offers such cooperation from the world is required at the level of rationality rather than at the non-rational level. All that McDowell does is import the problematic truth condition into the notion of a reason, thereby simply shifting the focus of the problem rather than presenting us with the resources to answer that problem—on both the hybrid picture and the McDowellian picture the essential dependence upon epistemic luck is the same. Accordingly, the sceptic's claim that our 'knowledge' of the external world is imbued with reflective epistemic luck and thus not genuine knowledge at all is unaffected by the McDowellian account.

With this in mind, it is unsurprising that the McDowellian account of reasons fails to have the antisceptical implications that McDowell intends it to have. For the factive reasons regarding what one sees to perform an antisceptical role they would need to yield something that non-factive reasons do not, viz. an epistemic entitlement for one's beliefs in the denials of sceptical hypotheses. This is not possible, however, since these reasons only serve the role that they do in supporting our perceptual beliefs given the framework of hinge certainties which already includes the denials of sceptical hypotheses. In terms of the issue of reflective epistemic luck, factive reasons could only serve an antisceptical role if they could be used to show how, in the best case, our knowledge was not subject, in any substantive way, to reflective epistemic luck after all. But as McDowell admits in his discussion of epistemic luck, no such conclusion is in the offing. Knowledge is irredeemably subject to this form of epistemic luck, and this means that it is always subject to the (in part) undetectable cooperation of the world. Far from putting forward an alternative philosophical picture in light of which the sceptical problem disappears, McDowell is in fact merely presenting us with a different account of our perceptual knowledge which is no less subject to the sceptical challenge. It is hardly surprising, then, that his content externalism is unable to offer us a resolution to the sceptical problem.[15]

9.3. A Pragmatic Response to Scepticism

One claim that Wittgenstein is emphatic about in *On Certainty* is how doubting the denials of radical sceptical hypotheses, either directly or via doubt of a local hinge proposition such as that one has two hands, leads one into absurdity. Some have seen in this claim a possible basis for supplying an epistemic legitimation of our belief in the denials of radial sceptical hypotheses and thus in hinge propositions more generally.[16] Clearly, however, that it is incoherent to doubt a certain proposition is not thereby an *epistemic* reason to believe that proposition. There is, for example, a strong prima facie case for supposing that it is incoherent to doubt that one has free will, in that the very act of doubting it only makes sense given that one is already taking oneself to be capable of free action. Nevertheless, even granted this point, it remains that this is not an *epistemic* reason in support of one's belief that one has free will since it offers no grounds for thinking that the claim that one has free will is *true*. Similarly, the incoherence of sceptical doubts at best only shows that endorsement of the conclusion of the radical sceptical argument cannot coherently form part of a philosophical position, but we knew *that* already. Indeed, the force of scepticism when it is set out as an argument (rather than just a series of sceptical techniques) lies in the fact that it is *paradox* rather than a thesis—that it is a series of claims which we would all independently assent to but which, when taken collectively, lead to an intellectually devastating conclusion. In effect, the antisceptical version of Wittgenstein's thesis merely comes down to the claim that sceptical doubts are absurd, but that is just to reiterate that we are dealing with a paradox here, and certainly does not suffice to *answer* that paradox.[17]

Nevertheless, although Wittgenstein's claim that entertaining sceptical doubts commits one to absurdity will not supply the desired *epistemic* answer to scepticism, it can help us to identify a possible *pragmatic* response to the problem. Recall that the problem is that we must take it for granted that sceptical possible worlds are far off if we are to be able to coherently ascribe internalist knowledge of everyday propositions. Crucially, however, we can never have sufficient reflectively accessible grounds that would indicate to us that this assumption is legitimate. Moreover, unless that assumption is legitimated then the whole practice of offering evidential support is called into question. Even everyday beliefs concerning, for example, that one has hands, are problematic unless one is able to make this assumption. And Wittgenstein's point is that to entertain a doubt of this sort is not to play the 'game' of offering grounds in a more austere way than is usual but rather to stop playing the 'game' altogether. Just as one cannot offer grounds in support of one's belief in a hinge proposition—because these grounds will be more questionable than the belief that they are meant to be grounds for—similarly, one can never offer grounds for *doubt* in a hinge proposition either, because these grounds for doubt will also be more questionable than the belief doubted. If one wishes to play the 'game' of offering reasons for belief or doubt, then one must be willing to accept certain propositions where one's belief in those propositions can never be coherently open to rational doubt or rational support.

There is nothing in this line of thought which offers an epistemic legitimation of the antisceptical assumptions which guide our reason-giving practices, but it does offer us a strong pragmatic motivation for accepting these assumptions. For whilst the Wittgensteinian discussion of hinge propositions grants that we must assume that the world is pretty much as we take it to be if our evidential practices are to be coherent (and that we necessarily lack reflectively accessible grounds to support this assumption), it also highlights the manner in which doubt of a certain sort is epistemically futile in that it takes us out of the very epistemic 'game' itself.

Initial reflection on the sceptical problem might tempt us to suppose that sceptical standards are simply a more demanding extension of everyday standards (this was the conception of scepticism that we saw informing the infallibilism-based treatments of the sceptical argument that we considered in Chapter 1, and which also underlay the sensitivity-based and attributer contextualist responses to scepticism that we looked at in Chapter 2). In contrast, what

Wittgenstein is identifying in *On Certainty* is the sense in which sceptical standards, far from being extensions of everyday standards, are in fact the rejection of *any* standard. That is, a more demanding epistemic standard would be one in which a more rigorous set of criteria was employed regarding what is tested relative to what. In contrast, the sceptic is rejecting the very practice of testing our beliefs relative to other beliefs that we hold, because in light of her doubt there is nothing that can count as fixed relative to what is tested. In this sense, then, engaging in sceptical doubt does not so much raise the epistemic standards as completely undermine the possibility of there being such standards in the first place (see, for example, Wittgenstein 1969: §§115, 450, 490, 613).

If this is right, then it follows that if one is to engage in an epistemological enterprise at all—if one is to attempt to track the truth—then it is essential that one takes the falsity of sceptical hypotheses as given. The choice then becomes between allowing this assumption to stand and (if certain external conditions obtain) being in a position to engage in evidential practices in forming one's beliefs in such a way that one's beliefs tally with the way the world is; or not allowing this assumption and closing off any possibility of engaging in such evidential practices, no matter what the actual circumstances might turn out to be. So construed, the choice is between the possibility of knowledge which admits of a quasi-evidential grounding and the impossibility of knowledge of this sort.[18]

We can make this point more precise (and more compelling, I think), by considering it in light of a proposal made some years ago by Hans Reichenbach (1938, 1949) regarding the problem of induction. Reichenbach was happy to accept that there was no epistemic response available to this problem. Nevertheless, he argued that to doubt induction was incoherent in the sense that no seeker of truth could ever coherently entertain such a doubt. One of the analogies that he gave to illustrate this was that of the blind man who must choose between what could well be a path that would take him down from the mountain, and what he knows for sure is not a path. Even if the grounds he has for believing the former are weak and inadequate, the former course of action is clearly preferable to the latter if saving one's life is one's aim (see, for example, Reichenbach 1949: 469–82). Elsewhere, he offered the following analogy of the dying man:

An example will show the logical structure of our reasoning. A man may be suffering from a grave disease; the physician tells us: 'I do not know whether an operation will save the man, but if there *is* any remedy, it is an operation.' In such a case, the operation would be justified. Of course, it would be better to know that the operation will save the man; but, if we do not know this, the knowledge formulated in the statement of the physician is a sufficient justification. If we cannot realize the sufficient conditions of success, we shall at least realize the necessary conditions. (1938: 355)

That is, to cash out the analogy in play here, taking it as given that the actual world is induction-friendly and using induction as a result will at least put one in the position of *potentially* gaining the wide class of true beliefs that induction provides in induction-friendly worlds (i.e. we will meet one of the necessary conditions of successfully employing induction). In contrast, not employing induction on the grounds that one lacks an epistemic justification for its use would almost certainly *guarantee* that one would never gain such a wide class of true beliefs, regardless of whether the world in question was an induction-friendly or an induction-hostile world (i.e. we would not even meet one of the necessary condition for successfully employing induction). Employing induction is thus preferable to not employing induction if the epistemic goal of gaining true beliefs is one's aim.

This strategy only works at the most general of levels, of course, in that it only validates the use of some version of inductive reasoning over the non-employment of inductive reasoning, rather than validating any particular employment of an inductive method of belief-formation. But this is all that we need for our purposes. The parallel to the sceptical case is that whilst there are not the desired epistemic grounds available for blocking the underdetermination-based sceptical argument, there is an overwhelming pragmatic case for adopting the strategy of being non-sceptical over being sceptical. If the actual world is indeed much the way that we suppose it to be, then we will have a great deal of (at least brute) knowledge and our everyday epistemic practices will be entirely in order in the sense that the evidence that we offer in favour of what we believe will, in general, perform the role we take it to perform in quotidian contexts. In contrast, if this 'initial condition' assumption is false, then we will fail to know anything of consequence and our evidential practices will be of no epistemic use to us whatsoever. (And note that if it is false, then it doesn't really matter all that much from an epistemic point of view what we believe.) Crucially, however, adopting the sceptical conclusion would mean that we give up on even the *possibility* that we have knowledge and that our evidential practices are reliable guides as to the nature of the world. The choice is thus between the possibility of knowledge and the useful employment of our evidential practices on the one hand, and the guarantee of no knowledge and no useful employment of our epistemic practices on the other. Faced with such a choice, it is easy to see that there is an overwhelming pragmatic motivation for disregarding scepticism and taking the antisceptical 'initial condition' assumption for granted. One might put the matter this way: whilst we lack epistemic grounds for believing the antisceptical assumption, such a belief is clearly practically rational, given the alternatives.

With this assumption in play we can then allow our evidence to perform the usual supporting roles. What Wittgenstein's comments on hinge propositions highlight is the manner in which we take this assumption for granted along with how even everyday claims to know illustrate this general assumption that guides our evidential practices. We might suppose that, since the initial condition assumption is only directly focused on the denial of sceptical hypotheses, it is only when it comes to, for example, claiming knowledge of the falsity of sceptical hypotheses that the sceptical challenge makes itself felt. In contrast, what the discussion of hinge propositions reveals to us is the way in which this assumption informs all of our epistemic practices, even those regarding—better: *especially* those regarding—those propositions that we most take for granted.[19]

This does not mean that we have an answer to the Pyrrhonian problematic that we outlined above, however—much less that we have an answer to the underdetermination-based sceptical argument—in that it is still true that in the sceptical conversational context in which the Pyrrhonian challenge is made it will be improper to respond with claims to know. Moreover, it remains true that, strictly speaking, our beliefs are subject to a substantial degree of reflective epistemic luck and thus that we lack internalist knowledge of the everyday propositions that we believe. Nevertheless, what this pragmatic antisceptical strategy does ensure is that our everyday epistemic practices of claiming knowledge are in order as they are, for whilst they are not sufficiently epistemically grounded, they are pragmatically legitimated. Our beliefs, when true, are reflectively lucky—and this makes our holding them epistemically problematic—but this does not mean that we ought not to hold these beliefs where the 'ought' here is construed broadly so that it includes both epistemic and pragmatic considerations.

9.4. Epistemic *Angst*

There is, of course, an obvious problem with this merely pragmatic legitimation of our epistemic practices, which is that a pragmatic legitimation of this sort seems inadequate to license the *beliefs* needed by the agents involved. That is, whilst one can imagine such a pragmatic legitimation sufficing to license one's *acceptance* of the propositions in question, once one has recognized that one lacks any adequate epistemic grounds to believe these propositions it is then far from obvious that one could (much less should) believe these propositions, even despite the presence of a pragmatic ground for such belief.

In order to see this point in more detail, we need to clarify at least two very different ways in which this problem might manifest itself. Consider first the beliefs of those who have not engaged in the kind of epistemological theorizing that we have undertaken here and so have not considered the sceptical problem. Such agents will believe all manner of everyday propositions even though, as we have seen, these beliefs are of their nature ultimately lacking in epistemic support. Moreover, we can also expect that these agents will believe at least some antisceptical propositions, or at least be disposed to believe them if the relevant logical connections between their everyday beliefs and alternative sceptical hypotheses are highlighted to them, and these beliefs will also be lacking in epistemic support. We would expect, however, that these agents will not have any theoretical beliefs about the nature of their epistemic practices (they simply engage in them), and so there is not the added concern here about the status of their beliefs in this regard, such as the second-order belief that one's beliefs are, in the main, evidentially grounded in the manner that one supposes.

As regards those uninitiated to the philosophical project regarding knowledge, the pragmatic legitimation of our epistemic practices can supply some comfort (though only, of course, to those who *are* initiated to the project). Whilst these philosophically unreflective agents labour under a false consciousness of sorts, they are engaging in the right kind of (general) epistemic practices, all things considered. Furthermore, there is also the additional consideration here regarding the psychological necessity of our forming certain beliefs. Plausibly, we are psychologically compelled to regard our beliefs as being 'hooked-up' to the world in roughly the manner that we typically suppose, in that those agents who lose this kind of conception of how their beliefs relate to the world don't form different beliefs as a result but tend to simply embark on a path that leads very quickly to madness. If this is right, then the lack of doxastic choice here further removes a degree of epistemic blame from these agents, since it is not as if an alternative doxastic strategy is open to them.[20]

This last point also applies to those who have reflected on our epistemic condition, of course, though here the difficulty is accentuated by this very reflection. We who have followed the sceptical train of thought to its conclusion become aware of the epistemic deficiency in our beliefs, and it is now problematic for us to retain such beliefs, even despite our uncovering along the way a pragmatic legitimation for our doxastic commitments. At the very least, it seems, one must lose one's optimistic theoretical beliefs about the manner in which one's beliefs are evidentially grounded, though even here it may be that one is under a psychological compulsion, in the limited sense that if one is to take any doxastic attitude in this respect at all, then it must be one of belief, and reflection on our epistemic practices forces one to take a doxastic attitude. If such a compulsion is lacking, however, then it seems that what will remain will not be belief based on pragmatic grounds but rather merely an *acceptance* of the relevant propositions that is accompanied by non-belief. The more important question, however, is what happens to our beliefs in non-theoretical propositions, such as our beliefs in everyday and antisceptical propositions. Even if one grants that we are psychologically compelled to conceive of our beliefs as being roughly related to the world in the manner that we typically suppose, this is small comfort if such a conception coexists with a recognition that adequate grounds are lacking for thinking that this is true.

In the light of this it seems that reflection on the epistemic aspect of the human condition inexorably leads to a kind of epistemic bad faith, and thus to an associated *epistemic angst*. That is, in the light of philosophical reflection, we discover that our beliefs are ineliminably subject to reflective epistemic luck and thus that we are unable to take the kind of cognitive responsibility for our beliefs which we typically suppose ourselves to possess. That there are pragmatic grounds for participating in our usual epistemic practices in the same vein as an agent would who had not become aware of this philosophical discovery is little comfort given this realization, nor would the philosophically reflective subject take any great solace from the fact that we may be psychologically compelled to retain a substantial proportion of our beliefs regardless of their evidential grounds.

The moral of scepticism is thus not simply that our knowledge is prone to a degree of epistemic luck, since as we have seen there are varieties of luck that might be considered epistemic that are entirely compatible with knowledge possession. Moreover, neither is the moral of scepticism that our knowledge is irredeemably prone to *all* of those varieties of problematic epistemic luck, since we have seen that there is a plausible conception of knowledge cast along externalist lines that is able to meet one of the problematic species of epistemic luck, veritic luck. The moral of scepticism instead comes down to the fact that our knowledge is prone to that particular problematic variety of epistemic luck that we have labelled here *reflective* epistemic luck, and that this is an unavoidable feature of our epistemic condition. As I have emphasized at several junctures, this contention alone does not license the conclusion that knowledge is impossible, only that a certain form of fine-grained knowledge which meets the relevant internalist conditions is impossible, though this is problem enough.

Indeed, we can be even more specific about the nature of the sceptical attack. For as we have seen, the knowledge that meets an internal epistemic condition will be immune to reflective epistemic luck just so long as the sceptical error-possibilities are indeed as modally far off as we take them to be. In effect, just so long as the actual world is pretty much as we typically suppose it is—and, in particular, just so long as there are no sceptical possible worlds in the modal neighbourhood—then our reflectively accessible grounds will be a good guide to what is the case. There is thus a general 'initial condition' that must be in place if we are to have internalist knowledge, and the sceptic highlights to us that we can never have adequate reflectively accessible grounds for thinking that it is in place. Our epistemic position is thus akin to a high-wire acrobat who is unable to be sure that the safety net has been erected below. For sure, it *looks* as if it has, but it would look that way even if it hadn't been erected. This gives rise to a certain epistemic anxiety regarding our epistemic position. In so far as we can take it for granted that the world is pretty much as we suppose it to be, then the knowledge that we can access via reflection is (at least in the best case) a good guide as to the nature of our epistemic position. Crucially, however, we do not have adequate reflectively accessible epistemic grounds to license this assumption, and therein lies the source of the anxiety about our epistemic position.

9.5. Concluding Remarks

We noted at the beginning of this book that there is in the epistemological literature a certain ambivalence regarding the epistemic luck platitude that knowledge is incompatible with luck. On the one hand, there are those who endorse such a claim seemingly without qualification. On the other, there are those who seem to want to say that knowledge is compatible with a certain (perhaps variable) degree of epistemic luck, and that, indeed, 'epistemic luck permeates the human condition'. It should be clear now what was underlying this apparent conflict of intuitions. There is a variety of epistemic luck that is unquestionably incompatible with knowledge possession, and that is veritic epistemic luck. In so far as we genuinely are knowers, then, epistemic luck of this sort does not permeate the human condition to *any* degree. Nevertheless, what is right (but poorly expressed) about the comments of those who seem to reject the (unqualified) epistemic luck platitude, is that there is a variety of epistemic luck—reflective epistemic luck—that is epistemically undesirable and perhaps also (claims the epistemic internalist) incompatible with knowledge possession. In this sense epistemic luck *does* permeate the human condition.

It should be noted, however, that our conclusion here has an air of absurdity about it. Whilst we have discovered that our unreflective everyday epistemic practices are legitimate, we have also discovered, in the context of reflection, that the sense of 'legitimate' at issue in this regard is ultimately pragmatic rather than, as we would have hoped, epistemic. What happens, then, when one moves from a sceptical conversational context back to a quotidian context? Recall that, for the attributer contextualist, the epistemic status of one's beliefs after engaging with the sceptic (after moving to a sceptical conversational context) will be much the same as they were in the conversational context that one was in prior to engaging with the sceptic. On this view, one preserves one's epistemic 'innocence' save for the temporary state of ignorance brought about by the consideration of the sceptical challenge.[21]

On the view outlined here, however, there is no such return to epistemic innocence once one has considered the challenge posed by radical scepticism. Whilst it is of course true that, prior to becoming apprised of the sceptical challenge, one will be unaware of the manner in which one's evidential practices rest upon ungrounded assumptions, consideration of the sceptical predicament shatters the illusion that is in play here. Once the challenge has passed and one returns to a quotidian conversational context, the implicit awareness remains that one's epistemic position is not what one thought it was. This is when the epistemic *angst* sets in. Since our everyday epistemic practices function in such a way as to disguise the ultimately groundless nature of our belief (for example, they never bring doubt about local or global hinge propositions into focus), one could be forgiven for never becoming conscious of this fact—never overcoming one's epistemic false consciousness to recognize the true nature of one's epistemic predicament.[22] Nevertheless, what we have seen is that our epistemic condition is unavoidably subject to an epistemic *angst*, and that this *angst* turns upon the fact that our beliefs are ineliminably subject to reflective epistemic luck.

Notes

1. Though whether or not Wittgenstein himself would have endorsed this reading is another matter entirely. In the main, commentators on *On Certainty* have tended to interpret Wittgenstein as arguing that we *lack* knowledge of hinge propositions. See, e.g., Strawson (1985: ch. 1); Wright (1985, 1991); McGinn (1989, 2002); Travis (1989, 2003); Putnam (1992: ch. 8); Stroll (1994); Ribeiro (2002*a*); and Moyal-Sharrock (2004). There are two main reasons that motivate this 'non-epistemic' interpretation. The first is that some see in Wittgenstein an implicit commitment to epistemological internalism such that where we

cannot offer adequate grounds in favour of certain propositions, and thus cannot properly claim knowledge of these propositions, then we cannot know them at all. This line of argument is most explicit in Ribeiro (2002*a*), though it is notable, I think, that the textual support that Ribeiro offers for this interpretation is simply three passages—(Wittgenstein 1969: §§14, 91, 243)—and in each case the focus of Wittgenstein's remarks is on a claim to know rather than on knowledge itself. Given the fact that an externalist account of knowledge would be committed to claming that there is a substantial difference between the conditions under which one can properly claim knowledge and the conditions under which one knows, this interpretation of *On Certainty* is bound to beg the question against the externalist.

The second reason why commentators take Wittgenstein to be arguing that we lack knowledge of hinge propositions is because in places he is clearly drawn to an austere epistemic theory of truth such that propositions which cannot be supported by grounds cannot be true or false (and thus, a fortiori, they cannot be known). He writes, for example:

> The reason why the expression 'true or false' has something misleading about it is that it is like saying 'it tallies with the facts or it doesn't', and the very thing that is in question is what 'tallying' is here.
>
> Really 'The proposition is either true or false' only means that it must be possible to decide for or against it. (Wittgenstein 1969: §§199–200)

And later, 'If the true is what is grounded, then the ground is not *true*, nor yet false.' (Wittgenstein 1969: §205) This interpretative approach is most explicit in the work of such figures as McGinn (1989, 2002), Travis (1989, 2003) and Moyal-Sharrock (2004). Significantly, however, both of these quotations are ambiguous since neither of them explicitly states that hinge propositions are neither true nor false. Interestingly, the only passages where Wittgenstein is clear that 'propositions' of a certain contested sort which are relevant to the sceptical debate are neither true nor false is when it comes to 'philosophical' propositions such as, 'There are physical objects' (see, e.g. Wittgenstein 1969: §§35–6). The reason why these 'propositions' are treated as neither true nor false by Wittgenstein, however, is not because they are necessarily groundless, but because, as Wright (1985) and Williams (2003*b*) point out, they are nonsense and therefore completely fail to express a proposition at all.

For more on Wittgenstein's *On Certainty*, see Morawetz (1979) and Williams (1991, 2003). I offer an extended discussion of some of the textual issues in play here in Pritchard (2001*c*, 2005*e*).

2. This is not to say, of course, that Wittgenstein was a sceptic, only that there is nothing in his account of reasons which would support an antisceptical thesis.

3. Although, of course, the issue then becomes whether we are able to know that we have those mental states which have externally individuated contents. In general, the question that content externalism raises is how we are to have any special epistemic access to our mental states where the content of these states is (at least in part) externally individuated. For some of the key recent discussions of this issue, see the papers collected in the volume edited by Nuccetelli (2003). I discuss this problem in Pritchard (2002*a*).

4. Content externalism will probably have ramifications for other forms of scepticism as well, such as scepticism about other minds, but I will be focusing here on the specific sceptical issue of whether it is possible for us to have any widespread knowledge about the external world because this is the variety of scepticism that is most obviously affected by content externalism. (In any case, it is this form of scepticism that has been the focus of this book.)

5. For more on the supposed antisceptical implications of the Davidsonian view, see Klein (1986), Williams (1988–9), and Craig (1990*a*).

6. For more on Putnam's BIV argument, and on the general antisceptical consequences of the content externalist approach that he and Davidson propose, see Brueckner (1992), Christensen (1993), Warfield (1998), and Wright (1994).

7. Critical appraisal of McDowell's response to the sceptic has been fairly limited, though for two interesting—and very recent—discussions of McDowell in this respect, see Macarthur (2003) and Greco (2004).

8. See Sellars (1997).

9. I will not be taking issue with this claim that McDowell makes. He has defended this thesis in a number of places, principally McDowell (1994*b*).

10. For a development of this line of thought, see McDowell (1986).

11. McDowell sometimes expresses his point by saying that we do not need to adduce a non-question-begging argument in order to cogently support our perceptual beliefs with reasons, where for an argument to be 'cogent' means something like 'rationally persuasive'. For example, he writes that

> someone who sees that things are a certain way, has an excellent reason for taking it that things are that way; the excellence comes out in the fact that from the premise that one sees that things are thus and so, it follows that things *are* thus and so. The epistemic positions themselves put their occupants in possession of reasons for their beliefs; those reasons do not need to be supplemented with less cogent arguments from non-question-beggingly available premises. (McDowell 1994*a*, 201)

So, e.g. whilst the inference from *I see that I have two hands* to *I have two hands* (where knowledge of the premiss is meant to support knowledge of the conclusion) is clearly question-begging (since the truth of the conclusion is presupposed in the premiss), McDowell argues that it is no less cogent for that. The present discussion grants McDowell this point, at least when the inference in made in abnormal circumstances, but contends that the cogency of such inferences is due to the fact that they take place against a backdrop of shared certainties which already presupposes the denials of the very sceptical hypotheses that would make such inferences questionable (and so lacking in cogency). Accordingly, whilst it grants the in-principle cogency of these sorts of inferences, it takes issue with the supposed antisceptical implications of them. In particular, it takes issue with the subsequent inference that McDowell makes from *I have two hands* to, say, *I am not a (handless) BIV* (where, again, knowledge of the premiss is meant to support knowledge of the conclusion). Whilst the former inference is question-begging in the trivial sense that it ungroundedly takes a framework of hinge beliefs as given, the latter inference is question-begging in the more specific sense that it attempts to adduce the conclusion of an inference which was only cogent because it took place relative to a background of hinge beliefs as a reason for believing one of the very ungrounded hinge beliefs that made the previous assertion permissible in the first place. On the view presented here, then, there is more than one way in which an inference can be question-begging, and the exact manner in which it is question-begging will determine whether or not the inference in question is cogent.

12. In recent work, Williamson (2000*a*) has put forward an externalist account of content that also (he claims) has the effect of neutralizing the sceptical problem and which shares a number of key features of the McDowellian picture. In particular, like McDowell, Williamson argues that what epistemically supports one's beliefs in the 'good'

(non-deceived) case as opposed to the indistinguishable 'bad' (deceived) case is not, *contra* the sceptic, the same. Despite this surface similarity between the two antisceptical views, however, the line of critique applied to McDowell here is not directly applicable to Williamson's argument because of how the crucial supporting notion for Williamson is not reasons but an epistemologically externalist conception of evidence as knowledge. Nevertheless, although the Williamsonian account avoids this particular problem, by being an epistemologically externalist response to the sceptic it is therefore subject to the line of critique that I have applied to externalist antisceptical accounts elsewhere in this book. I discuss the Williamsonian response to scepticism in Pritchard (2006).

13. Interestingly, in a recent article McDowell notes, in passing, that there are certain affinities between his general position and the Wittgensteinian account of 'hinge' propositions in *On Certainty*. He remarks that his conviction that he is reliable—and hence authoritative—in his judgements about green objects should not be understood such that the epistemic standing of his judgements in this regard inferentially depends on the epistemic standing of his belief in his reliability, as if they were the conclusions of an argument. Rather they have, he writes, 'a sort of status that Wittgenstein considers in *On Certainty*'. He continues that this conviction is 'held firm for me by my whole conception of the world with myself in touch with it, and not as the conclusion of an inference from some of that conception' (McDowell 2002: 26). These brief remarks are, I think, telling. For one thing, they imply that whilst McDowell might back up his assertions about green objects by simply offering factive reasons about what he sees, he grants that this practice of offering reasons rests upon a background of certainties which serve a special role. Although McDowell doesn't spell this out, the further Wittgensteinian implication of this is clearly that the beliefs which make up this 'whole conception of the world and myself in touch with it' are not themselves supported by reasons since their standing fast is what allows the practice of offering reasons to have the cogency it does in the first place. Accordingly, one does not counter the sceptic with reasons at all, properly speaking, but merely with one's antisceptical convictions. McDowell was in this article responding to Brandom (1995), who was in turn responding to an earlier article by McDowell (1995).

14. I develop this critique of McDowell at greater length in Pritchard (2003*a*: §2).

15. I explore this point in more detail in Pritchard (2003*a*: §3).

16. See, e.g. Strawson (1985: ch. 1); McGinn (1989); Putnam (1992); Stroll (1994); and Wright (1985, 2003*a*, 2003*b*).

17. In any case, I don't think that it was even *Wittgenstein's* intention to argue for an antisceptical thesis in *On Certainty*. Indeed, in so far as one can discern anything concrete about Wittgenstein's intentions from reading these fragmentary remarks, then it seems that his focus is on the language-games that govern the propriety of claims to know, rather than on the actual possession conditions for knowledge, and this would certainly accord with the general trend of his later writings. I argue for this claim in Pritchard (2005*e*, 2001*c*), where I also present a critical appraisal of some of the main antisceptical readings of Wittgenstein in the contemporary literature.

18. Indeed, not allowing the assumption might also affect one's 'brute' knowledge of certain propositions, though I doubt that this is in fact possible because of the resistance of our most basic beliefs to the dictates of reason. For more on this point, and how it relates to a Humean conception of belief (at least in certain propositions), see Ribeiro (2002*b*).

19. Williams (1991) offers a similar reading of Wittgenstein, and goes on to argue for a general epistemological thesis which he calls epistemological contextualism, although

it is very different from the form of attributer contextualism discussed in Part I. Significantly, however, whilst he makes most of the same moves that I make here, he regards the epistemological view that results as completely *anti*sceptical in tone. I critically examine the differences between Williams's contextualism and the kind of attributer contextualism discussed in Chapter 2 in Pritchard (2002*e*), and further discuss Williams's position in Pritchard (2001*c*, 2004*a*, 2004*d*, 2005*e*).

20. A related claim in this respect is, of course, the so-called 'Principle of Charity', as defended by, e.g. Davidson (1986). One of the consequences of this principle is that one could not coherently regard an agent as having beliefs at all unless one took that agent to have beliefs which were mostly true. Supposing an agent to have mostly false beliefs is thus conceptually incoherent (though note that this does not mean, in itself, that an agent's beliefs could not be mostly false, only that one could not coherently regard them as such).

21. In Pritchard (2001*a*), I argue that epistemological attributer contextualists cannot maintain this claim even by their own lights. Brueckner (2003) argues for a similar conclusion.

22. That said, one can see inklings of possible confused and partial realizations of what our true epistemic situation is amongst those who haven't explicitly considered the sceptical challenge. For example, it is often noted that, independently of sceptical concerns, people sometimes get quickly convinced of such incoherent doctrines as relativism about truth, and one explanation could well be that what is motivating this pseudo-scepticism is an implicit awareness of our epistemic position. This is a sociological-cum-psychological story, however, and extends far beyond the reaches of this book.

10

Postscript: Moral Luck

10.0. Introduction

Our focus in this book has been on the phenomenon of epistemic luck. Interestingly, however, some of the key discussions regarding luck in the recent philosophical literature have been about a supposedly analogous form of luck that affects the moral status of our actions—the so-called problem of 'moral luck'. Although, as with epistemic luck, one can trace the source of this problem back to issues discussed in ancient philosophical works, the contemporary stimulus for this debate is an exchange between Bernard Williams (1976) and Thomas Nagel (1976).[1] Significantly, both of these authors raise the problem of moral luck in a way that overlaps with epistemic luck, since they each see the issue as ultimately resting upon an inability for agents to take the appropriate responsibility for their actions, whether those actions are such that they fall under the remit of moral or epistemic evaluation (or both).

In this postscript I offer some general remarks concerning the extent to which the strategy outlined in this book as regards epistemic luck can be employed to resolve the parallel issue of moral luck. As we will see, applying the conclusions we have drawn from our discussion of epistemic luck to the moral case is not straightforward because there does not seem to be a distinctive problem of moral luck at all, or at least there does not seem to be a problem that can be stated independently of the problem of reflective epistemic luck that we have identified.

10.1. Nagel on Moral Luck

Nagel describes the phenomenon of moral luck as being concerned with the following types of scenario where

a significant aspect of what someone does depends on factors beyond his control [and] yet we continue to treat him in that respect as an object of moral judgement. (Nagel 1979: 25)

So, for example, the consequences of my decision to reverse out of my driveway without checking first to see if anyone is approaching along the pavement are, to a certain extent at least, subject to luck. Nevertheless, I will be held to account for those consequences even if they are the result of luck. If, for example, it just so happens that an elderly gentleman is walking past my drive-way as I reverse out of it, and I hit him and kill him, then (intuitively at least) I will be subject to a greater level of moral censure than if he had not happened to be there and I had exited my driveway without incident. It thus seems that my moral responsibility extends even to 'lucky' factors that I have no control over, and this is contrary to a widespread intuition that (roughly) we are only morally responsible for what is in our control.

Whilst there has been a tremendous amount of critical appraisal of the general notion of moral luck, what has been noticeably lacking in the literature is an assessment of the manner in which Williams and Nagel employ the concept of luck in their arguments.[2] Neither of them offers an explicit account of the notion, with Williams remarking (almost in passing) that he will 'use the notion of "luck" generously [and] undefinedly' (Williams 1981b: 22). Commentators have followed suit and thus been likewise inclined to treat the concept as an undefined primitive of which we may legitimately take ourselves as having a clear grasp.

What little Nagel and Williams do say about luck tends to identify it with a lack of control on the part of the agent, as in the quotation from Nagel just cited. Similarly, in one of the few passages in his paper where he mentions luck in isolation from moral luck, Williams writes that 'what is not in the domain of the self is not in its control, and so is subject to luck' (Williams 1981b: 20). Clearly, however, as we saw in §5.1, this could only be (and is only intended to be) a very partial account of luck since all sorts of events—such as the celestial movements of the planets—are beyond our control, but are not thereby considered lucky as a result. With this in mind, it is worthwhile considering the examples of moral luck that Nagel and Williams offer in the light of the account of luck that is presented here. As we will see, this has some surprising results. We will begin by looking at Nagel's article on the problem.

Perhaps the most famous example that Nagel offers in favour of moral luck is that of the drunk-driver. He writes that

there is a morally significant difference between reckless driving and manslaughter. But whether a reckless driver hits a pedestrian depends on the presence of the pedestrian at the point where he recklessly passes a red light. (1979: 25)

And since the presence of the pedestrian at that particular point and at that particular time is a matter of luck, so luck alone can make a morally significant difference (the difference between (mere) reckless driving and manslaughter). We are thus asked to imagine two drunk-drivers who are counterparts in every respect except that the former has the bad luck to hit a pedestrian whilst the latter has the good luck not to, and where these differences in consequences are morally significant.[3]

Of course, simply noting the difference between the *crimes* of reckless driving and manslaughter is not enough to establish the point that Nagel wishes to argue for. After all, it is not in itself contentious to suppose that two agents could be equally morally at fault (and otherwise identical) and yet the one agent be guilty of a lesser criminal offence (and so subject to a less severe punishment). There are a number of reasons why this might be so. For one thing, the role of punishment is standardly understood such that it should do more than merely reflect moral disapproval (indeed, some might argue that punishment should not reflect moral disapproval at all). For similar reasons, it is even less obvious that the extent of the punishment should match the extent of the moral opprobrium in each case. Moreover, punishments can vary in line with there being a victim to the crime in question (and thus vary in response to the extent of the suffering of the victim). Whether rightly or wrongly, we might wish to punish one criminal more severely than another for committing the same crime for the sole reason that the first criminal's act, whilst otherwise identical, resulted in more suffering and we want our punishments to (somehow) represent this differing extent of suffering. And since there is this logical gap between moral opprobrium and punishment, the onus is on Nagel to do more than merely show that there is a difference in terms of the crimes that we attribute to the agents in question (and thus the punishments we inflict) if he is to show that there is a genuine moral difference in these cases.

One response to the putative examples of moral luck that Nagel and others have proposed has thus been to put pressure on this potential gap between moral opprobrium and legal punishment (in the form of the crimes attributed to the agent, and the punishments incurred by the agent as a result). This style of counter-argument essentially involves taking the examples offered at face value and trying to show how the intuitions that they give rise to can be reinterpreted so that our initial 'intuition' of there being a moral difference can be explained away.[4] In contrast, I contend that the focus of our counter-argument should, as it were, be one stage back by not taking these examples of moral luck at face value in the first place. The claim is that such examples are, on closer inspection, controversial because they trade on diverse—and, in this case, incompatible—claims about luck. As we will see, once the role of luck in these examples is made clear we will have a way of responding to the putative phenomenon of moral luck that both supplements and strengthens the more conventional critique offered by those who merely note the gap between moral opprobrium and legal punishment.

There are many possible ways of filling out the details of Nagel's drunk-driver example and, depending on what detail we add, the example may not end up involving luck at all (at least regarding whether or not the agent hits the pedestrian). Indeed, using the account of luck that we put forward in §5.1, we can imagine two extreme cases, one where there is a lot of luck involved and one where there is hardly any (and perhaps none at all), with most other cases lying on a continuum between these two extremes. At the 'non-lucky' end of the continuum will be those cases where the agent in question regularly takes risks of this sort and where he is taking a great risk in driving under the influence like this, perhaps because he is about to drive down a crowded street. If this is how we are to understand the example, however, then it would be odd to say that the driver is unlucky to hit a pedestrian, since we would *expect* him to hit a pedestrian, not just in this world but in most nearby possible worlds where the relevant initial conditions are the same (where, for example, his reckless character remained unchanged). At the other end of the continuum is the genuinely unlucky drunk-driver who isn't taking much of a risk (it is a rural area, say, with very few pedestrians), and who rarely takes risks of this sort (his reckless behaviour is, we might say, out of character). Here we do have a case of bad luck since although the driver hits a pedestrian in the actual world, we would not expect him to hit a pedestrian in most nearby possible worlds where the relevant initial conditions are the same. In these worlds, we would expect him to either come to his senses and not drive, or else drive and not hit a pedestrian.

So we can either understand the drunk-driver example in such a way that he is clearly unlucky to hit a pedestrian, or we can understand it in such a way that the driver's actions having this consequence isn't a matter of luck at all. Clearly, there is a moral difference between these two drivers even if the consequences of their actions turn out to be the same. For example, if they both end up hitting a pedestrian then I think that we would subject the unlucky driver to a lesser degree of moral censure than his non-lucky counterpart. Part of the reason for this is that, unlike the non-lucky driver, the unlucky driver acted out of character. Moreover, he acted in such a way that was far less reckless than the actions of the non-lucky driver.

Of course, this kind of moral contrast between the unlucky and non-lucky drunk-driver is of no use to Nagel because the surrounding facts of the situation are substantively different in each case. Accordingly, he will not be able to employ this contrast in order to motivate the desired conclusion that luck alone is affecting the kind of moral evaluation that is being offered. It thus appears that if Nagel is to get the unambiguous example of moral luck that he wants, then he is going to have to consistently understand the drunk-driver case along one of the two lines outlined above. In the one case (the driver who acted out of character) we would have an agent who was genuinely unlucky to hit a pedestrian, unlike his (non-lucky) counterpart. In the other, we would have an agent who was lucky to *not* hit a pedestrian, unlike his non-lucky counterpart. The issue thus concerns whether the two counterparts consistently understood in either of these ways should be subject to a different moral evaluation. We will take the cases in turn. First, the driver who is unlucky to hit a pedestrian, unlike his counterpart who doesn't.

Although there is obviously a difference in consequences here, and thus a difference in the crime that the driver will be charged with in each case (manslaughter in the former case, rather than just reckless driving), once we had reflected on the details of the scenario we would, I think, feel a certain sympathy for the unlucky driver that his lack of care should have had such tragic consequences. In particular, I think that we would feel sympathy for this driver precisely because of the fact that his actions were out of character and would not normally have led to anyone being harmed. That is, the fact that the agent is genuinely unlucky in having run over a pedestrian would temper our moral disapproval of him. That our response to the dire consequences brought about (in part) by luck should be one of sympathy itself suggests that we are willing to 'factor-out' the role of luck in our moral assessment of an agent's actions. Whilst we might recognize the need for an appropriate legal censure which is greater than his counterpart, this need not reflect any conviction that the unlucky driver has committed a morally worse action than his counterpart.

Similar remarks apply to the other case, that of the drunk-driver who was not acting out of character and who was taking a great risk by driving home drunk on roads where there are lots of pedestrians. Suppose that the agent in question has the good fortune to not hit a pedestrian, unlike his counterpart who, as we would expect, does. Would this lead to a different moral assessment of the two agents? Again, I think that we would answer in the negative, even though we would grant that the crimes committed by these agents (and thus the punishments that they should incur) would be different. If we knew that the agent who was lucky to not hit a pedestrian was acting in character in taking such an inordinate risk with other people's lives, then I think that we would regard him as behaving in a way that was no less subject to moral censure than his counterpart. Indeed, we could imagine, for example, this lucky agent being condemned in court by the judge for behaving in a way that was, morally, no different from someone who had actually run over a pedestrian (even whilst passing a different sentence to that which he would have passed to a counterpart driver who did run over a pedestrian).

So if Nagel wants to make use of our clear intuition that there is a moral difference in the drunk-driver example, then he needs to vary the details of the example so that we are making a comparison between the 'out-of-character' driver who isn't being especially reckless (or some analogue) and the 'in-character' driver who manifestly is being reckless (or some analogue). Crucially, however, this contrast involves more than just a difference in the luck involved in each case, since it also illicitly varies circumstantial features of the scenario at issue. In so far as Nagel sticks to examples which do not vary circumstantial features of the scenario and simply varies the luck involved, however, as in examples that consistently stick to either the out-of-character or the in-character template, then he doesn't get the clear moral intuitions that he is trying to motivate.

The same goes for the other examples that Nagel offers, though the details are different in each case. The example of the drunk-driver is an instance of what Nagel calls 'resultant luck', which is 'luck in the way one's actions and projects turn out' (Nagel 1979: 27). This is contrasted with what he terms 'circumstantial luck', which is luck involved in the 'kind of problems and situations one faces' (Nagel 1979: 27).[5] The main example that Nagel offers to illustrate this kind of luck is of the 'unlucky' Nazi and the 'lucky' German expatriate:

[W]hat we do is ... limited by the opportunities and choices with which we are faced, and these are largely determined by factors beyond our control. Someone who was an officer in a concentration camp might have led a quiet and harmless life if the Nazis had never come to power in Germany. And someone who led a quiet and harmless life in Argentina might have become an officer in a concentration camp if he had not left Germany for business reasons in 1930. (1979: 25)

We are clearly meant to suppose that it is the same agent in each of these cases, though faced with different situations. Accordingly, we are to imagine an agent who would have led a harmless life if the Nazis had never come to power, or if he had emigrated to Argentina for business reasons in 1930, but who in fact became an officer in a Nazi concentration camp.

In these, and other examples that Nagel offers, reflecting on the role of luck in the example does not just undermine the force of our initial intuitions in favour of moral luck, as it does in the drunk-driver case, but actually completely undercuts them. For suppose we take seriously the idea that had our protagonist been 'lucky' enough to have avoided being present when the Nazis were in power, then he would have led a relatively blameless life. According to the understanding of luck offered here, this means that we have to suppose that there are a great number of nearby possible worlds in which this agent lives under the Nazi rule and so commits atrocities as a result. If this is to be taken completely at face value, then I think we would agree, on reflection, that there is no clear moral difference between the Nazi officer and his 'peaceful' Argentinean counterpart. Indeed, we often find out key moral truths about agents by getting a 'glimpse' of how they might have behaved had circumstances been different (we might observe, for example, their surprising degree of callousness when faced with an injured animal, or their cruel disregard for another's feelings). Of course, part of the problem of evaluating such cases is that we have such shaky epistemic access to the relevant counterfactual facts. Our 'hunches' about our 'peaceful' expatriate German neighbour in Buenos Aires are only that, and it is rare that we would have evidence of any definitive sort to justify such a damning verdict about someone who did not actually commit the crimes in question. Nevertheless, in so far as we are entitled to take the relevant facts as known, as Nagel implicitly asks us to do, then the putative moral difference disappears.[6]

In contrast, when the situation is described so that we are willing to suppose that there is a moral difference between the peaceful German expatriate and his Nazi counterpart, then luck no longer seems to be playing the desired role. For example, were it to be stipulated that there are very few (if any) nearby possible worlds in which our naturalized Argentinean commits such atrocities, then our intuition that there is a moral difference between the peaceful expatriate German and his Nazi counterpart would be re-established, but at the expense of this no longer being an example that illustrates moral luck. After all, since we have now stipulated that the possibility that the agent could have been a Nazi is remote, it follows that it is not a matter of luck that the agent leads the peaceful—as opposed to wicked—life that he does. Indeed, given the remoteness of the possibility, it is now a contentious issue whether we are talking about the same agent in each case (or, at least, relevantly similar agents). So either Nagel can get the relevant moral difference but in doing so loses the sense in which luck is involved, or else he retains the role of luck in the example but at the expense of completely undermining our intuition that there really is a moral difference between the two counterpart agents.

The reason why reflecting on the role of luck in this example has a more dramatic effect than it does in the case of the example of resultant luck considered above is that whereas the focus in the drunk-driver case is on our moral assessment of the actions of the driver, in the expatriate case it is more on the agent himself. This makes a substantive difference because although we can (though with difficulty, as it turns out) conceive of scenarios in which two otherwise identical agents engage in the same act and yet, due to luck, that act seems to be subject to differing moral evaluations, it is far harder (if not impossible) to imagine two otherwise identical agents engaging in lifestyles that, again, due to luck, are so drastically divergent in their moral status. That is, to suppose that two agents are otherwise identical is to thereby suppose that whilst luck might influence their resultant behaviour in different ways, they are not, *qua* agents, subject to a different moral assessment as a result.

So whilst it might be a matter of luck that an agent does not end up being an officer in a Nazi concentration camp, it will not be a matter of luck that the agent displays behaviour that is subject to moral censure (and indicative of a generally morally corrupt character) in other ways. Similarly, in cases such as the drunk-driver example, although focusing upon the actions might seem to present some (albeit, as we have seen, inconclusive) grounds for thinking that luck can influence our moral assessment of an agent's actions, it would still remain true that we would hold the protagonist and his counterpart as equally at moral fault *qua* agents.

It is thus significant that Nagel motivates his case for the circumstantial luck that (putatively) affects our assessments of agents via the less contentious (though still problematic) case of resultant luck.[7] Whereas the latter merely trades upon ambiguous claims about luck that, once disambiguated, substantially weaken his argument, the former trades upon the supposed truth that there exist genuine cases of resultant moral luck in order to establish the even more contentious claim that there exist cases of circumstantial moral luck also.

10.2. Williams on Moral Luck and Rational Justification

As we have seen, Nagel's examples fail to work because he doesn't keep the relevant details of the examples fixed. We cannot simply extend this critique of Nagel to Williams's own treatment of the issue, however, because Williams offers a very different account of what is involved in the putative phenomenon of moral luck. What Williams explicitly does (and which Nagel only does implicitly), is treat the problem of moral luck as being derivative on the problem of epistemic luck.[8] That is, the issue for Williams is not how luck can undermine the moral status of actions, but rather how it can undermine their 'rational justification' (Williams 1981b: 22).

261

The primary example of moral luck that Williams offers in his article is that of the painter Gauguin who deserts his family in order to pursue his ambition to be a great artist (Williams 1981*b*: 22ff.). Williams points out that Gauguin cannot be sure in advance that his project will be successful, and yet the success or otherwise of the project will determine how we morally evaluate his decision to desert his family. Williams writes:

[W]hether he will succeed cannot, in the nature of the case, be foreseen. We are not dealing here with the removal of an external obstacle to something which, once that is removed, will fairly predictably go through. Gauguin, in our story, is putting a great deal on a possibility which has not unequivocally declared itself. I want to explore and uphold the claim that in such a situation the only thing that will justify the claim will be success itself. If he fails—and we shall come shortly to what, more precisely, failure may be—then he did the wrong thing, not just in the sense in which that platitudinously follows, but in the sense that having done the wrong thing in those circumstances he has no basis for the thought that he was justified in acting as he did. If he succeeds, he does have a basis for that thought. (1981*b*: 23)

So if Gauguin's action does result in him becoming a great painter then that action will be rationally justified (despite the cost of this action to his family and others), whereas if he does not succeed then his action will not be rationally justified. Crucially, argues Williams, it can be a matter of luck that Gauguin's actions lead to success, and thus rational justification for one's actions can substantively depend upon luck. We will examine this claim in more detail in a moment. First, I want to dwell on just what is meant here by 'success'.

Williams is clear that not just any kind of failure will suffice to show that Gauguin's decision was unjustified. After all, as he points out:

if Gauguin sustains some injury on the way to Tahiti which prevents his ever painting again, that certainly means that his decision (supposing it now to be irreversible) was for nothing, and indeed there is nothing in the outcome to set against the other people's loss. But that train of events does not provoke the thought in question, that after all he was wrong and unjustified. He does not, and never will, know whether he was wrong. What would prove him wrong in his project would not just be that *it* failed, but that *he* failed. (Williams 1981*b*: 25, *italics mine*)

What is required for failure is thus some genuine test of Gauguin's choice which shows that he made the wrong decision, rather than merely an external obstacle preventing that choice from even being tested in the first place, and Williams's point is that luck can intervene even here. Williams does not give an example of luck that is, as he puts it, 'intrinsic' rather than 'extrinsic' to

Gauguin's project, though he does offer a different example regarding Tolstoy's fictional heroine Anna Karenina:

Anna remains conscious in her life with Vronsky of the cost exacted from others, above all from her son. She might have lived with that consciousness, we may suppose, if things had gone better, and relative to her state of understanding when she left Karenin, they could have gone better. As it turns out, the social situation and her own state of mind are such that the relationship with Vronsky has to carry too much weight, and the more obvious that becomes, the more it has to carry; and I take that to be a truth not only about society but about her and Vronsky, a truth which, however inevitable Tolstoy makes it seem, could, relative to her earlier thoughts, have been otherwise. It is, in the present terms, a matter of intrinsic luck, and a failure in the heart of her project. But its locus is not by any means entirely in her, for it also lies in him. (Williams 1981b: 26–7)

So whilst Anna and Vronsky's relationship was not scuppered by extrinsic luck—they were, for example, able to be together as they wished—it was nevertheless ultimately unsuccessful, and unsuccessful because of failings within them—in particular, as Williams puts it, part of the reason why the relationship did not work out was Anna's 'state of mind'. This example of intrinsic luck suggests that intrinsic failure in the case of Gauguin's project would consist in Gauguin arriving in Tahiti and having the chance to make a solid sustained attempt at his painting—unencumbered by extrinsic luck—but ending up with disappointing results nonetheless.

Crucially, however, the failure at issue here is not meant to reflect a *mistake* on Gauguin's part regarding his original assessment of his abilities, since we are meant to suppose that, like Anna, relative to his 'state of understanding' when he made his decision that decision was based on entirely epistemically justified grounds. Rather, the failure consists in something other than that, though intrinsic to the project nonetheless. Finding uncontroversial examples here is difficult (which is probably why Williams does not even try), but one possibility might be that what Gauguin eventually discovers in Tahiti, contrary to the information that he had to go on whilst back in Europe, is that his abilities were in fact dependent upon the stresses and hardships that life with his family brought him.

With the problem so construed, however, it is far from clear that there is a difficulty regarding *moral* luck here at all, since the concern about the moral status of actions seems to collapse into the issue of how luck can afflict the epistemic status of certain judgements that will be assessed retrospectively. That is, it collapses into the issue of how one can never, given the possibility of intrinsic luck, have the appropriate epistemic justification *in advance* to adequately rationally justify setting out on a project of this sort. Indeed,

Williams is aware of this, noting that even if Gauguin's project were to be rationally justified in the way that he imagines, this does not mean that Gauguin will thereby have 'any way of justifying himself to others, or at least to all others' (Williams 1981*b*: 23) and, plausibly, an ability to offer such a justification is constitutive of one's actions enjoying a positive moral status.[9] So even if one could evade the problem of intrinsic luck at issue here and recover one's rational justification, this need not have any effect on the moral status of one's actions (i.e. Gauguin's actions could rightly be regarded as immoral regardless of whether he is successful in his project). Accordingly, unlike the examples that Nagel offers, there is no clear reason for thinking that the presence of luck can affect the moral status of one's actions.

Furthermore, even the underlying epistemological problem that Williams alludes to is unclear. For let us suppose, for the sake of argument, that the beliefs upon which Gauguin's decision is made (his beliefs about what his artistic abilities are, for example), are all true and enjoy an adequate positive epistemic status which suffices to ensure that his decision is based on knowledge. The problem is that in so far as Gauguin really does know that he has the great talent that he thinks he has, and in so far as we exclude in advance the possibility of extrinsic luck so that his project is genuinely tested, then it is hard to see how he could possibly fail in this enterprise. Wouldn't failure in this regard simply indicate that he lacked the relevant knowledge after all? Put another way, to have one's projects frustrated by intrinsic luck alone seems to imply that the beliefs upon which that project was based were epistemically faulty in some way, and an ascription of knowledge to the propositions in question rules out this possibility.

So what then is the epistemic problem that Williams is focusing upon here? I think that we get an idea of what he has in mind in the following passage:

[T]here might be grounds for saying that the person who was prepared to take the decision, and was in fact right, actually knew that he would succeed. ... But even if this is right for some cases, it does not help with the problems of retrospective justification. For the concept of knowledge here is itself applied retrospectively, and while there is nothing wrong with that, it does not enable the agent at the time of his decision to make any distinctions that he could not already make. As one might say, even if it did turn out in such a case that the agent did know, it was still luck, relative to the considerations available to him at the time ... that he should turn out to have known. (1981*b*: 25–6)[10]

Reading between the lines here, one can take it that the 'considerations [that were] available to [Gauguin] at the time' he made his decision were those considerations that were reflectively accessible to him. Williams's point

264

therefore comes down to the claim that in terms of what the agent is able to know by reflection alone, it is a matter of luck that the agent knows that the decision in question is the right decision. That is, that no matter how good the reflectively accessible grounds are upon which an agent bases his decision, it will still be possible for a substantial degree of intrinsic luck to intervene such that his beliefs, though well founded, were not knowledge after all (and thus that his decision was not rationally justified).

Williams thus seems to have the specific problem of reflective epistemic luck in mind. The epistemic worry that Williams is giving expression to appears to concern how no matter what the pedigree is of the reflectively accessible grounds that, say, Gauguin can adduce when making his life-changing decision to abandon his family, it will remain that his belief that he will succeed will be luckily true, if true at all. Given the account of reflective epistemic luck that we have offered here, this means that the problem with Gauguin's belief that he will succeed is that, even if it turns out to be true, it will nevertheless be the case that there will be a wide class of nearby possible worlds—where those worlds are ordered solely in terms of what he knows by reflection alone—in which this belief is false.

Interestingly, on the issue of whether or not this reflective epistemic luck should undermine the possibility of his knowing that he will succeed, Williams is ambivalent. He notes that there 'might be grounds for saying that the person who was prepared to take the decision, and was in fact right, actually knew that he would succeed', and then further remarks that 'even if it did turn out in such a case that the agent did know, it was still luck, relative to the considerations available to him at the time...that he should turn out to have known' (Williams 1981*b*: 25–6). Williams thus does not definitively take sides on the issue of whether the elimination of reflective epistemic luck is necessary for knowledge, and thus, given only his remarks in this paper, his position does not come down on either side of the epistemic externalism–internalism distinction.

Nevertheless, it should be clear from how Williams puts matters in this way that it must be reflective epistemic luck that is at issue, since the point seems to be that from the agent's point of view at the time that he made the decision he has, perforce, insufficient reflectively accessible grounds in support of his belief to exclude luck, even though, provided he does indeed meet the relevant external epistemic conditions, then he may well have such knowledge (at least by the lights of an externalist account of knowledge). The ambivalence thus relates to the possibility of taking two different viewpoints as regards the knowledge in question—one which is 'internal' and only takes into account what the agent has reflective access to; and one which is 'external' and takes other relevant facts (such as whether or not his belief is safe) into account.

Clearly these two viewpoints will roughly map onto our distinction between reflective and veritic epistemic luck, in that in the former case the possible worlds are ordered 'internally' in terms of only what the agent can know by reflection alone rather than in terms of the actual facts of the situation. Williams's point is thus that whether or not the agent in the case that he imagines knows that he will succeed is subject to reflective epistemic luck.

There is clearly something right about Williams's claim here, but it will not do as it currently stands. The reason for this is that the kind of reflectively accessible grounds that the agent has *will* suffice to eliminate reflective epistemic luck in any substantive degree from his knowledge, at least in so far as such reflective luck is ever eliminable. Compare, for example, Gauguin's belief that he will succeed with that of the enlightened chicken-sexer. Just as the enlightened chicken-sexer, unlike her naïve counterpart, evades the problem posed by reflective epistemic luck by having excellent reflectively accessible grounds in favour of her belief, so the same should be true of Gauguin in the example that Williams offers. If he does really have the supporting grounds in question, and his belief ends up being true, then the nearby possible worlds on the 'reflective' ordering should be such that in most of them he continues to form a true belief (in the same way as in the actual world) about whether or not he succeeds. Of course, his belief might not be knowledge because it is not safe (or not, in the actual world, true), but that is to take it out of the market for knowledge altogether, by the lights of an externalist *or* an internalist theory of knowledge. So what then is the problem that Williams is giving expression to here?

I think that the answer lies in the fact that, as we saw in §8.1, we only count the enlightened chicken-sexer as eliminating reflective epistemic luck from her beliefs because we are implicitly bracketing the sceptical possibility that her reflectively accessible grounds might bear no relation to the world *whatsoever*. Imagine, for example, that the enlightened chicken-sexer was, unbeknown to her, a BIV being 'fed' her experiences by neuroscientists. Clearly in this case the reflectively accessible grounds that she has in favour of her beliefs are wholly unreliable since they are in no way indicative of the truth. Provided that we do not 'factor-out' such sceptical scenarios, however, then the ordering of the possible worlds that only takes into account the agent's reflective knowledge will include a wide class of nearby possible worlds in which the agent is the victim of a sceptical scenario since, as the sceptic famously points out, we do not have any adequate reflectively accessible grounds for thinking that we are not the victim of a sceptical hypothesis. Accordingly, her beliefs—even when well supported by reflectively accessible grounds—cannot help but be subject to reflective epistemic luck to a substantive degree.

The same goes for Gauguin. Unless we exclude the sceptical scenarios from our calculations of how the possible worlds should be ordered given only what he knows by reflection alone, then there will be a wide class of nearby possible worlds in which he forms his belief in the same way as in the actual world and yet forms a false belief as a result because he is the victim of a sceptical error-possibility (e.g. he is a BIV who has been tricked into thinking that he has the abilities that he took himself to have).

The crucial point for our purposes is that the problem that Williams raises as regards Gauguin makes no mention of the problem of scepticism at all. Accordingly, it is odd to discover that one can only make sense of that problem by understanding it in the light of sceptical concerns. It seems, then, that Williams not only (perhaps intentionally) fails to distinguish between the problem of moral luck and the analogue problem of epistemic luck, but that he also (seemingly unintentionally) fails to recognize that the problem of epistemic luck that he raises (in so far as we can make sense of it at all) is really the very specific issue about epistemic luck highlighted by the sceptic.

10.3. Nagel on Epistemic Luck and Scepticism

A closer inspection of Nagel's paper on moral luck further reveals how his argument for the existence of moral luck, like Williams's, in fact implicitly draws on the problem of epistemic luck and, in particular, the specific problem of reflective epistemic luck identified by the sceptic. For example, at one point in the paper Nagel argues that the problem of moral luck

resembles the situation in another area of philosophy, the theory of knowledge. There too conditions which seem perfectly natural, and which grow out of the ordinary procedures for challenging and defending claims to knowledge, threaten to undermine all such claims if consistently applied. Most sceptical arguments have this quality: they do not depend on the imposition of arbitrarily stringent standards of knowledge, arrived at by misunderstanding, but appear to grow inevitably from the consistent application of ordinary standards. There is a substantive parallel as well, for epistemo-logical scepticism arises from consideration of the respects in which our beliefs and their relation to reality depends on factors beyond our control. External and internal causes produce our beliefs. We may subject these processes to scrutiny in an effort to avoid error, but our conclusions at the next level also result, in part, from influences which we do not control directly. The same will be true no matter how far we carry the investigation. Our beliefs are, ultimately, due to factors outside of our control, and the impossibility of encompassing those factors without being at the mercy of others

Epistemic Luck

leads us to doubt whether we know anything. It looks as though if any of our beliefs are true, it is pure biological luck rather than knowledge. (1979: 26–7)

Two points are primarily significant here. The first is the dialectical observation that the remarks in this passage are being used to *motivate* the examples of moral luck that are subsequently offered, which implies that it is the phenomenon of epistemic luck that possesses the greater intuitive force. Moreover, unlike Williams, Nagel is in this quotation explicitly identifying the problem of epistemic luck with the specific version of that problem raised by the sceptic. Thus, it is not the problem of epistemic luck *simpliciter* that is meant to be motivating his further (and as we saw above, erroneous) contentions regarding moral luck, but rather the particular sceptical use of this problem.

The second point to note is that the initial focus in this passage is on knowledge *claims*, as if what one knows one can, at least typically, properly claim to know. As we have seen at various junctures in this book, to put the emphasis on knowledge claims in this way is to thereby focus on knowledge of a very specific sort—knowledge where the agent has met an internal epistemic condition. The reason for this is that the kind of 'brute' knowledge allowed by the externalist where the agent has no (or hardly any) reflectively accessible grounds in support of her beliefs will not be of a sort to allow the agent to properly claim that knowledge (think, for example, of the naïve chicken-sexer in this respect). This is because a claim to know is only conversationally appropriate if (*inter alia*) the agent concerned can offer adequate supporting grounds and brute knowers precisely lack such supporting grounds for their beliefs. All parties to the epistemological externalism–internalism dispute should thus be willing to grant that, *ceteris paribus* of course, meeting an internal epistemic condition is essential if one is to be in a position to properly claim knowledge. That Nagel views the problematic form of epistemic luck as undermining the propriety of knowledge claims thus indicates that it is a specifically reflective variety of epistemic luck that he has in mind.

Indeed, Nagel's remarks about 'lack of control' and the 'internal' and 'external' determinants of belief in this passage would seem to suggest that there are factors that are relevant to the epistemic status of an agent's beliefs but which are not reflectively knowable by the agent. That is, that the factors relevant to knowledge that we are able to control—the 'internal' and thus, we might suppose, reflectively knowable factors—will not suffice to determine whether or not we do in fact have knowledge. Instead, external factors (and thus non-reflectively knowable) factors will also be relevant. Nagel's point thus appears to be on a par with Williams's, in that he is contending that, in terms of the 'internal' reflectively accessible grounds possessed by the agent alone, it is a matter of reflective epistemic luck that his belief is true.[11]

In later works, where Nagel is explicitly dealing with the problem of scepticism rather than the problem of moral luck, he is much clearer about what this issue regarding reflective epistemic luck amounts to. He argues that objectivity involves attaining a completely impartial view of reality, one that is not tainted by any particular perspective. We aspire, he contends, to 'get outside of ourselves', and thereby achieve the impossible task of being able to 'view the world from nowhere from within it' (Nagel 1986: 76). We realize that the initial appearances present to a viewpoint can be unreliable guides to reality and therefore seek to modify our 'subjective' view with a more 'objective' perspective that is tempered by reason and reflection. As Nagel points out, however, the trouble with this approach is that

if initial appearances are not in themselves reliable guides to reality, [then] why should the products of detached reflection be any different? Why aren't they . . . equally doubtful . . . ? . . . The same ideas that make the pursuit of objectivity seem necessary for knowledge make both objectivity and knowledge seem, on reflection, unattainable. (1986: 76)

Of course, what Nagel means by 'perspective' here essentially involves what the agent is able to know by reflection alone—i.e. our reflectively accessible grounds for believing what we do—which means that the problem he poses is that our demand for objectivity imposes a requirement that, in the best case at least, what we are able to know by reflection alone will entail that the world is the way we take it to be. Such a requirement cannot be met, however, since our reflectively accessible grounds are always going to be consistent with the truth of a sceptical scenario. Nagel thus draws the pessimistic conclusion that the problem of scepticism 'has no solution, but to recognize that is to come as near as we can to living in the light of truth' (Nagel 1986: 231). We are therefore back to the problem of reflective epistemic luck posed by the sceptic.

It is important to note that if Nagel understands the problem of scepticism as being the problem of the possibility of knowledge *simpliciter*, then this conclusion goes much further than that advanced by Williams. As we saw above, Williams merely presents a problem for our ordinary understanding of knowledge, in that the 'knowledge' that we putatively possess turns out to be subject to a significant degree of reflective epistemic luck. Nagel, however, is here drawing the stronger sceptical conclusion from this observation—that since knowledge is incompatible with reflective epistemic luck, so we must lack the knowledge we take ourselves to have after all. In effect, Nagel is endorsing a form of epistemological internalism which demands the complete elimination of reflective epistemic luck and therefore concluding, since such a complete elimination is impossible, that the genuine possession of knowledge is impossible also.

In any case, what is important to the present discussion is that it is a certain conception of the sceptical problem that is motivating Nagel's general concerns about epistemic luck which, in turn, are being used to motivate the putative problem of moral luck. If one takes away the underlying problem regarding epistemic luck—specifically, regarding *reflective* epistemic luck—then the problem of moral luck disappears with it.[12]

10.4. Concluding Remarks

Ultimately, both Williams and Nagel implicitly motivate their examples regarding moral luck—examples which we have found to be on reflection inconclusive—via an appeal to the sceptical problem of reflective epistemic luck. The immediate import of this observation is that the problem of moral luck identified by Williams and Nagel, in so far as they identify a difficulty at all, is not what they take the problem to be. By being clear about the true nature of the sceptical challenge we are thus able to cast light on debates that are outside epistemology. Indeed, the fact that it is the specific sceptical quandary regarding reflective epistemic luck that is being used to motivate the problem of moral luck further reinforces the claim made earlier that such scepticism is without a solution (without an *epistemic* solution, at any rate).

The secondary import of this observation is that the epistemological sceptical problem regarding reflective epistemic luck poses a general existential difficulty that has not only an abstract impact on our doxastic practices but also a concrete effect by undermining our ability to fully legitimate the life-changing courses of actions that we opt for. This highlights the sense in which the problem of scepticism is an *ethical* problem, in the broad sense of that term, a conclusion which, whilst familiar to the classical sceptics (such as the Pyrrhonians), is not so familiar to the contemporary philosophical mind-set. In general, the sceptical worry that this form of luck presents us with concerns our inability to take a robust form of cognitive responsibility for our beliefs and, as this discussion of the problem of moral luck has shown, this has ramifications which extend beyond the realm of epistemology.

Notes

1. These papers were subsequently reprinted (in a slightly altered form) as Nagel (1979) and Williams (1981*b*), and it is these versions of the papers—which have each been reprinted since in a number of different anthologies—that I shall focus upon here.
2. That said, in a very recent article by Latus (2003) one does find the beginnings of a discussion of this sort, one that is focused on the specific issue of constitutive luck (see note 5 below for a definition). For some of the key discussions of the exchange between Williams and Nagel, see the papers collected in the anthology edited by Statman (1993*b*).
3. Nagel actually begins the article by simply talking about a morally lucky reckless driver, without specifying that the recklessness in question has anything to do with drink. Later on, however, he specifically mentions an example of a reckless driver who is drunk. For convenience, rather than take these as two different examples, I will simply regard them as one example where the recklessness is in both cases due to drink.
4. For examples of responses along these general lines, see Jensen (1984), Rescher (1993), Richards (1993), and Thomson (1993). For discussion specifically on the relationship between moral luck and punishment, see Browne (1992) and Duff (1996: ch. 12).
5. Nagel also distinguishes these two types of luck in turn from what he terms 'causal' and 'constitutive' luck. These are, respectively, 'luck in how one is determined by antecedent circumstances' and the luck involved in a person's having the 'inclinations, capacities and temperament' that he does (Nagel 1979: 27). For the sake of brevity I will not be extending this discussion to cover examples of these kinds of luck here, although I do think that it can be applied. In any case, much of the focus of Nagel's article is on resultant and circumstantial luck.
6. Both Rescher (1993) and Richards (1993) argue that all that cases of moral luck highlight is merely an epistemic lack on our part regarding what the appropriate moral judgement of someone's actions should be. That is, as Statman (1993*a*: 17) expresses the point, 'luck does not affect one's *deserts* but only our *knowledge* of them.' See also Zimmerman (1987).
7. Nagel begins his article by discussing cases like the drunk-driver example, and then moves on to consider examples of circumstantial luck like the example of the German expatriate.
8. Williams wouldn't put the point in these terms, of course, since his ultimate goal is to deflate the three-way distinction between the moral, the ethical, and the practically rational. For more on this point, see Williams (1981*a*, 1993).
9. Elsewhere in the paper Williams describes the Kantian view that he is opposed to as demanding that in terms of 'the agent's reflective assessment of his own actions . . . it cannot be a matter of luck whether he was justified in doing what he did' (Williams 1981*b*: 23).
10. The reader should note that I've deleted a *caveat* from this quotation that might be thought to be significant. This is where Williams notes that the successful agent might have known that he would have succeeded 'however subjectively uncertain he may have been' at the time. I've removed this phrase since it ought not to be relevant to the case in hand. If Williams is right, then it should be possible to construct a Gauguin-type example where it is explicitly stipulated that the agent is subjectively certain of the correctness of his decision. The *caveat* thus only serves to add a complication to the proceedings that is irrelevant to the main thrust of the argument.
11. This interpretation of Nagel is further confirmed once one considers the famous example that Nagel mentions in a footnote to back up his points about epistemic luck where he

notes that 'the Nobel Prize is not awarded to people who turn out to be wrong, no matter how brilliant their reasoning' (Nagel 1979: 183–4). The implication of this remark is that what the agent is in control of extends only so far as meeting the relevant internal conditions—such as ensuring that her reasoning is as impeccable as it can be—but that what ultimately determines knowledge (and thus enables one to be in the market for a Nobel Prize) goes beyond this to implicate external factors such as (primarily) whether or not the belief in question is true. That said, it should also be noted that Nagel (1979: *passim*) doesn't think we have complete control over the 'internal' realm either, so the distinction here is clearly going to be one of degree rather than kind.

12. I offer an extended discussion of the supposed problem of moral luck posed by Nagel and Williams in Pritchard (2004*c*).

Bibliography

Annas, J., and Barnes, J. (eds.) (1985). *The Modes of Scepticism: Ancient Texts and Modern Interpretations*. Cambridge: Cambridge University Press.

Annis, D. B. (1978). 'A Contextualist Theory of Justification', *American Philosophical Quarterly* 15: 213–19.

Armstrong, D. M. (1973). *Belief, Truth and Knowledge*. Cambridge: Cambridge University Press.

Austin, J. L. (1961). 'Other Minds', in his *Philosophical Papers*, ed. J. O. Urmson and G. J. Warnock. Oxford: Clarendon Press.

Axtell, G. (1997). 'Recent Work on Virtue Epistemology', *American Philosophical Quarterly* 34: 1–26.

—— (2000). *Knowledge, Belief, and Character: Readings in Virtue Epistemology*. Lanham, Md.: Roman & Littlefield.

—— (2001). 'Epistemic Luck in Light of the Virtues', in *Virtue Epistemology: Essays on Epistemic Virtue and Responsibility*, ed. A. Fairweather and L. Zagzebski. Oxford: Oxford University Press.

—— (2003). '*Felix Culpa*: Luck in Ethics and Epistemology', *Metaphilosophy* 34: 331–52; and reprinted in Brady and Pritchard (2003).

Ayer, A. J. (1956). *The Problem of Knowledge*. Harmondsworth: Pelican.

Bach, K. (2004). 'The Emperor's New "Knows"', in *Contextualism in Philosophy: On Epistemology, Language and Truth*, ed. G. Preyer and G. Peter. Oxford: Oxford University Press.

Bailey, A. (2002). *Sextus Empiricus and Pyrrhonian Scepticism*. Oxford: Clarendon Press.

Barnes, J. (1982). 'The Beliefs of a Pyrrhonist', *Proceedings of the Cambridge Philological Society* 208: 1–29.

Black, T. (2002). 'A Moorean Response to Brain-In-A-Vat Scepticism', *Australasian Journal of Philosophy* 80: 148–63.

—— (2003). 'Contextualism in Epistemology', *Internet Encyclopædia of Philosophy*, www.iep.utm.edu/c/contextu.htm.

BonJour, L. (1985). *The Structure of Empirical Knowledge*. Cambridge, Mass.: Harvard University Press.

—— (1987). 'Nozick, Externalism, and Skepticism', in *The Possibility of Knowledge: Nozick and his Critics*, ed. S. Luper-Foy. Totowa, NJ: Rowman & Littlefield.

BonJour, L., and Sosa, E. (2003). *Epistemic Justification: Internalism vs. Externalism, Foundations vs. Virtues*. Oxford: Blackwell.

Bibliography

Brady, M. S., and Pritchard, D. H. (eds.) (2003). *Moral and Epistemic Virtues*. Oxford: Blackwell.

Brandom, R. (1994). *Making It Explicit*. Cambridge, Mass.: Harvard University Press.

—— (1995). 'Knowledge and the Social Articulation of the Space of Reasons', *Philosophy and Phenomenological Research* 55: 895–908.

—— (1998). 'Insights and Blindspots of Reliabilism', *The Monist* 81: 371–92.

Brown, J. (2005). 'Adapt or Die: The Death of Invariantism?', *Philosophical Quarterly* 55: 37–52.

Browne, B. (1992). 'A Solution to the Problem of Moral Luck', *Philosophical Quarterly* 42: 345–56.

Brueckner, A. (1991). 'Unfair to Nozick', *Analysis* 51: 61–4.

—— (1992). 'Semantic Answers to Skepticism', *Pacific Philosophical Quarterly* 73: 200–19.

—— (1994). 'The Structure of the Skeptical Argument', *Philosophy and Phenomenological Research* 54: 827–35.

—— (2004). 'The Elusive Virtues of Contextualism', *Philosophical Studies* 118: 401–5.

Burnyeat, M. (1980). 'Can the Sceptic Live His Scepticism?', in *Doubt and Dogmatism: Studies in Hellenistic Epistemology*, ed. J. Barnes, M. Burnyeat, and M. Schofield. Oxford: Clarendon Press.

—— (1982). 'Idealism and Greek Philosophy: What Descartes Saw and Berkeley Missed', *Philosophical Review* 40: 3–40.

—— (ed.) (1983). *The Skeptical Tradition*. Berkeley, Calif.: University of California Press.

—— (1984). 'The Sceptic in his Place and Time', in *Philosophy in History: Essays on the Historiography of Philosophy*, ed. R. Rorty, J. B. Schneewind, and Q. Skinner. Cambridge: Cambridge University Press.

Card, C. (1990). 'Gender and Moral Luck', in *Identity, Character, and Morality*, ed. O. Flanagan and A. Rorty. Cambridge, Mass.: MIT Press.

Cavell, S. (1979). *The Claim of Reason: Wittgenstein, Skepticism, Morality and Tragedy*. New York: Oxford University Press.

Chisholm, R. (1989). *Theory of Knowledge*, 3rd edn., Englewood Cliffs, NJ: Prentice-Hall.

Christensen, D. (1993). 'Skeptical Problems, Semantical Solutions', *Philosophy and Phenomenological Research* 53: 301–21.

Code, L. (1984). 'Toward a "Responsibilist" Epistemology', *Philosophy and Phenomenological Research* 44: 29–50.

—— (1987). *Epistemic Responsibility*. Hanover, NH: University Press of New England.

Cohen, S. (1998*a*). 'Contextualist Solutions to Epistemological Problems: Scepticism, Gettier, and the Lottery', *Australasian Journal of Philosophy* 76: 289–306.

—— (1998*b*). 'Two Kinds of Skeptical Argument', *Philosophy and Phenomenological Research* 58: 143–59.

—— (1999). 'Contextualism, Skepticism, and the Structure of Reasons', *Philosophical Perspectives* 13: 57–90.

—— (2000). 'Contextualism and Skepticism', *Philosophical Issues* 10: 94–107.

—— (2002). 'Basic Knowledge and the Problem of Easy Knowledge', *Philosophy and Phenomenological Research* 64: 309–29.

Conant, J. (1998). 'Wittgenstein on Meaning and Use', *Philosophical Investigations* 21: 222–50.

Conee, E., and Feldman, R. (1998). 'The Generality Problem for Reliabilism', *Philosophical Studies* 89: 1–29.

Craig, E. (1989). 'Nozick and the Sceptic: The Thumbnail Version', *Analysis* 49: 161–2.

—— (1990*a*). 'Davidson and the Sceptic: The Thumbnail Version', *Analysis* 50: 213–14.

—— (1990*b*). *Knowledge and the State of Nature: An Essay in Conceptual Synthesis*. Oxford: Clarendon Press.

Dancy, J. (1985). *Introduction to Contemporary Epistemology*. Oxford: Blackwell.

Davidson, D. (1986). 'A Coherence Theory of Truth and Knowledge', in *Truth and Interpretation: Perspectives on the Philosophy of Donald Davidson*, ed. E. LePore. Oxford: Blackwell.

Davies, M. (1998). 'Externalism, Architecturalism, and Epistemic Warrant', in *Knowing Our Own Minds: Essays on Self-Knowledge*, ed. C. J. G. Wright, B. C. Smith, and C. Macdonald. Oxford: Oxford University Press.

—— (2000). 'Externalism and Armchair Knowledge', in *New Essays on the A Priori*, ed. P. Boghossian and C. Peacocke. Oxford: Oxford University Press.

—— (2003). 'The Problem of Armchair Knowledge', in *New Essays on Semantic Externalism and Self-Knowledge*, ed. S. Nuccetelli. Cambridge, Mass.: MIT Press.

—— (2004). 'Epistemic Entitlement, Warrant Transmission and Easy Knowledge', *Proceedings of the Aristotelian Society* 78 (supp. vol.): 213–45.

Dennett, D. (1984). *Elbow Room: The Varieties of Free Will Worth Wanting*. Cambridge, Mass.: MIT Press.

DePaul, M., and Zagzebski, L. ed. (2002). *Intellectual Virtue: Perspectives from Ethics and Epistemology*. Oxford: Oxford University Press.

DeRose, K. (1995). 'Solving the Skeptical Problem', *Philosophical Review* 104: 1–52.

—— (1996). 'Knowledge, Assertion and Lotteries', *Australasian Journal of Philosophy* 74: 568–80.

—— (1999). 'Contextualism: An Explanation and Defence', in *Epistemology*, ed. J. Greco and E. Sosa. Oxford: Blackwell.

—— (2000). 'How Can We Know that We're Not Brains in Vats?', *Southern Journal of Philosophy* 38: 121–48.

—— (2002*a*). 'Knowledge, Assertion, and Context', *Philosophical Review* 111: 167–203.

—— (2002*b*). 'Sosa, Safety, Sensitivity, and Skeptical Hypotheses', in *Sosa and His Critics*, ed. J. Greco. Oxford: Blackwell.

DeRose, K., and Grandy, R. (1999). 'Conditional Assertions and 'Biscuit' Conditionals', *Noûs* 33: 405–20.

Descartes, R. (1984). *The Philosophical Writings of Descartes* (vol. 2), tr. J. Cottingham, R. Stoothoff and D. Murdoch. Cambridge: Cambridge University Press.

Bibliography

Diogenes Laertius. (1925). *Lives of the Philosophers* (2 vols.), tr. R. D. Hicks. London: Heinemann.

Dretske, F. (1970). 'Epistemic Operators', *Journal of Philosophy* 67: 1007–23.

—— (1971). 'Conclusive Reasons', *Australasian Journal of Philosophy* 49: 1–22.

—— (1981). *Knowledge and the Flow of Information*. Oxford: Blackwell.

—— (1983). 'The Epistemology of Belief', *Synthese* 55: 3–19.

Duff, R. A. (1996). *Criminal Attempts*. Oxford: Clarendon Press.

Engel, M. (1992). 'Is Epistemic Luck Compatible with Knowledge?', *Southern Journal of Philosophy* 30: 59–75.

Fairweather, A., and Zagzebski, L. (eds.) (2001). *Virtue Epistemology: Essays on Epistemic Virtue and Responsibility*. Oxford: Oxford University Press.

Fogelin, R. (1994). *Pyrrhonian Reflections on Knowledge and Justification*. Oxford: Oxford University Press.

Foley, R. (1984). 'Epistemic Luck and the Purely Epistemic', *American Philosophical Quarterly* 21: 113–24.

—— (1987). *A Theory of Epistemic Rationality*. Cambridge, Mass.: Harvard University Press.

Frede, M. (1987a). 'The Skeptic's Beliefs', in his *Essays in Ancient Philosophy*. Minneapolis, MN: University of Minnesota Press.

—— (1987b). 'The Sceptic's Two Kinds of Assent and the Question of the Possibility of Knowledge', in his *Essays in Ancient Philosophy*. Minneapolis, MN: University of Minnesota Press.

Fumerton, R. (1990). 'Metaepistemology and Skepticism', in *Doubting: Contemporary Perspectives on Skepticism*, ed. M. D. Roth and G. Ross. Dordrecht, Holland: Kluwer.

—— (1995). *Metaepistemology and Skepticism*. Lanham, Md.: Rowman & Littlefield.

Gaukroger, S. (1995). 'The Ten Modes of Aenesidemus and the Myth of Ancient Scepticism', *British Journal for the History of Philosophy* 3: 371–87.

Gettier, E. (1963). 'Is Justified True Belief Knowledge?', *Analysis* 23: 121–3.

Gjelsvik, O. (1991). 'Dretske on Knowledge and Content', *Synthese* 86: 425–41.

Goldman, A. (1976). 'Discrimination and Perceptual Knowledge', *Journal of Philosophy* 73: 771–91.

—— (1979). 'What is Justified Belief?', in *Justification and Knowledge*, ed. G. S. Pappas. Dordrecht, Holland: D. Reidel.

—— (1986). *Epistemology and Cognition*. Cambridge, Mass.: Harvard University Press.

—— (1988). 'Strong and Weak Justification', *Philosophical Perspectives* 2: 51–69.

—— (1993). 'Epistemic Folkways and Scientific Epistemology', *Philosophical Issues* 3: 271–84.

Greco, J. (1993). 'Virtues and Vices of Virtue Epistemology', *Canadian Journal of Philosophy* 23: 413–32.

—— (1995). 'A Second Paradox Concerning Responsibility and Luck', *Metaphilosophy* 26: 81–96.

—— (1999). 'Agent Reliabilism', *Philosophical Perspectives* 13: 273–96.

—— (2000). *Putting Skeptics in Their Place: The Nature of Skeptical Arguments and Their Role in Philosophical Inquiry*. Cambridge: Cambridge University Press.

—— (2002). 'Knowledge as Credit for True Belief', in *Intellectual Virtue: Perspectives from Ethics and Epistemology*, ed. M. DePaul and L. Zagzebski. Oxford: Oxford University Press.

—— (2003). 'Virtue and Luck, Epistemic and Otherwise', *Metaphilosophy* 34: 353–66; and repr. in Brady and Pritchard (2003).

—— (2004). 'Externalism and Skepticism', in *The Externalist Challenge: New Studies on Cognition and Intentionality*, ed. R. Shantz. New York: de Gruyter.

Greene, R., and Blamert, N. A. (1997). 'Two Notions of Warrant and Plantinga's Solution to the Gettier Problem', *Analysis* 57: 31–6.

Grice, H. P. (1989). *Studies in the Way of Words*. Cambridge, Mass.: Harvard University Press.

Grimm, S. (2001). 'Ernest Sosa, Knowledge and Understanding', *Philosophical Studies* 106: 171–91.

Hall, B. J. (1994). 'On Epistemic Luck', *Southern Journal of Philosophy* 32: 79–84.

Harman, G. (1973). *Thought*. Princeton, NJ: Princeton University Press.

Harper, W. (1996). 'Knowledge and Luck', *Southern Journal of Philosophy* 34: 273–83.

Hawthorne, J. (2004). *Knowledge and Lotteries*. Oxford: Oxford University Press.

Heller, M. (1999*a*). 'Relevant Alternatives and Closure', *Australasian Journal of Philosophy* 77: 196–208.

—— (1999*b*). 'The Proper Role for Contextualism in an Anti-Luck Epistemology', *Philosophical Perspectives* 13: 115–30.

Hetherington, S. (1998). 'Actually Knowing', *Philosophical Quarterly* 48: 453–69.

Hookway, C. (1994). 'Cognitive Virtues and Epistemic Evaluations', *International Journal of Philosophical Studies* 2: 211–27.

Jensen, H. (1984). 'Morality and Luck', *Philosophy* 59: 323–30.

Jones, W. (1997). 'Why Do We Value Knowledge?', *American Philosophical Quarterly* 34: 423–40.

Klein, P. (1981). *Certainty: A Refutation of Scepticism*. Minneapolis, MN: University of Minnesota Press.

—— (1986). 'Radical Interpretation and Global Skepticism', in *Truth and Interpretation: Perspectives on the Philosophy of Donald Davidson*, ed. E. LePore. Oxford: Blackwell.

—— (1987). 'On Behalf of the Skeptic', in *The Possibility of Knowledge*, ed. S. Luper-Foy. Totowa, NJ: Rowman & Littlefield.

—— (1995). 'Skepticism and Closure: Why the Evil Genius Argument Fails', *Philosophical Topics* 23: 213–36.

—— (1998). 'Foundationalism and the Infinite Regress', *Philosophy and Phenomenological Research* 58: 919–26.

—— (2003). 'How a Pyrrhonian Skeptic Might Respond to Academic Skepticism', in *The Skeptics: Contemporary Essays*, ed. S. Luper. Aldershot, UK: Ashgate.

Bibliography

Kornblith, H. (ed.) (2001). *Epistemology: Internalism and Externalism*. Oxford: Blackwell.

Kvanvig, J. (1992). *The Intellectual Virtues and the Life of the Mind: On the Place of the Virtues in Contemporary Epistemology*. Savage, Md.: Rowman & Littlefield.

—— (1998). 'Why Should Inquiring Minds Want to Know?', *The Monist* 81: 426–51.

—— (2003). *The Value of Knowledge and the Pursuit of Understanding*. Cambridge: Cambridge University Press.

—— (2004). 'Nozickian Epistemology and the Value of Knowledge', *Philosophical Issues* 14.

Latus, A. (2000). 'Moral and Epistemic Luck', *Journal of Philosophical Research* 25: 149–72.

—— (2003). 'Constitutive Luck', *Metaphilosophy* 34: 460–75.

Lehrer, K., and Paxson, T. (1969). 'Knowledge: Undefeated Justified True Belief', *Journal of Philosophy* 66: 225–37.

Lewis, D. (1979). 'Scorekeeping in a Language Game', *Journal of Philosophical Logic* 8: 339–59.

—— (1996). 'Elusive Knowledge', *Australasian Journal of Philosophy* 74: 549–67.

Loux, M. (ed.) (1979). *The Possible and the Actual*. Ithaca, NJ: Cornell University Press.

Macarthur, D. (2003). 'McDowell, Scepticism, and the "Veil of Perception"', *Australasian Journal of Philosophy* 81: 175–90.

McDowell, J. (1982). 'Criteria, Defeasibility, and Knowledge', *Proceedings of the British Academy* 68: 455–79.

—— (1986). 'Singular Thought and the Extent of Inner Space', in *Subject, Thought, and Context*, ed. P. Pettit and J. McDowell. Oxford: Clarendon Press.

—— (1994*a*). 'Knowledge by Hearsay', in *Knowing from Words: Western and Indian Philosophical Analysis of Understanding and Testimony*, ed. B. K. Matilal and A. Chakrabarti. Dordrecht, Holland: Kluwer.

—— (1994*b*). *Mind and World*. Cambridge, Mass.: Harvard University Press.

—— (1995). 'Knowledge and the Internal', *Philosophy and Phenomenological Research* 55: 877–93.

—— (2002). 'Knowledge and the Internal Revisited', *Philosophy and Phenomenological Research* 64: 22–30.

McGinn, M. (1989). *Sense and Certainty: A Dissolution of Scepticism*. Oxford: Blackwell.

—— (2002). 'What Kind of Senselessness is This? A Reply to Conant on Wittgenstein's Critique of Moore', in *Scepticism and Interpretation*, ed. J. Conant and A. Kern. Stanford, Calif.: Stanford University Press.

Merricks, T. (1995). 'Warrant Entails Truth', *Philosophical and Phenomenological Research* 55: 841–55.

—— (1997). 'More on Warrant's Entailing Truth', *Philosophy and Phenomenological Research* 57: 627–31.

Montmarquet, J. (1987). 'Epistemic Virtue', *Mind* 96: 487–97.

—— (1993). *Epistemic Virtue and Doxastic Responsibility*. Lanham, Md.: Rowman & Littlefield.

Moore, G. E. (1925). 'A Defence of Common Sense', in *Contemporary British Philosophy* (2nd series), ed. J. H. Muirhead. London: Allen & Unwin.

—— (1939). 'Proof of an External World', *Proceedings of the British Academy* 25: 273–300.

—— (1959). 'Certainty', in his *Philosophical Papers*. London: Allen & Unwin.

Moore, A. W. (1990). 'A Kantian View of Moral Luck', *Philosophy* 65: 297–321.

Morawetz, T. (1979). *Wittgenstein & Knowledge: The Importance of On Certainty.* Cambridge, Mass.: Harvester.

Morillo, C. R. (1984). 'Epistemic Luck, Naturalistic Epistemology, and the Ecology of Knowledge', *Philosophical Studies* 46: 109–29.

Moyal-Sharrock, D. (2004). *Understanding Wittgenstein's On Certainty*. London: Palgrave Macmillan.

Nagel, T. (1976). 'Moral Luck', *Proceedings of the Aristotelian Society* (supp. vol.) 76: 136–50.

—— (1979). 'Moral Luck', in his *Mortal Questions*. Cambridge: Cambridge University Press.

—— (1986). *The View from Nowhere*. Oxford: Oxford University Press.

Neta, R. (2002). 'S Knows that P', *Noûs* 36: 663–81.

—— (2003). 'Contextualism and the Problem of the External World', *Philosophy and Phenomenological Research* 63.

Norman, A. P. (1999). 'Contextualism: Its Past, Present, and Prospects', *Philosophia* 27: 1–28.

Nozick, R. (1981). *Philosophical Explanations*. Oxford: Oxford University Press.

Nuccetelli, S. (ed.) (2003). *New Essays on Semantic Externalism and Self-Knowledge.* Cambridge, Mass.: MIT Press.

Percival, P. (2003). 'The Pursuit of Epistemic Good', *Metaphilosophy* 34: 29–47; and repr. in Brady and Pritchard (2003).

Plantinga, A. (1988). 'Positive Epistemic Status and Proper Function', *Philosophical Perspectives* 2: 1–50.

—— (1993*a*). *Warrant: The Current Debate*. New York: Oxford University Press.

—— (1993*b*). *Warrant and Proper Function*. New York: Oxford University Press.

—— (1993*c*). 'Why We Need Proper Function', *Noûs* 27: 66–82.

—— (1997). 'Warrant and Accidentally True Belief', *Analysis* 57: 36–40.

Pritchard, D. H. (2000*a*). 'Closure and Context', *Australasian Journal of Philosophy* 78: 275–80.

—— (2000*b*). 'Doubt Undogmatized: Pyrrhonian Scepticism, Epistemological Externalism, and the 'Metaepistemological' Challenge', *Principia—Revista Internacional de Epistemologia* 4: 187–218.

—— (2000*c*). 'Is "God Exists" a "Hinge" Proposition of Religious Belief?', *International Journal for Philosophy of Religion* 4: 187–214.

—— (2000*d*). 'Understanding Scepticism', *Sats—Nordic Journal of Philosophy* 1: 107–24.

—— (2001*a*). 'Contextualism, Scepticism, and the Problem of Epistemic Descent', *Dialectica* 55: 327–49.

Bibliography

Pritchard, D. H. (2001*b*). 'Meta-Epistemological Constraints on Anti-Sceptical Theories', *Facta Philosophica* 3: 101–26.

—— (2001*c*). 'Radical Scepticism, Epistemological Externalism, and "Hinge" Propositions', in *Wittgenstein-Jahrbuch 2001/2002*, ed. D. Salehi. Berlin: Peter Lang.

—— (2001*d*). 'Scepticism and Dreaming', *Philosophia* 28: 373–90.

—— (2001*e*). 'The Opacity of Knowledge', in *Essays in Philosophy*, vol. 2: *The Internalism/Externalism Debate in Epistemology*, ed. H. B. Shaeffer. Humboldt, Calif.: Humboldt University Press.

—— (2002*a*). 'McKinsey Paradoxes, Radical Scepticism, and the Transmission of Knowledge across Known Entailments', *Synthese* 130: 279–302.

—— (2002*b*). 'Radical Scepticism, Epistemological Externalism, and Closure', *Theoria* 68: 129–61.

—— (2002*c*). 'Recent Work on Radical Skepticism', *American Philosophical Quarterly* 39: 215–57.

—— (2002*d*). 'Resurrecting the Moorean Response to Scepticism', *International Journal of Philosophical Studies* 10: 283–307.

—— (2002*e*). 'Two Forms of Epistemological Contextualism', *Grazer Philosophische Studien* 64: 97–134.

—— (2003*a*). 'McDowell on Reasons, Externalism and Scepticism', *European Journal of Philosophy* 11: 273–94.

—— (2003*b*). 'Reforming Reformed Epistemology', *International Philosophical Quarterly* 43: 43–66.

—— (2003*c*). 'Virtue Epistemology and Epistemic Luck', *Metaphilosophy* 34: 106–30; and repr. in Brady and Pritchard (2003).

—— (2004*a*). 'Epistemic Deflationism', *Southern Journal of Philosophy* 42: 1–32.

—— (2004*b*). 'Epistemic Luck', *Journal of Philosophical Research* 29: 193–222.

—— (2004*c*). 'Moral and Epistemic Luck', *typescript*.

—— (2004*d*). 'Neo-Mooreanism, Contextualism, and the Evidential Basis of Scepticism', in *Contextualism* (special issue of *Acta Analytica*), ed. D. Suster. New York: Rutgers University Press.

—— (2005*a*). 'Contextualism, Scepticism and Warranted Assertibility Manoeuvres', in *Knowledge and Skepticism*, ed. J. Keim-Campbell, M. O'Rourke, and H. Silverstein. Cambridge, Mass.: MIT Press.

—— (2005*b*). 'How to be a Neo-Moorean (and not a Contextualist)', *Grazer Philosophische Studien* 67 (special issue on *Contextualism*).

—— (2005*c*). 'Scepticism, Epistemic Luck and Epistemic *Angst*', *Australasian Journal of Philosophy* 83.

—— (2005*d*). 'The Structure of Skeptical Arguments', *Philosophical Quarterly* 55: 37–52.

—— (2005*e*). 'Wittgenstein's *On Certainty* and Contemporary Anti-Scepticism', in *Investigating On Certainty: Essays on Wittgenstein's Last Work*, ed. D. Moyal-Sharrock and W. H. Brenner. London: Palgrave Macmillan.

—— (2006). 'Externalism, Skepticism and Luck', in *Internalism and Externalism in Semantics and Epistemology*, ed. S. Goldberg. Oxford: Oxford University Press.

—— and Smith, M. (2004). 'The Psychology and Philosophy of Luck', *New Ideas in Psychology* 22: 1–28.

Pryor, J. (2000). 'The Skeptic and the Dogmatist', *Noûs* 34: 517–49.

—— (2001). 'Highlights of Recent Epistemology', *British Journal for the Philosophy of Science* 52: 95–124.

Putnam, H. (1981). *Reason, Truth and History*. Cambridge: Cambridge University Press.

—— (1992). *Renewing Philosophy*. Cambridge, Mass.: Harvard University Press.

Quine, W. V. O. (1953). 'Two Dogmas of Empiricism', in his *From a Logical Point of View*. Cambridge, Mass.: Harvard University Press.

Ravitch, H. (1976). 'Knowledge and the Principle of Luck', *Philosophical Studies* 30: 347–9.

Reichenbach, H. (1938). *Experience and Prediction: An Analysis of the Foundation and the Structure of Knowledge*. Chicago, Ill.: University of Chicago Press.

—— (1949). *Theory of Probability*. Berkeley, Calif.: University of California Press.

Rescher, N. (1993). 'Moral Luck', in *Moral Luck*, ed. D. Statman. Albany: State University of New York Press.

—— (1995). *Luck: The Brilliant Randomness of Everyday Life*. New York: Farrar, Straus & Giroux.

Ribeiro, B. (2002*a*). 'Cartesian Skepticism and the Epistemic Priority Thesis', *Southern Journal of Philosophy* 40: 573–86.

—— (2002*b*). 'Epistemological Skepticism(s) and Rational Self-Control', *The Monist* 85: 468–77.

—— (2002*c*). 'Is Pyrrhonism Psychologically Possible?', *Ancient Philosophy* 22: 319–31.

—— (2004). 'Skeptical Parasitism and the Continuity Argument', *Metaphilosophy* 35.

Richards, N. (1993). 'Luck and Desert', in *Moral Luck*, ed. D. Statman. Albany: State University of New York Press.

Riggs, W. (2002). 'Reliability and the Value of Knowledge', *Philosophy and Phenomenological Research* 64: 79–96.

Rosenberg, R. J. (2003). *Thinking About Knowing*. Oxford: Oxford University Press.

Russell, B. (1948). *Human Knowledge: Its Scope and its Limits*. London: Allen & Unwin.

Ryan, S. (1996) 'Does Warrant Entail Truth?', *Philosophy and Phenomenological Research* 56: 183–92.

Rysiew, P. (2001). 'The Context-Sensitivity of Knowledge Attributions', *Noûs* 35: 477–514.

Sainsbury, R. M. (1996). 'Crispin Wright: *Truth and Objectivity*', *Philosophy and Phenomenological Research* 56: 899–904.

Sainsbury, R. M. (1997). 'Easy Possibilities', *Philosophy and Phenomenological Research* 57: 907–19.

Sedley, D. (1983). 'The Motivation of Greek Skepticism', in *The Skeptical Tradition*, ed. M. Burnyeat. Berkeley, Calif.: University of California Press.

Bibliography

Sellars, W. (1997). *Empiricism and the Philosophy of Mind*. Cambridge, Mass.: Harvard University Press.

Sextus Empiricus. (1933–49). *Sextus Empiricus with an English Translation* (4 vols.), tr. R. G. Bury. London: Heinemann.

Shope, R. K. (1983). *The Analysis of Knowing: A Decade of Research*. Princeton, NJ: Princeton University Press.

Sinnott-Armstrong, W. (2004). 'Classy Pyrrhonism', in *Pyrrhonian Skepticism*, ed. W. Sinnott-Armstrong. New York: Oxford University Press.

Slote, M. (1979). 'Assertion and Belief', in *Papers on Language and Logic*, ed. J. Dancy. Keele: Keele University Press.

Sorenson, R. (1998). 'Logical Luck', *Philosophical Quarterly* 48: 319–34.

Sosa, E. (1985). 'Knowledge and Intellectual Virtue', *The Monist* 68: 224–45.

—— (1988). 'Beyond Skepticism, to the Best of our Knowledge', *Mind* 97: 153–89.

—— (1991). 'Intellectual Virtue in Perspective', in his *Knowledge in Perspective: Selected Essays in Epistemology*. Cambridge: Cambridge University Press.

—— (1993). 'Proper Functionalism and Virtue Epistemology', *Noûs* 27: 51–65.

—— (1994). 'Philosophical Scepticism and Epistemic Circularity', *Proceedings of the Aristotelian Society* (supp. vol.) 68: 263–90.

—— (1997). 'Mythology of the Given', *History of Philosophy Quarterly* 14: 275–86.

—— (1999). 'How to Defeat Opposition to Moore', *Philosophical Perspectives* 13: 141–54.

—— (2000). 'Skepticism and Contextualism', *Philosophical Issues* 10: 1–18.

—— (2001). 'Human Knowledge, Animal and Reflective', *Philosophical Studies* 106: 193–6.

—— (2002). 'Tracking, Competence, and Knowledge', in *The Oxford Handbook of Epistemology*, ed. P. K. Moser. Oxford: Oxford University Press.

—— (2003). 'Knowledge, Animal and Reflective: A Reply to Michael Williams', *Proceedings of the Aristotelian Society* (supp. vol.) 77: 113–30.

Statman, D. (1991). 'Moral and Epistemic Luck', *Ratio* 4 (new series): 146–56.

—— (1993*a*). 'Introduction', in *Moral Luck*, ed. D. Statman. Albany: State University of New York Press.

—— (ed.) (1993*b*). *Moral Luck*. Albany: State University of New York Press.

Steup, M. (2001). 'The Analysis of Knowledge', http://plato.stanford.edu/entries/knowledge-analysis/.

—— (ed.) (2002). *Knowledge, Truth, and Duty: Essays on Epistemic Justification, Responsibility, and Virtue*. Oxford: Oxford University Press.

Stevenson, L. (2000). 'Six Levels of Mentality', *Philosophical Explorations* 5: 105–24.

Stine, G. C. (1976). 'Skepticism, Relevant Alternatives, and Deductive Closure', *Philosophical Studies* 29: 249–61.

Strawson, P. F. (1985). *Skepticism and Naturalism: Some Varieties*. London: Methuen.

Stroll, A. (1994). *Moore and Wittgenstein on Certainty*. Oxford: Oxford University Press.

—— (1994). 'Scepticism, "Externalism", and the Goal of Epistemology', *Proceedings of the Aristotelian Society* (supp. vol.) 68: 290–307.

—— (1996). 'Epistemological Reflection on Knowledge of the External World', *Philosophy and Phenomenological Research* 56: 345–58.

Stough, C. (1984). 'Sextus Empiricus on Non-Assertion', *Phronesis* 29: 137–64.

Swain, M. (1974). 'Epistemic Defeasibility', *American Philosophical Quarterly* 11: 15–25.

Talbott, W. J. (1990). *The Reliability of the Cognitive Mechanism*. New York: Garland Publishing.

Teigen, K. H. (2003). 'When A Small Difference Makes A Large Difference: Counterfactual Thinking and Luck', in *The Psychology of Counterfactual Thinking*, ed. D. R. Mandel, D. Hilton, and P. Catellani. London: Routledge.

Thomson, J. J. (1993). 'Morality and Bad Luck', in *Moral Luck*, ed. D. Statman. Albany: State University of New York Press.

Travis, C. (1989). *The Uses of Sense: Wittgenstein's Philosophy of Language*. Oxford: Oxford University Press.

—— (2005). 'The Legacy of Cook Wilson', *Philosophical Quarterly* 55.

Unger, P. (1968). 'An Analysis of Factual Knowledge', *Journal of Philosophy* 65: 157–70.

—— (1971). 'A Defence of Skepticism', *Philosophical Review* 80: 198–219.

—— (1974). 'An Argument for Skepticism', *Philosophical Exchange* 1: 1–10.

—— (1975). *Ignorance: A Case for Scepticism*. Oxford: Clarendon Press.

—— (1984). *Philosophical Relativity*. Oxford: Blackwell.

—— (1986). 'The Cone Model of Knowledge', *Philosophical Topics* 14: 125–78.

Vahid, H. (2001). 'Knowledge and Varieties of Epistemic Luck', *Dialectica* 55: 351–62.

Vogel, J. (1990). 'Cartesian Skepticism and Inference to the Best Explanation', *Journal of Philosophy* 87: 658–66.

—— (1993). 'Dismissing Skeptical Possibilities', *Philosophical Studies* 70: 235–50.

—— (1999). 'The New Relevant Alternatives Theory', *Philosophical Perspectives* 13: 155–80.

—— (2004). 'Varieties of Skepticism', *Philosophy and Phenomenological Research* 68: 1–37.

Warfield, T. (1998). '*A Priori* Knowledge of the World: Knowing the World by Knowing our Minds', *Philosophical Studies* 60: 76–90.

Williams, B. (1976). 'Moral Luck', *Proceedings of the Aristotelian Society* (supp. vol.) 76: 115–35.

—— (1978). *Descartes: The Project of Pure Enquiry*. Harmondsworth: Pelican.

—— (1981*a*). *Moral Luck*. Cambridge: Cambridge University Press, Cambridge.

—— (1981*b*). 'Moral Luck', in his *Moral Luck*. Cambridge: Cambridge University Press.

—— (1983). 'Descartes's Use of Skepticism', in *The Skeptical Tradition*, ed. M. Burnyeat. Berkeley, Calif.: University of California Press.

—— (1993). 'Postscript', in *Moral Luck*, ed. D. Statman. Albany: State University of New York Press.

—— (2002). *Truth and Truthfulness: An Essay in Genealogy*. Princeton, NJ: Princeton University Press.

Williams, M. (1986). 'Descartes and the Metaphysics of Doubt', in *Essays on Descartes' Meditations*, ed. A. Rorty. Berkeley, Calif.: University of California Press.

Bibliography

Williams, M. (1988). 'Scepticism without Theory', *Review of Metaphysics* 41: 547–88.

—— (1988–9). 'Scepticism and Charity', *Ratio* (new series) 1–2: 176–94.

—— (1991). *Unnatural Doubts: Epistemological Realism and the Basis of Scepticism*, Oxford: Blackwell.

—— (1999). 'Skepticism', in *Epistemology*, ed. J. Greco and E. Sosa. Oxford: Blackwell.

—— (2001*a*). 'Contextualism, Externalism and Epistemic Standards', *Philosophical Studies* 103: 1–23.

—— (2001*b*). *Problems of Knowledge: A Critical Introduction to Epistemology*. Oxford: Oxford University Press.

—— (2003*a*). 'Mythology of the Given: Sosa, Sellars and the Task of Epistemology', *Proceedings of the Aristotelian Society* (supp. vol.) 77: 91–112.

—— (2003*b*). 'Wittgenstein's Refutation of Idealism', in *Wittgenstein and Scepticism*, ed. D. McManus. London: Routledge.

Williamson, T. (1996*a*). 'Cognitive Homelessness', *Journal of Philosophy* 93: 554–73.

—— (1996*b*). 'Knowing and Asserting', *Philosophical Review* 105: 489–523.

—— (1997). 'Knowledge as Evidence', *Mind* 424: 717–41.

—— (2000*a*). 'Scepticism and Evidence', *Philosophy and Phenomenological Research* 60: 613–28.

—— (2000*b*). 'Scepticism, Semantic Externalism and Keith's Mom', *Southern Journal of Philosophy* 38: 148–57.

—— (2000*c*). *Knowledge and Its Limits*. Oxford: Oxford University Press.

—— (2001). 'Comments on Michael Williams' 'Contextualism, Externalism and Epistemic Standards', *Philosophical Studies* 103: 24–33.

Wittgenstein, L. (1969). *On Certainty*, ed. G. E. M. Anscombe and G. H. von Wright, tr. D. Paul and G. E. M. Anscombe. Oxford: Blackwell.

Wright, C. (1985). 'Facts and Certainty', *Proceedings of the British Academy* 71: 429–72.

—— (1991). 'Scepticism and Dreaming: Imploding the Demon', *Mind* 397: 87–115.

—— (1992). *Truth and Objectivity*. Cambridge, Mass.: Harvard University Press.

—— (1994). 'On Putnam's Proof that we are not Brains in a Vat', in *Reading Putnam*, ed. B. Hale and P. Clark. Oxford: Blackwell.

—— (1996). 'Response to Commentators', *Philosophy and Phenomenological Research* 56: 911–41.

—— (2000). 'Cogency and Question-Begging: Some Reflections on McKinsey's Paradox and Putnam's Proof', *Philosophical Issues* 10: 140–63.

—— (2002). '(Anti-)Skeptics Simple and Subtle: G. E. Moore and John McDowell', *Philosophy and Phenomenological Research* 65: 331–49.

—— (2003*a*). 'Some Reflections on the Acquisition of Warrant by Inference', in *New Essays on Semantic Externalism and Self-Knowledge*, ed. S. Nuccetelli. Cambridge, Mass.: MIT Press.

—— (2003*b*). 'Wittgensteinian Certainties', in *Wittgenstein and Scepticism*, ed. D. McManus. London: Routledge.

—— (2004). 'Warrant for Nothing (and Foundations for Free)?', *Proceedings of the Aristotelian Society* 78 (supp. vol.): 167–212.

Yalçin, U. D. (1992). 'Skeptical Arguments from Underdetermination', *Philosophical Studies* 68: 1–34.

Zagzebski, L. (1994*a*). 'Religious Luck', *Faith and Philosophy* 11: 397–413.

—— (1994*b*). 'The Inescapability of Gettier Problems', *Philosophical Quarterly* 44: 65–73.

—— (1996). *Virtues of the Mind: An Inquiry into the Nature of Virtue and the Ethical Foundations of Knowledge*. Cambridge: Cambridge University Press.

—— (1999). 'What is Knowledge?', in *Epistemology*, ed. J. Greco and E. Sosa. Oxford: Blackwell.

—— (2003). 'The Search for the Source of the Epistemic Good', *Metaphilosophy* 34: 12–28; and repr. in Brady and Pritchard (2003).

Zimmerman, M. J. (1993). 'Luck and Moral Responsibility', in *Moral Luck*, ed. D. Statman. Albany: State University of New York Press.

Index

Index

Index

CPSIA information can be obtained
at www.ICGtesting.com
Printed in the USA
BVHW040358121019
560939BV00011B/55/P